12

U 241 G56 2008

Global Insurgency and the Future of Armed Conflict

Global Insurgency and the Future of Armed Conflict examines the meaning of the rising tide of terrorism and guerrilla warfare, which increasingly dominates world-wide military planning. After the 1991 war with Iraq, it seemed that the 'Revolution in Military Affairs' would assure the United States and its allies of ever greater military dominance. However, rapid victories like the toppling of the Afghan Taliban in 2001 and Saddam Hussein in 2003 now seem like isolated events in a long struggle. For the first time since the Vietnam War ended, the problems of insurgency have leapt to the top of the international security agenda. Coalition forces in Afghanistan and Iraq are bogged down by insurgency, while virtually every country is struggling to ensure its domestic safety against terrorist threats.

In this edited book, some leading advocates of 'Fourth-Generation Warfare', led by T.X. Hammes and Bill Lind, maintain that irregular warfare is evolving into the dominant form of conflict. However, other strategic thinkers, such as Lawrence Freeman and Antulio Echevarria, argue that the novelty of irregular warfare has been exaggerated. Others examine the lessons of warfare in Afghanistan and Iraq, and the ability of military organizations to deal with the new challenge. Case studies from the United States, India, Israel, NATO and others reveal military thinkers working at the limits of their trade to adapt old institutions and assumptions to address the rising challenge.

Terry Terriff is Reader in International Security in the Department of Political Science and International Studies at Birmingham University, UK. **Aaron Karp** is Instructor of Political Science at Old Dominion University, Virginia. He is co-editor of the journal *Contemporary Security Policy*. **Regina Karp** is Associate Professor at Old Dominion University, Virginia. She is co-editor of the journal *Contemporary Security Policy*.

Routledge global security studies

Series editors: Aaron Karp, Regina Karp and Terry Terriff

Global Insurgency and the Future of Armed Conflict

Debating fourth-generation warfare

Edited by
Terry Terriff, Aaron Karp and
Regina Karp

Routledge
Taylor & Francis Group

LONDON AND NEW YORK

First published 2008
by Routledge
2 Park Square, Milton Park, Abingdon, Oxon OX14 4RN

Simultaneously published in the USA and Canada
by Routledge
270 Madison Ave, New York, NY 10016

Routledge is an imprint of the Taylor & Francis Group, an informa business

Typeset in Times by Wearset Ltd, Boldon, Tyne and Wear
Printed and bound in Great Britain by TJI Digital, Padstow, Cornwall

British Library Cataloguing in Publication Data
A catalogue record for this book is available from the British Library

Library of Congress Cataloging in Publication Data
Global insurgency and the future of armed conflict: debating fourth-
generation warfare/edited by Terry Terriff, Aaron Karp and Regina Karp.
p. cm.
Includes bibliographical references and index.
1. Counterinsurgency. 2. War on Terrorism, 2001—I. Karp, Aaron. II.
Cowen Karp, Regina. III. Terriff, Terry, 1953–
U241.G56 2007
355.02'18–dc22
2006101900

ISBN10: 0-415-41357-5 (hbk)
ISBN10: 0-203-08927-8 (ebk)

ISBN13: 978-0-415-41357-2 (hbk)
ISBN13: 978-0-203-08927-9 (ebk)

Contents

Preface

If there is one theme that typifies the changing character of war in the twenty-first century, it is complexity and non-linearity. Hence, it is no surprise that the origins of this volume are complex as well, to say the least. With three editors, and more than 20 contributors, including several of the originators of the concept of Fourth Generation Warfare, any effort to trace particular claims of maternity and paternity for the volume is deeply problematic and probably futile. The proximal genesis nonetheless can be traced to the publication in 2004 by T.X. Hammes of *The Sling and the Stone: On War in the 21st Century*. In the wake of September 11, Fourth Generation Warfare gained unprecedented prominence. Yet it was far from clear that the concept was truly understood by many of those who used it. Moreover, it was evident that the concept was controversial. Hammes' book went a long way towards clarifying what was Fourth Generation Warfare, as well as bringing the idea to a broader public audience. The editors of this volume approached Hammes to write an article on Fourth Generation Warfare as the centrepiece for a symposium debating the concept. Hammes was enthusiastic about having his argument subjected publicly to critical scrutiny. The result was the symposium, 'Debating Fourth Generation Warfare', published in the August 2005 issue of *Contemporary Security Policy*.[1] Publication of this debate elicited considerable positive response, which encouraged us to expand the discussion. Thus, this volume owes its gestation to Hammes and the nine scholars who agreed to comment critically on his work.

The particular aim of this volume is not only to contribute specifically to the debate on the idea of Fourth Generation Warfare, but also to the wider debate on the changing character of war and what we need to do to meet its challenges. The concept of Fourth Generation Warfare remains contested on several grounds, which were very well articulated in the *Contemporary Security Policy Symposium*, reprinted here. For this volume, William S. Lind was invited to provide an additional critical commentary on Hammes' conceptualization, for he does differ on some aspects, addressed in his contribution. The rest of the contributions in the volume focus on the features of Fourth Generation Warfare or on what we may and should do to meet their challenges. The former analyses focus on particular current conflicts from a range of different perspectives. Some of these contributions seek to challenge the idea of Fourth Generation Warfare, while others emphasize elaborating or extending features of Fourth Generation Warfare – but all contribute to our understanding of the evolving nature of war.

We would like to extend our sincerest appreciation, again, to Hammes for his original article and to the nine original respondents for their willingness to comment on his argument in the *Contemporary Security Policy* symposium. We would also like to extend our sincere gratitude to William S. Lind, Chet Richards, Greg Wilcox, Gary I. Wilson, Avi Kober, Warren Chin, Paul Jackson, Frank Hoffman, Don MacCuish, Frans Osinga, Diego Ruiz Palmer, and Rajesh Rajagopalan and, yet again, Thomas X. Hammes for their willingness to furnish original contributions to this volume.

Aaron Karp, Regina Karp and Terry Terriff

Note

1 In addition to Hammes, the *Contemporary Security Policy* symposium featured commentary by Martin van Creveld, Antulio J. Echevarria II, Michael Evans, John Ferris, Lawrence Freedman, Edward N. Luttwak, David S. Sorenson, Rod Thornton, and James J. Wirtz.

Part I

Introduction

1 The Fourth Generation Warfare debate

Aaron Karp, Regina Karp, and Terry Terriff

We are all strategists now

It was not supposed to be this way. Most countries emerged from the Cold War into an era of unprecedented peace and stability. After the round of fierce, brutal ethnic fighting unleashed by the collapse of the world's last empire, warfare began a steady decline. Today, traditional warfare, the various forms that preoccupied princes and governments for centuries, is historically distant and geographically remote. Not only do democracies almost never fight each other, virtually no state of any stripe fights another.[1] Armed conflict ceased to mean war and became associated with ever more nebulous events in ever remoter regions. The major use of most countries' armed forces was helping out others by maintaining the peace. It was not the millennium of prophesy, but for most of humankind, it was pretty good.

Then on September 11 we woke to find that one of those far away nebulous armed conflicts had directly engaged the world's sole superpower. Afterwards Bali, Madrid, London, and Bombay joined the list of cities subsequently victimized; traditional armed forces seemed increasingly helpless to prevent attack. These were not the threats they were created to repel. Nor were the new adversaries ones that the armed services knew how to defeat. Statistically, humanity currently is safer from the worst dangers of the past four centuries than ever, but a seemingly novel threat left many feeling as insecure as ever. Adding to the confusion, when governments tried to use their armed forces to enhance their own security objectives, the results were frustrating at best, catastrophic at worst. Afghanistan, Iraq, and Lebanon became symbols of the ineffectiveness of the world's most professional armed forces, while less conspicuous conflicts droned on remorselessly.

The new demon has many names, none of them completely satisfactory: insurgency, guerrilla warfare, terrorism, non-state actors, the long war, global war on terrorism (GWOT), and so on and so forth. *Fourth Generation Warfare* is neither the most elegant nor parsimonious term, but it conveys better than the others the evolving nature of global armed conflict. More so than the other synonyms for post-Cold War fighting, it is a self-conscious critique of the weaknesses of current military and security planning. Unlike the more neutral terms,

Fourth Generation Warfare comes with an agenda, simultaneously diagnosing the problems posed by contemporary security dangers and recommending a particular path to overcome them.

This book is both about how we think about those security dangers and how to deal with them. Unlike alternative descriptors, Fourth Generation Warfare is steeped in strategic conceptualization. One of the most immediate effects of the Fourth Generation Warfare debate has been epistemic, accelerating a renaissance in Western strategic thought that had been slowly gathering momentum since the late 1970s.[2] This process was subtle enough to go largely unremarked, but it is deep enough to affect virtually all thought on the use of force. It has influenced and informed the intellectual debate on the character of war in ways completely unprecedented. Maybe it has not ameliorated the ashen prose of government reports – that would ask too much – but it compelled even bureaucratic efforts to grapple with the fundamentals of armed violence. Only the most passive warriors and citizens are unaware of this trend. Although our talents and insights vary, we are all strategists now, probing difficult questions of military goals and means.

It is a measure of the change that even the recent past now looks incredibly alien. Preoccupied throughout the Cold War by the problems of nuclear deterrence, strategic thought became an intellectual backwater, so much so that the word strategy became a synonym for nuclear, and all other uses of force were – quite literally – "non-strategic." The efforts of isolated intellectuals helped to sustain an otherwise forgotten field, but their efforts were not enough to foster a broad interest in strategy, much less in its development. In retrospect such exercises seem arbitrary and out of touch with events.

Michael Howard and Peter Paret's English translation of Carl von Clausewitz's *On War*, published in 1976,[3] reminded military professionals and security analysts of the decline of strategic thought. The book did remarkably well for a dense and incomplete philosophical work of German idealism, but sales undoubtedly benefited most from romantic fascination. It was a book that one was supposed to have read. In retrospect it is obvious that most copies of the fat white volume sat untouched, largely because to most it still seemed irrelevant. Military self-perception offered little room for uniformed intellectuals.[4] In an era that stressed unity of effort, it was easy to dismiss strategic introspection as doubt. Writers such as Paret and Howard made Western security planners aware of what they were not doing, but they could not actually make them do it. Except for isolated dens of genuine innovation – the US Army's Training and Doctrinal Command in the late 1970s, and the US Marine Corps University in the mid to late 1980s – security thought concentrated on the problem of maintaining stability, not on anticipating and preparing for change.

Welcome to Fourth Generation Warfare

Only with the end of the Cold War and the weirdness of a world swamped by ethnic conflict were conditions ripe for a return to basics. This was trumpeted by the appearance in 1989 of *The Changing Face of War: Into the Fourth Genera-tion* by William S. Lind, Keith Nightengale, John F. Schmitt, Joseph W. Sutton, and Gary I. Wilson. Although their article received scant attention when origin-ally published, today it ranks with Fukuyama's *End of History* and Huntington's *Clash of Civilizations* as an essential guide to post-modern world affairs.

Reproduced here, *The Changing Face of War* has lost none of its ability to startle. Lulled into confusing strategic thought with debate over the design of the perfect airplane, ship, or tank, far too many of us missed their growing irrelevance. These were merely the artifacts of Third Generation Warfare (maneuver warfare), a form of armed violence that emerged in the twentieth century that has been widely embraced by our military organizations. Major weaponry and procurement politics – the dominant strategic discourse of the Cold War era – actually was any-thing but strategic. Reaffirmation of old assumptions through a preoccupation with material symbols is a mistake that we cannot afford to make anymore. Emphasiz-ing no particular technologies, but the enormous advantages available to irregular forces preying on the weakness of contemporary society, Fourth Generation Warfare undermines our ability to protect ourselves. Older forms of warfare might continue – they always do – but they would not matter as much.

So long as the attacks on civil society that distinguish Fourth Generation Warfare happened mostly to other people, Western observers could afford to overlook its significance. *The Changing Face of War* was largely forgotten through the 1990s,[5] when its implications seemed to mean little more than ever-messier peacekeeping operations or to use the US term, ever-messier 'military operations other than war' (MOOTW). Only after September 11 transformed the choice of peacekeeping operations and MOOTWs into the necessity for counter-terrorism, did the menace of Fourth Generation Warfare win broader recogni-tion.

T.X. Hammes has been an important figure in propelling these concepts into the center of Western strategic dialogue. With September 11 and Iraq in the foreground, he had the advantage of audiences whose assumptions about war already were beginning to shake.[6] Few still confused modern war with the bat-tlefields of the Eastern Front and Okinawa. But what had war become? And how much control did we have over its evolution? On one side of the new debate stood Donald Rumsfeld with demands for military transformation, based on a vision that owed much to the "Revolution in Military Affairs" debate about whether rapid advances in information technology were in the process of chang-ing the nature and character of warfare. But his efforts to assert a template over processes beyond his control only bamboozled listeners who never quite under-stood what he was talking about. The intense discussion on transforming means did not make sense without a comparable elaboration of goals. In practice this meant finding a suitable enemy, something politically unacceptable and practic-ally impossible. In retrospect the exercise seems arbitrary and wayward. The Secretary of Defense finally connected his war fighting concept to President George Bush's determination to launch a preventive invasion of Iraq. The result was misleading in the short run and disastrous in the long run.

Hammes came closer than anyone to explaining publicly the new strategic logic.[7] Summarized here in his essay *War evolves into the fourth generation*, his interpretation of 4GW is the fulcrum of this volume.[8] Unlike earlier diagnoses, which tended to fail because they saw strategic change as a goal to be pursued, Hammes understands change as an environmental condition. Instead of leading change, we must struggle to keep up. Like William Lind and his co-writers, Hammes recognized that it was Western militaries and political leaders who were being forced to adapt to pressures imposed by more adroit enemies. But more explicitly than Lind and others, he argues that irregular warriors are evolving even faster due to their better recognition and exploitation of the opportunities afforded by ongoing political, social, cultural, and technological change.

Through the twentieth century, he explains, guerrillas learned to accomplish more and more with less and less. Much more nimble than state military establishments, the irregulars learned much quicker how to tailor the use of force. Crafting their techniques to rely less on actual killing and destruction, the most successful guerrillas and terrorists came to rely more on the political effects of their attacks. What began in the mid-twentieth century with the massive guerrilla armies of Mao Tse-tung ended with Osama bin Laden challenging the world's sole superpower with an army of hundreds or dozens. The extraordinary power of a carefully designed Fourth Generation Warfare campaign can make tiny bands the equals of great powers and sometimes their masters. Bin Laden may be the one hiding in a Waziristan cave, but we are the ones who are wracking our brains.

It is the critics of Hammes who bring the debate fully to life, as can be seen in Part III. Respondents to Hammes' argument fall into two general categories. None deny the salience of the techniques of Fourth Generation Warfare, but they disagree about the extent of its advantages and whether it is a decisive change in the use of force. Those who find 4GW claims persuasive worry that existing armed forces will have to struggle for effectiveness. The rituals of classical Westphalian warfare, they maintain, have become a sideshow. State-to-state warfare with its single-purpose armies may continue, but with less frequency and importance. Instead warfare is destined to be shaped more by insurgent-like actors[9] whose methods are easier, more adaptable and no less effective.

The most incisive question is historical insights. They emphasize not the radical disjuncture of a new generation of warfare from the old but the gradual evolution of a guerrilla threat that undoubtedly has existed as long as violent conflict. Far from amounting to something new, they argue, today's irregular war adheres to ancient patterns and can be overcome through age-old techniques.

The end of unity of effort

The historical critique of Fourth Generation Warfare – stressing the permanence of guerrilla concepts and their antidotes – is undeniable. This explains the continuing utility of studying lessons from past counterinsurgency campaigns and, indeed, furnish cogent reasons for the continuing utility to reflect critically on the history of war and warfare.[10] But it misses equally significant changes in the character of asymmetric warfare and the demands on those who face it. One of Hammes' greatest insights is that of the differences between today's guerrilla warfare and earlier manifestations. Through the twentieth century, the practitioners of guerrilla warfare have become more politically astute and more tactically adroit. As a result they have achieved comparable goals with ever smaller forces and thinner external support. Compared to the Spanish guerrilla forces that ravaged Napoleon's force, the peasant armies of Mao Tse-tung or the Viet Cong, al Qaeda is a mosquito and Hezbollah a sideshow. But shrewd political and cultural insight make Osama bin Laden and Hassan Nasrallah every bit their equals.

For military planners, the Fourth Generation Warfare critique emphasizes both a shift in the predominant forms of warfare and evolutionary development of its effectiveness. Seen from this point of view, the rise of insurgency is not temporary or secondary but permanent and fundamental. As shown by the contributors in Part IV who address some of the wider implications of Fourth Generation Warfare, any serious military organization now requires a fully-developed, large-scale counterinsurgency component. But as many also show, there are limits to the process. One limit is that there is no one form of 4GW, in part because regional variations in history, politics, culture, and society result in different environmental conditions, and in part because of an almost Darwinian process of adaptation and change. Another limit is that, even though it has diminished, the risk of inter-state war remains. Older-style forces still must be cultivated. The result is not an either/or choice in strategic doctrines but a less/more problem of unsolvable uncertainty. There is no alternative to rethinking military organizations so they can cope with both.

As military professionals never tire of pointing out to their civilian counterparts, cultivating the ability to fight more than one kind of war simultaneously is much harder than it sounds. Soldiers trained for counterinsurgency operations are poorly suited to high-tempo mechanized operations. Units trained to fight on traditional battlefields may be worse than useless on the streets of a post-modern conflict. Asking units to cross over invites disaster. The Vietnam War was replete with talented officers who understood the needs of counterinsurgency, but were unable to make their traditional organizations adapt.[11] The fiasco of the US Army's 4th Infantry Division, the first unit sent into Iraq in 2003 after the fall of Baghdad, deployed especially for occupation and stabilization, showed how little had changed in 35 years.[12] Wholesale retraining of American units who deploy to face the Iraqi insurgency has helped, but as subsequent events show, it remains far from sufficient. So long as units are expected to retain their capabilities for traditional battlefields – even if only in the distant future – they will not excel on post-modern ones.

One of the strongest recommendations echoing through Part V of this book is that major states no longer can afford to maintain single-purpose military organizations. The differences in the dominant forms of warfare can only be mastered through parallel career specialization. For their armed forces there is no alternative to a painful stretching of personnel, missions, and imaginations. The new era rules out the Napoleonic commandment of unity of forces. Militaries have divided their forces this way before, but usually only temporarily as an expedient. The great counterinsurgency campaigns of the past – George Crook in the 1880s against the Apaches, Britain in the Malayan Emergency of 1948–1960 – were not central efforts but temporary expedients. Now planning for similar diversions must become permanent. For air forces, and to an even lesser extent for navies, there is not much radical adjustment to be made; they will continue to play vital, but supporting roles. But for ground forces, long wedded to the unity of effort, developing advanced skills in Fourth Generation Warfare, while preserving traditional battlefield capabilities, can be achieved only by redesigning traditional military organizations.

Each form of warfare requires fully dedicated specialists. Nor can the problem be solved through traditional compartmentalization. The armed services, especially ground forces, must fundamentally change educational, training and promotion systems, and ultimately their basic organizational design. Civilian organizations, especially foreign affairs and development agencies, must overcome their traditional bureaucratic propensities in order to be fully integrated into planning and operations. And civilian leaders must learn to think in ways that give equal importance to all these dimensions. For American and Asian leaders this means learning to take the non-military aspects of war seriously again. For European leaders it means relearning the importance of military operations.

Beyond Fourth Generation Warfare

It is difficult to know at this point in time whether or not Fourth Generation Warfare will become an enduring element of the world's military lexicon. Increasingly commonplace use suggests that it has become a cliché, cited even by writers with only a hazy grasp of its implications. Whether the concept serves as a stepping stone or becomes a strategic premise in its own right, however, our understanding of war and security policy has been permanently affected. Unfairly, perhaps, the field is far too dynamic to allow the last word to even its keenest students like William Lind and T.X. Hammes, among others, not even on a concept of their own creation. But no telling of the evolution of military ideas and debates can be complete without acknowledging their important contribution.

Perhaps their single greatest contribution has been to remind us of the obvious that we seemingly managed to forget; the character of warfare (and those who wage it) is subject to constant change. Fourth Generation Warfare will continue to evolve and at some point eventually be superseded as the dominant way of warfare by yet another, "fifth generation", form, which may possibly be old or may possibly be new, but we need to be attentive to this reality.

Notes

1 *Human Security Report 2005: War and Peace in the 21st Century* (Oxford: Human Security Centre, University of British Columbia and Oxford University Press, 2006) ch. 5, "Why the dramatic decline in armed conflict?"

2 The originators of the concept of Fourth Generation Warfare were strongly influenced by Col. John Boyd, particularly the sophisticated version of his Observation – Orientation – Decision – Action (OODA) Loop. Boyd and his work were very influential from the late 1970s providing conceptual coherence to maneuver warfare as adopted by the US Army and the US Marine Corps. On Boyd's thought, see Grant T. Hammond, *The Mind of War: John Boyd and American Security* (Washington and London: Smithsonian Instituion Press, 2001) esp. pp. 118–174; and Frans Osinga, *Science Strategy and War: The Strategic Theory of John Boyd* (London and New York: Routledge, forthcoming).

3 Carl von Clausewitz, *On War*, edited and translated by Michael Howard and Peter Paret (Princeton, NJ: Princeton University Press, 1976).

4 An unusually explicit fictional interpretation is the portrayal of the bookish Lieutenant M.R. Ring, played by Boyd Gaines in Clint Eastwood's movie, *Heartbreak Ridge* (1986, screenplay by James Carabatsos).

5 Five years after the initial article, the *Marine Corps Gazette*, under the editorship of Col. John Greenwood, USMC (ret.), published a number of articles on 4GW. See John E. Greenwood, "Editorial: Into the fourth generation," *Marine Corps Gazette*, Quantico: Sep 1994. Vol. 78, Issue 9 (September 1994) p. 2; Robert J. Bunker, "The transition to fourth epoch war," *Marine Corps Gazette*, Vol. 78, Issue 9 (September 1994) p. 20ff; and Thomas X. Hammes, "The evolution of war: The fourth generation," *Marine Corps Gazette*, Vol. 78, Issue 9 (September 1994) p. 35ff. Three of the five authors of the original 1989 piece on 4GW subsequently updated their argument in response; see William S. Lind, John F. Schmitt, and Gary I. Wilson, "Fourth generation warfare: Another look," *Marine Corps Gazette*, Vol. 78, Issue 12 (December 1994) p. 34ff.

6 Many individuals continuously sought to argue and develop the concept of Fourth Generation Warfare through the 1990s. A key outlet for their work was Defense and the National Interest, a website featuring extensive analyses and commentary on 4GW. See Defense and the National Interest: Fourth Generation Warfare, at: www.d-n-i.net/second_level/fourth_generation_warfare.htm.

7 See Hammes, *The Sling and the Stone: On War in the 21st Century* (St. Paul, MN: Zenith Press, 2004).

8 The concept of Fourth Generation Warfare is advocated and articulated by many different individuals, and while they may share a common broad conceptualization and even nomenclature, there are variations, at times significant differences, in the details and implications drawn. For some examples of other writings on or based on 4GW, see: Chet Richards, *Neither by the Sword: Conflict in the Years Ahead* (Washington, DC: Center for Defense Information, 2006); John Robb's blog, 'Global Guerrillas' (globalguerrillas.typepad.com/globalguerrillas/); and the work of William Lind, Greg Wilcox, and many other authors on the Defense and National Interest website, www.d-n-i.net/second_level/fourth_generation_warfare.htm.

9 States may well also adopt 4GW-like techniques, tactics, and procedures. For a potential example of a state adopting similar approaches, see Col. Qiao Liang, PLA and Col. Wang Xiangsui, PLA, *Unrestricted Warfare: China's Master Plan to Destroy America* (Panama City, Panama: Pan American Publishing Company, 2002). *Unrestricted Warfare* was first published in 1999 by the People's Liberation Army Literature and Arts Publishing House.

10 On the broader utility of studying history, see Williamson Murray and Richard Hart Sinnreich, eds, *The Past as Prologue: The Importance of History to the Military Profession* (Cambridge and New York: Cambridge University Press, 2006).

11 See for example, Andrew F. Krepinevich, *The Army and Vietnam* (Baltimore and London: Johns Hopkins University Press, 1986) and John A. Nagl, *Counterinsurgency Lessons from Malaya and Vietnam: Learning to Eat Soup with a Knife* (Westport and London: Praeger Publishers, 2002).
12 Thomas E. Ricks, *Fiasco: The American Military Adventure in Iraq* (New York: Penguin, 2006).

Part II

The re-discovery of Fourth Generation Warfare

2 The changing face of war[1]

Into the fourth generation

*William S. Lind, Colonel Keith Nightengale (USA),
Captain John F. Schmitt (USMC), Colonel
Joseph W. Sutton (USA) and Lieutenant Colonel
Gary I. Wilson (USMCR)*

The peacetime soldier's principal task is to prepare effectively for the next war. In order to do so, he must anticipate what the next war will be like. This is a difficult task that gets continuously more difficult. German Gen Franz Uhle-Wettler writes:

> At an earlier time, a commander could be certain that a future war would resemble past and present ones. This enabled him to analyze appropriate tactics from past and present. The troop commander of today no longer has this possibility. He knows only that whoever fails to adapt the experiences of the last war will surely lose the next one.

The central question

If we look at the development of warfare in the modern era, we see three distinct generations. In the United States, the Army and the Marine Corps are now coming to grips with the change to the third generation. This transition is entirely for the good. However, third generation warfare was conceptually developed by the German offensive in the spring of 1918. It is now more than 70 years old. This suggests some interesting questions: Is it not about time for a fourth generation to appear? If so, what might it look like? These questions are of central importance. Whoever is first to recognize, understand, and implement a generational change can gain a decisive advantage. Conversely, a nation that is slow to adapt to generational change opens itself to catastrophic defeat.

Our purpose here is less to answer these questions than to pose them. Nonetheless, we will offer some tentative answers. To begin to see what these might be, we need to put the questions into historical context.

Three generations of warfare

While military development is generally a continuous evolutionary process, the modern era has witnessed three watersheds in which change has been dialectically qualitative. Consequently, modern military development comprises three distinct generations.

First generation warfare reflects tactics of the era of the smoothbore musket, the tactics of line and column. These tactics were developed partially in response to technological factors – the line maximized firepower, rigid drill was necessary to generate a high rate of fire, etc. – and partially in response to social conditions and ideas, for example, the columns of the French revolutionary armies reflected both the élan of the revolution and the low training levels of conscripted troops. Although rendered obsolete with the replacement of the smoothbore by the rifled musket, vestiges of first generation tactics survive today, especially in a frequently encountered desire for linearity on the battlefield. Operational art in the first generation did not exist as a concept although it was practiced by individual commanders, most prominently Napoleon.

Second generation warfare was a response to the rifled musket, breech-loaders, barbed wire, the machinegun and indirect fire. Tactics were based on fire and movement, and they remained essentially linear. The defense still attempted to prevent all penetrations, and in the attack a laterally dispersed line advanced by rushes in small groups. Perhaps the principal change from first generation tactics was heavy reliance on indirect fire; second generation tactics were summed up in the French maxim, "the artillery conquers, the infantry occupies." Massed firepower replaced massed manpower. Second generation tactics *remained* the basis of US doctrine *until* the 1980s, and they are still practiced by most American units in the field.

While ideas played a role in the development of second generation tactics (particularly the idea of lateral dispersion), technology was the principal driver of change. Technology manifested itself both qualitatively, in such things as heavier artillery and bombing aircraft, and quantitatively, in the ability of an industrialized economy to fight a battle of materiel *(Materialschlacht)*.

The second generation saw the formal recognition and adoption of the operational art, initially by the Prussian army. Again, both ideas and technology drove the change. The ideas sprang largely from Prussian studies of Napoleon's campaigns. Technological factors included von Moltke's realization that modern tactical firepower mandated battles of encirclement and the desire to exploit the capabilities of the railway and the telegraph.

Third generation warfare was also a response to the increase in battlefield firepower. However, the driving force was primarily ideas. Aware they could not prevail in a contest of materiel because of their weaker industrial base in World War I, the Germans developed radically new tactics. Based on maneuver rather than attrition, third generation tactics were the first truly nonlinear tactics. The attack relied on infiltration to bypass and collapse the enemy's combat forces rather than seeking to close with and destroy them. The defense was in depth and often invited penetration, which set the enemy up for a counterattack.

While the basic concepts of third generation tactics were in place by the end of 1918, the addition of a new technological element – tanks – brought about a major shift at the operational level in World War II. That shift was blitzkrieg. In the blitzkrieg, the basis of the operational art shifted from place (as in Liddell-Hart's indirect approach) to time. This shift was explicitly recognized only recently in the work of retired Air Force Colonel, John Boyd and his "OODA (observation–orientation–decision–action) theory."

Thus we see two major catalysts for change in previous generational shifts: technology and ideas. What perspective do we gain from these earlier shifts as we look toward a potential fourth generation of warfare?

Elements that carry over

Earlier generational shifts, especially the shift from the second to the third generation, were marked by growing emphasis on several central ideas. Four of these seem likely to carry over into the fourth generation, and indeed to expand their influence.

The first is mission orders. Each generational change has been marked by greater dispersion on the battlefield. The fourth generation battlefield is likely to include the whole of the enemy's society. Such dispersion, coupled with what seems likely to be increased *importance* for actions by very small groups of combatants, will require even the lowest level to operate flexibly on the basis of the commander's intent.

Second is decreasing dependence on centralized logistics. Dispersion, coupled with increased value placed on tempo, will require a high degree of ability to live off the land and the enemy.

Third is more emphasis on maneuver. Mass, of men or fire power, will no longer be an overwhelming factor. In fact, mass may become a disadvantage as it will be easy to target. Small, highly maneuverable, agile forces will tend to dominate.

Fourth is a goal of collapsing the enemy internally rather than physically destroying him. Targets will include such things as the population's support for the war and the enemy's culture. Correct identification of enemy strategic centers of gravity will be highly important.

In broad terms, fourth generation warfare seems likely to be widely dispersed and largely undefined; the distinction between war and peace will be blurred to the vanishing point. It will be nonlinear, possibly to the point of having no definable battlefields or fronts. The distinction between "civilian" and "military" may disappear. Actions will occur concurrently throughout all participants' depth, including their society as a cultural, not just a physical, entity. Major military facilities, such as airfields, fixed communications sites, and large headquarters will become rarities because of their vulnerability; the same may be true of civilian equivalents, such as seats of government, power plants and industrial sites (including knowledge as well as manufacturing industries). Success will depend heavily on effectiveness in joint operations as lines between responsibility and mission become very blurred. Again, all these elements are present in third generation warfare; the fourth generation will merely accentuate them.

A potential technology-driven fourth generation

If we combine the above general characteristics of fourth generation warfare with new technology, we see one possible outline of the new generation. For example, directed energy may permit small elements to destroy targets they could not attack with conventional energy weapons. Directed energy may permit the achievement of EMP (electromagnetic pulse) effects without a nuclear blast. Research in superconductivity suggests the possibility of storing and using large quantities of energy in very small packages. Technologically, it is possible that a very few soldiers could have the same battlefield effect as a current brigade.

The growth of robotics, remotely piloted vehicles, low probability of intercept communications and artificial intelligence may offer a potential for radically altered tactics. In turn, growing dependence on such technology may open the door to new vulnerabilities, such as the vulnerability to computer viruses.

Small, highly mobile elements composed of very intelligent soldiers armed with high-technology weapons may range over wide areas seeking critical targets. Targets may be more in the civilian than the military sector. Front-rear terms will be replaced with targeted-untargeted. This may in turn radically alter the way in which military Services are organized and structured.

Units will combine reconnaissance and strike functions. Remote, "smart" assets with preprogrammed artificial intelligence may play a key role. Concurrently, the greatest defensive strengths may be the ability to hide from and spoof these assets.

The tactical and strategic levels will blend as the opponent's political infrastructure and civilian society become battlefield targets. It will be critically important to isolate the enemy from one's own homeland because a small number of people will be able to render great damage in a very short time.

Leaders will have to be masters of both the art of war and technology, a difficult combination as two different mindsets are involved. Primary challenges facing commanders at all levels will include target selection (which will be a political and cultural, not just a military, decision), the ability to concentrate suddenly from very wide dispersion, and selection of subordinates who can manage the challenge of minimal or no supervision in a rapidly changing environment. A major challenge will be handling the tremendous potential information overload without losing sight of the operational and strategic objectives.

Psychological operations may become the dominant operational and strategic weapon in the form of media/information intervention. Logic bombs and computer viruses, including latent viruses, may be used to disrupt civilian as well as military operations. Fourth generation adversaries will be adept at manipulating the media to alter domestic and world opinion to the point where skillful use of psychological operations will sometimes preclude the commitment of combat forces. A major target will be the enemy population's support of its government and the war. Television news may become a more powerful operational weapon than armored divisions.

This kind of high-technology fourth generation warfare may carry in it the seeds of nuclear destruction. Its effectiveness could rapidly eliminate the ability of a nuclear-armed opponent to wage war conventionally. Destruction or disruption of vital industrial capacities, political infrastructure and social fabric, coupled with sudden shifts in the balance of power and concomitant emotions, could easily lead to escalation to nuclear weapons. This risk may deter fourth generation warfare among nuclear armed powers just as it deters major conventional warfare among them today.

A major caveat must be placed on the possibility of a technologically driven fourth generation, at least in the American context. Even if the technological state of the art permits a high-technology fourth generation and this is not clearly the case – the technology itself must be translated into *weapons* that are effective in actual combat. At present, our research, development and procurement process has great difficulty making this transition. It often produces weapons that incorporate high technology irrelevant in combat or too complex to work in the chaos of combat. Too many so-called "smart" weapons provide examples; in combat they are easy to counter, fail of their own complexity or make impossible demands on their operators. The current American research, development and procurement process may simply not be able to make the transition to a militarily effective fourth generation of weapons.

A potential idea-driven fourth generation

Technology was the primary driver of the second generation of warfare; ideas were the primary driver of the third. An idea-based fourth generation is also conceivable.

For about the last 500 years, the West has defined warfare. For a military to be effective it generally had to follow Western models. Because the West's strength is technology, it may tend to conceive of a fourth generation in technological terms.

However, the West no longer dominates the world. A fourth generation may emerge from non-Western cultural traditions, such as Islamic or Asiatic traditions. The fact that some non-Western areas, such as the Islamic world, are not strong in technology may lead them to develop a fourth generation through ideas rather than technology.

The genesis of an idea-based fourth generation may be visible in terrorism. This is not to say that terrorism is fourth generation warfare, but rather that elements of it may be signs pointing toward a fourth generation.

Some elements in terrorism appear to reflect the previously noted "carry-overs" from third generation warfare. The more successful terrorists appear to operate on broad mission orders that carry down to the level of the individual terrorist. The "battlefield" is highly dispersed and includes the whole of the enemy's society. The terrorist lives almost completely off the land and the enemy. Terrorism is very much a matter of maneuver: the terrorist's firepower is small, and where and when he applies it is critical.

Two additional carryovers must be noted as they may be useful "signposts" pointing toward the fourth generation. The first is a component of collapsing the enemy. It is a shift in focus from the enemy's front to his rear. Terrorism must seek to collapse the enemy from within as it has little capability (at least at present) to inflict widespread destruction. First generation warfare focused tactically and operationally (when operational art was practiced) on the enemy's front, his combat forces. Second generation warfare remained frontal tactically, but at least in Prussian practice it focused operationally on the enemy's rear through the emphasis on encirclement. The third generation shifted the tactical as well as the operational focus to the enemy's rear. Terrorism takes this a major step further. It attempts to bypass the enemy's military entirely and strike directly at his homeland, at civilian targets. Ideally, the enemy's military is simply irrelevant to the terrorist.

The second signpost is the way terrorism seeks to use the enemy's strength against *him*. This "judo" concept of warfare begins to manifest itself in the second generation, in the campaign and battle of encirclement. The enemy's fortresses, such as Metz *and* Sedan, became fatal traps. It was pushed further in the third generation where, on the defensive, one side often tries to let the other penetrate so his own momentum makes him less able to turn and deal with a counterstroke.

Terrorists use a free society's freedom and openness, its greatest strengths, against it. They can move freely within our society while actively working to subvert it. They use our democratic rights not only to penetrate but also to defend themselves. If we treat them within our laws, they gain many protections; if we simply shoot them down, the television news can easily make them appear to be the victims. Terrorists can effectively wage their form of warfare while being protected by the society they are attacking. If we are forced to set aside our own system of legal protections to deal with terrorists, the terrorists win another sort of victory.

Terrorism also appears to represent a solution to a problem that has been generated by previous generational changes but not really addressed by any of them. It is the contradiction between the nature of the modern battlefield and the traditional military culture. That culture, embodied in ranks, saluting uniforms, drill, etc., is largely a product of first generation warfare. It is a culture of order. At the time it evolved it was consistent with the battlefield, which was itself dominated by order. The ideal army was a perfectly oiled machine, and that was what the military culture of order sought to produce.

However, each new generation has brought a major shift toward a battlefield of disorder. The military culture, which has remained a culture of order, has become contradictory to the battlefield. Even in the third generation warfare, the contradiction has not been insoluble; the *Wehrmacht* bridged it effectively, outwardly maintaining the traditional culture of order while in combat demonstrating the adaptability and fluidity a disorderly battlefield demands. But other militaries, such as the British, have been less successful at dealing with the contradiction. They have often attempted to carry the culture of order over onto the battlefield with disastrous results. At Biddulphsberg, in the Boer War, for example, a handful of Boers defeated two British Guards battalions that fought as if on parade.

The contradiction between the military culture *and* the nature of modern war confronts a traditional military Service with a dilemma. Terrorists resolve the dilemma by eliminating the culture of order. Terrorists do not have uniforms, drill, saluting or, for the most part, ranks. Potentially, they have or could develop a military culture that is consistent with the disorderly nature of modern war. The fact that their broader culture may be non-Western may facilitate this development.

Even in equipment, terrorism may point toward signs of a change in generations. Typically, an older generation requires much greater resources to achieve a given end than does its successor. Today, the United States is spending $500 million apiece for stealth bombers. A terrorist stealth bomber is a car with a bomb in the trunk – a car that looks like every other car.

Terrorism, technology and beyond

Again, we are not suggesting terrorism is the fourth generation. It is not a new phenomenon, and so far it has proven largely ineffective. However, what do we see if we combine terrorism with some of the new technology we have discussed? For example, what effectiveness might the terrorist have if his car bomb were a product of genetic engineering rather than high explosives? To draw our potential fourth generation out still further, what if we combined terrorism, high technology and the following additional elements?

- A non-national or transnational base, such as an ideology or religion. Our national security capabilities are designed to operate within a nation-state framework. Outside that framework, they have great difficulties. The drug war provides an example. Because the drug traffic has no nation-state base, it is very difficult to attack. The nation-state shields the drug lords but cannot control them. We cannot attack them without violating the sovereignty of a friendly nation. A fourth-generation attacker could well operate in a similar manner, as some Middle Eastern terrorists already do.
- A direct attack on the enemy's culture. Such an attack works from within as well as from without. It can bypass not only the enemy's military but the state itself. The United States is already suffering heavily from such a cultural attack in the form of the drug traffic. Drugs directly attack our culture. They have the support of a powerful "fifth column," the drug buyers. They bypass the entire state apparatus despite our best efforts. Some ideological elements in South America see drugs as a weapon; they call them the "poor

man's intercontinental ballistic missile." They prize the drug traffic not only for the money it brings in through which we finance the war against ourselves – but also for the damage it does to the hated North Americans.

• Highly sophisticated psychological warfare, especially through *manipulation* of the media, particularly television news. Some terrorists already know how to play this game. More broadly, hostile forces could easily take advantage of a significant product of television reporting – the fact that on television the enemy's casualties can be almost as devastating on the home front as are friendly casualties. If we bomb an enemy city, the pictures of enemy civilian dead brought into every living room in the country on the evening news can easily turn what may have been a military success (assuming we also hit the military target) into a serious defeat.

All of these elements already exist. They are not the product of "futurism," of gazing into a crystal ball. We are simply asking what would we face if they were all combined? Would such a combination constitute at least the beginnings of a fourth generation of warfare? One thought that suggests they might is that third (not to speak of second) generation militaries would seem to have little capability against such a synthesis. This is typical of generational shifts.

The purpose of this chapter is to pose a question, not to answer it. The partial answers suggested here may in fact prove to be false leads. But in view of the fact that third generation warfare is now over 70 years old, we should be asking ourselves the question, what will the fourth generation be?

Note

1 Reprinted by permission of *Marine Corps Gazette.*

3   War evolves into the fourth generation

Thomas X. Hammes

Since the early 1990s, the Pentagon has been promulgating its vision of a new form of war. While the name of the vision has changed from year to year, the concept remains the same. High-technology, light forces will dominate the battlefield through a tightly connected network that allows US commanders to see everything, decide rapidly and execute immediately. The foundation of this concept is information dominance. It will come from the application of new technology.

The latest manifestation of this concept is "Transformation," in which:

> Information age military forces will be less platform-centric and more network-centric. They will be able to distribute forces more widely by increasing information sharing via a secure network that provides actionable information at all levels of command. This, in turn, will create conditions for increased speed of command and opportunities for self-coordination across the battlespace.[1]

Transformation is simply an updated version of four earlier concepts – the Chairman of the Joint Chiefs Joint Vision 2010, the Revolution in Military Affairs, the Navy's Network Centric Warfare and Joint Vision 2020 (JV 2010's updated version). All these concepts saw a future where "systems of systems" dominate the battlefield through high-technology sensors linked to precision weapons by a sophisticated and highly automated command and control system. All disregard any action taken by an intelligent, creative opponent to negate the technology.

Initial results in Afghanistan and Iraq seemed to validate that vision. Relatively small, high-technology forces smashed the Taliban and the Ba'athist regime. Unfortunately, in both cases, the enemy refused to accept defeat. Instead, they turned to insurgency. They drew us into the political, protracted conflict that is a fourth generation war (4GW).

This kind of warfare is not new or surprising, rather it has been evolving around the world over the last seven decades. In fact, America has lost to 4GW opponents three times: Vietnam, Lebanon and Somalia. This form of warfare has also defeated the French in Vietnam and Algeria and the USSR in Afghanistan. It continues to bleed Russia in Chechnya and the United States in

Iraq, Afghanistan and around the world against al-Qaeda. The consistent defeat of major powers by fourth generation opponents makes it essential that we understand this new form of warfare and adapt accordingly.

There is nothing mysterious about 4GW. Practitioners created it, nurtured it and have continued its development and growth. Faced with enemies they could not possibly beat using conventional war, they sought a different path.

Mao was the first to define insurgency as primarily a political struggle and use it successfully. Each practitioner since has learned from his predecessors or co-combatants in various places in the world. Then, usually through a painful process of trial and error, each has adjusted the lessons to his own fight. Each added his own refinement, and the cumulative result is a new generation of war. The anti-coalition forces in Iraq, the Taliban, the Chechens, the Palestinians and the al-Qaeda network are simply the latest to use an approach that has been developing for decades.

The question this chapter will seek to answer is whether the current insurgencies are merely aberrations or if the insurgencies represent the evolution of a new generation of war, one that is different from the Pentagon's vision of the future of warfare.

Theorists

While the Pentagon has commissioned numerous studies that predict warfare will evolve to the high-technology future asserted in its official documents, independent authors have disagreed.

As early as 1993, J. Arquilla and D. Ronfeldt outlined two possible forms of future warfare in their article "Cyberwar is Coming." One, cyberwar, envisioned a high-technology, short duration war where technology is vital and essentially machines fight machines. The other, netwar, envisioned complex, long-term conflicts.[2]

Martin van Creveld in his essay, "Through a Glass Darkly," points out the last 50 years have led to a fundamental erosion of the state's monopoly on the use of force.

> The roughly three-hundred-year period which was associated primarily with the type of political organization known as the state – first in Europe, and then, with its expansion, in other parts of the globe as well – seems to be coming to an end. If the last fifty years or so provide any guide, future wars will be overwhelmingly of the type known, however inaccurately, as "low intensity."[3]

In 1989, Bill Lind, G.I. Wilson and their co-authors, published "The Changing Face of War: Into the Fourth Generation." They stated three previous generations of modern warfare had evolved over the last few hundred years. The first was based on line and column, the second on firepower and the third was maneuver warfare.[4]

Theirs was one of the first, if not the first, attempts to understand how modern warfare was actually changing. They evaluated modern eras where the dominant military force was distinctly different from each previous era. In proposing the concept that these differences represent different generations of war, they outlined a very useful model. That model will allow us to study why and how the generations evolved and then see if we can detect similar evolutionary changes taking place in today's warfare.

From this very brief survey, it is clear that numerous authors have seen that warfare was changing. Those associated with the Department of Defense (DOD) have concentrated on the technological changes driving warfare. Others, primarily historians, have a broader interpretation of the reasons for change. They contend that such change requires changes in all major aspects of a society – political, economic, social and technical – to bring about a generational change in warfare.

In this chapter, I intend to show that a new form of war has, in fact, evolved. It is visible and distinctly different than the forms of war that preceded it. It evolved in conjunction with the political, economic, social and technological changes that are modifying our world.

Further, I intend to show that, like its predecessors, this new form of war did not arrive on the scene as a fully developed instrument but has evolved over decades and continues to evolve at widely scattered locations. We are not in the midst of a revolution of military affairs but rather an evolution. We can trace that evolution by examining our recent past.

For clarity in terminology and to provide a framework for study, I will adopt the generations model laid out by Lind, Wilson and compatriots. Like all models, it is not a perfect representation of reality. But it provides a framework to examine how previous generations evolved. First, we will examine the factors that drove the development of and transition to the first three generations of modern war. Then we will conduct a very brief survey of the political, economic, social and technological changes since third generation warfare evolved. Next, we will trace the development and evolution of 4GW. In doing so, we can develop a clear view of how this form of warfare has evolved and allows superior political will to defeat greater military and economic power.

First generation war

Lind, Wilson and fellow authors stated that each of the first three generations evolved in response to technical solutions to specific tactical challenges.

While technical advances clearly had an impact, attributing the generational changes in warfare primarily to technical factors oversimplifies the problem. The first generation of war grew not just from the invention of gunpowder, muskets and cannon but also from the political, economic and social structures that developed as Europe transitioned from a feudal system to states ruled by monarchs.

The transition from the feudal to Napoleonic warfare required centuries. It required not only reliable firearms but, more importantly, the political system, the wealth generating national economies, the social structures and the technologies capable of sustaining the mass armies of the Napoleonic era.

Politically, it required the evolution of the nation state to raise, train, equip and sustain its huge armies. Economically, major advances in agriculture and transportation were absolutely essential to generating the wealth and resources required to field, move and sustain them. Both the population[5] and the GDP per person[6] were increasing significantly faster than prior to 1500. The combination increased the overall wealth of the nation, provided additional food for major armies and freed manpower from agriculture for mobilization.

As the wealth and trade of European society increased, so did the road and inland barge transportation networks essential to move and sustain the much larger armies across Europe. In 1415 at Agincourt, a maximum of about 55,000 men fought.[7] In contrast, by 1812 Napoleon took almost 450,000 men with him into Russia.[8]

Socially, the development of patriotism was essential to enable Napoleonic warfare. Growing out of the French Revolution, patriotism allowed the poorly trained French columns to smash other nation's lines. With the success of the French, the Allies had to widen the base of their forces and the concept of nationalism overtook the other nations of Europe.

Technically, the mass production of the reliable smoothbore musket and the development of lightweight artillery contributed to the change in war. In short, it required changes across the political, economic, social and technical arenas to field the armies and massed direct fire weapons that marked the culmination of the first generation of war at Waterloo.

Second generation war

Similarly, the second generation of war did not grow just from improvements in weaponry. It too required changes across the spectrum of human activity. While the political structure of the nation state was essentially in place at the end of the Napoleonic Wars, the states' power to tax and enforce taxes increased dramatically during the 100 years between Waterloo and the Marne. More important than an increase in the ability to levy and collect taxes was the fact there was much vaster wealth to tax. The GDP per person in Western Europe almost tripled from 1800 to 1915 while the population increased about 50 percent.[9] The combination of increased GDP per person, major population increases and significantly better government control greatly increased the wealth available to the national governments of Europe.

Second generation war also required massive industrial output to produce the weapons and the huge quantities of ammunition they consumed. Further, transportation systems also had to mature. In particular, extensive rail systems and their supporting telegraph networks were necessary to move, control and coordinate the armies and their mountains of supplies. The strengths of national armies increased from hundreds of thousands to millions of men.

All of these factors – political, economic, social and technical – came together in a way that allowed massed firepower to dominate the battlefield by World War I.

Transition to third generation warfare

In 1939, Germany shocked the world with Blitzkrieg. While it made use of aircraft, armor and radio communication, all European nations had access to the same technology. So why did the Germans develop Blitzkrieg while the French and British did not?

The political and social atmospheres of the opposing sides were a critical aspect in the difference in development. While the politically unified state that permitted 3GW still existed throughout Europe, the social contract between governed and governors had been dramatically altered by World War I.

In the democracies, people no longer had blind faith in the institutions of government. Virtually every family in Britain and France had lost at least one male relative to the apparently pointless slaughter of the trenches. The Allies had mobilized almost 28 million men and suffered almost 12 million casualties.[10] The populace of the Allied nations rightly blamed these staggering losses on failures of both their governments and their militaries and would not support a military buildup.

The German people, despite suffering proportionately heavier casualties – six million of 11 million mobilized, did not react in the same fashion at all.[11] They never withdrew support from their armed forces. In fact, the armed forces remained a respected institution in the German government. Over time, the Germans developed the myth of the "stab in the back." They came to believe their army had not been defeated on the field of battle but rather betrayed by subversive elements in the civilian sector.

Thus, the political conditions were very different in the interwar period. Hitler was able to use the myth as part of his drive to power. The political will of Hitler allowed the German Army to begin rebuilding years ahead of the Allies. In contrast, the Chamberlain government in Britain did not begin rebuilding until February 1939, only seven months before the outbreak of hostilities.

For their part, the French were content to focus their assets on the deeply flawed concept of the Maginot Line. They prepared for the war they wanted not the war that was coming.

While the political climate varied greatly between the future belligerents, the economic factors were similar for all the nations involved. The fact is that despite the Great Depression all three nations, as well as the United States, had the economic base to build the combined arms forces that made Blitzkrieg possible. Since the end of World War I, each nation had developed a society capable of producing the equipment and the mechanics, drivers, electricians necessary to run it.

Only the Germans had the political will, intellectual honesty and strategic imperative to build a complete combined arms team to execute the tactics the Germans had developed in World War I.

While the Germans' new tactics failed to win World War I, they introduced an entire generation of German officers to the idea of mission type orders, reconnaissance pull and exploiting penetration. The Germans studied the war intensely and honestly. They came to understand what had actually happened and built on the foundation of 1918 so they were ready to exploit the technological improvements in 1939.

The French also conducted an intensive study of World War I seeking doctrinal and organizational lessons. Unfortunately, the institutional bias toward "methodical battle" ensured the study was limited to those battles that "proved" that a tightly-controlled, centrally-directed battle that emphasized firepower was the key to victory. Reinforcing the institutional bias was the requirement that "all articles, lectures, and books by serving officers had to receive approval by the high command before publication."[12] The uninspired interwar Army leadership, the stifling of discussion and the emphasis on the "methodical battle" ensured the French Army completely missed the evolution that drove Blitzkrieg.

It is interesting to note the similarities in the French interwar "discussion" and our current DOD "discussion" of future war. The French General Staff defined the discussion and then ensured all "experiments" and "developments" adhered to that definition. Currently, the DOD has defined the future as technology and is driving all experiments and developments in that direction. Much like the French, the DOD has not seen the evolution of war taking place in our time but instead insists war is evolving according to its pre-conceived technological vision.

Summary of the first three generations

In tracing the evolution of the first three generations of war, a few facts leap out. The first is that none of them came from a sudden transformation. Second, each new generation required developments across the spectrum of society. Each required major changes in the political, economic, social and technological arenas to create the conditions necessary for the next generation to evolve. Finally, each succeeding generation made use of the changes in society to reach deeper into the enemy's rear. If 4GW is a logical progression, it must reach much deeper into the enemy's forces in seeking victory.

Societal changes

Since war evolves along with society, a key question is, has society changed enough since the evolution of 3GW to allow an entirely new generation to evolve?

This chapter is too short to provide a definitive list of the enormous changes since World War II but a sampling of those changes will stimulate thought concerning the breadth and types of changes in society since the 1940s – and lead the reader to consider how those changes have affected warfare during the same period.

There have been extensive changes across the range of human activity since 3GW evolved in 1939. Politically, there are vastly more players in the arena. In 1945, there were 51 states in the UN, today there are 191.[13] Beyond the increase in states there are numerous other players. For instance, transnational groups such as Greenpeace, Islamic Brotherhood and drugs organizations influence decision making in even the most powerful countries. A situation not even conceived of in 1939.

Economically, powerful states used to control their own investment, tariff and trade policies. Today, various international organizations – such as the North American Free Trade Organization, the European Union, the World Bank and others – severely limit every nation's ability to set those policies independently. An even bigger economic change has resulted from what Thomas Freidman has called "Supermarkets" and "Electronic Herds."[14] Today, they dominate international trade and commerce. In fact, "by the end of 1997 twenty-five Supermarkets controlled 83 percent of the world's equities under institutional management and accounted for roughly half of global market capitalization – around $20 trillion."[15] Yet no state controls them.

Socially, the world is dramatically smaller. In 1945, the vast majority of people in the world knew only their own village. Even in developed nations, most knew only what they read in their newspapers and had little or no contact with people of other nations. Today, citizens of developed nations communicate with and travel freely around the globe. Small generators and satellite TV have delivered the world to even isolated, primitive villages. People's perception of what life should entail have changed dramatically.

The basic changes in technology are so obvious as to not need reviewing but one should consider a few examples. In 1939 when 3GW came to the fore, there was not a functioning computer on the planet, international communication was very expensive and the first transoceanic flights had just started.

It is obvious to any observer that there has been extraordinary change in the last 60 years. While not all sectors of a society are evolving at the same rate, they are all moving in the same direction. As we moved into the industrial era, governments, business, social organizations all moved to a hierarchical structure that was often national in scale. In the same way, as we move into the information age, all sectors of society are becoming networked on an international scale.

What is less obvious is the fact that the rate of change has been accelerating – and not just over the last 60 years but over the recorded history of man. In warfare, change is also accelerating. It took hundreds of years for first generation warfare to evolve. Second generation warfare evolved and peaked in the 100 years between Waterloo and Verdun. Third generation came to maturity in less than 25 years. Clearly, third generation warfare cannot be the leading edge of war over 60 years later. So what form of warfare has been evolving and where?

Mao and the birth of fourth generation war

Given the fact insurgency has often defeated third generation powers since 1945, we have to examine its evolution to see if it is leading us to fourth generation war.

The first practitioner to both write about and successfully execute a 4GW, Mao Tse-tung was a product of the intense turmoil that characterized China in the early twentieth century. Nineteen when the last emperor of the Qing Dynasty abdicated in 1912, he grew up under the collapsing imperial system. He was intensely interested in what form of government would fill the vacuum.

From joining the Communist Party in 1921 until he led their forces to victory in 1949, Mao developed and tested his theories of government and war constantly. He did not develop these theories in an academic setting. He lived them. During this period, he rose from activist to army commander to supreme commander. He understood he must avoid direct confrontation with superior warlord and government forces and he needed the peasants on his side to win. He developed a strategic approach around those two precepts.

> This was summed up in a pithy folk rhyme, which conveyed the essence of the Red Army's future strategy. In its final form, drawn up by Mao and Zhu,[16] and popularized throughout the army in May, it contained sixteen characters:
>
> > Di jin, wo tui, [When the] enemy advances, we withdraw,
> > Di jiu, wo roa, [When the] enemy rests, we harass,
> > Di pi, wo da, [When the] enemy tires, we attack,
> > Di tui, wo jui, [When the] enemy withdraws, we pursue.
>
> Meanwhile the guidelines for the army's treatment of civilians, which Mao had first issued at Sanwan in September 1927, were expanded into what became known as the "Six Main Points for Attention." Soldiers were urged to replace straw bedding and wooden bed-boards after staying at peasant homes overnight; to return whatever they borrowed; to pay for anything they damaged; to be courteous; to be fair in business dealings; and to treat prisoners humanely.[17]

Mao saw revolution as a political struggle where he must pay great attention to maintaining the good will of the people. He knew only the peasants could provide an unbeatable intelligence network and a constant source of manpower and resources in the form of food and labor.

As the first practitioner to define insurgency, Mao, like Clausewitz, understood war is fundamentally a political undertaking. However, he went much further than Clausewitz stating: "The problem of political mobilization of the army and the people is indeed of the utmost importance ... political mobilization is the most fundamental condition for winning the war."[18] He further emphasized the primacy of political efforts when he stated. "This is a matter of the first magnitude on which the victory primarily depends."[19]

After firmly establishing the overriding political character of insurgency, Mao outlined his famous three phases for the successful conduct of insurgency. Phase one is political mobilization. Phase two is guerrilla warfare to wear down the government. Phase three is the destruction of the government using conventional forces.

Mao knew insurgents could not match the government's conventional military forces initially. Therefore, he conceived the careful buildup of political, social and economic power during Phase I and II. His goal was nothing less than to change the "correlation of forces" between the government and the insurgent. Only after that shift would the insurgent be ready to move to Phase III, the final destruction of the government by conventional forces.

"People's War" was correctly hailed as a new form of war. Mao was the first to envision political power as the key to insurgency. Mao also understood that networked, interlocked, mass organizations were the key to political power. He advanced warfare by showing how powerful maneuver forces could be beaten by political strength applied over time. His was the fundamental work upon which the fourth generation of war would be built.

The Vietnamese modification

Necessity being the mother of invention, the next major modification of communist insurgency doctrine was developed and employed by Ho Chi Minh and Vo Nguyen Giap. Faced with defeating a powerful outside government, they developed a very interesting twist to the concept of People's War. While maintaining the Maoist model of a three-phase insurgency based on the peasants, they refined the model to include an aggressive attack on the national will of their real principle enemy – first, France and then the United States. Ho and Giap developed the ability to take the political war to their distant enemy's homeland and destroy his will to continue the struggle. They were greatly aided in their efforts by both the French and US inability to understand the type of war they were fighting. A decade after the war ended, Colonel Harry Summers wrote "There are still those who would attempt to fit it into the revolutionary war mold and who blame our defeat on our failure to implement counterinsurgency doctrine."[20]

Yet both the First and Second Indochinese Wars made use of People's War – as explicitly stated by Ho Chi Minh. In his address to the Second National Congress of the Viet-Nam Worker's Party in 1951, Ho summarized the Viet Minh revolution to date.

> Our Party and Government foresaw that our Resistance War has three stages. In the first stage, … all we did was to preserve and increase our main forces. In the second stage, we have actively contended with the enemy and prepared for the general counteroffensive. The third stage is the general counteroffensive.[21]

Ho categorically stated he was using People's War to defeat France and then did so.

Following the defeat of the French, the United States subsequently decided to back the South Vietnamese government and incrementally increased our commitment until we had over 500,000 troops in Vietnam. Confronted with a much more powerful foe, Ho did not change his strategy. As he explained in 1962 to Bernard Fall, French author and expert on the Indochina conflict:

> Sir, you have studied us for ten years, you have written about the Indochina War. It took us eight years of bitter fighting to defeat you French in Indochina.... The Americans are stronger than the French. It might perhaps take ten years but our heroic compatriots in the South will defeat them in the end. We shall marshal public opinion about this unjust war against the South Vietnamese.[22]

He openly explained how he expected to beat the US/South Vietnamese alliance. He planned a war of attrition accompanied by intensive national and international propaganda to weaken American resolve. After accurately explaining what he planned, Ho then executed that plan. Ho had advanced 4GW another step. He twice defeated massively superior military and economic powers despite the fact he could neither threaten their homelands nor even fully defeat the military forces they sent to Vietnam.

The Sandinistas refinement

In Nicaragua, the Sandinistas, through evolutionary steps, further increased the emphasis on political development driving the battlefield outcome. They refined the Maoist doctrine by making political strategy itself the end game. In the Sandinista strategy, political maneuvering would not be the precursor to a conventional invasion – it would serve as the invasion itself by destroying external support for the Nicaraguan National Guard. However, like previous innovations, it took time, mistakes and numerous false paths before the Sandinistas found the solution to seizing power.

Founded in 1961, the Sandinistas initially had no clear concept on how they would take power. They tried, in turn, a "foco"[23] insurgency, an urban based insurgency and then a rural peasant based one (three times). In each case, their organizations were quickly identified and attacked with disastrous results for the insurgents.

After all these failures, Humberto Ortega chose a very different course for the movement. Ortega's bold solution was to create a "third way" between the competing urban and peasant proponents. He formed a broad-front, urban based coalition whose strength rested in a network of middle-class businessmen, entrepreneurs, unemployed students and urban poor of the shantytowns. On May 4, 1977, he published a new FSLN (Sandinista National Liberation Front) strategy paper that,

> contained the basic insurrectional strategy, including (1) development of a program without leftist rhetoric; (2) creation of a broad anti-Somoza front

with non-Marxist opposition groups; (3) creation of mass organizations to support the FSLN; (4) agitation to bring about the radicalization of the moderate opposition; (5) action to undermine the integrity of the National Guard; and (6) unification of the three FSLN factions under a joint leadership.[24]

His emphasis on concealing the FSLN's leftist doctrine combined with active propaganda for a moderate coalition allowed him to convince a wide range of Somoza's opponents to join the coalition.

His real innovation was that, despite the appearance of a broad front, Ortega ensured the key elements of power, namely all of the coalition's military and security elements, remained firmly in the hands of the communist leaders.

Much more important to the revolution than activities within the country was the work the Sandinistas did to further undermine support for the Somoza regime in the international community. They showed true strategic vision and operational finesse in orchestrating this campaign while simultaneously consolidating their control on the "popular front" that was opposing the regime.

After the war, a Sandinista leader explained why the revolution was successful:

An armed element is still a key requirement for revolution wherein the cadres are educated and "blooded." We earn our leadership positions in the new order by paying our dues in Sierra. The mass appeal of broad-front political organization is also a must in which disaffected non-Marxists and non-Marxist–Leninists are brought into the movement. This ensures not only better and wider internal support but outside support that does not have a Cuban, Eastern Bloc or Soviet taint can also be obtained.

Because of the superior unity and discipline of the Party, the real power will not be shared with those who provide essentially window dressing for the revolution.

The Church, by now heavily infiltrated with Liberation Theologists, gives us guerrillas the moral high ground we've never enjoyed before.[25]

This honest appraisal shows clearly how the Sandinistas advanced the art of war. Notice he never claimed the guerrillas were essential to victory. Rather he stated that, like all insurgents before them, the leaders earned their positions by fighting. So, although the Sandinistas consistently failed in the efforts to instigate a rural insurgency, the rural efforts provided a crucible to toughen the leaders who would lead the guerrilla elements of the insurgency.

He is very clear that the broad-front political organization was essential to both attract people to the movement and to ensure external support from non-communist bloc countries. He states that the Party (the FSLN) was the real power behind the coalition at all times – and had no intention of ever sharing the power with the moderate coalition members. The moderates were simply window dressing. Finally, he clearly states that the Sandinistas used the priests and philosophy of Liberation Theology to provide unassailable moral high ground for the insurgency.

The Sandinistas' unique contribution was to eliminate the requirement for the final conventional military offensive. Their political efforts so severely changed "the correlation of forces" that the government collapsed and they occupied the vacuum.

Intifada

The next evolution in 4GW came out of the Palestinian Intifada. Ignited by a spontaneous uprising, the Intifada demonstrated both networking and emergence as new characteristics of insurgency. The isolation of Yasser Arafat and his Palestinian Liberation Organization in Tunisia forced the local Palestinian leadership to take charge of the uprising. Although they could draw upon existing self-help organizations that provided medical services, education and social services, the Palestinians had no national organization in the Occupied Territories when the Intifada literally exploded onto the political landscape.

In response, the local organizations rapidly formed a coalition that provided local guidance to the people in each area. In turn, these local organizations were guided by a self-organizing, self-appointed national council via regularly published "night letters." The Palestinians knew they could not defeat the Israelis militarily, so they

> concentrated on out administering, not outfighting the enemy. The aim ... is not simply to inflict military losses on the enemy but to destroy the legitimacy of its (the Israeli) government and to establish a rival regime.[26]

They targeted different messages to the three primary groups involved in the struggle. To the Palestinian people the message was simple, "We are continuing to fight." They hammered the point home that the Palestinian people, fighting by themselves, had lasted longer than all the Arab states put together. The Palestinians knew the will of their people was critical and they worked very hard to maintain it.

The message to the Israelis was different but also simple. "As long as the Israelis occupy the territories there will be no peace." Since most Israelis serve in the armed forces, Israeli parents knew their sons and daughters would face continual unrest. While these parents were prepared for their sons and daughters to fight to preserve Israel, they were not as certain they wanted them to face continual bombardment with rocks, bottles and hate in a questionable attempt to hold onto the Occupied Territories. The casualty figures reinforced Israeli reluctance to continue the occupation. While such figures are a source of much controversy, the Israeli group, B'Tselem, states that during the Intifada only eighty Israeli civilians were killed while 1,019 Palestinian civilians were killed.[27] Israelis could not reconcile their self image as a liberal democracy with the actions necessary to suppress the uprising in the Occupied Territories. The Palestinian message reinforced this unease.

Finally, there was the message for international consumption. It was: "The Palestinians are an oppressed, impoverished but very brave and resolute people fighting for human dignity. They asked only to have the occupying power go home and allow the Palestinians to be citizens of their own country." The constant repetition of this theme accompanied by daily media coverage of teenagers in jeans and t-shirts armed only with rocks confronting tanks changed the image of Israel in the world's eyes. Israel was no longer seen as a tiny state surrounded by a sea of hostile Arabs but rather as a brutal occupying power denying legitimate Palestinian aspirations for their own nation.

The Palestinians used a network of anonymous leaders to sustain the movement through six long years. They remained focused on the will of the Israeli voters and in the end, those voters replaced Likud with Labor. Labor negotiated the 1993 Oslo Accords. For the first time in history, an Arab organization had forced the Israelis to give up territory and they did so without a military force or a centralized command. Rather a coalition of the willing, united by an idea sustained by a network defeated the dominant military power in the Middle East.

Al Aqsa Intifada

With the Oslo Accords on September 13, 1993, the Palestinians had apparently started down the path to a state of their own. After decades of conflict, it appeared that the Palestinians would finally have a territory to call their own. The six-year Intifada set the internal and external conditions necessary for both sides to accept the unthinkable – recognition of the blood enemy. Yet, at the time of this writing, that dream has faded to dust.

The obvious question is what happened? How did the Palestinians go from a well executed fourth generation campaign to the bloody war of attrition that is the al Aqsa Intifada.

In short, Arafat returned and reasserted his authority. Between Arafat and the Israeli security services, the new Palestinians leaders were neutralized and Arafat's corrupt, inflexible regime took charge. As the Oslo Accords fell apart (with significant help from both Palestinian and Israeli radicals), the Palestinians reverted to the current bombing campaign. Motivated by the Israeli withdrawal from Lebanon, the radicals became convinced they could force the Israelis from the West Bank.

Unfortunately, for the Palestinians, the message they sent to both Israelis and the West was the desire to completely destroy Israel. No Israeli government can negotiate in the face of such a threat and no Western government could pressure them to. They had completely abandoned 4GW and reverted to pure terror.

The Israelis, on the other hand, had learned from the Intifada. This time, they had multiple messages. For the international community, they projected a reasonable approach of a democracy under attack. They stated they could not negotiate with people who bombed their children intentionally. They allowed full media coverage of attack sites so the impact was passed to the Western world.

To their own population, they repeated the Palestinian message of utter destruction. When faced with that threat, the Israelis had no choice but to support the harsh Likud methods.

Under the cover of these 4GW messages, the Israelis continued a rapid expansion of settlements on the West Bank. Sticking to Sharon's long-term strategy, they established "facts on the ground." Using security requirements as the reason, they built roads and outposts that cut the West Bank into economically unviable enclaves.

In short, the situation is completely reversed since the end of Intifada I. Israel is back to being the oppressed nation fighting for its survival, Palestinians are terrorists again and the US policy on the struggle could have been written in Jerusalem. The rapid reversal of fortunes shows the political message and image are central to 4GW. The Israelis mended theirs for the international and domestic audiences – with a great deal of assistance by bad Palestinian decisions. Projecting the image of a small, brave nation struggling for survival, they have been able to virtually recreate apartheid without any significant Western outcry.

In contrast, the Palestinians have managed to project the worst possible image to their own people, the Israelis and the Western community. They have ensured that even their legitimate grievances are buried in the avalanche of outrage over the suicide bombing campaign and stated desire to destroy Israel. Compounding the damage, the actions are being taken by corrupt, incompetent leaders who clearly care more about themselves than about their people. The Palestinians have proven to be their own worst enemy.

The death of Arafat may provide an opportunity for the Palestinians to abandon their disastrous approach. The election and the initial steps of the new Palestinian administration give reason for hope but it will require patience and courage from both sides to pursue peace.

Common sense

Common sense virtually demands that movements seeking political and social change will use 4GW. Since World War II, wars have been a mixed bag of conventional and unconventional. Conventional wars – the Korean War, the Israeli–Arab wars of 1956, 1967 and 1973, the Falklands (Malvinas) War, the Iran–Iraq War, and the first Gulf War – have ended with a return to the strategic status quo. While some territory changed hands and, in some cases, regimes changed, in essence each state came out of the war with largely the same political, economic and social structure with which it entered.

In sharp contrast, unconventional wars – the Communist revolution in China, the First and Second Indochina Wars, the Algerian War of Independence, the Sandinista struggle in Nicaragua, the Iranian revolution, the Afghan–Soviet War of the 1980s, the first Intifada, and the Hezbollah campaign in South Lebanon – display a markedly different pattern. Each ended with major changes in the political, economic and social structure of the territories involved. While the changes may not have been for the better, they were distinct changes. Even those unconventional wars where the insurgents lost (Malaya, Oman, El Salvador) led to significant changes. The message is clear for anyone wishing to shift the political balance of power: only unconventional war works against established powers.

This brief survey of history, societal changes, current events and common sense, all indicate warfare has moved beyond high-technology maneuver war.

4GW

Beginning with Mao's concept that political will defeats superior military power and progressing to Intifada I's total reliance on the mass media and international networks to neutralize Israel's military power, warfare underwent a fundamental change. It shifted from an industrial age focus on the destruction of the enemy's armed forces to an information age focus on changing the minds of the enemy's political decision makers. With the al Aqsa Intifada and al Qaeda, we have seen that 4GW can develop a variety of strategies depending on the goals of the practitioner. In Iraq, we have seen that 4GW can hold its own even against the most technologically advanced and militarily powerful nation in the world.

Moreover, states have recognized that many of the 4GW techniques used by insurgents to neutralize superior military power are also available to them. Even a dictator as isolated as Saddam Hussein attempted to use some of these techniques. To build Islamic support, he posed as a protector of Islam, as a supporter of the Palestinians. To muddle the discussion in the UN, he claimed to have complied with the UN inspectors while using a series of delaying tactics to keep the inspection option open. He also worked to split the West focusing his efforts on France and Russia. While none of these actions prevented the invasion of his country, they did force the Bush Administration to expend significant political capital in responding to them.

China has also taken note of the potential for shifting the conflict to a wide range of fields rather than focusing on the military aspects. In "Unrestricted War," Qiao Liang and Wang Xiangsui ridicule the US focus on "military technical" war and propose that war must be expanded to six other fields: diplomatic, economic, financial, cyber, media/information and network. While working to improve their own conventional forces, they also seek expansion into all these fields to neutralize the US advantage in high-technology weaponry.

Recent history indicates that a new form of war has arrived. One that can defeat the previous generation, maneuver warfare, by making use of superior political will employed over time.

War has entered a new generation. Unfortunately for the West, it is not the high-technology war that plays to our strengths but rather an evolved form of insurgency that attacks our weaknesses.

Fourth generation war uses all available networks – political, economic, social, and military – to convince the enemy's political decision makers that their strategic goals are either unachievable or too costly for the perceived benefit. It is rooted in the fundamental precept that superior political will, when properly employed, can defeat greater economic and military power. 4GW does not attempt to win by defeating the enemy's military forces. Instead, combining guerrilla tactics or civil disobedience with the soft networks of social, cultural and economic ties, disinformation campaigns and innovative political activity, it directly attacks the will of enemy decision makers. Historically, fourth generation wars are lengthy – measured in decades rather than months or years.

Fourth generation war is a very different concept from the short, intense war the Pentagon has envisioned and focused on for the last 15 years. Unfortunately, it is the type of war that we see actually being fought in the world today.

Strategic aspects of 4GW

Strategically, 4GW does not attempt to achieve superiority on the battlefield. The first through the third generation objective of destroying the enemy's armed forces and his capacity to regenerate them is not how 4GW enemies plan to defeat their opponents. Both epic, decisive Napoleonic battles and wide-ranging high-speed maneuver campaigns are irrelevant to 4GW. Instead, 4GW will target specific messages to policy makers and to those who can influence the policy makers. Although tailored for various audiences, each message is designed to achieve the basic purpose of war: change an opponent's political position on a matter of national interest. The fights in Iraq and Afghanistan show these characteristics. In each, the insurgent is sending one message to his supporters, another to the mass of the undecided population and a third to the Coalition decision makers. The message to their supporters is that they are "defending the faith and their country against outside invaders." The message to their uncommitted or pro-coalition countrymen is that it is "a fight between us and the invaders. Stay out of it or you will get hurt. You know the Americans will eventually leave and we will still be here." Finally, their message to the Coalition, particularly to Americans, is that, "unless you withdraw, you are engaged in an endless and costly fight."

4GW is not bloodless. In fact, we have seen in Iraq, Afghanistan, Chechnya and Palestine that most 4GW casualties will be civilians. Further, many will not be victims of military weapons but rather of materials made available within the society. This is an aspect of 4GW that we must understand. The 4GW opponent does not have to build the warfighting infrastructure essential to earlier generations of war. As displayed in the Beirut bombings, the Khobar Tower bombing, the Northern Ireland campaign, the African Embassy bombings, 9/11 and the ongoing bombing campaign in Iraq, 4GW practitioners are making more and more use of materials made available by the society they are attacking. This allows them to take a very different strategic approach. It relieves the 4GW practitioner of the strategic necessity of defending core production assets, leaving them free to focus on offense rather than defense. It also relieves them of the logistics burden of moving supplies long distances. Instead, they have to move only money and ideas – both of which can be digitized and moved instantly.

Even at the strategic level, the importance of the media in shaping the policy of the participants will continue to increase. We saw a demonstration of this when US interest in Somalia, previously negligible, was stimulated by the repeated images of thousands of starving Somali children. Conversely, the images of US soldiers being dragged through the streets ended that commitment. The media will continue to be a major factor from the strategic to the tactical level. In fact, worldwide media exposure can quickly give a tactical action strategic impact.

Political aspects of 4GW

In the political arena, 4GW warriors will seek to use international, transnational, national and sub national networks for their own purposes. Internationally there are a growing variety of networks available – the United Nations, NATO, the World Bank, OPEC and dozens of others. Each organization has a different function in international affairs; but each has its own vulnerabilities and can be used to convey a political message to its leadership and from there to targeted capital cities. While these international organizations may not be capable of directly changing the minds of national leaders, they can be used to slow or paralyze an international response.

Their obvious use is to create a political paralysis in both the international organizations (not usually a difficult task) and in the target nation (difficulty varies with the nation being targeted.) However in addition to normal political attacks, 4GW planners can influence other aspects of the target society. They know that the security situation in a country has a direct effect on the ability of that nation to get loans. The international marketplace is a swift and impersonal judge of credit worthiness. This gives the attacker a very different avenue to effect the position of a nation – the mere threat of action may be enough to impact the financial status of the target nation and encourage them to negotiate. Thus, if his objective is simply to paralyze the political processes of a target nation, he can use a number of avenues to create that effect. Recent attacks on oil production infrastructure in Iraq have painfully illustrated this fact. The Nigerian rebels have also used the threat to oil production to force negotiation on the Nigerian government. The fact oil prices were at an all time high gave the rebels more leverage because each day's delay increased the costs to the Nigerian government. As the world becomes ever more interconnected, the potential for varied approaches increases and the effects may reinforce each other.

A coherent 4GW plan will also include transnational elements in a variety of ways. They may include belief-based organizations like Islamic Jihad and mainline Christian churches; nationalistic organizations such as the Palestinians and Kurds; humanitarian organizations; economic structures such as the stock and bond markets; and criminal organizations such as narco-traffickers and arms merchants. The key traits of transnational organizations are that none are contained completely within a recognized nation state's borders; none have official members that report back to nation states and they owe no loyalty to any nation – and sometimes very little loyalty to their own organizations.

The use of such transnational elements will vary with the strategic situation. But they provide a variety of possibilities. They can be a source of recruits. They can be used – at times unwittingly – as cover to move people and assets. They can be an effective source of funds – charitable organizations have supported terrorists as diverse as the IRA and al Qaeda. During the 1970s, Irish bars on the east coast of America often had jars where patrons could donate to the "cause." The jars indicated the money was to provide support to Irish families when in fact much of the money went directly to support IRA insurgent operations. At times, entire organizations can be used openly to support the position of the 4GW operator. Usually this is done when the organization genuinely agrees with the position of one of the antagonists but false flag operations are also viable. Such support can lend great legitimacy to a movement and even reverse long held international views of a specific situation.

National political institutions are primary targets for 4GW messages. The Congress of the United States was both a target of and a network for the North Vietnamese, the Sandinistas and the Palestinians. They knew Congress controls the US budget. If the Congress cut off funds, the US allies would lose their wars. Thus, Congressmen were targeted with the message that "the war was unwinnable and it made no sense to keep fighting it." The Sandinistas even worked hard to make individual Congressmen part of their network by sponsoring trips for Congressional aides and mainline church groups to insurgent held areas in Nicaragua. If they could convince their guests that Somoza's government was indeed corrupt, they would actively lobby Congress to cut off aid to Somoza.

Non-governmental national groups have also been major players in shaping national policies – churches, diaspora associations, business groups and even lobbying firms. We must assume 4GW opponents will continue these efforts.

Sub national organizations can both represent groups who are minorities in their traditional homelands such as the Basques and those who are self-selecting minorities such as Sons of Liberty and Aryan Nation. These groups are in unusual positions. They can be either enemies or allies of the established power. It depends on who best serves their interests. Even more challenging, since they are not in fact unified groups, one element of a sub national group may support the government while another element supports the insurgent.

Political alliances, interests and positions among and between insurgents will change according to various political, economic, social and military aspects of the conflict. While this has been a factor in all wars (Italy changed sides in the middle of the biggest conventional war of all time), it will be prevalent in 4GW. It is much easier for non-nation state entities (tribes, clans, businesses, criminal groups, racial groups, sub national groups, transnational groups) to change sides than it is for nation states or national groups. A government usually ties itself to a specific cause. It has to convince decision makers or its people to support it. Thus it can be very awkward for that government to change sides in mid-conflict without losing the confidence of its people. Often, the act of changing sides will lead to the fall of the government. In contrast, non-state entities get involved only for their own needs and if these needs shift, they can easily shift loyalties. In Somalia, Afghanistan, Iraq and innumerable skirmishes in Africa, alliances shift like a kaleidoscope.

Operational level techniques for 4GW

To succeed, the 4GW operational planner must determine the message he wants to send; the networks best suited to carry those messages; the actions that will cause the network to send the message; and the feedback system that will tell him if the message is being received. He must seek different pathways for his messages. Traditional diplomatic channels, both official and unofficial are still important but are no longer the only pathway for communication and influence. Other networks rival the prominence of the official ones.

The media has become a primary avenue as has been painfully obvious in Vietnam, the West Bank and Iraq. Professional lobbying groups have also proven effective. An increasingly important avenue is the internet and the power it provides grass roots campaigns. Whether the anti-land mine campaign or Zarkawi's terror campaign in Iraq, the internet provides an alternate channel for high impact messages unfiltered by editors or political influence. It can also be used to raise money.

A key factor in a 4GW campaign is that the audience is not a simple unified target. It is increasingly fragmented into interest groups who shift sides depending on how a particular campaign affects their issues. During Intifada I, the Palestinians tailored different messages for different constituencies. The Israelis are doing the same during al Aqsa Intifada, as are the Anti-Coalition Forces in Iraq and Afghanistan.

To date, the US has not understood the importance of messages in 4GW. As recently as last year, military spokesmen kept insisting that the insurgent attacks on US troops in Iraq were "militarily insignificant." This was at a time each attack was on the front page of major daily newspapers in the United States and Europe. While the actual casualties may have been few, each story reached the decision makers in Congress and the public.

In contrast, 4GW practitioners have used networks successfully for a variety of reasons. In Kosovo, the seizure of UN hostages was the first step of a cycle. The media was then used to transmit images of them chained to a bridge. Then the insurgents watched TV to determine the response of the various governments. It allowed them to commit the act, transmit it via various channels, observe the response and then decide what to do. All this occurred much faster than the bureaucratic reporting processes of NATO could complete the same cycle.

During Intifada I, the Palestinians made an operational decision to limit the use of violence. They confronted the Israeli Army not with heavily armed guerrillas but with teenagers armed only with rocks. By doing so, they neutralized

US support for Israeli action, froze the Israeli defense forces and influenced the Israeli national election which led to the Oslo Accords.

Similarly, the series of bombings conducted by the Iraqi insurgents throughout the fall and winter of 2003–2004 carefully targeted the organizations most helpful to the Coalition Provisional Authority – police, UN, NGOs, coalition partners, the Kurdish political parties and Sh'ia clerics. Each event was tactically separated by time and space, but each tied together operationally to attack America's strategic position in the country.

The campaign continues even today with each attack designed to prevent a stable, democratic government from emerging. Not all have succeeded but they did drive the UN and many NGOs out of the country. Further, the coalition is shrinking and the insurgency has clearly impacted the price of oil. The threat of instability spreading to the rest of the Gulf increases the upward pressure on oil prices.

To complicate matters, 4GW will include aspects of earlier generations of war in conjunction with those of fourth generation. Even as Israelis struggled with the Intifada, they had to be constantly aware that major conventional forces were on their border. Similarly in Vietnam, the United States and later South Vietnam had to deal with aggressive, effective fourth generation guerrillas while always being prepared to deal with major North Vietnamese Army (NVA) conventional forces. Clearly 4GW seeks to place an enemy on the horns of this dilemma. Just as clearly, this is an intentional approach and goes all the way back to Mao.

Action in one or all of the fields above will not be limited to the geographic location (if any) of the antagonists but will take place worldwide. Al Qaeda has forcefully illustrated this to us. Though some elements will be more attractive as targets, no element of US society, no matter where it is located in the world is off limits to attack.

The range of possible 4GW opponents is broad. It is important to remember that such an opponent does not need a large command and control system. At a time when US forces are pouring ever more money and manpower into command and control, commercial technology makes worldwide, secure communications available to anyone with a laptop and a credit card. It also provides access to 1-meter resolution satellite imagery, extensive information on US troop movements, immediate updates on national debates and international discussion forums. Finally, it provides a worldwide, fairly-secure financial network. In fact, with the proliferation of internet cafes, one does not need either the credit card or the laptop. All one needs is an understanding of how email and a browser work and some very basic HUMINT tradecraft.

At the operational level, all that an opponent has to move is ideas and funds. He can do so through a wide variety of methods from email to snail mail to personal courier to messages embedded in classified advertisements. He will try to submerge his communications in the noise of the every day activity that is an essential part of a modern society. He will disguise the movement of material and funds as commerce – using commercial sources and vehicles. His people will do their best to merge into whatever civil society they find themselves in.

As a result, it will be extremely difficult to detect the operational level activities of a sophisticated 4GW opponent.

Tactical considerations

Tactically, 4GW takes place in the complex environment of low intensity conflict. Every potential opponent of the United States has observed the Gulf War, Operation Iraqi Freedom and Afghanistan. They understand that if you provide America with clear targets, no matter how well fortified, those targets will be destroyed. Just as certainly, they have seen the success of the Vietnamese and the Somalis. They have also seen and are absorbing the continuing lessons of Chechnya, Palestine, Afghanistan and Iraq. They will not fight us conventionally.

In attempting to change the minds of key decision makers, antagonists will use a variety of tactical paths to get their message through to presidents, prime ministers, members of cabinets, legislators and even voters. Immediate, high impact messages will probably come via visual media – and the more dramatic and bloody the image, the stronger the message. Longer-term, less immediate but more thought provoking messages will be passed via business, church, economic, academic, artistic and even social networks. While the messages will be based on a strategic theme, the delivery will be by tactical action such as guided tours of refugee camps, exclusive interviews with insurgent leaders, targeted kidnappings, beheadings, car bombings, assassinations, etc.

Tactically, 4GW will involve a mixture of international, transnational, national and sub national actors. Since the operational planner of a 4GW campaign must use all the tools available to him, we can assume that we will have to deal with actors from all these arenas at the tactical level as well. Even more challenging, some will be violent actors and others will be non-violent. In fact, the very term non-combatant applies much more easily to conventional conflicts between states than fourth generation war involving state and non-state actors. Non-violent actors, while being legally non-combatants, will be a critical part of tactical actions in 4GW. By using crowds, protestors, media interviews, internet web sites and other "non violent" methods, the 4GW warrior can create tactical dilemmas for their opponents. It will require tactical resources in police, intelligence, military, propaganda and political spheres to deal with the distractions they create.

Tactical military action (terrorist, guerrilla or, rarely, conventional) will be tied to the message and targeted at various groups. The August 19, 2003 bombing of the UN facility in Iraq convinced the UN it was too costly to continue to operate in Iraq. The August 19, 2004 burning of the southern Iraq oil buildings had an immediate effect on the per barrel price of oil. These were two tactical actions with very different messages for very different target audiences; yet, they both support the strategic goal of increasing the cost to the United States of staying in Iraq.

War evolves along with society. Recent history, current events and common sense all point to the fact a new generation of war has evolved. It evolved as practical men solved real problems in an attempt to win against a militarily more powerful force. Fourth generation war has been the result and it is being used by intelligent, ambitious men across the world.

Characteristics of 4GW

Fourth generation war uses all available networks – political, economic, social and military – to convince the enemy's political decision makers that their strategic goals are either unachievable or too costly for the perceived benefit. It is rooted in the fundamental precept that superior political will, when properly employed, can defeat greater economic and military power. 4GW does not attempt to win by defeating the enemy's military forces. Instead, combining guerrilla tactics or civil disobedience with the soft networks of social, cultural and economic ties, disinformation campaigns and innovative political activity, it directly attacks the enemy's political will.

Fourth generation war spans the spectrum of human activity – political, economic, social and military. Politically, it involves transnational, national and sub-national organizations and networks to convey its message to the target audiences. Strategically, it focuses on breaking the will of decision makers. It uses different pathways to deliver different messages for different target audiences. The messages serve three purposes: to break the enemy's will; maintain the will of its own people; ensure neutrals remain neutral or provide tacit support to the cause. Operationally, it delivers those messages in a variety of ways from high impact, high profile direct military actions to indirect economic attacks such as those designed to drive up the price of oil. Tactically, 4GW forces avoid direct confrontation if possible while seeking maximum impact it uses materials present in the society under attack. To minimize their logistics requirements they can attack using industrial chemicals, liquefied natural gas tankers or fertilizer shipments. Finally, 4GW practitioners plan for long wars – decades rather than months or years.

In sum, 4GW is political, socially (rather than technically) networked and protracted in duration. It is the anti-thesis of the high-technology, short war the Pentagon is preparing to fight.

Final caution

Let me close with a final thought. Fourth generation war has been around for over seventy years. No doubt fifth generation warfare (5GW) is evolving even as we attempt to deal with its predecessor. We may not recognize it as it evolves around us. Or we may look at several alternative futures and see each as fifth generation.

One possible form of 5GW is represented by the anthrax and ricin attacks on Capitol Hill. Although similar to fourth generation attacks, they seem to have been conducted by an individual or, at most, a very small group. It is much too early to tell if these were fifth generation attacks, but super-empowered individuals or small groups conducting such an attack would be in keeping with several emerging global trends – the rise of biotechnology, the increasing power of the knowledge worker and the changing nature of loyalties. Each of these trends increases the destructive potential of small groups and makes the DOD's current structure less and less relevant. It is essential that we remain alert to these changes and examine all aspects of them rather than the purely technological ones.

Super-empowered individuals are only one possible form of future war. Yet the very fact these new attacks took place reinforces the requirement to look at actual conflicts rather than remain wedded to our own high-technology cyberwar vision of the future. In short, America needs to understand that war evolves rather than transforms. But if America can develop the force to fight a fourth generation war, that force will also have the flexibility to adapt to the fifth generation as it evolves.

Notes

1 "DoD Transformation Planning Guidance," Department of Defense, April 2003, p. 9.
2 Arquilla, John and Ronfeldt, David, "Cyberwar is Coming," *Comparative Strategy*, November 1, 1993, Vol. 12, p. 34.
3 Van Crevald, Martin, "Through the Glass Darkly"; *Naval War College Review*; Autumn, 2000.
4 Lind, William, Nightengale, Keith, Schmitt, John, Sutton, Joseph and Wilson, Gary I.; "The Changing Face of War: Into the Fourth Generation," *Marine Corps Gazette*, October, 1989, pp. 22–26.
5 Staff Writers, "Like Herrings in a Barrel," *The Economist*, Special Millennium Edition, p. 13.
6 Staff Writers, "The Road to Riches," *The Economist*, Special Millennium Edition, p. 11.
7 Seward, D., *The Hundred Years War*, Athenaeum, New York, 1978, p. 164.
8 Chandler, D.G., *The Campaigns of Napoleon*, MacMillan Publishing Company, New York, 1966, p. 754.
9 Ibid, same pages.
10 Dupuy, Colonel T.N., *A Genius for War: The German Army and General Staff, 1807–1945*, Hero Books, Fairfax, VA; 1984, p. 177.
11 Ibid., p. 147.
12 Ibid., p. 34.
13 "Growth in United Nations Membership," www.un.org/Overview/growth.htm.
14 Freidman, T., *The Lexus and the Olive Tree*, Farrar, Strauss, Giroux, NY, 2000, p. 111.
15 Ibid., p. 113.
16 Zhu De – co-commander of the Zhu–Mao Army in 1928. This army consisted of about 8,000 men.
17 Short, P., *Mao: A Life*, Henry Holt and Company, NY, 1999, p. 222.
18 Mao Tse-tung, *On Protracted War*, People's Publishing House, Peking, 1954, p. 137.
19 Ibid., p. 77.
20 Summers, H.S., *On Strategy: A Critical Analysis of the Vietnam War*, Presidio Press, Novato, CA, 1982, p. 83.
21 Ho Chi Minh, *On Revolution: Selected Writings, 1920–66*, Westview Press, Boulder, CO, 1984, p. 316.
22 Ibid., p. 355.
23 The "foco" theory of insurgency states that by creating a small focus group of armed

guerrillas, an insurgent group will be able to stimulate a spontaneous uprising of the mass of the people and rapidly overthrow the government.

24 Ibid., p. 44.
25 Waghelstein, Colonel J., "A Latin American Insurgency Status Report," *Military Review*, February 1987, Vol. LXVII, No. 2, p. 44.
26 Hiltermann, J., *Behind the Intifada*, Princeton University Press, Princeton, NJ, 1991, p. 13.
27 The Israeli Center for Human Rights in the Occupied Territories, "Total Casualties," www.btselem.org/English/Statistics/Total_Casualties.asp#Anchor-Total-23522.

Part III

Evaluating Fourth Generation Warfare theory

4 Politics with guns

A response to T.X. Hammes' "War evolves into the fourth generation"

James J. Wirtz

I would like to offer a few thoughts about why US military professionals are so disturbed by the prospect of Fourth and Fifth Generation Warfare and then identify a flaw in the analysis offered by Thomas Hammes in his essay, "War Evolves into the Fourth Generation." Although I do not disagree with Hammes in fundamental ways, I think he exaggerates both the novelty of Fourth Generation Warfare and its effectiveness against more conventionally organized and equipped militaries. I also think that Hammes is attempting to break down the dichotomy between war and politics that exists in the minds of many US military officers, but his essay actually seems to reinforce that dichotomy. The locus of the problem he identifies is not Fourth Generation Warfare, but an unwillingness on the part of many military officers to confront the fact that war is ultimately a political contest. In any event, Hammes makes several important points in his essay, so the reader might forgive me for placing his argument in a slightly different context. After all, an issue is completely covered only when everyone gets to restate the same idea in his or her own words.

The professional military bias

Hammes' analysis betrays a bias that is often shared by US military professionals. It is a tendency to privilege considerations of "warfighting" over the political sphere that dominates war. This bias is embedded in the way the history of warfare was divided into periods by Bill Lind, G.I. Wilson and their co-authors in 1989.[1] First, Second and Third Generation Warfare are typologies that reflect the ability of military organizations to harness political, industrial and technological developments to maximize their size and effectiveness against similarly equipped and trained militaries on the battlefield. The Lind–Wilson framework reflects the modes of fighting favored by the most accomplished and professional militaries of their time and traces the evolution of modern combined arms operations. It is a story about how some militaries mastered complex operations and destroyed smaller, or more often, larger but less professional and technically proficient armies. It is not surprising that military professionals tend to become preoccupied with how best to use contemporary political, industrial and technological resources to maximize combat effectiveness, but war ultimately is not a story about military prowess alone. It is a story about how militaries use force to achieve political objectives.

Although Hammes makes reference to the role of politics in war, and the greater role played by society in warfare since Napoleon harnessed the energy of the French revolution to create First Generation Warfare, his analysis reflects a nagging doubt that troubles thoughtful military professionals: military prowess, even victory on some distant battlefield, is no guarantee of victory in war. Militaries are not the only actor, and sometimes they are not the most significant actor, on the stage known as war. But this is not a recent development. The guerrillas that plagued Napoleon's soldiers in Spain, Lawrence's Arab forces, or the Soviet partisans that harassed Nazi supply lines, have all proven to be politically and even militarily significant during First, Second and Third Generation Warfare. Mao's peasant armies were just the most recent example of how politically motivated, non-professional "armies" can sometimes dominate their conventionally trained, equipped and more professional opponents. Despite the fact that no military on the planet today would serve as more than cannon fodder to the highly professional air-sea-land-space-information force at the disposal of the United States, overwhelming military prowess alone still cannot *guarantee* victory in war. The fact that highly professional militaries are sometimes seriously harassed or even defeated by motivated amateurs is a fact that cuts across the Lind–Wilson typology. It is this problem that has set Hammes' pen to paper.

At various moments in history – and this is one of them – conventional militaries can appear to be relatively ineffective. US military personnel, for instance, seem to be just another target, not an effective counter, to the wave of bombings that is sweeping Iraq. The US military has no readily available solution to the problem of international terrorism. If the locus of conflict moves away from the conventional combat operations to other fields, then the use of military force will have increasingly less influence on the outcome of the contest. And since the emergence of First Generation Warfare, war has continuously enlarged its sphere of conflict away from traditional battlefields. Publics everywhere have become increasingly politically mobilized and better informed, making it all the more likely that media images, stirring political oratory or self-aggrandizing propaganda will effect the outcome of war. The information revolution has now even given individuals abilities to communicate, organize and travel around the planet that were not even possessed by governments fifty years ago. The information revolution, and the ideology embedded in the new technology, provides "super-empowered individuals" or small groups of malcontents with the capability and sanction to take matters into their own hands (i.e. Fifth Generation Warfare).[2] The surge in the number and variety of potentially significant new political actors is staggering and these actors often emerge in unexpected ways and from unexpected places. The unprofessional and badly led soldiers who photographed themselves abusing Iraqi prisoners at Abu Ghraib prison hurt the US war effort in Iraq far more than Iraq's conventional military units. Who thought that a few reservists could have that kind of impact on the Coalition war effort? The fact that people, events and images unrelated to battle itself can trump extraordinarily effective combat forces gives military professionals fits.

Clausewitz to the rescue

Hammes' alarm about the rise of Fourth Generation Warfare is understandable given his bias as a military professional. He is wrong, however, to credit peasant armies, guerillas, mujahideen, terrorist networks or individual fanatics with universal and permanent superiority over their more conventional opponents. War is a dialectic, the outcome is produced by the interaction of forces, ideas and wills. This Clausewitzian conception of war suggests that Hammes has overestimated the military and political strength of fourth generation warriors by treating their effectiveness as a constant in the every changing duel known as war. Clausewitz would suggest that it is imperative to judge the effectiveness of fourth generation warriors against their opponents. Mao's armies faced Chiang Kai-Shek's Kuomintang units, which never achieved much combat effectiveness even after decades of continuous war and an outpouring of US material and technical support. By contrast, Mao's peasant armies suffered devastating casualties when they encountered competent US units during the Korean War. The Communist effort to unify Vietnam also was undertaken at a horrendous cost and succeeded only because Hanoi could count on the Soviet Union for unlimited material support and China as a deterrent to a direct US invasion of North Vietnam. Moreover, when the end finally came for Saigon, mechanized units, not peasant armies, stormed the Presidential Palace.[3] The Sandinistas defeated the forces of a deeply corrupt kleptocracy that could only muster the political support it could buy. It is probably a bit hasty to conclude that non-traditional forms of warfare will always best traditional forces. In any event, Hammes' claim that Fourth Generation Warfare is an unstoppable problem for traditional militaries is not based on a net assessment of the fighting prowess of both sides in the conflicts he surveys.

Another issue raised by Hammes' analysis is that not all of the fourth generation warriors are equally gifted in terms of their ability to translate operational success in battle into political success. As Hammes notes, the al Aqsa Intifada has hurt the political standing of the Palestinians. Similarly, Iraqi insurgents are slowly but surely turning world public opinion against them as they seek to disrupt the emergence of an Iraqi democracy, a democracy that is favored by the majority of Iraqis. Al-Qaeda's brilliant operational success in launching the terrorist attacks against the United States on September 11 was not accompanied by an equally brilliant campaign plan to achieve clearly defined political objectives. In a sense, fourth generation warriors, like their more conventionally minded and equipped counterparts, still must find a way to translate battlefield accomplishments into political success. An ability to launch innovative or increasingly deadly attacks does not guarantee that political objectives can be achieved.

Fifth Generation Warfare?

For good reasons, Fifth Generation Warfare should strike terror in all of us. If super-empowered individuals wield deadly chemical, biological or radiological weapons they cannot only injure or kill thousands of people, they can cause enormous disruption to the economic and social life of entire nations. These individuals can emerge at random – motivated by some real or imagined insult – or they can emerge as fourth generation organizations that are pulverized by the steady attritional warfare practiced by states and professional militaries and police forces. Fifth generation warriors, however, will encounter overwhelming problems when it comes to translating some spectacular operational success into a lasting political result because direct violent action by individuals has been criminalized by most of the international community, making it virtually impossible for super-empowered individuals to cease hostilities. There is virtually unanimous international agreement that individuals have no right as individuals to use force to achieve political objectives. Super-empowered individuals might be able to change the course of history through some especially outrageous and diabolical act of terrorism or to punctuate acts of terror with political demands, but it is more difficult to imagine that they can harness acts of terror to achieve political objectives, especially objectives that would be realized in peace time. If Osama Bin Laden came out of hiding to reach a negotiated solution with the US or Saudi government, for example, he would be quickly arrested, tried and convicted for his foray into Fifth Generation Warfare. Fifth generation warriors might be able to use violence to make political statements, but their ability as individuals to perform as true political actors will be limited by their nearly universal criminal status.

Fifth Generation Warfare probably marks a turning point in the expansion of the scope of warfare that began with the French Revolution. Individuals now can unleash more death and destruction than the *Grande Armée* might have inflicted on an opposing force in a sustained battle, but it is hard for them to use this capability to achieve political objectives. People can, of course, be political actors, but violent acts by super-empowered individuals, witness the fate of Timothy McVeigh or Ted Kaczynski, tends to discredit the individual and their political demands. Individuals, or small groups of people, cannot use violence alone to achieve political objectives without first building a political or social movement, which would effectively transform their fifth generation outburst into a fourth generation organization. The "insurgency" in Iraq or al-Qaeda will fail ultimately because they have not built a social or political movement to capitalize on their battlefield success. Violence alone – whether it is unleashed by professional militaries, Maoist insurgents, terrorist syndicates or a lone gunman – is no guarantee of political victory.

Toward the future

The Vietnamese communists referred to their soldiers as "armed politicians" and they called war "politics with guns." I have always thought that these terms were both wonderfully accurate and generally alien to the way that US military officers thought about war. For US officers, the height of their profession is the conception and execution of brilliant combined-arms operations. This sort of thinking is at the heart of the Lind–Wilson typology and Hammes' concern about the rise of a new group of armed politicians. Fourth Generation Warfare, however, is not combat effective against a modern combined-arms military. But, as Hammes correctly notes, it does pose a political challenge. This challenge would best be met not by devising ever more splendid combat evolutions, but by thinking more about how the use of force can be used to achieve political objectives. The problem with fourth generation warriors is not that they are better soldiers than today's military professionals are; it is that they are better politicians.

Notes

1 Lind, William, Nightengale, Keith, Schmitt, John, Sutton, Joseph, Wilson and Gary I., "The Changing Face of War: Into the Fourth Generation," *Marine Corps Gazette*, October, 1989, pp. 22–26.
2 There is a rich literature on the effect of the information revolution on society. Several critics are especially provocative. See Rochlin, Gene I., *Trapped in the Net: The Unanticipated Consequences of Computerization* (Princeton, NJ: Princeton University Press, 1997; Theodore Roszak, *The Cult of Information* (Berkeley, CA: University of California Press, 1986); and Postman, Neil, *Technopoly: The Surrender of Culture to Technology* (New York: Vintage Books, 1993).
3 For a discussion of how the North Vietnamese slowly abandoned the doctrine of People's War see Lomperis, Timothy J., *The War Everyone Lost – and Won: America's Intervention in Viet Nam's Twin Struggles* (Baton Rouge, LA: Louisiana State University Press, 1984).

5 A brief note on "Fourth Generation Warfare"

Edward Luttwak

Any refocusing of military resources and attention on "Fourth Generation Warfare" would imply that terrorists and insurgents are fit targets for US military action. They are not. Terrorists never win, and often hardly try to do so: they are venting emotions, they seek satisfaction in being seen to inflict suffering on others. All they do is to increase the cohesion of those they attack to war-like levels – without inflicting war-like levels of damage. War and revolution – mass action – or the leveraged power of coups can achieve external or internal victories. Terrorism never – the damage it inflicts is a loss for the victims, not a gain for the perpetrators.

Moreover, terrorism is rarely more than an irritant – as compared to wartime levels of destruction. September 11, 2001 was an exception, and increasingly isolated in retrospect. The only reason so much attention is devoted to terrorism is the unusual and probably temporary absence of Great Power conflictuality. Nuclear-weapon terrorism could be catastrophic of course and probably will be one day, but only political, administrative and security arrangements can keep nuclear weapons from falling into the hands of terrorists – not military forces of whatever kind. As for insurgencies, there is only one sovereign remedy: the ungrateful do not deserve to be occupied by the armed forces of the United States of America. Given that American ideas, goods, services, fashions and brand-names are globally influential, it makes no sense for Americans to hold on to bits of foreign territory where they are not wanted.

To refocus military resources on "Fourth Generation Warfare" would be especially unfortunate for the United States. During the next few decades, while China attains the per capita standard of living of Portugal, its leaders will be choosing between peaceful and military investments. If the United States neglects its large-scale warfare forces and systems to chase futile terrorists and localized insurgents, Chinese leaders might well be tempted to invest heavily in military power, because parity or even superiority might become attainable goals. It is important therefore that the United States retains a position of unassailable superiority, to make competition seem quite hopeless, and thus not worth the cost of trying.

There is also another consideration. The United States is good at destroying objects and armed forces that assemble into conveniently targetable mass formations. It is not good at espionage, covert operations, para-military action and so on. It all worked very well in Afghanistan against the grotesque Taliban, but that merely induced delusions of adequacy exposed in Iraq. There are apparently insurmountable difficulties with languages – even officially qualified speakers usually have only a pathetically rudimentary knowledge of even the easiest languages. The US is regularly embarrassed or worse around the world because its diplomats, CIA officers and military personnel stationed overseas for terms of years cannot be bothered to learn local languages, as their foreign counterparts are routinely required to do. I have seen the CIA drop the ball in Latin America because its operatives cannot muster Spanish, never mind Aymara or Guarani. There are apparently equally insurmountable career-management obstacles – how can John go undercover in X-land if Jane cannot get a job there? The resulting lack of societal penetration, the absence or incapacity of covert operators, leave us with excellent Special Operations capabilities – including some really good commandos – who cannot go beyond the hidden-in-nature clandestine realm, because if they infiltrate there is never anybody waiting to meet them on the other side. That is why, even while exaggerated attention is being paid to terrorism, so few terrorists have been hunted down. We should remain focused on global strategy to preserve the imbalance of military strength that dissuades Great Power competition, leaving terrorists to police forces and staying clear of insurgencies.

6   It will continue to conquer and spread

Martin van Creveld

Fifteen years after Bill Lind and his associates wrote that Fourth Generation Warfare (4GW) was about to replace Third Generation Warfare (3GW); twelve years after this author wrote that non-trinitarian War was replacing that of trinitarian War; five years after Mary Kaldor published *New and Old Wars*; four years after Robert Kaplan had turned his original *Atlantic Magazine* article into a book entitled, *The Coming Anarchy*; and a year after Secretary of Defense Donald Rumsfeld, in a memorandum to his aides, admitted that the military establishment set up to wage the Cold War was not suited for the wars of the twenty-first century – after all this, even the US Armed Services are latching on to Madame History's skirt. They are waking up to the fact that the world has changed and will continue to change, though not necessarily in the direction they expected and prepared for. The harbinger of this somewhat less than astonishing news is Thomas X. Hammes. Hammes is a Marine Corps Colonel on active duty with something called "functional area expertise in low intensity conflict" (Google.com). That means he helped train insurgents in several, unspecified, countries as well as serving in Somalia; it was the latter experience, he says, which really forced him to open his eyes.

To Hammes' credit, it must be said that he is no newcomer to the field. He started thinking about all this as far back as 1988, when he published an article in the *Marine Corps Gazette* entitled, "Insurgency: The Forgotten Threat." As the fact that he refers to 4GW rather than any of the other above-mentioned terms shows, essentially he is a disciple of Lind. Lind is a Washington-based political and military analyst with strong conservative views. He is also a brilliant maverick, and the author of the best single work ever written about maneuver warfare. In his book, Hammes does what Lind never did; namely, provide a full-length, coherent, account of the phenomenon.

The way he describes it, First Generation Warfare was that which was waged by Napoleon with the aid of muzzle-loading artillery, muskets, and columns and lines of infantrymen. Second Generation Warfare was waged by commanders from Moltke to Foch with the aid of the massive firepower made possible by the new, quick-firing weapons. Third Generation Warfare originated in the new German light infantry tactics of 1918. During the inter-war period it donned armor, and in 1940–1941 it climaxed in the form of the great German Blitzkrieg campaigns. It was still much in evidence when the Israelis defeated the Egyptians in 1967. Since then, however, it has almost turned into an extinct species. Though Hammes does not say so, the most important reason for this is nuclear weapons (which he does not mention even in the index). As the example of North Korea has recently reminded us, we have long reached the point where any country with the necessary industrial, technological and military infrastructure needed for waging 3GW will also be able to obtain nukes. And experience shows that, wherever nukes appear, large scale conventional war disappears.

As will be seen, the backbone of all three generations discussed so far is formed by technological, tactical, and operational developments. It is to Colonel Hammes' great credit that, following his mentor Lind, he does not content himself with this but seeks to bring out the political, economic, social, and cultural background as well. As this author explained in *The Transformation of War*, the first three "generations" Lind and Hammes write about – in fact, all major European wars as they have developed since the second half of the seventeenth century – were all "trinitarian." By that I meant that they were waged by states, against states, on the basis of a threefold division of labor between the government that rules and directs, the uniformed armed forces that fight and die, and the people whose job it is to pay and suffer.

As the shift from Third Generation to Fourth Generation takes hold, this is no longer true. As I, using the term "non-trinitarian," and Hammes and Lind, using their own terminology, have described the phenomenon, the new kind of warfare is distinguished precisely by the fact that it is *not* waged either by states, or on the basis of the "trinitarian" division of labor, or by means of uniformed armies operating in the open. Instead, on at least one side and sometimes on both, it is waged by completely different organizations; such as, depending on taste, may be characterized as warlords, or bandits, or terrorists, or guerrillas, or freedom fighters, or patriots, or the Martyrs of Allah. Whatever they are called, the members of the organizations in question do not come directly under a government (though in some cases they may be directed by one, as when Hezbollah acted in concert with Syria to oust Israel from southern Lebanon). Not coming under a government, they are not bureaucratically organized and do not wear uniform. Instead they blend into the surrounding population as much as they can; and do most of their fighting under cover rather than overtly.

In *The Sling and the Stone*, Colonel Hammes provides a brief history of 4GW as well as a detailed explanation of its nature. Its origins, he says, are to be found with Mao Tse-tung who used it during the 1930s in order to resist the Chinese government of Jiang Jiesi (Chiang Kai Shek) as well as the Japanese occupation. Personally I would rather turn to Tito and his partisans in German-occupied Yugoslavia; that, however, is quibbling. From then on 4GW has spread over much of the globe, achieving an unprecedented chain of victories. One after the other, the world's most powerful, most advanced, technologically sophisticated forces tried to cope with it but were defeated; often this was done at the hands of people who possessed hardly any formal military training, went barefoot, and could barely read. The losers include the British in Palestine, Kenya,

Malaysia, Cyprus, and Aden, the French in Indochina and Algeria, the Portuguese in Angola and Mozambique, the Americans in Vietnam and Somalia (and now in Iraq), the Soviets in Afghanistan, the Israelis in Lebanon ... the list is almost endless. Contrary to Hammes, I would add that the Israelis have lost not only their struggle against the First Intifada but against the Second (al Aqsa) one too. Or why else does he think they are even now preparing to pull out of Gaza and parts of Samaria?

All this is good and well, and Hammes is to be congratulated on his effort to open our eyes to the nature of the problem much of the world is facing. It is, however, not enough. As just noted, Hammes himself says that developed countries with all the advanced military technology at their disposal do not have the answer to 4GW (neither do most developing ones, but that is their problem). Apart from telling us that "the future is flexibility," he does not provide a detailed case study that might tell us how 4GW can be defeated; all he does is point toward the US effort in Afghanistan. As Hammes himself recognizes, though, as of early 2005 whether Afghanistan is indeed a US "success" remains in doubt. With Iraq claiming most of America's resources as well as those of al Qaeda and other Muslim terrorist groups, Afghanistan has been turned into a backwater. The Taliban have been dispersed, but they still exist. Much of the country is in the hands of warlords. With their activities, such as opium-growing, only rarely interfered with either by the US military or by the Karzai Government in Kabul, they do not bother to fight them too often. Karzai, in spite of having been democratically elected, only rules Kabul, and then only by day. But for his American bodyguards, he would probably not survive for twenty-four hours.

In explaining the nature of 4GW, Hammes has done us a service. In pointing out that it is going to be *the* most important form of twenty-first century armed conflict, he is almost certainly right. In taking events in Iraq as proof that the brainwaves generated by the US military since 1990 or so – the Revolution in Military Affairs (RMA), Military Transformation, Network-Centric Warfare, etc. – are not going to solve the problem, he is also right. In all this, however, he does little more than elaborate on what he himself, the above-listed authors, and many others have been saying – unfortunately, to ears that were mostly deaf – for over a decade. As General Zinni, who provided a blurb on the front cover, says, to win a war one must first understand its nature. Knowingly or not, Zinni was echoing Marx: philosophers have explained the world, the father of Communism once wrote, but the point is to change it.

Seventy years after Mao and sixty after Tito, people should take Marx's advice and stop chewing old cud. Phrases such as "we should use the tremendous potential of networked systems to ensure a common understanding of the commander's intent and concept of operations" are not helpful. Not only do they sound suspiciously like those mouthed by Hammes' opponents, the proponents of the RMA and "network centric warfare"; but experience shows that terrorists and guerrillas are at least as good at using communications technology to build "networks" as regular armed forces are. It is high time for Hammes and other professional officers like him to start earning their pay. They should stop beating around the bush, and come up with viable solutions instead. Or else we may be certain that 4GW, "non-trinitarian" warfare, or whatever one may choose to call the new form of armed conflict, instead of going away as most civilized people hope it does, will continue to conquer and spread.

7   Deconstructing the theory of Fourth-Generation Warfare

Antulio J. Echevarria II

Although Colonel Hammes rightly takes the Pentagon's vision of future warfare to task for being too technologically oriented and for not taking into account the countermeasures an intelligent, adaptive enemy could employ, the model of Fourth-Generation Warfare (4GW) that he and others have put forth has serious problems of its own.[1] The real shame is that the model itself is unnecessary; in fact, it only serves to undermine the credibility of those who employ it in the hope of inspiring the right kinds of change. Change is taking place despite, not because of, this theory. If the old adage is true, that correctly identifying the problem is half the solution, then the theorists of 4GW have gotten only half the problem right, and that they did by repeatedly reinventing their own concept. It is hardly news that non-state actors – whether insurgents, terrorists, guerrillas, street gangs, or other nefarious characters – will try to avail themselves of the increased mobility of people, weapons, and ideas that has come about with globalization. This is, in fact, all there is to the phenomenon that 4GW calls a "super-insurgency," or a "new generation" of war. Throughout history, terrorists, guerillas, and similar actors have typically aimed at an opponent's will to fight rather than his means; the difference now is that they enjoy enhanced access to that will.

That being the case, it is somewhat curious that the history and analyses that 4GW theorists hang on this phenomenon should be so deeply flawed. Fortunately, Colonel Hammes' recommendations for countering the phenomenon – the revitalization of counterinsurgency doctrine, better cultural and linguistic education for US troops, and the greater coordination of political, military, social, and economic efforts – though not entirely original, are surely steps in the right direction. His chapter here, however, does not expound on potential solutions as much as his book does.[2]

For his part, and to his utter credit, Colonel Hammes sees the theory of 4GW as little more than a vehicle, a tool, to generate a vital dialogue centering on deficiencies in US military doctrine, training, and organization. He has shown a willingness to roll up his sleeves and do the hard work necessary to promote positive change. Hence, these comments are not directed at him, but at the vehicle itself, and those who seem bent on claiming that it correctly predicted the future.

This essay argues that we need to drop the theory of 4GW altogether; it creates more confusion than it is worth. The concept itself is fundamentally and hopelessly flawed. It is based on poor history and only obscures what other historians, theorists, and analysts have already worked long and hard to clarify. Walter Laqueur, Ian Beckett, and many others have devoted considerable time and intellectual energy to understanding the phenomena of guerrilla warfare, insurgencies, terrorism, and their various combinations and evolutions.[3] The energy spent trying to prove the emergence of a new generation of warfare should instead be directed toward finding solutions that help broaden the scope and increase the depth of Defense Transformation in the United States.

The idea of 4GW emerged in the late 1980s as a vague sortie of "out of the box" thinking, an accumulation of speculative rhapsodies that blended a maneuver-theorist's misunderstanding of the nature of terrorism with a futurist's fascination with "high technology."[4] However, the high technology included directed energy weapons and robotics, rather than cell phones and the internet, and the terrorism that was described sought to collapse its enemy from within, rather than to defeat, or change, its political will by attacking defenseless non-combatants. The original theory also posited that 4GW might have a "nonnational or transnational base, such as an ideology or a religion." The problem with this proposition, of course, is that it also describes many conventional conflicts of the past, such as the ideologically driven World War II, which was fought within a transnational framework of opposing alliances; it also applies to the Cold War, which had these same characteristics. It is more than a little puzzling, therefore, that the architects of 4GW should have asserted that US military capabilities are "designed to operate within a nation-state framework and have great difficulties outside of it."[5] The US military actually seems to have handled two recent global wars, both requiring it to operate within transnational alliances, quite well.

To be sure, out-of-the-box thinking is to be applauded; militaries do not do enough of it, for a variety of reasons. However, its value diminishes when that thinking hardens into a box of its own, and its architects become captured by it.

By the mid-1990s, the theory of 4GW had taken up Martin van Creveld's egregious misrepresentation of the Clausewitzian trinity and his overemphasis of the significance of the 1648 Treaty of Westphalia, both of which appeared in the much lauded *Transformation of War*.[6] Interestingly, the theory's proponents claimed that van Creveld had actually expanded upon *their* ideas with regard to the concept of "non-trinitarian" war.[7] By taking ownership of this concept, they actually reinvented their theory again, proclaiming that the "first idea" that shapes 4GW is the thesis that "future war will increasingly be non-trinitarian and waged outside the nation-state framework."[8]

The problem with the idea of non-trinitarian war is that it does not understand the thing it purports to negate, that is, so-called trinitarian war. The notion of trinitarian war is actually a myth. It resulted from a misinterpretation of Clausewitz's "wondrous (*wunderliche*) trinity," a construct he used to describe the dynamic and changeable nature of war. Clausewitz portrayed the nature of war in terms of three tendencies, or forces: basic hostility, which if unchecked would make war spiral out of control; chance and uncertainty, which defy prescriptive theories and make war unpredictable; and the attempt to use war to achieve a purpose, to direct it toward an end.[9] Indeed, his portrayal appears accurate, for we find these forces present, in varying degrees, in every war, ancient or modern, traditional or otherwise. These tendencies, Clausewitz said, generally correspond to three institutions: the first to the populace, the second to the military, and the last to the government. However, as Clausewitz also noted, each of these institutions has taken various forms over time. The government, for example, can be the head of a clan or a tribe, or the king of Prussia.[10] The trinity consists of the actual *forces* themselves, which are universal, and not the institutions, which are just particular representations of them. Thus, those who, like van Creveld, refer to Clausewitz's trinity as people, military, and government, do not understand it.

Strictly speaking, there is no such thing as trinitarian war, because the three forces are present in *every* war, not just the wars of nation-states. If they are present in every war, then the term falls out as a discriminator. It follows, then, that since there is no such thing as trinitarian war, there can be no such thing as non-trinitarian war; the initial concept or idea has to exist first before the "non" that negates it can come into being. Non-trinitarian war is, therefore, nothing more than the negation of an idea that never existed in the first place. The proponents of 4GW failed to perceive this flaw in their theory because they decided not to read Clausewitz through for themselves, relying instead on van Creveld's misinterpretation of him.

They also bit rather deeply into the fruit van Creveld offered them with his exaggeration of the significance of the Treaty of Westphalia, which ended the Thirty Years' War.[11] They asserted that one of the key ideas of 4GW is that the "nation-state is losing its monopoly on war," a monopoly supposedly established by the Treaty of Westphalia.[12] However, what the treaty actually did, aside from granting or confirming the possession of certain lands by Europe's major powers, was to break-up the central authority of the Holy Roman Empire, and in its place grant territorial sovereignty to some 300 German and central European princes. It is more accurate to regard the treaty as a "new constitution" for the Empire that balanced religious and political concerns, than as a concerted effort to establish an enduring state system.[13] The principalities were not nation-states by any stretch, and Europe had several centuries to go before the notion of national identity would become associated with the idea of the state as a political organization. The sovereignty granted to the princes included, among other things, the right to declare war and to enter into treaties with foreign powers; any war that should break out among the princes would, thus, be considered an international affair, rather than a civil war within the Empire. The sovereignty of the princes was not absolute, however, despite the teaming rhetoric that claims the opposite. The princes could not enter into any treaty that was "against the Emperor, and the Empire, nor against the Publik Peace, and this Treaty, and without prejudice to the Oath by which everyone is bound to the Emperor and the Empire," for instance, and any prince who changed his religion would forfeit his lands.[14] The kind of sovereignty granted by the treaty did not preclude intervention by outside powers, therefore, and did not provide a legal basis for autonomy.

What the treaty did not do was give states a monopoly, legal or otherwise, on the waging of war.[15] Even van Creveld admits that "cities and coalitions of cities, religious leagues, and independent noblemen, to say nothing of robbers" continued to make war.[16] Rather, the Thirty Years' War itself showed that war had become extremely costly to wage, even for major powers.[17] Thus, the sheer expense of war tended to push it beyond the capacity of smaller states, and many non-state actors, except, of course, as mercenaries. Even the larger states had to reorganize themselves in order to wage war more effectively, but this reorganization did not amount to a monopoly on war.[18] Once again, therefore, the theory of 4GW is undercut by its poor use of history.

In late 2001, 4GW was reinvented again when one of the theory's principal proponents proclaimed that 9/11 was "Fourth-Generation Warfare's First Blow."[19] This claim was both clever – in that it exploited a moment of strategic surprise for the United States – and supremely arrogant, revealing the extent to which 4GW theorists had become preoccupied with proving their ability to predict the future, rather than understanding the motives and methods of America's terrorist enemies. 4GW was now "broader than any technique," and it was, in effect, the "greatest change in war since the Peace of Westphalia."[20] Forgotten was the fact that the theory initially started out as nothing more than a collection of muddled speculations about hypothetical combinations of tactics and techniques.

The theory has gained more attention of late as a result of the publication of Colonel Hammes' book, *The Sling and the Stone*, and the recent transition to insurgency–counterinsurgency operations in the war in Iraq. Now, the theory's proponents claim that 4GW is an "evolved form" of insurgency, like the one that has emerged in Iraq:

> The first generation of modern war was dominated by *massed manpower* and culminated in the Napoleonic Wars. The second generation, which was quickly adopted by the world's major powers, was dominated by *firepower* and ended in World War I. In relatively short order, during World War II the Germans introduced third-generation warfare, characterized by *maneuver*. That type of combat is still largely the focus of U.S. forces ... [4GW is an] evolved form of *insurgency* [that] uses all available networks – political, economic, social, military – to convince the enemy's decision makers that their strategic goals are either unachievable or too costly for the perceived benefit [emphasis added].[21]

Unfortunately, this new conception fares no better than previous ones, and actually repeats many of the old errors, some of which we have not yet discussed. First, the theory's sequencing of the so-called generations of war is both artificial and indefensible. Portraying changes in warfare in terms of "genera-tions" implies that each one evolved directly from its predecessor, and, as per the natural progression of generations, eventually displaced it. However, the generational model is an ineffective way to depict changes in warfare. Simple displacement rarely takes place, significant developments often occur in parallel. Firepower, for example, played as much a role in World War II, and the Korean and Vietnam conflicts as did maneuver, perhaps more so. In fact, insurgency as a way of waging war actually dates back to classical antiquity, and thus predates the so-called second and third generations (firepower and maneuver) as described by 4GW theorists. Insurgents, guerillas, and resistance fighters figured large in many of the wars fought during the age of classical antiquity.

Contrary to what 4GW-theorists assert, Mao Tse-tung was not the first, nor even the most important, theorist to articulate the virtues of insurgency, or Peoples' War, as it was sometimes called.[22] We know that Mao read Sun Tzu and Clausewitz; the former did not address guerrilla warfare directly, but dis-cussed certain tactics and principles that one could easily apply to that form of warfare.[23] Clausewitz, on the other hand, addressed it directly, calling it a "reality (*Erscheinung*) of the nineteenth century," and provided some valuable insights into its nature; he even delivered a number of lectures on the subject, based on his observations of the Spanish insurrection against Napoleon's forces, to the Prussian War College (*Allgemeine Kriegsschule*) in 1810 and 1811.[24] Insurgency did, after all, help the American colonies win independence from the British crown, and it nearly thwarted the ultimate Prusso-German victory over France in the war of 1870–1871. It played an important role in the histories of many Latin American states, and in Western Europe and the Soviet Union during World War II, as well as enabling the emergence of Israel in the late 1940s.

Second, even if it were valid to portray major changes in the conduct of war as an evolutionary progression from 1GW to 3GW, the next logical step in that progression would not be the sort of "super-insurgency" that 4GW theorists have tried to depict so opportunistically. Instead, the generation of warfare that succeeds 3GW would actually have to be closer to the vision of Network-centric warfare once propounded by some within the US Department of Defense, that is – small, high-tech forces networked together in knowledge-based systems that enables them to act rapidly and decisively.[25]

To their credit, the advocates of 4GW rightly criticize Network-centric warfare, and its vacuous theoretical offshoots, such as rapid decisive operations and effects-based operations, for being too dependent on high technology, and for being too inflexible to accommodate a thinking opponent. Yet, and quite ironically, this is the very direction in which the logic of their particular theory of military evolution would lead them, if they were true to it. Early on, in fact, proponents of the Revolution in Military Affairs, Network-centric warfare, and Defense Transformation made a point of using the so-called German blitzkrieg model as a way to articulate their goals. That they misunderstood blitzkrieg itself is beside the point; they wanted to create a form of "super-maneuver," through a combination of new technologies and new operational concepts, capable of rapidly and decisively defeating an adversary.[26] Ergo, the Pentagon-style of warfare that Hammes and others rail against, however justifiably, is actually the logical extension of 3GW – and it was, curiously enough, not too far removed from the direction in which 4GW theorists were initially headed. What this means for 4GW theorists, though, is that the evolutionary logic they use to explain key developments in the conduct of war actually undermines their case. That they failed to perceive this flaw in a theory they have been developing, or more accurately reinventing, for more than a decade is not a good sign.

Third, by comparing what essentially amount to military means or techniques – such as "massed manpower," "firepower," and "maneuver" – on the one hand, to what is arguably a form of warfare – such as insurgency – on the other, the advocates of 4GW only bait us with a proverbial apples-versus-oranges sleight-of-hand. In other words, they establish a false comparison by which they wish us to conclude that most of the wars of the modern age, which they claim were characterized by firepower or maneuver, were narrowly focused on military power and, unlike the super-insurgencies of the information age, rarely involved the integration of political, economic, and social power.

Yet, even a cursory review of the Napoleonic, and the First and Second World wars reveals that this is not true. Clausewitz thought that Napoleon had in fact brought warfare as close to its "absolute" form as anyone could, meaning that he had mobilized the French populace and exploited its potential by a variety of means, not the least of which was via the control of information. In Napoleon, the full political and military powers of the French state were brought together in one person.

The major wars of the twentieth century also show that political, social, and economic capabilities were, in many cases, employed to the maximum extent possible. Some historians, in fact, go so far as to maintain that World War I and II were, in effect, examples of "total" war precisely because of the extent to which the major combatants mobilized the elements of their national power.[27] Even the theoretical offshoots of Net-centric warfare, which 4GW rejects, recognize the need to integrate all the elements of national power in the pursuit of strategic aims. The problem is that this notion of total integration has become the new mantra; the idea itself has almost been elevated to a panacea for the various ills plaguing the American way of war. The fundamental rub, which even 4GW advocates do not address, is how to coordinate diverse kinds of power, each of which operates in a unique way and according to its own time-line, to achieve specific objectives, and to do so without at least the most egregious of unintended consequences. It is one thing to assert that all the elements of power must be coordinated to meet the challenges of this century; it's quite another to think through the next level of the problem and figure out how.

In sum, there is no reason to reinvent the wheel with regard to insurgencies – super or otherwise – and their various kin. A great deal of very good work has already been done, especially lately, on that topic, to include the effects that globalization and information technologies have had, are having, and are likely to have, on such movements. We do not need another label, as well as an incoherent supporting logic, to obscure what many have already made clear. The fact that 4GW theorists are not aware of this work, or at least do not acknowledge it, should give us pause indeed. In any case, the wheel they are trying to invent will not turn.

Notes

1 This tendency was particularly evident in the early white papers regarding Rapid Decisive Operations and Effects-Based Operations. It is also evident in the initial principles associated with Transformation: speed, knowledge, jointness, and precision. There is some evidence that this technocratic emphasis is changing, however. Greg Jaffe, "Rumsfeld Details Big Military Shift in New Document: Drive for Preemptive Force, Wider Influence Will Trigger Changes in Strategy, Budget," *Wall Street Journal*, March 11, 2005. In fact, some of the original proponents outside the Pentagon now admit that the initial scope of Defense Transformation was too narrow. Compare: Max Boot, "The New American Way of War," *Foreign Affairs* Vol. 82, no. 4 (July/August 2003): 41–58, to his more recent argument Max Boot, "The Struggle to Transform the Military," *Foreign Affairs* Vol. 84, no. 2 (March/April 2005): 103–118.
2 Thomas X. Hammes, *The Sling and the Stone: On War in the 21st Century* (St. Paul, MN: Zenith, 2004); see also Thomas X. Hammes, "Insurgency: Modern Warfare Evolves into a Fourth Generation," Strategic Forum no. 214, Institute for National Strategic Studies, January 2005.
3 The following old and new works are representative of such efforts: Walter Laqueur, *Guerilla Warfare: A Historical and Critical Study* (Boulder, CO: Westview, 1984); Ian F.W. Beckett and John Pimlott, eds, *Armed Forces and Modern Counterinsurgency* (New York: St. Martin's, 1985); Bard E. O'Neill, *Insurgency and Terrorism: Inside Modern Revolutionary Warfare* (Washington, DC: Brassey's, 1990); and Rohan Gunaratna, ed., *The Changing Face of Terrorism* (Singapore: Eastern Universities Press, 2004).
4 William S. Lind, Keith Nightengale, John F. Schmitt, Joseph W. Sutton, Gary I. Wilson, "The Changing Face of War: Into the Fourth Generation," *Marine Corps Gazette* (October 1989): 22–26.
5 Lind, *et al.*, "Changing Face of War," 26.
6 Martin van Creveld, *The Transformation of War* (New York: Free Press, 1991).
7 William S. Lind, Maj. John F. Schmitt, USMCR, and Colonel Gary I. Wilson, USMCR, "Fourth Generation Warfare: Another Look," *Marine Corps Gazette*, 78, no. 12 (December 1994): 34–37, here 34. Hammes provided some much needed intellectual heft to the theory at this time. Lieutenant Colonel Thomas X. Hammes, "The Evolution of War: The Fourth Generation," *Marine Corps Gazette* 78, no. 9 (September 1994): 35–44.
8 Lind, *et al.*, "Another Look," 36.
9 The trinity is only one aspect of Clausewitz's nature of war; he also described objective and subjective "natures" of war. The former includes those qualities that every war has – violence, chance, friction, etc. – while the latter consists of the means by which wars are fought. Similarly, his representation of the first trinity – consisting of the forces – corresponds with the objective nature of war, while the second trinity accords with the subjective nature of war. Carl von Clausewitz, *Vom Kriege. Hinterlassenes Werk des Generals Carl von Clausewitz*, 19th edn, ed. by Werner Hahlweg (Bonn: Ferd. Dümmlers, 1991), Book I, ch. 1, 212–213.
10 *Vom Kriege*, Book I, ch. 1, pp. 212–213. The term "government," as Clausewitz used

it, stands for any ruling body, any "agglomeration of loosely associated forces," or any "personified intelligence." Similarly, the military represents not only the trained, semi-professional armies of the Napoleonic era, but any warring body in any era. Likewise, Clausewitz's references to the "populace" pertain to the populations of any society or culture in any period of history. *Vom Kriege*, Book VIII, ch. 3B, pp. 962, 964–965.

11 The Treaty of Westphalia actually consisted of two treaties: the Treaty of Osnabrück, concluded between the Holy Roman Emperor and the Protestant King of Sweden; and the Treaty of Münster, concluded between the Emperor and the Catholic King of France. The treaties took seven years to negotiate, and fighting continued up to the last moment.

12 Lind, *et al.*, "Another Look," 34, 35; William S. Lind, "Understanding Fourth Generation War," *Military Review* 84, no. 5 (September/October 2004): 12–16, here 12.

13 Stephen D. Krasner, "Rethinking the Sovereign State Model," in Michael Cox, Tim Dunne, and Ken Booth, eds, *Empire, Systems and States: Great Transformations in International Politics* (New York: Cambridge University, 2001), 35. For other critiques of the treaty, see: Andreas Osiander, "Sovereignty, International Relations, and the Westphalian Myth," *International Organization* 55 (2001): 251–287; Stephane Beaulac, "The Westphalian Legal Orthodoxy – Myth or Reality," *Journal of the History of International Law* 2 (2000): 148–177; Derek Croxton, "The Peace of Westphalia of 1648 and the Origins of Sovereignty," *The International History Review* 21 (1999): 575–599.

14 Treaty of Münster, Article LXV; and Treaty of Osnabrück, Article VIII.1. The texts of the treaties are available in all major languages and in various sources.

15 Culturally, the treaty does represent a change in attitudes among Europe's elite: it reflected a new willingness to take matters in hand, instead of assuming that nothing could be done. Theodore K. Rabb, *The Struggle for Stability in Early Modern Europe* (New York: Oxford University Press, 1975), 78–79.

16 Van Creveld, *Transformation*, 192.

17 Paul Kennedy, *The Rise and Fall of the Great Powers: Economic Change and Military Conflict from 1500 to 2000* (New York: Random House, 1987), esp. 58–65.

18 This need to reorganize formed one of the pillars in Michael Roberts' argument that this period saw a military revolution. Michael Roberts, "The Military Revolution, 1560–1660," in Clifford Rodgers, ed., *The Military Revolution Debate: Readings on the Military Transformation of Early Modern Europe* (Boulder, CO: Westview, 1995), 13–36; Geoffrey Parker, *The Military Revolution: Military Innovation and the Rise of the West, 1500–1800*, 2nd edn, (Cambridge: Cambridge University Press, 1996), 45–82, points to the rising cost of supplying war.

19 William S. Lind, "Fourth-Generation Warfare's First Blow: A Quick Look," *Marine Corps Gazette* 85, no. 11 (November 2001), 72.

20 Lind, "First Blow," 72.

21 Thomas X. Hammes, "4th-Generation Warfare: Our Enemies Play to Their Strengths," *Armed Forces Journal* (November 2004): 40–44.

22 Mao Tse-tung, *On Guerrilla Warfare*, 2nd edn, trans. and intro. by Samuel B. Griffith II (Baltimore: Nautical & Aviation Publishing Co., 1992); and *Basic Tactics*, trans. and intro. by Stuart R. Schram, (New York: Praeger, 1966). Other theorists include: General Vo-Nguyen-Giap, *People's War, People's Army: The Viet Cong Insurrection Manual for Underdeveloped Countries* (New York: Praeger, 1962). Che Guevara, *Guerrilla Warfare*, 3rd edn, Brian Loveman and Thomas M. Davies Jr, eds (Wilmington, DE: Scholarly Resources, 1997).

23 Philip Short, *Mao: A Life* (New York: Henry Holt, 2000); Sun-tzu, *The Art of War*, trans. by Ralph Sawyer (New York: Westview, 1994).

24 Clausewitz, *Vom Kriege*, Book VI, ch. 26, 799. The lectures are reprinted in "Meine Vorlesungen über den kleinem Krieg, gehalten auf der Kriegs-Schule 1810 und

1811," in Werner Hahlweg, ed., *Carl von Clausewitz: Schriften–Aufsätze–Studien–Briefe* (Göttingen: Vandenhoeck & Ruprecht, 1966), Vol. I, 205–288.

25 David S. Alberts, John J. Gartska and Frederick P. Stein, *Network-Centric Warfare: Developing and Leveraging Information Superiority* (Washington, DC: National Defense University, 1999).

26 While contemporary military analysts and commentators, such as S.L.A. Marshall, *Blitzkrieg: Its History, Strategy, Economics, and the Challenge to America* (New York: William Morrow & Co., 1940), called the German style of fighting a "blitzkrieg" or lightning war and proclaimed it a revolution in warfare, their rhetoric had little substance and was intended primarily to arouse concern in the United States over events in Europe. In fact, no official blitzkrieg concept ever existed in German military doctrine. Instead, the methods employed by the German military were a natural continuation of the concept of a war of movement (*Bewegungskrieg*) as opposed to a war of position (*Stellungskrieg*), a distinction that was hammered out in the 1890s. The term itself appears to have been coined outside Germany; the picture of General von Brauchitch on the cover of the September 1939 issue of *Time* magazine along with the title "Blitzkrieger" may have been among the first instances. Even Guderian's own concept for the use of armored forces, as outlined in his book *Achtung – Panzer!* was organized around accomplishing a rather traditional mission, a breakthrough operation, which he saw as *the* most challenging operation of World War I. Hence, Guderian did little more than attempt to improve existing procedures or, in today's phraseology, re-fight the last war. In any case, the German success on the battlefield depended, more often than not, on such factors as thorough planning, good training, and decentralized leadership.

27 Roger Chickering and Stig Förster, eds, *Great War, Total War: Combat and Mobilization on the Western Front, 1914–1918* (New York: Cambridge University Press, 2000); Roger Chickering, Stig Förster, Bernd Greiner, eds, *A World at Total War: Global Conflict and the Politics of Destruction, 1937–1947* (New York: Cambridge University Press, 2005). These works are part of a series that has recently problematized the concept and reality of total war.

8   Elegant irrelevance revisited

A critique of Fourth Generation Warfare

Michael Evans

Since the end of the Cold War, a school of military theory has emerged that argues that non-state, low-intensity conflict represents the future of war. This new school rejects the salience of conventional inter-state armed conflict and Carl von Clausewitz's philosophy of 'trinitarian warfare' based on the nexus between people, government and military. Advocates of non-state forms of armed conflict such as Martin van Creveld, Kalevi J. Holsti and Mark Duffield argue that low-intensity warfare is the wave of the future. They believe that there is a serious disparity between the theoretical basis of military strategy – which is conventional – and the actual practice of war – which is unconventional.[1] In short, the problem of twenty-first-century security is not that of 'trinitarian' wars between states, but of 'non-trinitarian' wars waged by a variety of insurgents and irregulars in conflicts defined by ethnic differences and religious fundamentalism.[2]

The background to Fourth Generation Warfare theory

One radical strand of the post-Clausewitzian unconventional school of military theory is that of American Fourth Generation Warfare that dates from the late 1980s and which has made intermittent appearances in professional military journals over the last fifteen years.[3] Leading advocates of the Fourth Generation school include the maneuver warfare theorist, William S. Lind and a number of US Marine Corps officers – including the author whose essay is the subject of this symposium – Thomas X. Hammes.[4]

Before examining the content of Colonel Hammes' new essay, it is useful for background purposes, to make some observations on the Fourth Generation's basic ideas. In November 2001, Lind, perhaps Fourth Generation Warfare's leading theorist, stated:

> Fourth-generation warfare is the greatest change in war since the Peace of Westphalia in 1648, and it undoes what that treaty established: the state's monopoly on war. It also marks a return to a world of cultures, not merely states, in conflict, and the collapse of both the state and our traditional Western culture here on our own soil. Over time, it may prove as momentous as the fall of the Roman Empire.[5]

He went on to suggest that, from a Fourth Generation perspective, the al-Qaeda attacks on the United States of 11 September 2001 should have been followed by an American nuclear attack that 'wiped Taliban-held Afghanistan off the map'.[6]

Partly because of its radicalism and partly because of its clutch of idiosyncratic ideas and scattergun methodologies, Fourth Generation advocates have, so far, never succeeded in influencing the mainstream of American or Western military theory. The best critique of Fourth Generation Warfare was written in 1993 by Kenneth F. McKenzie Jr, and appeared in the US military journal, *Parameters*. In a memorable phrase, McKenzie described Fourth Generation Warfare as 'elegant irrelevance' – based on polemic rather than paradigm and on mantra rather than method. He highlighted its advocates' selective focus noting that the proposition of four generations of warfare omitted important areas of military history from analysis.[7]

McKenzie dryly wrote that, 'any theory of warfare that does not address the influence of the French Revolution, Republican France, and the First Empire stands in grave danger of being accused of historical myopia'.[8] He was also critical of the idiosyncratic, quasi-Marxist methodology of 'dialectical qualitatives' that underpinned the logic of a linear succession of generations of war stating that 'its [the Fourth Generation school's] methods are unclear, its facts contentious and open to widely varying interpretations, and its relevance questionable'.[9]

Continuing weaknesses of Fourth Generation Warfare theory

While Colonel Hammes' new essay, 'War Evolves into the Fourth Generation' is a reminder of the limitations of high technology in warfare, it merely restates original Fourth Generation thinking and shows little or no advance on the ideas criticized so effectively by McKenzie a dozen years ago. For example, Hammes retains the controversial methodology of the early Fourth Generation Warfare writers alongside a superficial and highly selective treatment of military history. The central tenet in Hammes' analysis is a Marxist-style division of warfare into distinct stages of massed manpower (First Generation Warfare), massed firepower (Second Generation Warfare), maneuver operations (Third Generation Warfare) and into low-intensity conflict or Fourth Generation Warfare.

Problems in strategic analysis and historical chronology

It is important to note that, while Colonel Hammes writes as a self-declared practitioner rather than as a military theorist, the Fourth Generation approach *is* an attempt to advance a general theory of war for the twenty-first century. Consequently, the theory of four generations of warfare must be tested against evidence that pays rigorous attention to strategic analysis and historical chronology if it is to be taken seriously. Based on reading Colonel Hammes' essay and his accompanying book, *The Sling and the Stone*, these considerations are not addressed in any depth.[10] It is, for instance not credible, as Hammes attempts to try to advance a theory of succeeding generations of warfare without some recourse to the vast scholarship on military change begun by Michael Roberts in the 1950s.[11] A belief in a linear sequence of three discrete generations of manpower, firepower and maneuver in the evolution of modern warfare cannot be sustained after reading the works of such scholars as Geoffrey Parker, Jeremy Black, MacGregor Knox, Williamson Murray and Colin S. Gray.[12]

These scholars have shown how developments in warfare often run parallel, or are uneven in character, so defying neat categorization. For example, in the history of war, it is difficult to draw a strict line between fire and maneuver. Combined arms warfare marked by fire and maneuver was first developed by the Swedish Army of Gustavus Adolphus in the seventeenth century – a period according to Fourth Generation theorists that is distinguished by reliance on manpower.[13] Moreover, the interdependence of firepower and maneuver was as central to Revolutionary and Napoleonic warfare as the use of large, conscript armies. Indeed, the use of mobile French army corps and the employment of massed artillery, was once described as 'the French secret weapon of the Napoleonic Wars'.[14] Similarly, firepower and maneuver played complementary roles at different times in both of the world wars.[15]

Hammes argues that insurgency, the incarnation of the Fourth Generation of war, is itself some seventy years old and dates from Mao Tse-tung's development of revolutionary warfare in the 1930s. Again, such an assertion requires an assessment of the evolution of insurgency. Yet the chapter draws on little from the huge literature on insurgency warfare. Important studies by Franklin Mark Osanka, Michael Elliot-Bateman, Tim Bowden, John Ellis and Walter Laqueur from the Cold War era or more recently those of Robert E. Harkavy and Stephanie G. Neuman and of Ian F.W. Beckett do not rate mention. Yet, collectively, it is such studies that have traced the growth of the nexus between politics and guerilla warfare. These works have demonstrated how different blends of insurgency warfare evolved – from China to Cyprus and from Ireland to Palestine – according to specific socio-political contexts and varying military methods.[16]

Colonel Hammes argues that Fourth Generation Warfare is symbolized by the mobilization of superior political will by insurgent forces. The author makes reference to an evolution in insurgency methods from Mao Tse-tung through Vo Nguyen Giap in Vietnam and Daniel Ortega in Nicaragua to the Palestinian *Intifada* and the contemporary Iraq insurgency. Yet grouping diverse conflicts from three different continents together is not a convincing explanation of the rise of insurgency and its place at the core of Fourth Generation Warfare. For instance, both Mao and Giap ultimately won their wars in China and Vietnam not by insurgency, but by converting their efforts from irregular to regular military operations through the doctrine of protracted warfare.[17]

Moreover, in terms of operational methods, the Iraq war cannot be related to Mao, Giap or Ortega. Indeed, armed conflict in contemporary Iraq reveals more similarities with the nationalist Algerian insurgency of the 1950s than with rural revolutionary warfare in Asia or Latin America. For this reason, the Pentagon has recently been screening Gille Pontecorvo's famous 1964 film, *The Battle of Algiers* for the benefit of US military officers. Finally, Hammes shows little recognition of the changes in insurgency since the end of the Cold War including the shift from Marxist–Leninist revolutionary war to forms of ethnopolitical conflict and wars of cultural identity that may involve population displacement and ethnic cleansing.[18]

Fourth Generation Warfare and the new security environment

The most serious weakness of Hammes' study is, however, its inability to situate warfare in the context of a new international security environment that has been reshaped by globalization and the information revolution. Contrary to the views of many non-state theorists, it is a simplification to suggest that the world has become post-Westphalian and post-Clausewitzian. Rather, what we have witnessed over the past fifteen years is the bifurcation of the contemporary international security system – that is, a split has occurred between a traditional twentieth-century state-centered paradigm and new twenty-first-century sub-state and trans-state strata.[19]

The result has been the rise of a new spectrum of conflict that reflects the merging of complex and overlapping modes of armed conflict. These modes are *post-modern* or RMA aerial precision strike warfare, *modern* or symmetrical, conventional warfare, and *pre-modern* or irregular, unconventional warfare. Conflicts such as Somalia, Afghanistan and Iraq have demonstrated how these different modes merge and interpenetrate. In Somalia, the tribal drums of warlord militia were used to signal the arrival of US Rangers in helicopters. In Afghanistan, post-modern American cruise missiles and pre-modern Afghan cavalry co-existed and modern US special operations forces operated with Northern Alliance tribal militia some of whom still carried Lee Enfield rifles inherited from colonial wars on the North-West Frontier. In Iraq, modern urban insurgency methods that recall the Algerian insurgency have been accompanied by suicide bombings in the name of a pre-modern form of political Islam.[20]

Understanding the twenty-first-century spectrum of conflict

It is important to understand the character of the new spectrum of conflict. In the West, for most of the Cold War, the notion of a spectrum of conflict was based on generic intellectual categories of *conventional* (high-intensity) and *unconventional* (low-intensity) conflict. The approach to war was often conceived in terms of separate worlds of conventional inter-state (or high-intensity operations) and unconventional intra-state (or low-intensity operations and counter-terrorism) military activity.[21] In bifurcated twenty-first-century conditions, such a view is no longer tenable. As the American analyst, Brian Michael Jenkins presciently argued in the early 1980s:

The three components of armed conflict – conventional war, guerrilla war and terrorism – will coexist in the future. Governments and subnational entities will employ them individually, interchangeably, sequentially, or simultaneously, and will be required to combat them.[22]

The spectrum of conflict that is rapidly emerging in the new millennium is distinguished by its merging categories, by its multidimensionality and by its unprecedented interaction.[23] Consequently, modern militaries in the early twenty-first century must prepare to confront a range of old, new and hybrid forms of armed conflict in multidimensional operations. As the US Hart-Rudman Commission on twenty-first-century security put it in 1999, the future of war is now based on 'the spectrum of symmetrical and asymmetrical threats we [in the US] anticipate over the next quarter century'.[24] As modes of operational activity increasingly merge and interpenetrate, the likelihood of the conventional and the unconventional, the symmetric and the asymmetric, appearing simultaneously increases. The US Marine Corps' doctrine of the 'three block war' – in which troops may be engaged in warfighting, peace operations and humanitarian relief simultaneously represents an attempt to grapple with this complex interaction.[25]

Thus, the intellectual challenge facing military professionals is not, as Fourth Generation Warfare advocates would have us believe, to consign Carl von Clausewitz and 2,000 years of Western military knowledge into the dustbin of history. Rather, the task is to learn how to fight what the leading Russian military theorist, Makhmut Gareev, has called 'a multi-variant war' waged across a new spectrum of conflict that is characterized by a 'high–low' mix of operations.[26] Gareev's approach is echoed by two leading American military theorists, Huba Wass de Czege and Richard Hart Sinnreich, who have noted that, 'clear distinctions between conventional and unconventional conflicts are fading, and any future major conflict is almost certain to see a routine commingling of such operations'.[27]

In advanced militaries, preparing for operations across a spectrum of conflict is best accomplished by having forces that are structured to confront the different opponents that may appear in the diverse alleys and valleys of contemporary warfare. If conventional and unconventional operations can occur almost simultaneously and overlap in time and space, then military force structures must be capable of rapid task force organization to provide a 'golf bag', or variety, of military capabilities. They must be able to fight Iraq's Republican Guard as well as Taliban militia forces, al-Qaeda terrorists and Iraqi urban insurgents in the Sunni Triangle.[28]

Conclusion

The difficulties with many contemporary 'end of inter-state conventional war' advocates – particularly Fourth Generation thinkers – are tendencies towards strategic generalization, poor military history and flawed conceptual analysis.

No single strategy and no linear interpretation of history can encompass the complex human experience of armed conflict. While it is true that inter-state war has occurred less frequently than intra-state war between 1945 and 1991, the same could be said for, say, the period between 1845 and 1891. In the latter period, there were more imperial 'small wars' and endemic civil conflicts from the Balkans through India to Africa than there ever were major inter-state wars.[29] The truth is, that, while major international wars may be infrequent, when they do occur they often tend to change the balance of world power. In short, most non-state war proponents tend to misunderstand, or to misrepresent, the complex workings of the *longue durée* of the history of arms.

It is difficult to avoid the conclusion that, as a theory of war, the Fourth Generation represents little more than a form of military dilettantism. The task before contemporary military theorists is not to seek artificial categorization based on alleged generations, or waves of activity, but to undertake an intellectual exploration of the growing interaction between inter-state, sub-state and trans-state conflict. The need is for analysts to conduct a rigorous investigation of the phenomenon of merging war forms – internal, international, post-modern, modern and pre-modern.

Such an approach requires that relevant features from the high-technology classical model of warfare associated with the Revolution in Military Affairs be carefully synthesized with the changing reality of conflict – both conventional and unconventional – as they present themselves at the beginning of the twenty-first century. Interaction has always been the outstanding feature of war and, in an age of networks and instant communications, the interactive character of war is likely to increase in importance. Armed conflict is far too complex a phenomenon to be evolving into a Fourth Generation that is defined by the single scenario of insurgency. Clausewitz was right when he wrote that war is a true chameleon 'that adapts its characteristics to the given case'.[30] In this, as in much else related to the theory of war, the great Prussian remains our most important teacher.

Notes

1   Martin van Creveld, *The Transformation of War*, The Free Press, New York, 1991, chap. 7; 'What is Wrong with Clausewitz?', in Gert de Nooy, ed., *The Clausewitzian Dictum and the Future of Western Military Strategy*, Kluwer Law International, The Hague, 1997, chap. 2; and 'The End of Strategy?' in Hugh Smith, ed., *The Strategists*, Australian Defence Studies Centre, University of New South Wales, 2001, chap. 10; Kalevi J. Holsti, *The State, War, and the State of War*, Cambridge University Press, Cambridge, 1996; Mark Duffield, *Global Governance and the New Wars: The Merging of Development and Security*, Zed Books, London, 2001. Both van Creveld and Holsti advance statistics to demonstrate that, during the Cold War only 20 per cent of the world's armed conflicts were inter-state in character.

2   See, for instance, van Creveld, 'The End of Strategy?', pp. 122–3; 'What is Wrong with Clausewitz', pp. 10–11; and Duffield, *Global Governance and the New Wars: The Merging of Development and Security*, chaps 1–2; 7–8.

3   William S. Lind, Colonel Keith F. Nightengale, Captain John F. Schmitt, Colonel

Joseph W. Sutton and Lieutenant Colonel Gary I. Wilson, 'The Changing Face of War: Into the Fourth Generation', *Marine Corps Gazette*, October 1989, Vol. 73, no. 10, pp. 22–8; and *Military Review*, October 1989, Vol. 69, no. 10, pp. 2–11; William S. Lind, Major John F. Schmitt and Colonel Gary I. Wilson, 'Fourth Generation Warfare: Another Look', *Marine Corps Gazette*, December 1994, Vol. 78, no. 12, pp. 34–7.William S. Lind, 'Fourth-Generation Warfare's First Blow: A Quick Look' and Colonel Gary I. Wilson, Major Frank Bunkers and Sergeant John P. Sullivan, 'The Next Conflict', *Marine Corps Gazette*, November 2001, Vol. 85, no. 11, pp. 72, 73–6.

4 Thomas X. Hammes, 'The Evolution of War: The Fourth Generation', *Marine Corps Gazette*, Vol. 78, no. 9, pp. 31–5; 'Insurgency: Modern Warfare Evolves into a Fourth Generation', *Strategic Forum*, Institute for National Strategic Studies, National Defence University, January 2005, no. 214, pp. 1–8.

5 Lind, 'Fourth Generation Warfare's First Blow: A Quick Look', p. 72.

6 Ibid.

7 Kenneth F. McKenzie Jr, 'Elegant Irrelevance: Fourth Generation Warfare', *Parameters: US Army War College Quarterly*, Autumn 1993, Vol. 23, no. 3, pp. 51–60.

8 Ibid., p. 55.

9 Ibid., p. 54.

10 Thomas X. Hammes, *The Sling and the Stone: On War in the 21st Century*, Zenith Press, St Paul, MN, 2004.

11 Michael Roberts, 'The Military Revolution, 1560–1660', in Clifford J. Rogers, ed., *The Military Revolution Debate: Readings in the Military Transformation of Early Modern Europe*, Westview Press, Boulder, CO, 1995, pp. 13–36.

12 Geoffrey Parker, *The Military Revolution and the Rise of the West, 1500–1800*, Cambridge University Press, Cambridge, 1988; Jeremy Black, *War: Past, Present and Future*, Sutton Publishing, Phoenix Mill, Gloucestershire, 2000; MacGregor Knox and Williamson Murray, eds, *The Dynamics of Military Revolution, 1300–2050*, Cambridge University Press, Cambridge, 2001; Colin S. Gray, *Modern Strategy*, Oxford University Press, Oxford, 1999; and *Strategy for Chaos: Revolutions in Military Affairs and the Evidence of History*, Frank Cass, London, 2002.

13 See Michael Evans and Alan Ryan, eds, *From Breitenfeld to Baghdad: Perspectives on Combined Arms Warfare*, Land Warfare Studies Centre, Canberra, Working Paper no. 122, July 2003.

14 David Chandler, *Napoleon*, Weidenfeld and Nicolson, London, 1973, p. 202.

15 G.D. Sheffield, 'Blitzkrieg and Attrition: Land Operations in Europe 1914–45', in Colin McInness and G.D. Sheffield, eds, *Warfare in the Twentieth Century: Theory and Practice*, Unwin Hyman, London, 1988, pp. 51–79.

16 Franklin Mark Osanka, ed., *Modern Guerrilla Warfare: Fighting Communist Guerrilla Movements, 1941–1961*, The Free Press of Glencoe, New York, 1963; Michael Elliot-Bateman, ed., *The Fourth Dimension of Warfare*, Manchester University Press, Manchester, 1970; Michael Elliot-Bateman, John Ellis and Tom Bowden, *Revolt to Revolution,* Manchester University Press, Manchester, 1974; Walter Laqueur, *Guerrilla: A Historical and Critical Study*, Weidenfeld and Nicolson, London, 1977; John Ellis, Robert E. Harkavy and Stephanie G. Neuman, *Warfare and the Third World*, Palgrave, New York, 2001; and Ian F.W. Beckett, *Modern Insurgencies and Counter-Insurgencies: Guerrillas and their Opponents since 1750*, Routledge, London, 2001.

17 See Michael Elliot-Bateman, *Defeat in the East: The Mark of Mao-tse Tung on War*, Oxford University Press, London, 1967; and John Ellis, *From the Barrel of a Gun: A History of Guerrilla, Revolutionary and Counter-Insurgency Warfare, from the Romans to the Present*, Greenhill Books, London, 1975, chaps 7–10.

18 See Mary Kaldor, *New and Old Wars: Organised Violence in a Global Era*, Polity Press, Cambridge, 1999; Avi Kober, 'Low-intensity Conflicts: Why the Gap between Theory and Practise?', *Defense and Security Analysis*, March 2002, Vol. 18, no. 1, pp. 15–38; and Harkavy and Neuman, *Warfare and the Third World*, especially chap. 5.

19 See Michael Evans, 'From Kadesh to Kandahar: Military Theory and the Future of War', *Naval War College Review*, Summer 2003, Vol. XVI, no. 3, pp. 132–50; Robert L. Pfaltzgraff Jr and Richard H. Shultz Jr, 'Future Actors in a Changing Security Environment', in Robert L. Pfaltzgraff Jr and Richard H. Schultz Jr, eds, *War in the Information Age: New Challenges for US Security Policy*, Brassey's, Washington DC, 1997, chap. 1; and Jean-Marie Guèhenno, 'The Impact of Globalisation on Strategy', *Survival*, Winter 1998–9, Vol. 40, no. 4, pp. 5–19.

20 Evans, 'From Kadesh to Kandahar: Military Theory and the Future of War', pp. 138–50; Robert J. Bunker and John P. Sullivan, *Suicide Bombings in Operation Iraqi Freedom*, Institute of Land Warfare, Association of the United States Army, Land Warfare Paper no. 46W, Arlington, VA, September 2004, pp. 7–14.

21 Ibid.

22 Brian Michael Jenkins, 'New Modes of Conflict', *Orbis: A Journal of World Affairs*, Spring 1984, Vol. 28, no. 1, p. 15.

23 Robert L. Pfaltzgraff Jr. and Stephen E. Wright, 'The Spectrum of Conflict: Symmetrical or Asymmetrical Challenge?', in Richard H. Shultz Jr and Robert L. Pfaltzgraff Jr, eds, *The Role of Naval Forces in 21st-Century Operations*, Brassey's, Washington, DC, 2000, pp. 9–28.

24 The United States Commission on National Security/21st Century, *Seeking a National Strategy: A Concert for Preserving Security and Promoting Freedom*, The Phase II Report on a US National Security Strategy for the 21st Century, The Commission, Washington, DC, 15 April 2000, p. 14.

25 Michael Evans, *The Continental School of Strategy: The Past, Present and Future of Land Power*, Land Warfare Studies Centre, Study Paper, no. 305, Canberra, June 2004, pp. 62–76, 120–32.

26 Makhmut Gareev, *If War Comes Tomorrow? The Contours of Future Armed Conflict*, Frank Cass, London, 1998, p. 94.

27 Huba Wass de Czege and Richard Hart Sinnreich, *Conceptual Foundations of a Transformed US Army*, Association of the United States Army, Institute for Land Warfare Paper no. 40, Washington, DC, March 2002, p. 6.

28 Evans, 'From Kadesh to Kandahar: Military Theory and the Future of War'.

29 For analysis of the incidence of small wars in the nineteenth century see Douglas Porch, *Wars of Empire*, Cassell & Co., London, 2000.

30 Carl von Clausewitz, *On War*, edited and translated by Michael Howard and Peter Paret, Princeton University Press, Princeton, NJ, 1976, p. 89.

9   Generations at war?

John Ferris

Thomas X. Hammes asks what power is and what war will be. His answers to these questions have strengths and weaknesses; weaknesses first.

The history is reductionist – Hammes loots the past for pedigree while discarding anything that does not fit his needs. His observations of current trends are intelligent, but he transmutes them into theory by dubious means. Implicitly, his case rests on ideas about "ages" and "generations", which he treats not as a loose means of categorization, but as tools to identify the essential characteristics of a time, from which one can predict what must happen, or cannot. Only a single generation can exist at a time, except when one is beating another to death. Ages have one and only one set of true characteristics – thus, his question whether current insurgencies are mere "aberrations", or indications of "the evolution of a new generation of war". Yet in reality, several generations coexist at any time, many things occur in any "age" which do not fit the name, and the world is filled with contrary trends. Hammes uses the concept of "age" exactly as do the advocates of "information age" warfare whom he criticizes.[1] That similarity indicates something about American thinking on strategy and war.

On the other hand, Hammes' critique of contemporary ideas about transformed forces is good. These ideas fail in practice, and in principle. They assume the United States can always play to its strengths, and never to its weaknesses. It is always convenient when an enemy chooses to be foolish or weak, or foolish and weak, but that is its choice, and you will be a fool to assume it must do what you wish. A smart but weak foe may refuse any game where you can apply your strengths, and make you play another one. A tough and able foe might turn the characteristics of your game into a strength of its own, by attacking any precondition for your system to work and then by imposing its rules on you. The Revolution in Military Affairs (RMA) has done many things, but not everything. It has multiplied American strengths but not reduced its weaknesses. It has increased the value of high technology and firepower in conventional war, but for little else; where these things matter, they do more than ever; where they do not, nothing has changed. In particular, the United States is as weak as ever against guerrillas.

This weakness lies at the heart of Hammes' theory, alongside claims about the transformation of insurgency. He argues that insurgents are more likely to win than before, because they apply means of organization and tactics which are new, and suited to their age. Fourth Generation Warfare (4GW), he claims, emerged 70 years ago, with Mao Tse-tung, though one may wonder whether Mao's theories mattered quite so much to the Chinese Communist Party's use of force as Hammes imagines. Then, he combines a standard counterinsurgent reading of the etymology of guerrilla theory and practice (from Mao to Giap to the Sandinistas), with ideas drawn from the original "4GW" theory, and David Arquilla and Jon Ronfeldt's concept of "netwar" (non-state actors using net-like organization and techno-political means on the internet). In essence, Hammes argues, 4GW combines guerrilla tactics with a sophisticated political strategy; insurgents win by making their foes play their game, a prolonged war of attrition won by willpower and politics rather than high technology and firepower; that approach has succeeded increasingly since 1940, and recently has taken a new form, as guerrillas draw on net-like modes of organization.

Hammes reads the success of guerrillas essentially as a function of military-political technique, or strategy; but it turns on a bigger matter, organization. Guerrillas do not win most of their wars, slowly; they lose most of them, fast. They can fight for decades with little popular support, while achieving nothing. They matter only when they can tap a large base of support and apply it in a prolonged and costly war of attrition, which their enemies cannot endure. In the nineteenth century, the only socio-political means available to rally peoples with loose organization beyond clans or villages were religious bodies: Sufi Muslim brotherhoods led the greatest insurgencies of that time, in Algeria and Chechnya-Daghestan. These movements were defeated fairly easily by western states. This situation changed after 1945 when guerrillas, the razor edge of well organized mass political movements, fought wars of national liberation. That political success escalated the price of counterinsurgency, and beat western states, unable to win easily and unwilling to fight hard. With the end of the colonial era, however, the situation changed again. Guerrillas were far more successful between 1945–65 than ever since. Guerrilla wars remained endemic in Asia, Africa and Latin America, but as a kind of civil conflict, generally long and inconclusive, with some spectacular exceptions. Governments with little popular support or outside help – as in Rhodesia and Nicaragua during the 1960s and 1970s – fought guerrillas more effectively than the colonial states or the superpowers. Defeat meant exile, impoverishment or death, and they had nowhere else to go.

Hammes argues that recent insurgents have adopted unusual military–political techniques. Guerrillas in the first Intifada played political judo; those in the second Intifada and Iraq used savage attacks on civilians; net-like means of organization featured in Iraq and the first Intifada. In fact, insurgents routinely use creative politics, the activities of the IRA or Irgun had shock value in their time, while netwar derives directly from a tactic dating back to 1880, "propaganda by the deed", the use of violence to catch media attention and bring your message directly to the people you want to rally or frighten. These techniques or strategies are not new, but something else is – the reduction in the entry cost of political organization needed for insurgency. During decolonization, guerrillas needed mass political movements in order to win; not today. The combination of ruthless leaders and militants, high explosives and the internet, lets small groups with tiny political bases fight awful and effective wars, reach their targets directly, and conduct propaganda of the deed with unprecedented success. Modern media, especially the internet, serve these groups as a means of publicity and to ensure that their acts of violence achieve political ends, so eroding (though not ending) their need for bureaucracy or mass support. These conditions increase the power of what, for want of a standard term, one might call "political warfare" or "terrorism", i.e. the use of violence for political means by non-state actors, whether Bolshevik or Black Hand, anarchist or al Qaeda; and also the number of organizations which can turn political struggle into war, and make us fight it. These techniques can be used against us abroad and at home, by jihadists or our equivalents of them (remember the Red Brigade?). The other side is stronger in an area where western militaries and states were weak to start with.

So, what of the theory as a whole? At any time over the past century, several "generations" of war have coexisted – conventional wars, guerrilla wars, and "political warfare". Over that period, the power of these "generations" has changed, but not in simple linear patterns of growth or decline; and none look dead yet. If conventional power seems less significant now than for the past century, that is simply because everyone knows what it can do, and who can do it. Yet it matters as much as ever, even when it is not used: overwhelming American power in the air and sea deters challenges from other peoples and underpins the world order as much as the Royal Navy did between 1815–1931. Since 1989, the conventional power of western states has risen, but so has that of insurgents against them. If the problem is that western governments cannot easily win guerrilla wars abroad, one solution may be – why bother trying? The western world has no vital interests in Afghanistan; we can evade guerrillas just as easily as they do conventional forces. Often, our weakness in this field may be real but irrelevant. But not in all cases – sometimes we will not be able to evade such wars, or they may follow us home. More broadly, Hammes touches on an area where strategic theory is weak, on the blurred boundaries between war by states and by non-state actors. We identify war with the state; yet non-states make war too. "Political warfare", the lower levels of force involving the state, terrorism and propaganda by the deed, the ability of non-state actors to make war without armies and make states respond with them, will be a growing area of war over coming generations. Our theories of strategy might pay attention to them.

Note

1 Cf. R.L. DiNardo and Daniel J. Hughes, "Some Cautionary Thoughts on Information Warfare", *Airpower Journal*, Winter 1995.

10 War evolves into the fourth generation

A comment on Thomas X. Hammes

Lawrence Freedman

The idea that warfare has been moving in recent decades into its fourth generation is normally associated with William Lind. It has been taken forward by
Thomas Hammes whose article usefully establishes the main features of the
thesis. He uses it effectively to explain the failure of the US to appreciate the
extent of the resistance it was facing in Iraq and to adjust its tactics accordingly,
and makes a compelling case that there are features of the war in Iraq that are
shared by other conflicts, past and present. His critique of what has been, at least
until now, the dominant mind-set in the Pentagon, is valuable. My concern in
this comment is with the underlying concept of fourth generation warfare
(4GW). I argue that the activities covered by 4GW are best viewed not as an
evolution from earlier, more conventional types of warfare but instead as aspects
of a separate process, reflecting strategies that the weak have long adopted in
conflicts with superior military powers. These activities, and their interaction
with regular forms of warfare, vary considerably in their size and scope, and in
the underlying politico-military assumptions that inform them. I conclude that
the category of 4GW is too diffuse and the historical analysis upon which it is
grounded is weak.

I

The attitudes with which the US armed forces approached the world after the Cold
War are normally assumed to have been shaped in reaction to Vietnam. This mis-
erable experience led to an internal consensus, particularly strong in the Army,
about what we can call 'proper war'. This assumed a comparative disadvantage
when it came to counterinsurgency operations but, with proper application of doctrine and technology, a comparative advantage in conventional operations. Proper
wars were therefore based on decisive battles between regular armed forces,
preferably operating without arbitrary political limits. There was a strong normative aspect: 'improper wars' distorted priorities and undermined preparations for
the proper and should not therefore be fought. So instead of the normal presump-
tion that military policy should follow foreign policy, the reverse had to be the
case. Civilians were expected to show restraint in not leading the US into improper
wars and in not interfering with the conduct of proper wars.[1]

The potential tension between military and foreign policy implied by this view was not fully addressed. This was partly because of the post-Vietnam mood, and a general wariness about the dangers of misguided foreign policy leading to more damaging military entanglements, but also because of the promulgation of a mistaken view of history, notably by Harry Summers. He suggested that the real failure in Vietnam was not to realize that in essence it was actually a proper war.[2] It was only with the 1983–4 debacle in Beirut that the possibility of a disconnection between military and foreign policy was addressed directly, in the great debate between the Pentagon and the State Department. As Secretary of Defense Caspar Weinberger had always been against any involvement in the Lebanese civil war, he used the experience to set down restrictive criteria for assessing future proposals for military interventions.[3] The State Department argued that engaging in only 'fun wars' would impose a severe constraint on the conduct of foreign policy.

At the time the main business of the armed forces could still be safely said to be deterring the Soviet Union and its allies, especially in Europe. With the end of the Cold War the main business was likely to change, for there was no longer any obvious need to prepare for a full-scale proper war. Then, along came the 1991 Persian Gulf War which appeared to confirm the validity of American military preferences, for it was fought successfully along wholly conventional lines. Military policy was to build on this success, with future force structure an extrapolation, though described as a 'revolution in military affairs'. This assumed a 'peer competitor', an enemy comparable in terms of size, organization and strategy. Yet in terms of military capacity the US had no peer. Any country that was drawn into a regular battle with the US was almost bound to lose. Even so, preparing for proper war was still deemed essential – for it was assumed that this would mean that the US could certainly deal with lesser enemies and even lesser operations (tellingly described as 'operations other than war'). So military policy focused on the contingencies for which conventional forces might be most useful – North Korea and another Iraq. In the event, the actual challenges of the 1990s were quite different. The reluctance of the US military to rise to these challenges, especially in the Balkans, led to Madeline Albright's famous question to Colin Powell (as Chairman of the Joint Chiefs of Staff): 'What's the point of having this superb military that you're always talking about if we can't use it?'[4]

The disconnect between military and foreign policy was thrown into even sharper relief after the attacks on the US of 11 September 2001. The military actions undertaken under the aegis of the 'war on terror' were, in the first instance, largely conventional. The defeat of the Taliban regime, and its al-Qaeda allies, for what had been launched from Afghanistan in the past, was followed by the defeat of Saddam Hussein's regime, for what might be launched from Iraq in the future. Yet these conventional military successes, in both cases relatively brief and painless (at least for US forces), were followed by much more problematic campaigns against insurgent forces. Once again the US forces found themselves having to cope with an enemy that intermingled with civil society, in wars that could not end with decisive battles but only with the collapse of political will. As the US 'will' had broken first in a number of relatively recent conflicts (Vietnam, Lebanon and Somalia), it was not unreasonable for its enemies (and potential friends) to suppose that it might break again.

The qualitative superiority that allowed the US to defeat with ease a larger, although generally third-rate, Iraq Army meant that it lacked the numbers on the ground to establish its presence and assert local authority after the war. Having begun with a legitimacy deficit, in terms of both domestic and international support for a war which was widely seen to have a contrived rationale, the US-led coalition struggled against an enemy as vicious as it was determined. With a doctrine encouraging a preoccupation with force protection and an over-reliance on firepower, US troops became alienated from the Iraqi people, thereby helping their enemies to acquire recruits and local sanctuaries. By preparing for the wrong sort of war, by not gearing military policy to the likely demands of foreign policy, the US armed force helped to aggravate an already difficult situation.

II

The 'fourth generation' school can see this state of affairs as a form of vindication. As the Cold War was coming to an end, William Lind with a number of military colleagues argued that the US needed to understand that warfare was undergoing a generational change.[5] The first three generations had developed in response to each other (line and column, massed firepower and blitzkrieg). Into the fourth generation was carried an increasingly dispersed battlefield, reducing the importance of centralized logistics and mass (either men or firepower), and a tendency for victory to come through the implosion of the enemy rather than its physical destruction. The essence of 4GW could be summed up as the blurring of boundaries – between war and peace, between civilian and military, between tactics and strategy, between order and chaos. Such war cannot be contained in either time or space.

This feature of 4GW is captured in the definition provided by Hammes:

> Fourth generation war uses all available networks – political, economic, social, and military – to convince the enemy's political decision makers that their strategic goals are either unachievable or too costly for the perceived benefit. It is rooted in the fundamental precept that superior political will, when properly employed, can defeat greater economic and military power. 4GW does not attempt to win by defeating the enemy's military forces. Instead, combining guerrilla tactics or civil disobedience with the soft networks of social, cultural and economic ties, disinformation campaigns and innovative political activity, it directly attacks the enemy's political will.

After discussing the implications of a form of warfare that spans the 'spectrum of human activity', the definition concludes: 'In sum, 4GW is politically, socially (rather than technically) networked and protracted in duration. It is the anti-thesis of the high-technology, short war the Pentagon is preparing to fight.'

This is simply too broad to be useful. Slightly reworked the first sentence could serve as a definition of grand strategy. It is hard to think of any recent conflict, including those involving clashes of regular forces, which did not involve the use of social, economic and political instruments in conjunction with the military. Influencing the enemy's cost–benefit calculation is central to any definition of strategic coercion. It is clear what is not included, but there are still many types of warfare quite different from the Pentagon's view of a proper war. It is also, as discussed below, not wholly accurate to pose tactics such as guerrilla warfare and civil disobedience against attempts to defeat enemy armed forces. The notion of networks, which stress inter-connectedness, also has to be treated carefully, because it can encourage an exaggerated and possibly illusory perception of linkages.

Lind's work demonstrates this latter danger. The original 1989 article is inevitably dated in some of its concerns, but also has a contemporary feel, for example, in its warning of the potential dangers of combining terrorism, high technology, and 'a non-national or transnational base, such as ideology or religion'. Yet there was still tentativeness around the discussion of what form 4GW would actually take. In particular there was a sense that anything corrosive of the cultural foundations of a society might be understood as part of such a war. Cultural damage appeared as the product of deliberate and hostile moves by enemies, aided and abetted by naive and wrong-thinking elements at home, rather than of broader and more diffuse social trends or economic imperatives. So the 1989 article worried about the impact of drug trafficking on the US and its vulnerability to highly-sophisticated psychological warfare. Lind has more recently, and controversially, presented culture as the key battleground for 4GW. In a 2004 article in the *Military Review* he talks of a 'world of cultures in conflict', describing Islam as 'the Christian West's oldest and most steadfast opponent' and bemoaning America's 'closed political system (regardless of which party wins, the Establishment remains in power and nothing really changes) and a poisonous ideology of multiculturalism'. This, he argues, makes the country 'a prime candidate for the homegrown variety of Fourth Generation war, which is by far the most dangerous kind'. As a 'true conservative' he has been a vigorous opponent of neo-conservatives, for he sees Afghanistan and Iraq as manifestations of exactly the sort of military thinking he opposes and gifts to America's cultural enemies.[6]

Hammes clearly is not seeking to press the cultural element of 4GW the way that Lind does. But the sort of arguments Lind makes about the nature of 4GW does point to a potential problem once the 'spectrum of human activity' is assumed to be employable in warfare. Take a proposition for which there is much support: the advisability of a 'hearts and minds' approach to counter-insurgency, whereby all military engagements, however small and local, must be evaluated by their political effects. The next stage is to observe that comparable political effects, relating to attitudes within the target population, can be achieved by non-military means even though undertaken by the military. This provides a case for civic action programmes and other activities with a humanitarian mission. The enemy may also be competing in the same way. The next stage in this line of thinking can pass the military by – noting how the battle for hearts and minds can be fought largely through the media and on the streets – taking the form of competition over values and beliefs. It is not a large step from that to accuse all those who tend to values and beliefs considered subversive to be seditious or what used to be called 'fifth columnists'.

In practice not all, or even most, contests between different belief systems are usefully considered wars, nor are all distasteful cultural developments the product of malign intent. Shifts in political attitudes and behaviour will come about through complex processes over time, involving changes in intellectual fashion and the impact of events. Those who seek to hurry them along through acts of violence are usually working at the margins. Only in situations where access to the political system has been denied will violent methods gain widespread support. In addition, the strategic reach of most political movements is limited and few can cope with the full spectrum of human activity. Only Marxists and religious fundamentalists ever believe they have succeeded in comprehending all the linkages and they are normally spectacularly wrong. The conditions which may help these movements prosper are not necessarily their own creations, and will develop in ways that they will be unable to control. The 4GW school correctly postulates the limits to state power, acknowledging the complexity of the environment. Yet this is even more so for non-state actors, whose ability to operate in a coherent manner across the spectrum of human activity will normally be quite modest. Non-state movements that adopt these methods often argue among themselves about which of a set of relatively hopeless strategies should be adopted. Mostly they fail, and those that succeed often do so not so much because they are able to create artificially a substantial political constituency but because this constituency already exists.

Hammes lists a range of non-military means available to dissident groups that want to coerce states. The use of such means may constitute a new form of politics, made possible by broader social, economic and technological changes, but not a new form of war. That involves organized violence for a political purpose. When a form of war is described which no longer depends on organized violence but instead involves using all the many forms of political pressure made possible in an interdependent, wired-up and media-intensive world, then it is not war. It is the case that movements and even individuals with quite radical objectives and marginal views have opportunities for making themselves heard that were denied their predecessors, but we are not at war with them as a result, unless we want to assign belligerent status to Greenpeace and Amnesty International. It is true that money and ideas can now be 'digitized and moved instantly', but that does not make the exploitation of all consequential possibilities to undermine the political status quo a form of warfare.

III

The notion of generational change is also problematic, attempting to impose clarity and order on multi-faceted processes. The evolutionary notion of 4GW is preferable to its peer competitors, such as 'the revolution in military affairs', in the battle for strategic ideas, for it is shaped by a sense of broad socio-economic and political change and not just technological. There is, however, still the same sense of sequences and historical progression. Hammes does not provide a definition of a generation. Lind has stated that generations are shorthand for a 'dialectically qualitative shift', but that does not really help much.[7] It is of course perfectly fair to state that the cumulative impact of broader changes must have an impact on the conduct of political and military affairs, but it would be surprising if these all pointed in the same direction. The view that warfare is being steadily refined to fit in with these broader changes ignores their often contradictory and paradoxical nature. The idea that there is something strikingly novel about groups that come together 'as networks to achieve short-term common goals and then go their own way' is bizarre. It is a common theme of political life, including much warfare, through the ages. How else would one describe the war-time alliance between the US, Britain and the Soviet Union?

The forms of warfare included under 4GW are not usefully understood as an evolution from previous generations of warfare. The first to third generations describe tendencies in thinking about regular battle.[8] Those who naturally tend to the activities included under 4GW do so precisely because they do not expect to win a regular battle. These are the weapons the weak might use against the strong, and in particular against military-powerful states. Those fighting a conventionally superior capability wish to avoid direct battle in order to survive over the long term. They must find ways to demoralize the enemy through constant harassment and ambush while building up political support, until a tipping point is reached and the balance of power shifts decisively. This is the approach of guerrillas, resisters, partisans, insurgents, subversives, insurrectionists, revolutionaries, secessionists and terrorists, and it has a long history. They are not a progression from forms of 'proper war', but instead constitute a parallel development. The category is a broad one, and not only includes activities far removed from proper war but also strategies that intersect with proper war, either because they complement regular forms of warfare (for example, working with partisan groups during the Second World War) or merge into such forms as the movements grow in military strength.

This misleading sense of sequence is found in Hammes' notion that 4GW is itself undergoing a progressive development. As he presents it, the approach was founded by Mao Tse-tung ('the first practitioner to write about and successfully execute a 4GW'), and then modified by the North Vietnamese who understood the need to attack the political will of the enemy in its home base, refined by the Sandinistas in Nicaragua who understood the importance of political developments driving the battlefield outcome, then the first Intifada, which concentrated on undermining the international legitimacy of the Israeli occupation, although the Palestinians somewhat lost their way during the second.

This is a very partial history. The whole history of colonialism is replete with encounters that would now come under the category of 4GW and it had many theorist-practitioners. Many are best known for counterinsurgency, but some were involved in successful insurgencies, including T.E. Lawrence (admittedly in the context of a much larger war).[9] It is a common theme in commentary on Iraq that American planners might usefully have looked back to the British attempts to pacify the country in the early 1920s. Moreover, as Hammes notes, the Chinese, and for that matter the Vietnamese, communists never planned to win without a decisive battle. The whole point about the early stages of political action and guerrilla warfare was to create the conditions for a final stage whereby the armed forces of the state, hopefully demoralized, would be defeated by a People's Army. The Vietnamese stumbled on the importance of American political will as a result of the 1968 Tet offensive which combined a disastrous military result with a probably unexpected political payoff. In addition, the two influential movements that did manage to win by using armed force to under-mine the enemy's political will rather than to defeat its army – Hezbollah in Lebanon and the Mujahideen in Afghanistan – are mentioned only in passing. Some of the most important theoretical influences (Franz Fanon, Che Guevara) are absent from this account but more importantly so are many of the seminal conflicts, such as Cuba and Algeria.

The Sandinistas in Nicaragua were a passing phenomenon and not generally considered to be strategic innovators. The theory of the foco, for example, which assumed that military force by itself could unlock, almost spontaneously, deep and natural revolutionary feelings, was based on a misreading of the Cuban revolution. It had already been applied calamitously in Bolivia by Guevara, and the Sandinistas initially made the same mistake until they accepted the need for a broad coalition. A broad coalition was in fact exactly what propelled Fidel Castro to power in Cuba, something conveniently forgotten by Castro after he decided to declare himself a Marxist–Leninist. This indicates the later role of myth-making in drawing lessons from successful guerrilla wars. In the Chinese case the coercive, intimidator aspects of force often employed by the commu-nists at a local level has been played down.

Another example of the unhelpfully broad nature of the 4GW category comes under the sub-heading of terrorism. This would include al-Qaeda's attempts to mount occasional but spectacular assaults, causing high casualties, and the IRA's much more focused campaign in Northern Ireland and the British main-land, which experimented with a range of targets, from political figures to mili-tary units to economic assets, as well as disrupting civilian life. Except at the most general level the techniques necessary to counter one campaign will be of limited value in attempts to counter the other.

Hammes argues that 4GW has an effectiveness that conventional war lacks. Thus with regard to the Arab–Israeli, Korean, Falklands and Iran–Iraq wars, 'in essence each state came out of the war with largely the same political, economic and social structure with which it entered'. Yet war had a profound effect on all the societies involved in these wars, even if the surface political changes were not always marked. The statement is not true at all with regard to Israel, changed forever by the acquisition of the West Bank territories and the Gaza strip, or Argentina, where the failure over the Falklands saw the end of the Argentine Military Junta. The point about the Korean and Iran–Iraq Wars was that they ended in stalemate, without either side being able to defeat the armed forces of the enemy. If they had succeeded then the character of the defeated states would have changed.

Nor is it the case that 'only unconventional war works against established powers'. The conventional wars were about territory: Argentina could not have taken the Falklands and Britain could not have recaptured them by unconventional means. The sort of wars that Hammes describes as 4GW were always about changing the internal status quo from inside the state rather than by external intervention. By definition they had to rely on unconventional means, at least initially. If we take Max Weber's 1919 definition of a state as 'a human community that (successfully) claims the monopoly of the legitimate use of physical force within a given territory,'[10] Then for any internal challenge to succeed that monopoly must be broken. Once it does so then the state is in trouble and will be facing a civil war. It is, therefore, not surprising to find that the forms of warfare put under this heading were developed in the face of major trends in international history, and in particular the struggles over colonization and decolonization, and the post-independence struggles for power. When the state successfully holds on to its monopoly of violence then externally-directed conventional force may be the only way of undermining it – as India did with Pakistan, leading to the formation of Bangladesh, or NATO did when it helped reduce the hold Serbia had over Bosnia and then Kosovo.

The Pentagon's notion of proper war deserves challenge. It must be hoped that recent experiences in Afghanistan and Iraq will lead to some basic changes in the conceptualization of contemporary warfare, and consequentially in doctrine, tactics and training. Unfortunately the idea that we have entered the Fourth Generation of warfare does not help in this process. It is founded on selective history and poor theory. It is ultimately futile as it attempts to capture the generality of contemporary unconventional conflict in a single category and so misses its diversity and complex interaction with more conventional forms of warfare. This problem is aggravated by the apparent reluctance to distinguish between conflicts which involve organized and politically purposive violence, that is war, and those that do not.

Notes

1 The belief that military policy should shape foreign policy existed prior to Vietnam. Although Korea was not as humiliating for the armed forces as Vietnam, and was fought on a largely conventional basis, it was frustrating, and reinforced military distrust of politically-imposed restraints. This led to the view that if wars were to be fought they must be fought on military terms, although the armed forces disagreed among themselves on what these terms might be. This was the position as the Kennedy administration debated its response to the communist challenge in Southeast

Asia in the early 1960s. This was reflected in the resistance to attempts to encourage a politically-sensitive ('hearts and minds') counter-insurgency campaign. I deal with this period in *Kennedy's Wars: Berlin, Cuba, Laos and Vietnam* (New York: OUP, 2000).

2 Harry G. Summers Jr, *On Strategy: A Critical Analysis of the Vietnam War* (Novato, CA, Presidio Press, 1982).

3 Weinberger's first test was that the US 'should not commit forces to combat overseas unless the particular engagement or occasion is deemed vital to our national interest or that of our allies'. The other tests referred to the need, once a commitment had been made to do so wholeheartedly and with the clear intention of winning, with clearly defined political and military objectives, continually reassessing the relationship between our objectives and the forces we have committed, with the support of the American people and their elected representatives in Congress, and as a last resort. Caspar W. Weinberger, *Fighting for Peace: Seven Critical Years in the Pentagon* (New York: Warner Books, 1990), pp. 453–4.

4 Colin Powell, *My American Journey*, (New York: 1995), p. 576.

5 William S. Lind, Colonel Keith Nightengale, Captain John F. Schmitt, Colonel Joseph W. Sutton and Lieutenant Colonel Gary I. Wilson, 'The Changing Face of War: Into the Fourth Generation', *Marine Corps Gazette*, October 1989, pp. 22–6.

6 William Lind, 'Understanding Fourth Generation War', *Military Review*, September–October 2004, 12–16. This reports the findings of a study group which he convened at his house. Lind's commentaries can be found at /www.lewrockwell.com/lind/lind-arch.html. On Lind's political stance see Bill Berkowitz, 'A Mighty Lind', 22 September 2003. www.workingforchange.com/article.cfm?ItemID=15659. After the Oklahoma bombing the *Washington Post* ('Militant Musings: From Nightmare 1995 to My Utopian 2050', 30 April 1995) reprinted an extract from a short story by Lind, written some time earlier. This involved a scenario which began in 2001 with a currency collapse ('Financial Weimar had followed cultural Weimar'), followed by an AIDS epidemic masked by officials so terrified of the 'gay lobby', that they insisted 'that "homophobia" was the real problem'. By 2005, when people 'demanded the quarantine of anyone diagnosed as HIV positive', the government instead 'classified the infected as "disabled", which made any preventive measures illegal discrimination'.

7 Lind, 'Understanding Fourth Generation War', p. 16.

8 Even here we might note that the concept barely does justice to the forms which regular battle can take, not only from attrition trench warfare to blitzkrieg, but from desert to jungle warfare, from urban combat to grand tank battles.

9 T.E. Lawrence, *Seven Pillars of Wisdom* (Ware: Wordsworth Editions, 1997). See also C.E. Caldwell, *Small Wars: Their Principles and Practice* (Lincoln and London: University of Nebraska Press, 1996).

10 Max Weber, *Politics as a Vocation*, (Kichener, ON: Fortress Press, 1972 [1919]).

11 Fourth Generation

A 'new' form of 'warfare'?

Rod Thornton

With *The Sling and the Stone* Colonel Hammes has written a work that has much to commend it. He displays an understanding of a current threat to Western societies and military organizations. He puts forward a conceptual framework for debate that is particularly pertinent to the US military. This being said, I have a concern. It is not whether the concept of Fourth Generation Warfare (4GW) per se is sound, rather, it is with the policy implications of the approach Hammes takes. Hammes is not able to set forth his policy proposals in his article as he does in his book, for the limitations of an article make this impossible. Hence my approach here may seem unfair, both to him and to readers of this symposium. Nonetheless, I think the point needs to be made that, although in looking at *insurgencies* in particular, he is sending the right messages, he is using a format that is not the most enlightening in terms of increasing the US military's counterinsurgency (COIN) capabilities.

In this regard, there are two particular points of contention that bear examination. The first refers to Hammes' idea that 4GW insurgencies are 'new' and have been slowly evolving since Mao Tse-tung in the 1920s. The issue here is that by saying there is a 'new' problem abroad, then the immediate reflex is to find 'new' ways of dealing with it. However, when you look closely, 4GW is just another term to describe what many a soldier has been dealing with for many a year – insurgencies. There is thus a wealth of experience going back several centuries and gathered from many quarters as to how to deal with insurgencies and thus *how to deal with 4GW*. Hammes' use of the term '4GW,' in his worthy desire to get US military thinkers focused on the current issues, risks excluding a huge corpus of valuable knowledge. The second issue I have relates to Hammes' use of the word 'warfare' in 4GW. Again, misleading nomenclature can skew analysis of the specific means to deal with insurgencies.

Learning from history

The basis of Hammes' argument is that 4GW, 'unlike previous generations ... does not attempt to win by defeating the enemy's military forces.' Rather, it aims to win through changing the minds of political decision makers.[1] There is a large element here, however, of *'twas ever thus*. Throughout history, most insurgencies have had two main characteristics: knee-jerk reflex actions against a foreign invader; and more thoughtful tactics bent on trying to change the minds of enemy political decision makers, in essence, through engaging that enemy's fielded military forces. It was done at least as far back as Roman times and it is being done today in Iraq and elsewhere.

For the insurgency we see today in Iraq that Hammes sees as 'clearly a 4GW struggle' is that of occupied against occupier.[2] It is this type of insurgency that we need to keep in mind as pertinent learning experiences and not really those directed against domestic governments (as in Mao's China or Ortega's Nicaragua). The insurgency directed against the occupier is the second variant in Robert Taber's typology of insurgencies.[3] The tendency in this variant is for the insurgents, alongside 'normal' reflex attacks, to send a message to the occupier that, while they may be weak, they will be around for a considerable period causing casualties and draining coffers. The conflict is then questioned in the occupier's domestic realm as the costs, seemingly without benefit, rise over time. For the insurgent it is all about enduring for long enough. It is as Henry Kissinger once observed: the conventional army loses by not winning, but the guerrilla wins by not losing.[4]

The insurgents in Iraq today are second-order insurgents. This must be recognized. As true second-order insurgents they blindly attack the occupier, but, in a more nuanced understanding of their craft, they also merely seek to show that they are not losing. And the US military in Iraq and elsewhere, à la Kissinger, appears to be losing by not winning. US forces are being 'defeated' on the ground and politicians have to react to a military that is not winning. The insurgents know this. Yes, it can be said that the insurgents are directing their campaign at political decision makers, but much of the pressure is applied on them via attacks on the *in situ* occupation forces. Harry Summers' well-worn anecdote bears repeating. He noted in his description of a post-Vietnam War conversation between a US colonel and a North Vietnamese officer that defeat is a debated concept. The US colonel he quotes as saying, 'You know you never defeated us on the battlefield.' The North Vietnamese colonel pondered this remark a moment, then replied, 'That may be so, but it is also irrelevant.'[5]

Examples of such second-variant insurgencies can be found far back in history and are not just products of the last 70 years. The earliest might be the campaign the Romans faced in what is now north Germany. Here, from AD 9 onwards, 'The Romans found themselves facing a strategic task of a completely peculiar type, such as we have never before been confronted with in … the history of warfare.' With its forces worn down by attacks from war-like tribes fighting in classic guerrilla style, Rome ordered a withdrawal.[6] This type of insurgency can also be recognized in the case of the original *guerrillas* (called *insurgé* by French officers of the time) in Spain trying to evict Napoleon's forces during the Peninsular Wars. These *guerrillas* undertook what Jan Read called 'a new form of warfare.' Between 1808 and 1813 they tied down many thousands of French troops and reportedly killed as many as 180,000.[7] The French withdrew. The likes of Bolivar and Martin, acting a few years later, used much the same tactics to drive Spain out of South America.[8] The influence of such insurgencies in 'modern' warfare caused even Clausewitz himself to comment on their effectiveness.[9]

Once the colonial period began in earnest, the number of insurgencies increased. Both Britain and France fought colonial campaigns against clever opponents who knew that they could not inflict battlefield defeat on the metropole's forces. They took the same view as their predecessors: inflict enough pain on the occupiers' forces and this will influence decisions in the domestic realm as to withdrawal.

Such insurgencies are basically the same as those we see today. Indeed, most of the characteristics of 4GW which Hammes sees as portending a 'novel' phenomenon are actually redolent of many past second-order insurgencies. And because there are such similarities then much can be *learnt* from insurgencies conducted well before Mao's time, as well as those after his campaign. We can derive lessons as to COIN tactics both from 2,000 years ago and from last year. A quick *tour d'horizon* of past campaigns will illustrate this.

Hammes sees, for instance, the loose alliances of indigenous groups formed against Americans in Iraq as indicative of 4GW.[10] But whenever a great power has tried to extend its influence abroad there has been generated what Eliot Cohen refers to as a 'swirl of hostility to the colossus.'[11] Whenever large powers expand they inevitably invite an opprobrium that acts as a unifying factor. Indigenous – and disparate – people have always united in loose affiliations to defend their own spaces against foreign intervention: the German tribes against the Romans, for instance. In more modern history examples include the experiences of the British East India Company in India in the late 1700s and the French as they moved into Algeria in the 1830s.[12] They were both opposed by forces composed of clans, tribes, and small groups who had banded together to repel the invader. Such activities were repeated many times in the spread of both European empires and of others; the Japanese for instance, who managed to draw together Nationalist and Communist elements in China in the 1930s. As a colossus expanding its influence then the US must expect to attract a unifying ire; it is not unique.

Hammes sees that attacks against UN and aid agencies workers in Iraq and against the oil industry as being something new. However, in their efforts to make their lands ungovernable it has always been an insurgent tactic to kill those who help run the occupation – government officials and key experts, for instance. And they have always targeted important industries that cause economic pain for the metropolitan power (rubber in Malaya and Indo-China, oil in Dutch East Indies, etc.). In this regard, it is natural to see once again such attacks happening in Iraq and it is important for the US to understand that COIN tactics begin, not with offensives against insurgents, but with the defending of vital assets.

The use of 'non-violent' actors, says Hammes, 'will be a critical part of tactical actions in 4GW.'[13] Ever since colonial powers developed liberal domestic governments then peaceful protest has become a cutting-edge weapon for those who wanted occupations to end. Most of the efforts to rid India of British rule from 1900 onwards were designed to put international pressure on the imperial power through peaceful, not violent, protest. One line taken was to get the British to open fire on crowds and thus to exacerbate the situation. Another was that taken by Gandhi. He proposed a non-violent approach that proved a most effective policy and which garnered tremendous support around the world.[14] The strategy behind the first Intifada as described by Hammes was merely a variation of that of Gandhi. Non-violent protests have always been part and parcel of resistance to occupation campaigns conducted against liberal states.

Where violence is used, Hammes sees a novelty in the fact that Fourth Generation warriors can now take their struggles into the homelands of those that are seen to oppress them – the terrorist attacks of September 11, 2001, for example. Again, though, the tactic is nothing especially new. As far back as the 1880s, for instance, the IRA (a truly 'networked' organization even then) unleashed on London a five-year-long bombing campaign that left the city under the 'daily ... threat ... of explosions' and which targeted cultural icons such as the Houses of Parliament, London Bridge, and the Tower of London. Indeed, it could be said that the Irish nationalist Fenian campaign of the 1880s and beyond fits snugly into Hammes' characteristics of a 4GW struggle:[15] attacking the political will of the British domestically; using 'submarines' against ships in American harbors to undermine British commerce; using transnational, national, and sub-national organizations to convey messages to target audiences; and 'using materials in the society under attack' by purchasing gunpowder and dynamite legally.[16] Indeed, the invention of dynamite was a technological improvement that changed the face of 'warfare' in that it offered then what the Fourth Generation warrior appears to have the capability to do today: i.e. the ability to collapse the enemy from within.[17] As the *New York Tribune* acknowledged in 1884, the advent of dynamite in the hands of Irish-Americans in Britain meant that 'the power of making war was no longer confined to governments.'[18]

Hammes talks of the 4GW environment as being one where the media now shape policy, forcing the US, for instance, to send troops to Somalia in 1992. But the media have always had the power to create such pressures. In 1854 the British media pushed the government into sending troops to the Crimea. It then almost drove the government to send troops to Bulgaria in 1876 to prevent Ottoman atrocities against Christians.[19] The force of the liberal press in the US had much to do with the invasion of Cuba and the Philippines in 1898.[20] The Boers made good use, again, of the British liberal press to limit British activities in the insurgency phase of the Boer War (1899–1902). Indeed, a long time before Ho Chi Minh, the Boers played on the domestic resolve in Britain to continue with this particular war.[21] The Boers also looked, as did many other oppressed nations, to the media to get their plight across to the world community which then put pressure on the British. And there was a world community to appeal to a long time before the League of Nations and the UN came into being. Such appeals are not unique to the Fourth Generation warrior. 'Information', used in whatever form and on whatever forum, has been influencing governments for a very long time. Yes, we are in an 'information age', but its advent has not unduly changed the nature of insurgencies. We tend to think in today's world that information flies around so quickly that everything becomes transformed. Information, though, still flew around many decades ago (the Crimea, the Boer War, etc.), just more slowly. The speed of passage, however, did not alter its ultimate effect.

Hammes creates the sense that powerful militaries such as that of the US have recently forced the Fourth Generation warrior into different tactics. He points out that opponents of the US 'understand that if you provide American forces with clear targets, no matter how well fortified, those targets will be destroyed.'[22] Again, such an understanding has been clear to many an insurgent body down the ages. The opponents of the French in Algeria from the 1830s onwards, for instance, soon realized that they should not present themselves en masse as targets to the large columns and artillery of their adversaries.[23] Once these forces, however, had adopted the right tactics, then the French realized that their own tactics, based on mass, availed them little when dealing with an elusive, will-o'-the-wisp enemy. Breaking down into smaller and more flexible groups was the key to French success in the long run. In essence, the aim was to become more like the enemy.[24] Many a COIN force down the years has copied the French. Technology, too, can mean little when faced with insurgent foes and always has done. Hammes is not saying something novel in his comments that, 'With Iraq and Afghanistan, we have seen that 4GW can hold its own even against the most technologically advanced and militarily powerful nation on earth.'[25] This sentence could have equally applied to Great Britain in 1920. In that year, this hyperpower, with the largest air force in the world at the time, was being battered by insurgents in Iraq while, at the same time, being given a bloody nose by tribesmen in Afghanistan.[26] *Plus ça change, plus c'est la même chose.*

Here we have situations, and it applies throughout the history of COIN operations, where both the French and British realized that the key to success was to become more like their adversaries in terms of flexibility and in their use of intelligence. And they were doing this and learning lessons that are useful today a long time before Mao. The point in all this history is that what Hammes sees as 4GW – and thus something which has only been evolving since Mao – is not 'new.' It therefore does not need some 'magic' new formula to deal with it. It has been dealt with in the past by many a former world colossus. Yes, there have been changes that have made insurgencies 'evolve' as Hammes says, but these do not alter the basic dynamics of second-order insurgencies or the way they should be countered. The insurgencies of today still seem to show the same main characteristics of previous iterations. Much of the insurgents' actions still appear to be based on knee-jerk, policy-blind reflexes to being occupied by a foreign power and, while there may be more actual thought put into pressuring policy makers today, it is not of a completely new order. And if insurgencies still 'look' the same then answers as to how to deal with them can still be gleaned from history. If military students can study ancient battles and wars and can read Sun Tzu and Clausewitz, why should they also not look at 'old' insurgencies and learn from them?

Insurgencies are not 'wars'

The way, however, of dealing with insurgencies is not the way of dealing with war. Hammes is right to point out that changes are needed in the US military's approach to COIN operations in Iraq and elsewhere. He himself, however, is in danger of making this more difficult by including insurgencies under the rubric of 'warfare' – as in Fourth Generation 'Warfare.' This terminology, given the fact that the idea of 4GW may become common parlance in the US military,[27] (see spelling in footnote) may not be his fault; but the fact is that it does dilute his message.

Many COIN operations in the past have made the mistake of treating insurgencies as if they were wars. Insurgencies and war are, in many ways, mutually exclusive. They require different vernaculars, psychologies, and approaches. At heart, insurgencies need to be *managed away* while wars need to be won. Insurgencies are, above all, as the COIN expert, Frank Kitson, once noted, 'a struggle for men's minds,' rather than a physical battle between opposing forces.[28] Pitfalls will inevitably result if an insurgency, which requires patience, endurance, and the application of extremely focused violence to expunge, is approached in the same way as a war, where winning requires mass, firepower, and panache.

Whenever COIN forces have attempted to 'win' second-order insurgencies the effect has often been the opposite of that intended. The French tried to win at Dien Bien Phu (1954) and in the 'Battle of Algiers' (1956[29]), and with their ideas of *guerre révolutionnaire*.[30] They lost. The British tried to win in Northern Ireland in the early years of the 'Troubles.' The means employed – harsh military tactics and internment without trial – backfired, however, and made the problem worse.[31] The US tried to win in Vietnam with big unit actions. The results were predictable. Striving for the quick fix is appropriate in 'war'; it is not, though, appropriate when tackling insurgencies. Hammes, and the US military in general, should be mindful of this nuance.

The full history of COIN campaigns against second-order insurgencies has shown what works and what does not. What appears to have worked over the course of COIN operations is a *patient* undermining of the insurgent cause. This would be done principally by investment in huge social improvements to make the lot of 'the sea' – the indigenous population – better. At one end of the temporal spectrum, the Roman tactic against its opposition was to show that the power of Rome could bring benefits in the mundane form of better roads, drains, irrigation systems, etc. This would be backed by a light military touch, but one which was pervasive. At the other end of the temporal spectrum, the British undercut the insurgency of the IRA by spending billions on social infrastructure that improved the lot of the Catholic population. The British also retained a fairly massive but restrained military presence. In many successful COIN campaigns in between these two the same tactics have been seen. The 'struggle for men's minds' was won, but won over many years. Troops would be killed, yes, and political pressure applied on domestic governments, but the necessary sense of patience to see the conflict through would undermine the idea of Kissinger's that a supposed absence of 'winning' means losing. His aphorism only applies when there is a lack of will to do what the insurgents themselves seek to do: *endure*. Thus, it really matters not what tactics any insurgents use: be they those of sophisticated Fourth Generation warriors or the ill-considered reflex actions of some Germanic tribe. What decides second-order insurgencies ultimately is how far the occupier is prepared to go to see that their own will prevails. It is always in their hands. They have the power, however defined. The key issue is, are they prepared to use it?

The problem for the US military now is that they have the power to kill lots of insurgents but little power to win over 'men's minds.' Hammes flags up some of the changes that this military needs to make but he can never get his message across accurately by packaging it under the label of 'warfare.' Insurgencies are managed to death, they are not 'won.'

Overall, Hammes is right to point out that there have been profound changes brought about by globalization and in the way societies are structured. This does alter the ways in which today's insurgents operate. Hammes does the US military a profound service by extolling the virtues of the new structures and mindsets that are needed to adjust to these 'new' realities. But the realities in question are not *that* new. Yes, there has been an 'evolving' of insurgencies recently but there is not some new beast to contend with. Only the focus of the insurgents has shifted slightly, not their general aims and *modus operandi*. This being so, there is a whole history to learn from vis-à-vis past successful and not so successful COIN operations. There are tried and trusted ways of dealing with the same types of situations we see today. Look in the right places and the valuable learning experiences as to how to deal with second-order insurgents are there. And learning experiences will be needed if the US is to continue, as it appears it might, to take offensive action against those states it deems to be in the 'axis of evil.' The US lashed out after 9/11; it may well do so again. Look past Mao, look at the 'right' types of insurgency that the US is likely to be faced with in the current era, and do not look at them through the prism of 'warfare.' Hammes in his work tells us where the US military should be going, and he is very right to do so; but the directions could be clearer.

Notes

1 Thomas Hammes, *The Sling and the Stone* (St Paul, MN: Zenith, 2004) p. 208.
2 Ibid, p. 188. With 130,000 troops in Iraq needed to keep control then 'occupation' does not seem too strong a term.
3 In the first type, the insurgency is against a domestic, discredited government (e.g. Cuba, 1959). The third type is where both insurgent and counter-insurgent forces clash in conventional battles (e.g. China in the 1930s and 1940s). Robert Taber, *The War of the Flea* (London: Paladin, 1970) pp. 44–58.
4 Tony Karon, 'Al Qaeda Today: Not Winning, But Not Losing Either,' *Time Magazine*, www.time.com/time/world/article accessed March 16, 2005.
5 Harry Glenn Summers, *On Strategy: The Vietnam War in Context* (Carlisle Barracks, PA: Army War College, Strategic Studies Institute, 1981) p. 1.
6 Hans Delbruck, *The Barbarian Invasions* (Lincoln, NB: University of Nebraska Press, 1980) p. 99.

7 Jan Read, *War in the Peninsular* (London: Faber and Faber, 1977) pp. 169–81.

8 See Margaret Woodward, 'The Spanish Army and the Loss of America, 1810–1824,' in Christian Archer (ed.), *The Wars of Independence in Latin America* (Wilmington, DE: Jaguar Books 2000).

9 Carl von Clausewitz, *On War* (Princeton, NJ: Princeton University Press 1976) pp. 482–3.

10 Hammes' chapter, 'War evolves into the fourth generation,' pp. 21–44 in this volume.

11 Eliot Cohen, 'History and the Hyperpower,' *Foreign Affairs*, 83/4, (Jul/Aug 2004) pp. 49–63.

12 Lawrence James, *The Rise and Fall of the British Empire* (London: Little, Brown and Co., 1994); and Abder-Rahmane Derradji, *The Algerian Guerrilla Campaign: Strategy and Tactics* (New York: Edwin Mellen Press, 1997) chap. 2.

13 Hammes (note 10) p. 48.

14 Judith Brown, *Prisoner of Hope: Gandhi* (New Haven, CN: Yale University Press, 1989).

15 Hammes, note 10.

16 K.R.M. Short, *The Dynamite Wars: Irish-American Bombers in Victorian Britain* (Dublin: Gill and Macmillan, 1979) p. 2.

17 See especially, William S. Lind, Colonel Keith Nightengale, Captain John F. Schmitt, Colonel Joseph W. Sutton, and Lieutenant Colonel Gary I. Wilson, 'The Changing Face of War: Into the Fourth Generation,' *Marine Corps Gazette* (Oct 1989) pp. 22–6.

18 Editorial in *New York Tribune*, April 18, 1884, quoted in ibid, p. 241.

19 William Miller, *The Ottoman Empire and Its Successors, 1801–1927* (London: Frank Cass, 1966).

20 Joseph Smith, *The Spanish American War* (New York: Longman, 1994).

21 Thomas Pakenham, *The Boer War* (London: Weidenfeld and Nicolson, 1979)

22 Hammes (note 10) p. 47.

23 Indeed, Mao seems to have been copying to some degree the approach of the leader of the insurgency against the French in 1840s' Algeria, Abdel Kader. He declared to the French that 'when your army moves forward we draw back, but it will be forced to withdraw and we will come back. We will fight when the time is suitable.' Derradji (note 12) p. 53.

24 Derradji (note 12).

25 Hammes (note 1) p. 208.

26 See Brian Robson, *Crisis on the Frontier: The Third Afghan War and the Campaign in Waziristan, 1919–20* (London: Spellmount, 2004).

27 Elaine M. Grossman, 'New Briefing Applies 4th Generation Warfare Ideas to Iraq Conflict,' *Inside the Pentagon*, December 23, 2004.

28 Frank Kitson, *Bunch of Five* (London: Faber and Faber, 1977) p. 282.

29 The attempt to root out terrorists in the Casbah district was a tactical success. It became a strategic failure, though, resulting in eventual French withdrawal from Algeria. The tough methods used were seen as excessive and meant lost public support for the French Army and thus loss of support for its mission in Algeria. See Bruce Hoffman, 'Nasty Business,' *Atlantic Monthly* (Jan 2002) www.theatlantic.com/doc/200201/hoffman accessed March 15, 2005.

30 *Guerre révolutionnaire* was a 1950s idea, conceived by David Trinquier and others, which held that the threat of communist subversion to French colonies was so great that it required an all-out military response that copied the terror tactics of the insurgents. David Trinquier, *Modern Warfare: A French View of Counter-Insurgency* (London: Pall Mall Press 1964).

31 Peter Taylor, *Brits: The War Against the IRA* (London: Bloomsbury, 2001).

12 The mythology of fourth-generation warfare

A response to Hammes[1]

David S. Sorenson

One of the most elemental pieces in political science education is learning to categorize. The subject of study fits into paradigms, waves, civilizations, generations, or something that gives certain distinctness to them. There are times when such categorization is essential for comparisons (across party or religious identities, for example), but when the categories weaken from the "mutually exclusive and exhaustive" criteria, they often are as likely to cloud the question under study as to elucidate it.

Such is the case with types of warfare. Thomas X. Hammes follows the efforts by Lind and others in breaking down war into four "generations," (and a potential fifth generation) which differ from each other because of developments in firepower, tactics, logistics, and certain societal factors like the growing ability to extract wealth from populations.[2] While Hammes acknowledges, "Like all models, it is not a perfect representation of reality,"[3] he repeats a number of weak assumptions in the original study. "Generational warfare" may have taken place roughly as the "generation" theorists argue in Europe, but because the generationists focus almost exclusively on European wars, they miss the many other wars in the world that hardly fit their typology. Less-developed countries fought wars with third generation weapons but first or second generation taxation systems (the Chaco War, or the 1948 Middle East War, for example). The Hutus and the Tutsis in Rwanda fought with second and third generation weapons in wars of mass attrition, while the Iranians and the Iraqis took third generation weapons into warfare that closely resembled that of Europe's World War I. Most of the twentieth-century Middle East wars had elements of both second and third generation warfare,[4] so which were they?

Fourth-generation warfare, for Hammes, began with Mao Tse-tung and his emphasis on the necessity to meld politics with strict military objectives to give the weaker side an advantage. Mao may have been an early theorist for the "people's war," linking traditional guerilla operations with his penchant for peasant-based revolution. However, beyond the theory, the differences between "People's War" and guerilla war, and, for that matter, fourth-generation warfare, are less clear, as is the very claim that Mao "invented" fourth-generation warfare. There have been numerous efforts at "people's war" throughout history, to include the thousand-year struggle by the Vietnamese against Chinese control

(111 BCE–939 CE), the guerilla war in Spain against Napoleon's forces, and numerous other small wars where popular support was a factor in the outcome.[5] Many of these were "people's wars," if that meant that a combination of skillful recruiting and ruthlessness by the dominant side brought popular participation to the war. That happened, for example, in Edward II's campaigns in Scotland in the twelfth and thirteenth centuries, the Philippine Insurrection of 1899–1902,[6] the "Arab Revolt" of 1916–17, and both the Algerian National Liberation Front (FLN) and Viet Minh wars against French occupation.

The question also remains as to whether Mao's principles of people's war were actually decisive or even significant when applied by the Chinese Communists in their campaign against the Kuomintang (KMT) or by the Vietnamese Communists in their wars against the French and the Americans. In the Chinese civil war, the Communists fought the primary warfare that broke the KMT with large-unit conventional military operations between massed armies (like the pivotal battles of Chinchou in October 1948, and the Huai-Hai Rivers campaign of late 1948–9), which the Communist armies won with military skill rather than peasant support.[7] Moreover, the KMT was weakened by its own political mistakes (economic mismanagement, and charges of collaboration with the Japanese).[8] The People's Republic of China (PRC) continued to advance the concept of people's war throughout the 1960s, but that was partly as a tactic in their contest for influence with the Soviet Union over revolutionary movements.[9] The Vietnamese Communists also adopted the logo of "people's war," and the Viet Cong applied it as a tactic in the south,[10] but the North Vietnamese stuck largely to conventional set-piece battles. They did avoid contact with clearly superior forces, instead biding their time until American political support finally waned. Then they swept out of the central highlands with conventional forces (including armor), and decimated the South Vietnamese forces. In the end, "people's war" was rarely fought or even supported by "people," but rather by soldiers. That America lost its public will might be attributed to the political side of "people's war," but more careful analysis suggests that Americans generally lose support for long, indecisive wars, as Mueller notes.[11] The US military is also more likely to lose or tie in wars that were, frankly, marred on the American side with policy squabbles between services[12] and civilian oversight of military operations, and air operations in particular.[13]

Hammes argues that the Sandinista victory in Nicaragua was a function of the successful adaptation of "fourth-generation warfare," which may be partially correct. It neglects, though, the utter incompetence of the Somoza forces and the corruption of the ruling regime that led to what was much more than a "people's war" but rather a popular explosion that Somoza could no longer contain.[14] Hammes also confuses the motives for the first Palestinian "Intifada" with "fourth-generation warfare," not realizing that the uprising (which really began in December 1987) was as much a revolt against the absent (then in Tunisia) Palestinian leadership as it was against the Israelis. Furthermore, it failed long before the beginning of the "al Aqsa Intifada" when a series of four suicide bombings in Israel in early 1996 led to Binyamin Netanyahu's Likud Party winning the subsequent election. Both "Intifadas" were less about clear political goals but instead were protracted campaigns of rage.[15] That may also be at least part of the motivation behind the insurgency in post-Saddam Iraq. The insurgents appear to be lashing out against a multitude of targets (US and coalition forces, Sh'ia citizens, Iraqis suspected of "collaboration," and in some cases just random targets like an elementary school in western Baghdad in March 2005). Their ranks include former Ba'athists, violent Islamists, and disaffected non-Iraqi Arabs, who hardly speak with one voice and thus there is hardly a unified strategy or anything even approximating one. This hardly qualifies as "fourth-generation war."

In sum, despite efforts to divide warfare into generations, "The nature of war in the 21st century is the same as it was in the 20th century, the 19th, and indeed, in the 5th century BC," as Colin Gray notes.[16] While Hammes outlines his "Characteristics of Fourth Generation Warfare" (p. 42), it must be asked how they differ from the objectives of warfare in general, with the notable exception of duration. *Forms* of warfare may wax and wane, as in the case of guerilla tactics, a form of war clearly preferred by poor combatants against wealthier opponents.

Having said all this, Hammes makes an important point in noting that the current Department of Defense (DoD) efforts at transformation appear misdirected. It seems to be focused largely on changing the military structure from the continuing reliance on Cold War-era systems and tactics to something lighter, more mobile, and presumably more affordable, given the ballooning size of the federal deficit.[17] The focus, in short, is inward over outward, more emphasis on the nature of current US systems instead of the types of conflict where they may be used. However, even here the efforts of the Office of Secretary of Defense to change this structure are half-hearted at best: the cancellation of the Army's "Crusader" artillery system, the possible reduction in Air Force F/A-22 attack aircraft, and the retirement of a single large carrier. The US has not really made significant adjustments for the "lessons learned" in operations like Operation Enduring Freedom in Afghanistan or Operation Iraqi Freedom. For Hammes, this means that the US needs to respond better to the tactics used by the insurgents in these two campaigns, including suicide bombs, beheadings, and efforts to portray the US as a crusading neo-imperialist state leading a Christian-inspired charge against the Muslim world.

It is certainly true that the US has failed dismally to counter these tactics and their resulting messages, but that is the smaller part of the problem. The larger part of the predicament is that the US plunged into both Afghanistan and Iraq (and Somalia, for different reasons) with a complete misunderstanding of the desired end-state, and, in the Iraqi case, with misinformation and the appearance of dishonesty that rendered American strategy vulnerable to the kinds of tactics used by the insurgents. Charges of US indifference toward civilian casualties, the alleged lust for Iraqi oil, the quixotic support for Iraqi leaders like Ahmed Chalabi, and the appalling situation of Abu Ghraib prison only enhanced the insurgents' campaign.[18]

So what are the real lessons for US military force planners? The first is that insurgency war planners plan long wars to exhaust their more powerful adversaries. Americans traditionally do not support long wars, and their support for them drops even more when they come to devalue the strategic objectives. Even in the Pacific theater during World War II, US military leadership felt compelled to accelerate air attacks against Japan to forestall a land invasion of Japan and the US public reaction to its expected high American casualties.[19] More to the point were the conflicts in Vietnam and Iraq that offer lessons for future strategic considerations. First, there must be a clear end-state that accommodates the possibility of insurgency warfare and the corresponding question about whether the US can both counter it and absorb its costs. Those costs are, it must be noted, always *relative*. The lower the perceived political value of the conflict, the higher the price of casualties. The US suffered a relatively low (by historical standards) casualty rate in Vietnam, and the Nixon administration lowered it even more by "Vietnamization," reducing the American loss rate while increasing the Vietnamese casualties. The casualty rate in both the Iraqi and Afghanistan campaigns is considerably lower, and even though the US death toll climbed to over 1,000 before the November presidential elections, it did not prevent George W. Bush from winning an even larger percentage of votes than he did in the 2000 contest. Most significantly, though, the insurgent tactics that Hammes labels "fourth generation warfare" have been unsuccessful in deterring the US from completing its Iraq and Afghanistan missions even though the former has not received robust public support after the first few months of combat.

The lessons of modern warfare for the US are that it should continue to plan for war *in all of its forms*. It also should avoid military engagements with little or no strategic value (like Lebanon in the 1980s and Somalia in the 1990s) because low value leads to low public and political support, and thus, vulnerability to even small numbers of casualties. Should political considerations push the US into such a conflict, then an air-only campaign like that waged against Milosevic is preferable since it is less vulnerable to insurgencies. Moreover there are still potential adversaries with large conventional forces (Iran and North Korea, for example) and smaller potential adversaries like the next Milosevich who will fight largely with conventional tactics with little emphasis on the kinds of guerilla tactics that Hammes cautions about. If the PRC and Taiwan square off in armed conflict, each side will likely use a full array of tactics and techniques, from strategic bombardment to propaganda instruments. Should the US become involved, it, too, will have to bring a full mix of force and political instruments to bear. Such wars require preparation across the full spectrum of capability, to include modern air and ground power for quick results against traditionally massed forces and infrastructure. They also must include preparation for post-conflict redevelopment, and clear rules on such things as Prisoner of War (POW) treatment, urban warfare in civilian proximity, and religious sensitivities.

However, the most basic lesson for American strategists to understand is the clear relationship between war and its strategic necessity. Thus the US will have to be much more careful in the future not to engage in situations like Vietnam or Iraq where politically-driven objectives overrode sound strategic choice, and thus making the US susceptible to insurgency warfare. Insurgency warfare is a thousand-year-old tactic used by the weak against the strong power, feeding often on their incompetence. The best way to prepare for insurgency is to avoid the mistakes upon which it feeds.

Notes

1 The views expressed here are those of the author, and do not necessarily reflect the positions of the US Air Force or any other government agency. Jeffrey Record and Judith Gentleman provided helpful comments.
2 Thomas X. Hammes, "War Evolves into the Fourth Generation," pp. 3–10.
3 Ibid., p. 4.
4 Kenneth M. Pollack, *Arabs at War: Military Effectiveness, 1948–1991* (Lincoln, NE and London: University of Nebraska Press, 2002).
5 Mao Tse-tung discusses theories of warfare in Mao Tse-tung, *On Protracted War* (Beijing: Foreign Language Press, 1967) (where the chapter "War and Politics" indicates that Mao is perhaps closer to Clausewitz than Marx or Lenin), and in "Problems of Strategy in Guerilla War Against Japan," "The Strategic Defensive and the Strategic Offensive in Guerilla War," and "The Role of the Chinese Communist Party in the National War," in *The Selected Works of Mao Tse-Tung*, Vol. II (Beijing: Foreign Languages Press, 1967), pp. 75–106; 195–212. See also Mao Tse-tung, *On Guerilla Warfare*, translated by Samuel B. Griffith (New York: Praeger Publishers, 1961); and Dick Wilson, *Mao Tse-Tung in the Scales of History* (Cambridge: Cambridge University Press, 1977), ch. 4.
6 The Philippine Insurrection had many elements that would later replay in Vietnam, including a charismatic leader, guerilla tactics, domestic opposition in the US, and popular support derived partly from American tactics that induced high civilian casualties. See Stuart Miller Creighton, *Benevolent Assimilation: The American Conquest of the Philippines, 1899–1902* (New Haven, CN and London: Yale University Press, 1982).
7 The best discussion of these campaigns is in William W. Whitson, *The Chinese High Command: A History of Communist Military Politics, 1927–71* (New York: Praeger Publishers, 1973). The CCP military leaders learned bitter lessons after the first application of "people's war" resulted in the disastrous failures of the "Autumn Harvest Uprisings" in central China in 1927. See Benjamin I. Schwartz, *Chinese Communism and the Rise of Mao* (Cambridge, MA: Harvard University Press, 1979).
8 Suzanne Pepper, *Civil War in China: The Political Struggle, 1945–1949* (Berkeley and Los Angeles, CA: University of California Press, 1978).
9 Chalmers Johnson, *Autopsy on People's War* (Berkeley and Los Angeles, CA: University of California Press, 1973), esp. chs 2 and 5.
10 The success of their tactics varied with conditions, but often they were aided by South Vietnamese officials and American troops who frequently mishandled or misunderstood the situations, creating antipathy for the anti-communist side, if not always sympathy and support for the Viet Cong. For a good example see Jeffrey Race, *War Comes to Long An* (Berkeley and Los Angeles, CA: University of California Press, 1972).
11 John E. Mueller, *Wars, Presidents, and Public Opinion* (New York: John Wiley & Sons, 1973).
12 For examples see Robert L. Gallucci, *Neither Peace nor Honor: The Politics of*

American Military Policy in Vietnam (Baltimore, MA: The Johns Hopkins University Press, 1975); Jeffrey Record, *The Wrong War: Why We Lost in Vietnam* (Annapolis, MD: The Naval Institute Press, 1998).

13 Benjamin S. Lambeth, *The Transformation of American Air Power* (Ithaca, NY and London: Cornell University Press, 2000), ch. 2

14 See John A. Booth, *The End and the Beginning. The Nicaraguan Revolution* (Boulder, CO: Westview Press, 1985), esp. chs 7 and 8.

15 One of Mao's basic principles of "people's war" was unity of purpose under the banner of the Communist Party (or at least some revolutionary party). But Palestinian loyalty was divided between the PLO, Hamas, and several Islamist organizations, and often did not extend beyond the neighborhood organization. Moreover most Palestinians knew about the alleged corruption of the PLO (and later PA), which weakened their support for it. See Ilan Pappe, *A History of Modern Palestine: One Land, Two Peoples* (Cambridge: Cambridge University Press, 2004); Baruch Kimmerling and Joel S. Migdal, *Palestinians: The Makings of a People* (Cambridge, MA: Harvard University Press, 1994); Hayim Gordon, Rivca Gordon, and Taher Shriteh, *Beyond Intifada: Narratives of Freedom Fighters in the Gaza Strip* (Westport, CT: Praeger Publishers, 2003); and Barry M. Rubin, *The Transformation of Palestinian Politics: From Revolution to State Building* (Cambridge, MA: Harvard University Press, 1999).

16 Colin S. Gray, "How Has War Changed Since the End of the Cold War?," *Parameters*, Vol. 35, no. 1 (Spring 2005), p. 17.

17 Typical of "transformational" systems is the Army's "Future Combat System," an effort to combine 53 "crucial technologies." According to one source, "The Army wants Future Combat to be a smaller, faster force than the one now fighting in Iraq. Tanks, mobile cannons and personnel carriers would be made so light that they could be flown to a war zone." The emphasis is on deployability, but there is little evidence that the Army's Future Combat System, like most other Rumsfeld-era transformations, are guided by threat assessment instead of a desire to increase the speed of force deployment. "An Army Program to Build a High-Tech Force Hits Snags," *The New York Times*, March 28, 2005. The emphasis on saving money was made emphatically by a former DoD Comptroller, Dov Zakheim, "Money Drives Rumsfeld's Changes," *London Financial Times*, March 29, 2005.

18 The most thorough discussion to date of the allegations involving manipulation and misuse of information on Iraq by the Bush administration for OIF is found in Chaim Kaufmann, "Threat Inflation and the Failure of the Marketplace of Ideas: The Selling of the Iraq War," *International Security*, Vol. 29, no. 1 (Summer 2004), pp. 5–48.

19 Geoffrey Perret, *Winged Victory: The Army Air Forces in World War II* (New York: Random House, 1993), pp. 457–8; Michael S. Sherry, *The Rise of American Air Power: The Creation of Armageddon* (New Haven, CN and London: Yale University Press, 1987), p. 333. This was obviously not the only or even the major reason for the air assault against Japan, but it was an increasingly troubling aspect of the war, particularly after the particularly bloody Okinawa campaign.

13 The will doesn't triumph

William S. Lind

Both in *The Sling and the Stone* and in his writings in this volume, Tom Hammes has made important contributions to our slowly growing understanding of Fourth Generation war. While his book is generally stronger in its descriptive than in its theoretical sections, it offers one very important addition to Fourth Generation theory, namely that with regard to John Boyd's OODA Loop (Observe–Orient–Decide–Act), accuracy of observation and orientation is more important in Fourth Generation situations than is the speed at which one cycles. Exactly how the OODA Loop works in the Fourth Generation remains an open question; it is possible that Fourth Generation entities can out-cycle states not by being faster, but by moving so slowly as to be unobservable. If that is true, it would put yet more weight behind Hammes' observation.

That said, I would note several areas where I disagree with Hammes. He dismisses the cultural aspects of Fourth Generation war, which in my view are central. Not only do other cultures fight differently from the West, which is part of the reason why the US and Britain are losing in Iraq and cannot comprehend how, they also use their cultures as weapons by coupling them with mass immigration into (formerly?) Western countries. In effect, more and more territory in European states is being occupied and governed by foreign non-state forces. The fact that the aspect of cultural Marxism known as "multiculturalism" renders the West unable to defend itself, or even acknowledge the threat, just makes the strategy of cultural invasion all the easier.

Another point on which I disagree with Hammes is his equating of Fourth Generation war with insurgency. This is too narrow, and it risks misleading us if we take it to mean that we only need to re-discover past counterinsurgency techniques in order to win. As Martin van Creveld has said, it is not how war is fought that changes in the Fourth Generation, more importantly what changes is who fights and what they fight for. At the core of Fourth Generation Warfare (4GW) is a crisis of legitimacy of the state itself and mere counterinsurgency cannot successfully address that crisis. Indeed, when the counterinsurgency effort is waged or controlled by foreign powers, the local state's crisis of legitimacy is exacerbated. While these are important points, I want to focus this short essay on what may be Hammes' most important misunderstanding of Fourth Generation war, a misunderstanding common in national capitals and central to the Bush administration's misconceived strategy for its "war on terrorism." It is Hammes' (and others') belief that all a government has to do to prevail against Fourth Generation opponents is maintain its "will."

Let me quote from Hammes' essay in this volume (he makes the same point in *The Sling and the Stone*):

> 4GW uses all available networks – political, economic, social and military – to convince the enemy's political decision-makers that their strategic goals are either unachievable or too costly for the perceived benefit. It is rooted in the fundamental precept that superior political will, when properly employed, can defeat greater economic and military power. 4GW does not attempt to win by defeating the enemy's military forces. Instead, combining guerrilla tactics or civil disobedience with the soft networks of social, cultural and economic ties, disinformation campaigns and innovative political activity, it directly attacks the will of enemy decision-makers.

Well, no. Fourth Generation forces do not win by convincing the decision-makers of hostile states that some strategic spreadsheet shows them making a loss. They win by pulling the states they are fighting apart at the moral level.

One of the most common myths about states' decisions to make war or make peace is that they are analogous to some sort of economic calculation. This myth supposes that at some point, a state's decision-makers in effect sit down around a big table and "go over the numbers," as if they were deciding on a hydro-electric project. If the war promises a "profit," they go to war. Or, if once in a war, the numbers suggest "their strategic goals are too costly for the perceived benefit," they shut down their subsidiary by making peace.

This theory of making war or peace was widely accepted in Europe immediately prior to World War I. After that war, which destroyed Europe for reasons that no one could quite recall, it was correctly regarded as bunk. Historians recognized that both deciding for war and deciding to make peace are vastly complex events in which non-rational factors, including what side of the bed key emperors, kings, premiers and foreign ministers happened to get up on that morning, play decisive roles. Far from war being a rational economic calculation, decision theory now recognizes that most corporate economic decisions are almost as non-rational as are states' decisions to go to war.

If we are to grasp how Fourth Generation war works, reviving a totally discredited theory of state decision-making is not likely to help us. Certainly no one observing the psychological dislocation of the Bush White House at this point in the Iraq war can visualize any sort of rational calculation going on there, at least outside the Univac mind of Karl Rove.

Rather, if we are to better understand the power of Fourth Generation forces, we need to combine two observations by two noted military theorists. The first is Colonel John Boyd's point that war is fought at three levels, the physical, the mental and the moral; of the three, the physical is the least powerful and the moral is the most powerful. The second observation is Martin van Creveld's:

the greatest power of Fourth Generation forces is the power of weakness. As van Creveld notes, at the physical level of war the power of states is usually vast compared to the power of those states' Fourth Generation, non-state opponents. The armed forces of the state have tens or hundreds of thousands of trained troops; they have tanks, artillery, attack helicopters and fighter-bombers; and they have at least half-serious systems for taking care of their troops who are wounded or disabled. In contrast, Fourth Generation forces have almost nothing. Instead of body armor, they wear bathrobes. Their weapons are either improvised or date, at least in terms of technology, to World War II. They have no tanks, no artillery, no aircraft, and if they are wounded, they are usually left to the tender mercies of their enemies.

But at the moral level, the situation is reversed. Precisely because the Fourth Generation elements are so weak physically, they are powerful morally. Every time the state uses its vast superiority to win physically, it loses at the more powerful moral level of war. Indeed, the state quickly faces a paradox: almost everything that works for it at the physical level of war works against it at the moral level, and the moral level is decisive. The state cannot avoid being seen as Goliath, and the secret of the Biblical parable is that in a contest between David and Goliath, David usually wins.

Van Creveld uses another analogy that is helpful here. He compares a state that is fighting a Fourth Generation opponent to an adult who administers a prolonged, vicious beating to a small child in a public place. The adult can get away with giving the child one good whack. But if he continues to beat the child, other adults are outraged. They intervene, the police are summoned and the adult is arrested. In the eyes of everyone else, he has committed a crime.

The key elements here are two: disproportion and time. When a vast disproportion is played out over time, the stronger force becomes the weaker and the weaker the stronger. It is not only in Fourth Generation where this is true, although it is true in virtually all Fourth Generation conflicts. The Vietnam War offers a state versus state example: it was precisely the combination of the disproportion between the physical power in war of the United States and that of North Vietnam and the length of the war that swung much of both world and American public opinion against the United States, despite the fact that North Vietnam represented a stultifying Communist dictatorship, which it promptly imposed on South Vietnam when it won.

In Fourth Generation conflicts, the result of the combination of disproportion and time is that the state, which holds all the military advantages at the physical level, is pulled apart internally at the moral level. Disgust at its own behavior spreads and grows within the state's own public and its own armed forces. Morale weakens, dissent from the war spreads and the public comes to desire only an end to the whole dirty business. Since the Fourth Generation opponent is just strong enough to keep the conflict going, there is only one way it can end, and that is for the state to give up. By the time its decision-makers conclude to do just that, they have no other option. They are the last, not the first, to be convinced, and their "will" is at that point wholly irrelevant.

If we need examples, Israel in southern Lebanon and, more recently, in Gaza, give us two. Or are we to regard Mr. Sharon as somehow lacking in will?

Thus, we see that the moral level of war is much more than some meaningless calculation of profit and loss on the part of a state's decision-makers. It is also more than "will," which seems to mean little more than stubbornness on the part of the state's leaders. If the Bush White House has one quality in abundance, it is stubbornness. Yet that will not change the fact that in Iraq, and in time in Afghanistan also, the "world's only superpower" will give up and go home. The weaker force, by the very power of its own weakness, inevitably holds the moral high ground, regardless of what it otherwise represents. On the moral level of war, the high ground is decisive.

14 Response

Thomas X. Hammes

First, I would like to thank those who commented on this chapter. The reader will recognize the names and realize they took time from very busy schedules to do so. I wrote the article which led to this symposium (and the book) for the purpose of stimulating discussion and their feedback clarifies both the strong and the weak points of my writing.

I felt we needed a discussion on the role of insurgency in the future of war because, with very little serious discussion, the Pentagon has spent almost fifteen years and hundreds of billions of dollars pursuing a purely high-technology future. This future envisions a single type of enemy – a state using conventional war. Only in the last few months have official Pentagon documents even discussed the possibility that our enemies may not choose to join us in that future. One of the primary purposes of the chapter is to provide a different future, a future that renders most of the high-technology equipment the Pentagon is purchasing obsolete.

I selected the Fourth Generation Warfare (4GW) model for both the book and the chapter for two reasons. First, unlike many of the models in current literature, it focuses on modern war. Second, it is a very simple model. The point of the chapter and book is to stimulate discussion among people interested in national security but not necessarily deeply read in history. The 4GW model provides a simple framework to illustrate how modern insurgents have evolved to defeat the very high-technology force the Pentagon proposes.

Some might say the fact that US forces have been tied down by insurgencies for three years should be sufficient proof. 4GW or other discussions are unnecessary because Iraq and Afghanistan show we need to change our vision of the future. Unfortunately, those who support conventional warfare are very resistant to change. Two of the respondents to this chapter, both very thoughtful, well read, and highly respected commentators, essentially wrote that insurgency is unworthy of serious study or effort. Dr. John Ferris stated, "If the problem is that western governments cannot easily win guerrilla wars abroad, one solution may be – why bother trying?" Dr. Edward Luttwak recommends "leaving terrorists to police forces and staying clear of insurgencies." This is exactly the line those who seek a high technology, big war military would like the United States to adopt. Unfortunately, the first concept is based on the outdated assumption that if we leave the insurgents alone, they will leave us alone. 9/11 should have put that concept to rest.

The other concept, that police are sufficient to deal with insurgents, may be true in well-governed parts of the world. Unfortunately, it is in the ungoverned spaces that insurgencies establish themselves and grow. Ignoring insurgents is no longer a viable option. Modern society allows insurgents to strike anywhere in the world if they decide it will help their cause. Iraq and Afghanistan show that even if a high-technology military takes down a regime, it will be faced with an insurgency if the people of that nation refuse to accept defeat. The Defense Science Board Summer Study *Transition To and From Hostilities* stated that there is a "high likelihood" the United States will find itself dealing with failed states, terrorists, and insurgencies.[1] In short, like it or not, the United States had better be prepared to deal with insurgents.

Unlike Bill Lind, I do not see 4GW as a cultural struggle.[2] That is much too narrow a lens through which to understand these fights. In fact, that approach distorts the history and greatly reduces the possibilities for successfully dealing with a 4GW enemy. If you have unalterable cultural conflicts, it is impossible to work toward a functioning, mutually acceptable government in the area of the conflict.

In his reply, Dr. Wirtz hit a critical reason we have to discuss how war has changed. Many military officers "are unwilling to accept the fact war is ultimately a political contest." One of the central arguments of 4GW is that insurgents have learned to use political power to neutralize military power. Prowess on the battlefield does not necessarily translate to desired political end states. In the first three generations of modern war, if military personnel succeeded in their primarily military functions, there was a high probability the war would turn out well. 4GW changes that. As Dr. Wirtz concluded "the problem with Fourth Generation warriors is not that they are better soldiers than today's military professionals are, it is that they are better politicians." We have to learn how to tie our military actions to the political goals of the fight.

Several of the replies expressed concern that I see the evolution of war as a linear progression with each generation superseding the previous. In fact, a quick survey of modern conflict shows that all generations of modern war and even pre-modern tribal war continue to take place today. This is in keeping with how war has evolved. While a newer generation is capable of defeating an earlier generation of war, that does not mean nations and even groups won't continue to use earlier generations. They simply may not be organizationally, socially or intellectually ready for a newer generation and thus unable to use it. One of my key arguments is the form of warfare a society uses is based on its political, economic, social and technical status. Clearly the tribal groups in West Africa cannot employ even first generation state war against each other; they lack the prerequisite political and social organization. In the same way, Saddam's Iraq could not employ maneuver-based 3GW because the entire concept is based on trust between leader and led.

Other replies were concerned that I see 4GW as post-Clausewitzian war.

While some 4GW writers have stated that interstate war is waning, I have never seen any who say that it eliminates the basic trinity of hostile forces trying to achieve a political goal in an arena filled with friction, fog, and chance. Mao himself acknowledged Clausewitz's insights in his essay "On Guerrilla War."[3] Vividly driving the point home, the conflicts in Iraq and Afghanistan show that no matter how rich, well-equipped or high-tech a force, it still faces uncertainty and friction in war. This fact is one of the main weaknesses of the Pentagon's *Joint Vision 2020* and high-technology gurus. They see technology as giving US and allied forces "information dominance." Many in the Pentagon continue to push such a concept despite our obvious information deficits in Iraq, Afghanistan, and the badly misnamed Global War on Terror.

By far the most consistent complaint about my presentation of 4GW was the identification of Mao as the father of this form of war. I am fully aware that guerrilla warfare dates back much further. J.F.C. Fuller's *The Generalship of Alexander the Great* (1958) provides an excellent account of the problems Afghan guerrillas caused in the fourth century BC. Robert B. Asprey's book *War in the Shadows: the Guerrilla in History* (1975) shows how guerrilla warfare remained an important approach to warfare throughout the subsequent eras. In the past, however, its practitioners fell back on guerrilla war due to the failure of their conventional forces – not as a preferred war winning effort. For the most part, these guerrillas fought in support of a national army that had been driven back or an international army coming to their aid. The exceptions are those tribal and colonial wars such as the Indian Wars in the US west. These people fought as primitives, with no clear idea of how to win against a much more powerful opponent. Although some tribes allied themselves with outside powers, often to defeat a tribal enemy, they did not choose insurgency as a political approach to war. Even if they had, political and social conditions of the time made it impossible for such a campaign to win.

History is full of examples of guerrillas fighting a wide variety of enemies under a wide variety of conditions. Therefore, asking why I give Mao credit for being the father of Fourth Generation war is a legitimate question. I do so simply because he was the first to write a clear, concise instruction manual that was widely distributed and followed, virtually as a recipe in some cases. Carlos Marigella and Ernesto "Che" Guevara also wrote guerrilla manuals but their ideas died with the people who tried to execute them.

Sun Tzu wrote about insurgency and Clausewitz discussed it. Both clearly influenced Mao. But Mao was the first to identify insurgency not just as an auxiliary form of war to be used when conventional forces have been defeated or to support an advancing allied army, but as a war winning approach in and of itself. Mao did not see guerrilla warfare as a war winner but rather as one phase of his three phase theory of insurgent warfare. From the beginning, Mao wrote that People's War would include elements of conventional war, guerrilla operations and terror.

Most important, Mao is the first to state unequivocally that "political mobilization is the most fundamental condition for winning the war."[4] While others had highlighted the importance of political motivation to guerrillas, Mao not only stated its primary importance but also organized both his theory of war and his forces around that idea.

Several authors contest the idea that Mao and Ho won with insurgents. They noted that their wars ended with the defeat of the government forces by the insurgent's regular forces. To which Mao and Ho would have replied, "Of course!" Each stated unequivocally that he would use conventional forces in the final phase of his insurgency.

Despite the fact each knew his war would end with conventional fights, each gave greater weight to and focused more on political than military strength. Victory by insurgents is not inevitable. In fact, most insurgents, even liberation movements, failed because they had not heeded Mao's admonition that political strength was the most important factor. They failed to build a solid political base and thus were easily eliminated by the government security forces.

The sequence of insurgencies I selected was not meant to be representative of the numerous insurgencies fought between Mao and today. Rather I selected them to illustrate the significant changes each introduced to Mao's theory. Each adapted insurgency to take advantage of the unique political, economic, social, and technical conditions they faced. As a result, insurgencies have evolved from Mao's monolithic, hierarchical insurgency to the diverse, networked insurgencies of today. Each step in this evolution was the result of practical men solving practical problems in order to insure their insurgency won. And, as has been true throughout modern war, the most successful adaptations were those that took advantage of changes in society.

It is essential that we understand the changes in insurgency if we are to deal with them. The most important is the fact that we no longer face monolithic organizations that respond to a single leader and are driven by a single concept. Instead, we face coalitions of the willing. In Afghanistan, Chechnya, Iraq, and Palestine, there was/is no single unifying political idea. Rather the varied groups that cooperated to fight agreed on only one thing – the foreign power had to go. All insurgent groups knew that when that goal was achieved they would then have to fight among themselves to determine which of their political visions would rule. Far from being monolithic, today's insurgencies are coalitions of opportunistic groups banded together for the single purpose of ejecting the outsider and then defeating the government. They know they lack the unity to establish an effective government and anticipate continued fighting even after the government is defeated.

The insurgent coalition of the willing in Iraq shows all the traits of these earlier coalition insurgencies. The volatile mix of former Ba'athists, Sadr's Sh'ia militia, violent Sunni fundamentalists, foreign jihadists, criminal gangs, revenge seekers, and unemployed, bored teens is what Mao's monolithic insurgency has evolved to. As with prior 4GW combatants, their lack of a unified strategy is both a strength and a weakness. It is a strength because it does not allow the government to develop a single counterstrategy. But it is a weakness because it deprives the rebels of a unifying idea – they have only the negative goal of driving out the outsider.

A second major trend has been the shift from a military end game to a political end game. While Mao and Ho stated the war would end with a large conventional fight where the insurgents destroyed the government, current insurgencies do not seek a military victory. Starting with the Sandinistas, who stated they had no military plan to seize the country, this trend was magnified during Intifada I (1987–1991) when the Palestinian leadership actually disarmed the protesters in the street, preferring the strategic advantages of pure victims to the ambiguity of losing combatants. It is also clear the Iraqi and Afghan insurgents do not see themselves as capable of defeating the United States and its allies militarily. They do not currently seem to plan for a classic Maoist Phase III. Rather they intend to use long-term resistance to wear down American will. They believe that the withdrawal of US support from their governments is the essential condition that will lead to their victory.

With this goal in mind, the priority of insurgent targeting in Iraq is not to destroy significant US forces. Rather their highest priority is to attack the will of the US and Iraqi populations. A primary technique is to insure the attacks are covered both in western and Arab media. This is a targeted media campaign with one set of videos for the Arab media and another for Western media. While the use of the media is not new, modern communications technology vastly increases the velocity and impact of its use.

Yet another trend is the truly transnational character of these conflicts. While one commentator stated World War I and II were transnational wars, I think they were actually international wars. Those wars were fought primarily by states operating, for the most part, under international law with the intention of militarily defeating their enemies. In contrast, the most ethereal transnational organizations have no fixed capital, no formal government, no recognized boundaries and report to no authority. They represent a very different enemy than a state. It requires distinctly different thought processes to deal with such enemies. Because they do not have to defend any particular geographic location, simple military defeat is largely ineffective. One must destroy their will to resist.

Each of these new characteristics of insurgency – coalitions, lack of a military campaign plan, targeting enemy decision makers directly through a variety of networks, and their transnational character – capitalize on the way society has evolved since Mao. The increased density of communications, particularly the Internet, has allowed very diverse coalitions to work together to defeat an outside power. The focus on political rather than military goals is only possible because there are so many paths available to convince enemy decision makers they cannot achieve their strategic goals. In Mao's time, the primary path was the grinding away of the security forces and the slow increase in the size of the territory the insurgents held. Today, insurgents do not need to hold major geographic areas in order to be effective. Instead, through media, the markets, international associations, and a worldwide network of sympathizers, the insurgent can drive his message home through a wide variety of paths.

Yet another concern expressed in the comments is the idea that I want to completely revamp western armed forces to fight 4GW enemies. Unfortunately, the article was not long enough to provide the range of recommendations of the book. In fact, I see the United States being required to maintain the ability to fight all generations of war. To do that, we first must accomplish what General Anthony Zinni refers to as the "transformation between the ears." No matter what force structure we have, we cannot use it correctly if we do not understand the particular conflict we are in.

Once we transform our thinking, the most important step is to develop true interagency capabilities to deal with all generations of war. This will require legislative action, extensive changes in personnel selection, promotion, and training policies and at least a decade to fully implement.

In the shorter term, well-balanced medium weight military forces such as a US Marine Expeditionary Force (MEF) will be the best approach to deal with the full spectrum of warfare. The MEF is a flexible tool kit, adaptable to a wide spectrum of contingencies. It has been used to build everything from the mechanized heavy force backed by hundreds of strike aircraft that entered Iraq in 2003 to a manpower heavy force that twelve years ago secured Somalia until it was turned over to the UN. In short, we should not build forces to fight a specific high-tech enemy or a specific type of war but to function well across the spectrum of conflict. It must be flexibly manned, trained, and equipped to deal with the far more unpredictable tasks at hand today.

To modify an old Marine Corps slogan "Nobody wants to know how to fight insurgents, but someone has to know how." The fact of the matter is those who wish to fight the United States have turned to 4GW – because it works. As Dr. Thornton stated in his comments, there is a danger in treating it as war because it will be left to the military. That is only true if you do not recognize the changes 4GW has brought to war. It was the same in World War I when both sides sent 1GW massed formations against the firepower of 2GW armies. They did not recognize the changes in war and paid a heavy price.

While not addressed in this short chapter, it is clear that states are also capable of using 4GW techniques to neutralize an opponent's combat power. Chinese authors have written that China should use diplomatic, economic, financial, cyber, media/information and network warfare to neutralize the West's advantages in the military/technical domain.[5] China's actions in political, economic, social, and military fields throughout Asia, the Middle East, and Africa indicate they are forming alliances to reduce western power and influence while assuring their access to raw materials, particularly, energy. The United States must think beyond conventional war with China and analyze how it, and other states, will use 4GW to neutralize our technical strengths.

How warfare is conducted has changed. Today, we have to understand that warfare is a multi-disciplined endeavor requiring a truly interagency effort. The United States and its allies must recognize that fact. 4GW, whether used by insurgents or another state, must be dealt with by a true interagency team, combining military and civilian capabilities to defeat adversaries. A purely military response is doomed to fail.

Notes

1 Defense Science Board Summer Study, *Transition To and From Hostilities*, (Washington, DC: Office of the Undersecretary of Defense for Acquisition, Technology and Logistics, December 2004).
2 Lind's views can be found in his 'On War' commentaries, which can be accessed via the 'Defense and the National Interest' pages devoted to 4GW at www.d-n-i.net/second_level/fourth_generation_warfare.htm.
3 Mao Tse-tung, *On Guerrilla Warfare*, trans. by S.B. Griffith II (Baltimore, MD: The National & Aviation Publishing Company of America, n.d.) p. 75.
4 Mao Tse-tung, *On Protracted War* (Peking: People's Publishing House, 1954) p. 137.
5 L. Qiao and X. Wang, *Unrestricted War* (West Palm Beach, FL: NewsMax.com, 2002).

Part IV

Fourth Generation wars

15 America in Peril

Fourth generation warfare in the twenty-first century

Colonel Chet Richards (USAF, Retired),
Lieutentant-Colonel Greg Wilcox (USA, Retired),
and Colonel G.I. Wilson (USMC, Retired)

Introduction

After the brilliant rapid-paced, low-cost, maneuver warfare demonstration that was the march up the Euphrates to Baghdad, the American military stalled-out. And we have been mired *in situ* for over three years in what is euphemistically called "stability operations." Moreover, it looks like this is going to be a long war for America.[1] This was not how it was supposed to be when we sliced into the country to depose a dictator who had:

- dissipated his country's great wealth in two wars;
- killed tens of thousands of Sh'ite Iraqi citizens after the 1991 Gulf War;
- killed thousands of Kurdish Iraqi citizens with gas;
- instituted a brutal dictatorship with none of the respect for human rights accorded even by other governments in the area, including the Kingdom of Saudi Arabia and the Islamic Republic of Iran.

Under these conditions you might not expect flowers, exactly, given the cultural and religious differences between our forces and the local population, but "Blackhawk Down: the Series" as Tom Barnett described it, was for the most part a huge surprise.[2] The only thing more surprising is the difficulty we are experiencing in bringing peace to the country against a pick-up insurgency that did not exist before the summer of 2003.

One group of analysts, however, was not surprised. They had predicted as far back as 1989 that the nature of war itself was changing, that state armies would not fight other state armies in replays of the Battle of Kursk so much as states would confront non-states in what some have called "insurgency on steroids." They also suggested that "clashes of cultures" would be a strong facilitator of such conflicts, from which one might conclude that when radically different cultures come into immediate and intimate contact – as US forces and Iraqi citizens did in 2003 – the possibilities for such state-versus-non-state conflict would be increased. The name they gave to this new form of organized conflict was "fourth generation warfare," and in the rest of this chapter, we will explore what is truly different about it, where it seems to be heading, and what options we have for dealing with it, particularly in Iraq.[3]

The Iraq war

The first combat phase went rather well: a conventional blitzkrieg that would have been familiar to Guderian, Manstein, Patton, or any previous practitioner of that art. On May 2, 2003, the President declared that major combat operations were over, and most people assumed that peace was at hand and rebuilding operations could begin. Fourth generation warfare theorists, however, were nervous. They recalled that in guerrilla-type insurgencies, getting in had been the easy part – think of the Soviets in Afghanistan or the US in Vietnam. General Anthony Zinni, for example, warned repeatedly about the aftermath as the hard part and its potential for undoing the initial "victory" of the taking of Baghdad.[4]

Things were "too quiet," in Iraq after the "March Up," but not for long.

To put it simply, the supporters of the Saddam regime may have been evil, but they were not stupid. Any Third World military would be quickly destroyed if it tried to stand and fight conventional battles with an advanced Western opponent, especially the United States. Apparently the Iraqi military understood this, if only instinctively. After an initial bloody nose, the Iraqi armed forces melted back into the population taking their weapons, and in some cases, their command system with them. In time, they were joined by "jihadists," religiously motivated fighters mostly from outside the country who were willing to carry out tactics such as suicide bombings on a large scale. By the end of 2003, an odd amalgam of unreconstructed Ba'athists, former Iraqi Army men, looters and criminals, and both outsider and insider Islamists had united if only opportunistically against the "occupiers," the Coalition Forces, that had invaded Iraq. Ultimately al Qaeda showed up on the scene in the form of Abu Musab al-Zarkawi, the Jordan-born self-professed leader of al Qaeda in Iraq. So while the war may not have started out as a fourth generation war, by May 2003, it was evolving into a fourth generation warfare (4GW) morass with plenty of outside help.

An observation

At a recent conference at the Army War College, a senior Army general stated that the difference between the radical Islamists and the Americans is that the American focus is on tactics while the al Qaeda focus is on strategy.[5] He likened it to two triangles. The Americans focus on expensive equipment and training to ensure the tactics are conducted correctly. The al Qaeda focus is on the strategy with very little emphasis on the tactics, which are perceived as a means to the end. The general presented a diagram much like that below to make his point.

The American over-emphasis on costly "things," mainly at the tactical level, is at the expense of placing the focus where it belongs, on people.

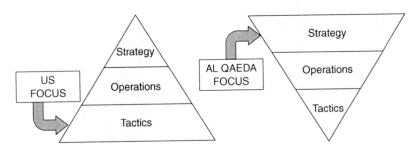

Figure 15.1 Construct of the differences between US and al Qaeda approaches to war

Americans like to talk to the three levels of war: tactics, operations, and strategy (including grand strategy). This convenient separation of the levels of war applies directly to the first three generations of warfare, which involve wars between the military forces of states, but in 4GW, these distinctions are mashed to the point of being unrecognizable as tactical or strategic. The "Strategic Corporal" identified by General Charles Krulak, former Commandant of the Marine Corps, best illustrates this phenomenon. This is a major difference between 4GW and "guerrilla warfare," which is normally contained within a state and where the separations of the levels of war are still relatively clear. For example, the strategic issues of Vietnam involved the Soviet and Chinese entry into the war. Operationally we limited our choices of combat methods with a clear eye toward the strategic implications. So we did not, for example, invade North Vietnam with American armored divisions or bomb it with nuclear weapons. This meant that we were forced to try to win the war at the tactical level: We wanted to not only win the hearts and minds, but also to kill the enemy. The focus was on the former and not the latter. There was, therefore, a well-defined sense of strategy, operations, and tactics, even though these were defined differently than they were in World War II.

In Iraq, after the fourth generation war had started, these distinctions began to blur. Just to cite one illustration, the tactical implications of what went on in Abu Ghraib had strategic implications and created more enemies than would have been the case in Vietnam. Through a global media, the "strategic corporals" of Abu Ghraib have adversely impacted support for the United States both abroad and at home. In other words, the actions of a few guards and interrogators in an obscure prison – whether authorized by their chain of command or not – had both strategic as well as grand strategic implications.

The threat

From April 2003 onward, there was growing resistance to the "occupiers" and this resistance largely employed 4GW tactics. These tactics are much more sophisticated than the tactics of guerrilla warfare in the past. In 4GW, information warfare reigns supreme, and the Islamists in particular are past masters at applying information warfare to the situation that exists in Iraq. Far more important than the kinetics, the message is the most important arrow in the enemy quiver, while the Americans continue to focus on the physical war. Months of building cultural bridges to the population can be quickly undone by rumor or propaganda. In the case of Danish members of the Coalition, the danger may come from cartoons published five months earlier in Copenhagen and held in waiting for the right opportunity. Such is the nature of 4GW.

Once activity like this begins, it is virtually impossible to control. Warned before the invasion by outspoken reformers, the United States did not see an emerging insurgency.[6]

> In the future, war will not be waged by armies but by groups whom we today call terrorists, guerrillas, bandits, and robbers, but who will undoubtedly hit on more formal titles to describe themselves. Their organizations are likely to be constructed on charismatic lines rather than on institutional ones, and to be motivated less by "professionalism" than by fanatical ideologically-based loyalties. While rooted in a "population base" of some sort, that population probably will not be clearly separable either from its immediate neighbors or from those, always the minority, by whom most of the active fighting is done.[7]

Once underway, the insurgency was fueled by not providing jobs for the many Iraqis of the defunct Iraqi Army nor was there any plan to co-opt them in the nation-building process. In the wake of the march to Baghdad there was little sense of urgency to shape Iraq's future other than to pump oil out of the ground to pay for this all. Nevertheless, the clock was ticking even before we invaded Iraq. We may have inadvertently planted the seeds of 4GW by not recognizing in advance the need for shaping and rebuilding immediately as we took down Baghdad.

So unemployed Iraqi soldiers found jobs as insurgents or in criminal activity, which was logical since there was hardly any legitimate economic activity for them. In 4GW, the distinctions between war, peace, and criminal are constantly blurred, and are often in the eye of the beholder: the government and its allies. In addition to the actual combatants, all guerrilla environments, including 4GW, involve "sympathizers" who will also be regarded as criminals by the government. Iraq is no different. Within the Iraqi security forces and Iraqi government and Iraqis working for the Coalition, these supporters provide excellent human intelligence (HUMINT) about US and Coalition operations without violently taking part in the insurgency. To win in a 4GW conflict, the government and its allies must infiltrate and break this cycle, although it cannot be pointed out often enough that the best strategy is not to let it begin in the first place.[8]

By the middle of 2004, the Coalition recognized the need to put an emphasis on building Iraqi security forces. Unfortunately by this time, the insurgency had had time to self-organize, and so provide recruits for the new Iraqi forces. The issue of vetting Iraqis working for Coalition forces and involved in the re-establishment of the Iraqi is one of denying the Iraqi 4GW foe his anonymity. It is very difficult to do, and is probably impossible for outsiders with little understanding of the language and culture. Attempts to vet Iraqis are also challenging because family, clan, and ethnic loyalties have made many supposedly loyal Iraqis become at least passive HUMINT sources for insurgents.

Everything is not going the insurgents' way, of course. Yet even when news is "good" it may not mean what we want it to mean. Insurgents, for example, continue to experience tactical defeats in greater Baghdad, Ramadi, Fallujah, and elsewhere, and suicide bombers tend to experience extremely high casualty rates. Yet, the discovery of large caches of munitions continues, and there is little evidence that the stream of insurgents or martyrs-to-be is declining. In fact, the estimates of the number of insurgents are increasing.[9] But perhaps more important, the number of Iraqis who say they support the insurgents appear to be increasing despite the outcome of the elections.[10]

Goals of the Iraqi 4GW forces

Iraq's fourth generation foes, generally referred to as "insurgents," appear to be everywhere in the region, connected not only by family, clan, and ethnic ties but by cell phones and the Internet as well. The Iraq 4GW foes have no desire for immediate peace – wanting only to increase casualties and create chaos to give the impression the new Iraqi government is incapable of providing security for the people. This 4GW adversary transcends borders and the nation-state paradigm. While Saddam loyalists press to destabilize Iraq to regain their lost authority, an irregular network of foreign and local terrorists in association with Islamic extremists strive to create internal strife and conflict for somewhat different purposes. At some point, of course, there will be a falling out between the secular ex-Ba'athists and the religious jihadists in the Sunni areas. For the short run, however, they appear to have enough of a common enemy in Coalition forces to suppress what would otherwise be mortal conflict between them.

A hybrid insurgency

So today, the insurgency is a mix of both secular and religious groups, among them former regime elements, Ba'athists, foreign jihadis, criminals, and Iraqi nationalists, all with a desire to disrupt the political process and drive US forces out of Iraq in order to pursue their own individual agendas. It is most important to understand that each group has its own unique motivations: former regime elements wanting to return to power, foreign fighters wanting Islamic dominance to restore an Islamic caliphate, criminals looking for opportunities to exploit, tribal leaders wanting to maintain their status quo, blood feud entities wanting to settle old scores, and foreign interlopers wanting to seed chaos. The collaboration and shifting alliances among the foreign interlopers, indigenous opportunists, Islamic extremists, and remnants of the Saddam regime is rather unique.

It is unique in the sense the insurgents have both secular and religious components. The secular group has its origin in remnants of the Ba'athist loyalists. The religious group ties are with the foreign jihadists who came to Iraq to fight the Great Satan – the United States. These foreign interlopers or jihadists are the chaos trainers of terrorist cells and handlers of suicide bombers inside Iraq.

Adaptive tactics

Although 4GW groups emphasize strategy, they still have to execute tactics, and in this area they are also making progress. Most worrisome for the Coalition, tactics and the nature of the insurgency itself are adaptive and constantly changing. This is characteristic of 4GW since they can operate in the anonymity of the population and share lessons learned via both their local networks of neighbors and relatives and over the Internet.

As a result, the astute enemy has continued to outpace us in the use of actions combined with information and backed up by more actions. Kidnappings followed by video tapes of beheadings are designed to shock and strike fear into the hearts of soldiers and civilians alike. Terrorist acts that target anyone working with US Coalition forces are aimed at preventing such cooperation. Destruction of pipelines is designed to give the population of Iraq the idea that the Coalition cannot secure anything. Improvised Explosive Devices (IEDs) are aimed at making the US forces, in particular, "heavy up" and avoid contact by staying in their base camps. Interestingly enough, these IEDs are frequently videotaped and put up on blog sites for the media to pick up for nightly news.

Strategic issues

As with all fourth generation conflicts, the operational arena in Iraq is not limited to the state that is under immediate attack, and the flows go out of as well as into the country(s). Fighters enter Iraq from neighboring countries, with or without official knowledge, and often with the support of established extremist organizations from elsewhere in the Middle East. The Muslim Brotherhood, for example, is a supranational organization with a long history of terrorism and the use of assassination throughout the Middle East. Although it has officially renounced violence, the Muslim Brotherhood is suspected of close association with the rise of the Islamist terrorists in Iraq. One of its chief theoreticians, Sayyid Qutb (1906–1966), created the theological justification for Osama Bin Laden's al Qaeda.[11] It is also recognized as the sponsor if not creator of Hamas.

It has been reported in the open press that Hamas has an office in Nasiriyah, and Hezbollah has offices in Basra and Safwan.[12] The political wings of both Hamas and Hezbollah are recruiting Iraqi youth with seminars that embrace their ideology and terrorist nature.[13]

And al Qaeda and other militant groups have set up Iraq as a training ground for future warriors so that training, experience, and networks from that war are exported to militant groups in other troubled states – Afghanistan and Pakistan, for example – as well as back to their home countries. The stakes are extremely high not only in Iraq, but also in the entire region.

It is not known, exactly, how the religious elements interact with the more secular Ba'athist insurgents, and their tactics may vary from group to group or even from incident to incident. We assume, for example, that the vast majority of the suicide bombers are from the extreme religious elements. But in some parts of the country, it would be nearly impossible for them to train for and carry out such attacks without the knowledge and perhaps support of the local Ba'athist insurgents.

It would be impossible for the radical religious elements to "take over" Iraq since 80 percent of the population are either Sh'ia or Kurd, neither of which have any use for Sunni salafism. The other 20 percent are split between a growing Sunni radical element, and the more secular remnants of the former Ba'athist regime (who seem to control most of the weaponry). Most analysts believe that the radicals are useful as suicide bombers, but will be quickly eliminated after Coalition forces leave.[14]

In addition, there are local complications involving Iran, which sees itself as a protector of Iraqi Sh'ites and also wants to ensure that Iraq does not develop a military force capable of threatening Iran again. The relation between the various Sh'ite players in Iraq is complex, involving at least two semi-organized military forces (the Mahdi Militia of Muqtada al-Sadr and the Badr Corps Militia of Supreme Council of Islamic Revolution in Iraq) and the religious influence of the Ayatollahs in Najaf. Readers should not place too much emphasis on the day-to-day machinations of these players, since positions and alliances can change overnight. What will not change is that like the United States and the Sunni Arab states, Iran is in a position to selectively aid various parties and will continue to do so. Although Iraqi Sh'ia do not seem to want to live under Iranian domination, Iran's influence guarantees that the emergence of another strong central government dominated by Sunnis is most unlikely.

No matter how the politics of Iraq evolve, the greatest near-term danger to the West will come from violent activities around the world by militants who have received some training and experience from their time in Iraq.

The al Qaeda bombings in Spain illustrate the careful intimidation of a nation-state – followed up by a "unilateral peace" offered by al Qaeda until the London bombings. The 4GW enemy has successfully used information to separate the United States from many of its Coalition partners, and it continues to do so. More "drop-outs" are forthcoming. This is not to say that the US Administration did not play into the hands of the Islamists, but the exploitation of the gaps using information warfare is truly unique. While the North Vietnamese were quite capable at manipulating the media, the Islamists have taken the art to a new level which the US has yet to recognize.

Near-term strategic issues

Like everything else associated with 4GW, there are ambiguities that can be exploited by all sides. Saddam was always willing to sell us oil, since that was the only way he could finance his repressive regime. It is possible that if a Sh'ite theocracy takes root in the south, and so controls a majority of the country's oil, they may be more willing to use the oil weapon, for example, to advance religious causes, provide support for Iran, and pressure the West on Israel. We cannot be sure what will happen.

The Islamic radicals also understand the importance of strategic issues, since many of the leadership were educated in the West and have advanced technical degrees. Al Qaeda has said that they intend to spend the US into bankruptcy, and they appear to be doing just that. The Congressional Research Service estimates that before the last American troops leave, the Iraq war will have cost more in inflation-corrected dollars than did Vietnam.[15] On the other hand, the war has cost al Qaeda practically nothing – in fact, their participation in Iraq may have ramped up donations from like-minded Muslims to "help protect Islam from Christian and Jewish invaders."

This situation illustrates one of the most peculiar aspects of 4GW: that military success on the ground – and the US has had many – may not translate into political success against the type of stateless threat represented by al Qaeda and other 4GW opponents.

In summary, the extremist focus is on the strategic ends, and they use tactical means to accomplish strategic goals. The American focus is on tactical things (i.e., Unmanned Aerial Vehicles, tanks, airplanes). Our friends and allies, notably the British, have tried to warn us of this mal-focus. Is this vulnerability in our thinking? Did we lay the foundation for the insurgency because of our Western quick-fix conventional thinking against a backdrop of a tribal culture we little understood? Could we have set expectations in the press and in the American culture that worked against us? One wonders if we did not set ourselves up with the "Shock and Awe" expectation; it being much greater than delivered. As a result, we are now experiencing Iraq Shock and Awe from suicide bombers and IEDs.

Why the US efforts are feeding the insurgency

Most American military forces were trained to fight a conventional war.[16] Only the Special Forces were trained to deal with insurgencies and counter-insurgencies. The focus on large armored formations moving across deserts was clearly our forte. We easily overwhelmed the Iraqi conventional army once again, due to a combination of excellent equipment and training in combined arms teams. But once we achieved the objectives of the conventional war, our conventional tactics failed us in the ensuing occupation and peace enforcement activities.

Even today, American forces are perceived by the Iraqis to be "heavy handed." Our soldiers understand little of the culture or the language, and as a consequence they treat everyone as potential enemies rather than potential friends.

Frequent raids on homes were conducted, starting immediately after the march up, looking for the high value Iraqi Ba'athist leaders. Mistakes were made by troops who manhandled women, dishonored Iraqi men, and left homes in shambles after non-productive searches. This resulted in what might be expected in the culture of Iraq: blood feuds. Most of the customs are now better understood, as they should be after three years. They are taught to our soldiers beginning in basic training, but the language and many less critical customs remain a problem. Still, the mistakes are hard to erase overnight, and the enemy keeps up the pressures not only by more sophisticated attacks, but also by more sophisticated information warfare.

The battles we fought in Fallujah in 2004 were justified through military press releases after finding large weapons caches and identifying that the mosques, once thought sacred and untouchable, were used as armories for the insurgents. But the long-term consequences of the attrition-style warfare conducted in Fallujah more likely resulted in the making of 300,000 enemies rather than destroying 1,000 insurgents. The fourth generation enemy invited this attack and the Americans took the bait. So now the insurgency grows aided and abetted by American mistakes.

Likewise the mistakes of Abu Ghraib and other like incidents convinced many Muslims that Americans were no different from Saddam's regime. Even while the Americans try desperately to get to the bottom of the moral lapses committed in Iraq, we are finding that there may have been policies from very high echelons which encouraged such actions, and Guantanamo may have been the basis of such outrages but that is still speculation. Many Muslims have already made up their minds, however, with insurgent-inspired suggestions and prodding.

While the enemy may not have to adhere to such high moral standards (and they do not), the Coalition must adhere to a higher moral standard in order to win the hearts and minds of the undecided and hopefully reverse the attitudes of those previously in the Islamist camp. This is one of the great and unequal dilemmas in any insurgency. It is okay for the terrorists to commit heinous crimes, but the established governments cannot without losing legitimacy. In guerrilla warfare, this is one of the very key objectives: to make the government forces commit amoral acts which will result in their insurgents' continued security among a doubting population.

American efforts at information operations are basically a pick-up game with little direction from the top and no coordination.[17] Former Secretary of Defense Donald Rumsfeld rued the absence of American capability in this regard in an article in the *Los Angeles Times*. The title of the article is: "War in the Information Age: In a 24/7 World, the US Isn't Keeping Up with Its Enemies in the Communications Battle."[18] Secretary Rumsfeld candidly stated: "Our enemies have skillfully adapted to fighting wars in today's media age, but for the most part we – our government, the media or our society in general – have not."[19] According to Robert D. Steele, writing in a monograph published by the Army War College,

> Modern IO is not about the old messages of psychological operations
> (PSYOPS), but rather about empowering billions of people with both
> information tools and access to truthful information. It is about education,
> not manipulation. It is about sharing, not secrecy. It is about human under-
> standing to create wealth and stabilize societies, not about the threat of viol-
> ence and the delivery of precision munitions. IO substitutes information for
> violence.[20]

Given the importance of information to the current stability operations, we
should also understand the critical value of the inputs: current intelligence.

Our lack of HUMINT, as opposed to technical intelligence, and the absence
of any Iraqi authority, helped create a vacuum in the post-combat period which
looters, insurgents, and foreign fighters exploited. Our President once said, "We
don't do nation building," and it was clear that American ground forces had no
intention of doing anything other than trying to round up the former Hussein
government.[21] We have since changed our minds with the recent publication of
US Government documents like "Victory in Iraq" and the "National Military
Strategic Plan for the War on Terrorism" (February 2006).[22] This change of attitude did not help us to begin collecting human intelligence, which was so long
ignored and is not rebuilt overnight. As any field intelligence specialist will tell
you, good HUMINT takes years to develop. We are again playing catch-up ball
with the Islamists who swim in the sea of urban populations.

United States military forces had very little cultural information on Iraq
despite having first supported them in the Iran–Iraq War in the 1980s, fighting
Iraq in Desert Storm in the early 1990s, and then surveillance with a continuous
air presence and International Inspectors for almost a decade. We assumed that
the Iraqis would welcome our presence after having rid the country of the dictator Saddam Hussein. There was very little consideration of the culture of Iraq or
the religious influence of Islam. Little wonder that Americans had very little
appreciation of Iraqis after the surrenders of hundreds of thousands of Iraqis in
Desert Storm. We were led to expect the same reaction upon an invasion of their
homeland. Sh'ia Iraqis gave us a taste of what was to come in Nasiriyah on the
march up to Baghdad, but that situation was dismissed as an aberration.

The Phase IV Stability Operation was never fully planned, despite the asser-
tions of high ranking generals, and once we became focused on the real problem
of stability, support, transition, and reconstruction, only a few inventive and
adaptive leaders looked to a holistic approach. Most just waited to turn over the
support, transition, and reconstruction effort to the Department of State or
whoever would follow the warriors into the next phase.[23] It is just this type of
approach, a holistic one, that is the essence of a winning strategy. It includes all
diplomatic, information, military, and economic (DIME) elements in an integrated practice. And while the State Department has recently stood up to the bar
for "Transformational Diplomacy," there have been few Foreign Service Officer
volunteers to participate in a distributed transformational diplomatic leadership
in Iraq and elsewhere.[24] This is a case of too little too late. What might be called

political arrogance or ignorance was evident in the break with our allies from the outset.

Despite past reliance on a wide range of allies, the United States decided to abandon its strategic principles to go it alone if need be in the decision to go to war. Fortunately, our friends the British and Australians agreed to come along for the ride in Iraq. We convinced a few other tentative allies to join the Coalition, but it was all too apparent that we were intent on going to war with Iraq with or without allies, and in the process, we left behind two of our former friends, France and Germany, who did participate with us in Desert Storm, leaving political breaches that are certainly damaging, perhaps irreparably. The "Coalition of the willing" was a joke from the start, and the "Coalition" has since shown its colors with disaffections and abandonment by many countries. The true cost of the war is being borne by the United States – exactly as Osama would have wanted had he been able to direct the outcome himself.

Broken arrow: the Information War

The coordination of military and non-military agencies has been a disaster. The Information War alone exemplifies the absolute lack of policy direction and coordination of the disseparate agencies, commands, and various elements.[25]

The 4GW enemy seems to understand that this war is not about bullets but rather about influence. Only lately have we come to realize the importance of the war of words.

What is different in 4GW for government forces trying to restore order in a chaotic situation is the realization that the objective is not the insurgent but rather the population that may either support the insurgent or be neutral. That places a heavy premium on protecting civilians – principally in urban areas. Otherwise, the government forces will be aiding their 4GW opponents by diminishing support for the war not only among its own population but also within its allies – in the case of Iraq, the Coalition, and particularly the United States.

The convincing of the Iraqi people that we are the good guys has been forgotten in the quest to find and kill the 4GW enemy, which is exactly what Osama wanted.[26] And the enemy has continually stayed ahead of our Observe, Orient, Decide, and Act cycles (OODA Loops), that is, they have been able to keep changing the circumstances on the ground faster than we can understand and react to them.[27] As the late American strategist, Colonel John R. Boyd, USAF, noted, when this situation persists, the result is increased levels of uncertainty, confusion, disorder, panic, and chaos leading to shattered cohesion, paralysis, and collapse. What this means for the Coalition is that we cannot keep fighting the insurgents' war by their rules indefinitely.

The American military focus is on things, not people or ideas, but we are a learning organization. Boyd continually emphasized that "People fight wars, not machines."[28] The question is, can US military forces "win" this peace in isolation without inter-agency support? Without the Administration? Without incorporation of our allies and friends?[29] One could sardonically suggest that this is exactly what our US Department of Defense has been forced into doing to date. Just recently, however, there has been an effort by the Administration to coordinate the affairs of different agencies in Iraq and elsewhere. The National Security Council published a pamphlet describing a "National Strategy for Victory in Iraq" and the President recently signed National Security Presidential Directive 15 to better coordinate the efforts of all agencies within Government.[30]

These actions are timely and necessary. They reflect the frustrations of the Administration with the progress of establishing peace and security in Iraq. In effect, it is an admission that things are not going so well, and we have to do better. Brigadier General Robert L. Caslen, the Pentagon's deputy director for the war on terrorism said on March 2, 2006, "Thirty new terrorist organizations have emerged since the September 11, 2001 attacks, outpacing US efforts to crush the threat."[31] Appearing before the Senate Armed Services Committee at its annual hearing on national security threats, the former Director of National Intelligence, John D. Negroponte, said in relation to Afghanistan, "The volume and geographic scope of attacks increased last year."[32] He also said that the Taliban had not been able to stop the democratic processes started in that country.

So what can be done?

Perhaps the American people will tire of this war and force a withdrawal before we can do anything significant, and there are signs that this may happen. If we are allowed to stay, we have to first recognize that the way to combat 4GW is with a large "D" for diplomacy, a large "I" for information operations, a small "m" for military efforts (meaning that military actions in stability, support, transition, and reconstruction operations have to be in support of the other more important political informational and economic efforts), and a large "E" for economic support: DImE. The base fact is, however, that perhaps the only institution capable of doing many of the things required of stability and support operations is the US Department of Defense. The other US Government agencies are simply not equipped or resourced to be able to handle the magnitude of such efforts, as Hurricane Katrina proved. What is missing is the leadership for these holistic efforts from the other agencies along with the coordination of an effective command and control system that will allow them to work in such environments along with Coalition partners and host nation governments.

We need good intelligence – most particularly HUMINT – to combat the 4GW enemy. To gain that intelligence, we cannot move our intelligence people into and out of areas as combat forces move. We need to establish regional information fusion centers with staying power. The composition of these fusion centers would be similar to Provisional Reconstruction Teams but very long standing and with a focus on information operations. The centers would include military and civilian staff with allied and host nation participation. These centers would be the beginning of good HUMINT for combat forces moving into or out of the area.

We need to trust our allies, including our hosts, and share intelligence routinely. Strong working relationships with allies are important in many ways. At the tactical level, alliances provide overflight rights and access to bases for refueling and maintenance. At the strategic level, allies can pool their strengths. This becomes especially important in intelligence, where countries like France and the UK often have better sources in their former colonies than does the United States. Perhaps most important, strong support from allies can help buttress moral strength, which Boyd defined as the "mental capacity to overcome menace, uncertainty, and mistrust," Under such circumstances, which are common when fighting an elusive insurgency, the support of allies can be critical in sustaining strong domestic support. To do this, we need to break up the stovepipes of the American intelligence community and share what can be shared with our friends. This would truly be a revolution in American governmental affairs.

We need to build an Iraqi Army and security force that is capable of fighting a fourth generation war, not a conventional war. For that, our US conventional forces are not the best trainers. Special Forces may be our best hope, but they are too few and far between. To augment them, we need a professional advisory corps. This advisory corps would be comprised of officers and non-commissioned officers who are trained in advising, training, and the language. The foundation of this advisory corps might be the Foreign Area Officer Program. The Military Training Teams (MITT) now being fielded are a response to this need.[33]

We need to train Iraqis to take over the fusion centers as well as the security force role. We also need trainers who are non-military for the para-military and non-military roles. So who trains them? This is a State Department role, and the Secretary of State published a document that calls for "Transformational Diplomacy" within the Department of State to adjust to the needs of combating what we are calling fourth generation warfare.[34]

To get ahead of enemy OODA Loops, we need a much smaller footprint. Otherwise insurgent forces will always be able to strike and regroup before our ponderous bureaucratic staffs can respond. So the very first requirement is to reduce the large headquarters. Cut the fat, not the meat. Reorganize staffs to provide thinkers. Choose and promote leaders who understand 4GW. Integrate our military with other interagency operators and multinationals. Educate our conventional army. Provide lateral entry into the military of cultural anthropologists and linguists. We must promote Information. We must get military intelligence specialists into the tactical units and have them accompany patrols. We need to live in the villages.

Information Operations have to be re-looked. It is too tech-centric and not sufficiently net-centric. It is not at all "people-centric." We need to invest in the understanding of this extremely important tool in winning the peace in stability and support operations. If we are ever to get ahead of the Islamist OODA Loops, we first have to learn about how to use information better. We also have to establish a firm policy to tell the truth, no matter how it may hurt. This is the essence of the moral high ground in the Information War. We need to consolidate the many different information venues into one information program, to include the highly independent military public relations sophists who may be doing more harm than good. We need information officers at every level of staff leading efforts to provide the "soft" bullets that may be more effective than actual combat operations. Most important, we should have information officers leading the long-term Provincial Reconstruction Teams by whatever name.

The military needs to re-examine the strategy for force employment in Iraq that exposes the troops to urban warfare at very close quarters while allowing insurgents and military supplies to flow freely into the country. The New Iraqi Army with American military advisory teams is best suited for operations within the cities. Best use of American forces and capabilities would be in surveillance of the borders and control of the lines of communication to include the Euphrates River.

We need to educate our military in "how to think," not "what to think," in order to provide for stability, support, transition, and reconstruction operations as well as military operations, and above all we must practise holistic approaches to combating 4GW. There is evidence that some of the military schools are doing better at this, but this pertains to only a few of the many educational systems. Our military educators need to learn 4GW from their students, and they can begin by hosting seminars where learning is shared, not preached from a platform. We need to revisit the mono-theistic theories of Clausewitz at the expense of all others. This may be one of our greatest weaknesses. Education is where it starts, and it may take years to change the fixed and doctrine driven thinking of the past. Cultural awareness ought to be one of the core subjects in every curriculum, especially in pre-commissioning programs. Only through combinations of these educational approaches can we begin to get inside the enemy OODA Loops.

It took General George Crook eight years to defeat the Chiricahuas; it took much longer for pacification of the Moros in the Philippines in the early 1900s, and even longer for the stabilization of Germany and Japan after World War II. How long will it take to allow a semblance of peace and security in Iraq? How long to inculcate the values associated with a democracy? Whatever the number is, it is a long time, and perhaps longer than the American public will allow.

Perhaps the biggest lesson yet to be learned is that 4GW is a company commander's war and it has to include all the resources of multi-nationals, interagency, and even non-governmental agencies combined at the very lowest level in a holistic approach. There are going to be no "Pattons" emerging from this type of war, and the generals have yet to understand that. We need to do a lot more thinking about how to combat 4GW and learn how to get ahead of the extremists' OODA Loops before we will come anywhere close to achieving our stated goals. The Clausewitzian objective of *defeating the enemy* has to be replaced by a focus on people, i.e., *separating the population base from the insurgents* worldwide. In stability operations or whatever we choose to call such operations, the focus must be on the population. We must deal with the 4GW enemy, but it is unlikely we will be able to change any of their minds; so we should concentrate on those we can. We have to emphasize the information war first.

These recommendations are provided with the knowledge that there have already been changes and there will continue to be changes in the approaches of the US and our Coalition allies to the problems of Iraq. Let us all hope for a Coalition breakthrough and a successful conclusion to this critical war for the Iraqis if not for ourselves in the near future.

The Islamists have proved one thing, however. There are no more superpowers.

Notes

1 See the US Department of Defense "Quadrennial Defense Review Report," Washington, D.C. February 6, 2006. The "QDR" lays out the case for global counter-terrorism operations in a long war.

2 Thomas P. Barnett, *The Pentagon's New Map: War and Peace in the Twenty-First Century*, New York: G.P. Putnam Sons, 2004, p. 290.

3 Readers interested in knowing more about 4GW are encouraged to visit www.d-n-i.net. The original 1989 article on 4GW in the *Marine Corps Gazette* by Lind, *et al.*, is posted to the site.

4 "General Anthony C. Zinni Interview: Conversations with History; Institute of International Studies, UC Berkeley," Harry Kriesler, Interviewer, March 6, 2001, "The Military's Role in a Changing World," globetrotter.berkeley.edu/conversations/Zinni/zinni-con4.html. Note that General Zinni has not identified himself as a 4GW theorist.

5 Remarks by the general were covered by a non-attribution policy at the Information Operations Workshop, Army War College, November 30, 2005.

6 Cf., Colonel G.I. Wilson, USMCR, Major Frank Bunkers, USMCR, and Sergeant John P. Sullivan, Los Angeles Police Department, "The Next Conflict," *Intum Magazine* (Summer 2001) and reposted on www.d-n-i.net.

7 Martin van Creveld, *The Transformation of War*, New York: The Free Press, 1991, p. 197.

8 A point made forcefully by Thomas P.M. Barnett in *Blueprint for Action*, New York: Putnam, 2005, particularly around p. 17ff.

9 Patrick J. McDonnell, "U.S. Apparently Underestimated Size of Insurgency, Top Commander Says," *Los Angeles Times*, January 27, 2005. Tony Capaccio, quoting from former DIA head, Admiral Lowell Jacoby at a Congressional Hearing indicated that the number might be in the 15,000 to 20,000 range. "Iraqi Insurgency May Include 20,000 People, U.S. Official Says," Bloomberg.com, March 17, 2005. At a hearing before Congress, Secretary of Defense Rumsfeld said the numbers were considerably lower than the estimated 40,000 insurgents and 200,000 supporters cited in one intelligence report, but he refused to provide the numbers citing classification of the information. Dana Priest and Josh White, "War Helps Recruit Terrorists, Hill Told," *The Washington Post*, February 17, 2005, p. 1.

10 A recent public opinion poll shows the Iraqis believe the Americans have no intention of ever leaving Iraq. www.worldpublicopinion.org/pipa/pdf/jan06/Iraq_Jan06_rpt.pdf.

11 Robert Dreyfus, "What 'Staying the Course' Really Means," *Asia Times Online*, (www.atimes.com), December 1, 2005.

12 Sharon Behn, "Hezbollah, Hamas Offices Reported in Iraq", *Washington Times*, www.washingtontimes.com/world/20040330–094233-2002r.htm.

13 Ibid.

14 A process that may already have started. See, John Ward Anderson, "Iraqi Tribes Strike Back at Insurgents," *Washington Post*, March 7, 2006, p. 12.

15 Cf., Brian Bender, "Economists Say Cost of War Could Top $2 Trillion," *Boston*

Globe, boston.com, January 8, 2006, www.boston.com/news/world/middleeast/articles/2006/01/08/economists_say_cost_of_war_could_top_2_trillion?mode=PF.

16 Brigadier Nigel Aylwin-Foster, British Army, "Changing the Army for Counterinsurgency Operations," *Military Review*, November–December 2005, p. 8.

17 US Government, Office of the Under Secretary of Defense for Acquisition, Technology, and Logistics, "Report of the Defense Science Board Task Force on Strategic Communication", Washington, D.C., September 2004. See also Greg Wilcox, "The Information Arrow," for a more robust discussion of the absence of an information component in the US arsenal. www.d-n-i.net.

18 Donald H. Rumsfeld, "War in the Information Age: In a 24/7 World, the U.S. Isn't Keeping Up with Its Enemies in the Communications Battle," *Los Angeles Times*, February 23, 2006.

19 Ibid.

20 Robert David Steele, "Information Operations: Putting the 'I' Back into DIME," US Army War College Strategic Studies Institute: Carlisle Barracks, PA, February 2006. www.strategicstudiesinstitute.army.mil/.

21 During a debate with then Vice President Al Gore on October 11, 2000, in Winston-Salem, N.C., Bush said: "I don't think our troops ought to be used for what's called nation-building... . I think what we need to do is convince people who live in the lands they live in to build the nations. Maybe I'm missing something here. I mean, we're going to have a kind of nation-building corps from America? Absolutely not." Wayne Washington, "Once Against Nation Building, Bush Now Involved," *Boston Globe*, March 2, 2004.

22 Note that in November 2005, the US Government (National Security Council) published a National Security Strategy for "Victory in Iraq." It is a well written and comprehensive document that if followed would eventually yield some positive results – in the perceptions of the authors of this article. Also see the National Military Strategy at: www.defenselink.mil/qdr/docs/2005-01-25-Strategic-Plan.pdf.

23 See Major "Ike" Wilson's paper: "Thinking Beyond War: Civil Military Operations Planning in Northern Iraq," paper delivered at the 2004 American Political Science Association (APSA) Annual Conference, September 3, 2004, Chicago, Ill. Accessed [On-Line] at www.einaudi.cornell.edu/PeaceProgram/calendar/index.asp?id=3989. See his forthcoming book: *Thinking Beyond War: Why America Fails to Win the Peace*, Naval Institute Press, June 2006.

24 US Department of State, Office of the Spokesman, "Fact Sheet: Transformational Diplomacy," January 18, 2006: 2006/54. Also see: Steven Komarow, "Iraq Reconstruction Plan Draws Criticism Following Delays: State Dept. Says Initiative Is Moving Forward," *USA Today*, March 7, 2006.

25 See for example, US Government, Office of the Under Secretary of Defense for Acquisition, Technology, and Logistics, "Report of the Defense Science Board Task Force on Strategic Communication," Washington, D.C., September 2004.

26 Cf., Michael Schuer, "How Bush Helps Jihaadists," *Washington Times*, March 13, 2006.

27 Colonel John Boyd, USAF, created the concept of the OODA Loop, and more information on Boyd and on the OODA Loop can be found at www.d-n-i.net.

28 See Chester W. Richards, *A Swift Elusive Sword: What if Sun Tzu and John Boyd Did a National Defense Review?*, Washington, D.C.: Center for Defense Information, 2001, pp. 36–37.

29 Note that in November 2005, the US Government (National Security Council) published a National Security Strategy for "Victory in Iraq." It is a well written and comprehensive document that if followed would eventually yield some positive results – in the perceptions of the authors of this article.

30 National Security Council, "National Strategy for Victory in Iraq," Washington: November 2005; Jason Sherman, "President Issues 'War on Terror' Directive to Improve Government Coordination," *Inside Defense*, March 8, 2006.

31 Sharon Behn, "Terrorist Growth Overtakes U.S. Efforts: Pentagon Deputy Warns of Decades-Long War," *Washington Times*, March 2, 2006, p. 13.

32 Walter Pincus, "Growing Threat Seen in Afghan Insurgency: DIA Chief Cites Surging Violence in Homeland," *Washington Post*, March 1, 2006; A08.

33 Gina Cavallaro, "Small Teams, Big Job: Military Transition Teams Will Assume a Pivotal Role in Iraq's Future – and U.S. Deployments," and "MITT Duty a Career-Booster for Soldiers Who Make Team," *Army Times*, February 6, 2006, pp. 8, 10.

34 See US Department of State Fact Sheet: "Transformational Diplomacy," January 18, 2006.

16 Fourth Generation Warfare in Afghanistan

Warren Chin

The aim of this chapter is to consider how far and to what extent the ongoing conflict in Afghanistan conforms to the paradigm of Fourth Generation Warfare (4GW). As such, it compares the ideal with the real in terms of the nature and conduct of fighting within the borders of this failed state and the extent to which it fits the new paradigm of 4GW. To this end the chapter examines 4GW in Afghanistan through the military prism of the levels of war to determine its most salient characteristics. Finally, the chapter looks at why the rag-tag forces thrown up by this conflict environment are causing so many problems for the international military coalition deployed to promote security and stability to Afghanistan.

The grand strategic context

A particular strength of 4GW is that it is not locked into a myopic technically driven vision of war which seeks to provide a 'silver bullet' in the conduct of operations. Rather it looks at the broader canvas or background in which wars are fought. Thus, as one analyst explained, it is not the revolution in military affairs, but the revolution in security affairs that is of most importance in the study of war. The most important drivers in shaping the nature and conduct of war are political, economic and social transformations rather than changes in technology, as the military tend to assume. Understanding this fact ensures that strategy has a basis in the real world and that challenges and obstacles to the use of force are addressed. 4GW is a concept that tries to encapsulate such change and one of its principal strengths is that it recognizes how developments in these other areas are impacting on the development of war.[1] The most obvious manifestation of such change can be seen in the increased incidence of state failure and collapse, which has created a fertile environment in which 4GW has flourished. While there is little doubt that one of the challenges that has confronted the international community in the post Cold War era has been the phenomenon of failed states, the actual scale of the problem is hard to quantify and estimates vary from between twenty to over sixty states currently which have collapsed or are about to.[2] In essence, while it is premature to speak of the end of the Westphalian system, it is under some stress and this is creating a complex strategic, operational and tactical context in which military power is exercised.

Afghanistan shows the hallmarks of being a failed state.[3] The state has been wrecked by nearly three decades of constant war between a variety of internal groups, and even trans-national actors like al Qaeda, the drug producers and organized crime have become embroiled in this conflict. However, it is important to note that a specific set of circumstances precipitated this collapse, which makes it difficult to extrapolate too much in terms of promulgating a general theory. In the case of Afghanistan the catalyst for this misery first began with the Soviet invasion in 1979. Although it is fair to say that the state was in crisis before this event, Soviet intervention resulted in the implementation of a radical reform programme that destroyed the existing political order and its ruling elite. The party and the system of government imposed were entirely alien to the country. Most of the ruling elite in the form of the Kahns were co-opted or destroyed by the communists. Land reform and the air war policy of 'rubbleiza-tion' eliminated the traditional sources of the Kahns' power and their failure to protect their supporters from the government eroded their authority. Over half the 24,000 villages in Afghanistan were destroyed as a result of the Soviet's 'rubbleization' strategy, adopted between 1980–1986 and intended to drive the population out of the rural areas and the control of the Mujahideen. Some 40 per cent of the population were made refugees and ten million anti-personnel mines were scattered throughout the country.[4] It is estimated that the Soviets killed 1.3 million Afghans over a decade of civil war.[5]

Afghanistan was also a society that became increasingly tolerant of violence. A process that the Pakistani press referred to as the 'Kalashnikovization' began to take place in the mid 1980s. This referred to the decline in law and order and the proliferation of small arms; in part caused by American arms transfers to the region. The result of this process was the emergence of petty warlords who extorted money from the local population, raped and pillaged. More and more of the country degenerated into chaos and it was in an attempt to deal with this problem that the Taliban came to the fore in the 1990s. However, this cult of violence exacerbated ethnic tensions, which reinforced the fragmentation of the nation state.[6]

Soviet withdrawal from Afghanistan in 1988 did not result in peace, stability or the emergence of a new national government. Instead the communist govern-ment remained in power until the Mujahideen captured Kabul in 1992. During that time the conflict mutated into a new civil war, one based on ethnicity rather than religion and ideology. This happened because, in contrast to the past, there was no single group capable of imposing its will on the other ethnic groups in Afghanistan. The traditionally dominant Pashtuns were at their weakest in 1992. They were the great majority of the 5–6 million refugees outside Afghanistan and, as a result, the Tajiks were probably the majority in the country at that time. The war also empowered new groups. The Uzbeks benefited from heavy Soviet investment in the development of non-Pashtun northern Afghanistan. The Hazaras who had been conquered and enslaved a century earlier, had their own militia and external support from Iran. A battle now emerged between Pashtuns and non-Pashtuns.[7] The emerging ethnic conflict undermined the UN's efforts to establish a new interim government between 1988–1992 and provided the political fuel that continues to feed conflict in the country to this day.

According to Saikal, the rise of the Taliban reinforced the ethnic power struggle between Pashtuns and non-Pashtuns, which made it almost impossible to unite the country around an acceptable religious or political ideology. The latter were forced to defend their heartlands from the Taliban, especially the Tajiks who were ethnically cleansed from the areas surrounding Kabul.[8] There is little doubt that in their efforts to secure control over the country the Taliban's actions also helped to exacerbate ethnic tensions within Afghanistan. For example, it is claimed that during their 1998 offensive against Mazari Sharif, the Taliban killed over 8,000 detainees from other ethnic groups. There were also concerns that the Taliban were contemplating the genocide of the Hazari Sh'ias.[9]

Rubin points out that inter ethnic conflict in Afghanistan was exacerbated by the international system's definition of states as political communities with fixed borders. Afghanistan's current borders derive from the political requirements of Britain and Russia at the end of the nineteenth century, defined in relation to the balance of power that existed at that time. The breakdown of the state and the arming of virtually the entire population of Afghanistan led to a distribution of power radically different from that which prevailed when the borders were first drawn. Before the advent of the contemporary state system, the Uzbek, Pashtun, Tajik and Hazara military leaders might have established Khanates in their own territories. The international recognition of Afghanistan condemns these groups to fight for Kabul.[10]

It is important to note that this spiral of fragmentation was exacerbated by the collapse of the Soviet Union, which resulted in the emergence of new states in Central Asia. Thus, state failure in Afghanistan was not simply the product of internal forces. 'On the contrary, failed states are states whose history leaves them vulnerable to shifts in the international power configuration.'[11] Of particular importance was the independence of former Soviet states like Kazakhstan, Uzbekistan and Tajikistan in Central Asia. These countries have significant ethnic groups living within Afghanistan's current borders and this magnified the problems of ethnicity within the country. New economic opportunities in the form of trade and the oil pipeline also drew other established regional powers like Pakistan and Iran more firmly into Afghanistan's internal affairs.[12]

Inter-ethnic conflict produced keen competition for control of the central government, especially between the Pashtuns and the Tajiks. Not only does such a prize provide access to scarce resources, equally important, it becomes possible to attack an opposing ethnic group under the veneer of legitimacy of the state. Thus, for example, in April 2005 the Tajik dominated government in Kabul used the hunt to stop poppy production to attack the farmlands of its Pashtun opponents which supported the Taliban in Maiwand province.[13] The human cost of endless civil war has been enormous. Although it is difficult to find accurate statistics it is estimated that between 600,000 and 1.2 million people were killed in fighting in the twelve years after the Soviet withdrawal.

Moreover, some five years after the fall of the Taliban, there are still over six million Afghan refugees living primarily in Pakistan and Iran.[14]

Since 2001 the international community has made an effort to eradicate the conditions that cause 4GW and establish a secure, stable and democratic state. However, in spite of the creation of a democratically elected government, which appears to be gaining the upper hand against key warlords, the Karzai Government exerts little real control over the country or its population. Equally important, in spite of the investment made to improve the internal security situation by increasing the size of the American contingent deployed to Afghanistan to 20,000 troops, the deployment of NATO, which began in 2003, and the creation and training of the Afghan National Army and an indigenous police force, the government so far has not established security for its people.

The strategic context

In the case of Afghanistan, it is difficult to generalize about strategy because of the sheer range of groups involved and because economic as much as political motivation appears to drive various conceptions of strategy. Although the political and economic domains of conflict may not neutralize each other, the dominance of the latter can cause distortions in the conduct of the war that reinforce the perception that such conflicts are entirely irrational, when, in fact, quite the opposite is the case. As Keen points out, warlords and drug producers probably cannot see the rationality of using war to achieve a better peace when they profit so much from war.[15] Equally important, ethnic tensions have also created a new grammar of war that is very different from our traditional understanding of how violence is used to achieve political ends.[16]

Although there are a myriad of warring groups in Afghanistan, each with its own political agenda, these elements can be combined into two broad coalitions based on a common political objective or strategic end state. In essence, there are those factions that support the international community's efforts to reconstruct the Afghan nation state and then there are those groups that oppose this process. To this end one of the principal objectives of the anti government faction has been to sabotage and destroy the construction of the state and more important its security apparatus.

According to Seth Jones, the Taliban and Gulbaddin Hekmatyr's Hezb-i-Islami are the primary indigenous resistance groups behind the anti government campaign. In the case of the Taliban, their specific aim is to re-install the theocracy they attempted to impose between 1996 and 2001. In contrast, Hekmatyr's ambition is focused on his own personal aggrandizement.[17] It seems that, in general, these factions are using a classic insurgent strategy to achieve their aims. As Jones explains, there is a civilian support network, i.e. a safe base, which provides logistical and medical support, and a source for recruitment. Equally important is the generation of intelligence on the activities of government and international forces operating in the local area. On top of this is an underground network or infrastructure which fulfils the functions of a shadow government. This seeks to undermine the existing government and generate a financial base for operations. Most frequently, this means becoming involved in the drug trade. Although Taliban participation in this activity contradicts their edicts issued in 2000 to destroy all poppy production, their willingness to help protect local farmers' opium crop has created a modicum of support for their actions in the region or at least a general tolerance for their presence. To the farmer, opium provides about ten times as much income as any alternative crop. Consequently, the Karzai government's policy of destroying poppy cultivation is not a popular measure.[18] Finally, there are the guerrilla fighters, who are organized into small tactical units that can hide easily among the population when necessary.[19]

An additional complication is the presence of foreign jihadists, most of whom are associated with al Qaeda. Most foreign volunteers are from Pakistan, Uzbekistan and Tajikistan. However, there are also representatives from Yemen, Chechnya, Somalia, Saudi Arabia and even Iraq. Again this force is organized in small units and they have significant freedom in the conduct of their day-to-day operations, but they do follow strategic direction which is provided by higher level commanders. Their aims differ fundamentally from those of the Taliban and Hezb-i-Islami in that their focus is not merely the defeat of the Afghan government, but more importantly, they see this local conflict as being part of the wider war against the United States and the 'West'.[20] An important distinction between this force and its indigenous counterparts is that its members are fulltime professional fighters and they are generally better trained and equipped than the local insurgent groups. According to Jones they play a key role as trainers, shock troops and surrogate leaders.[21]

The adoption of an insurgent strategy allows the Taliban and its allies to exploit the key weaknesses of the coalition deployed against it while maximising its own strengths. A good illustration of this can be seen from the asymmetry of interest that exists between the belligerents. This is not a war of national survival for the international coalition that has deployed to Afghanistan. As such, the more powerful actors involved are not prepared to pay an exorbitant cost to achieve their aims. The key to success, then, for the weaker opponent or insurgent is to bring about an escalation in the cost of the conflict by inflicting a constant stream of casualties against the forces or populations of the major powers involved. Equally important, is the need to create a sense of endlessness in terms of the time and effort that will be needed to achieve the goal of establishing a functional nation state so that even the hypothetical opportunity cost of this policy appears to be too high.

The deployment of NATO forces to Afghanistan offers a fertile opportunity for the Taliban and their cohorts to use this strategy to exploit the variables of time and cost and use the numerous networks available to them to persuade national governments to conduct a reassessment of their policies. The original mission given to the British Army was to work with the Foreign and Commonwealth Office and Department of International Development to create small security zones in which hearts and minds projects could be established. In April

2006, John Reid made his now famous declaration that British forces might leave after three years without having fired a shot. This optimism revealed how poor the intelligence picture was of the Taliban or their intentions.[22]

It is interesting that, although there was a resurgence of insurgent activity in the southern provinces of Afghanistan, the British Government did not believe that this represented a strategic threat to Afghanistan.[23] Estimates of Taliban strength in the south of the country were put at approximately 1,000 insurgents with only a very small al Qaeda representation.[24] However, between September 2005 and March 2006, 1,200 Afghan people and 900 police officers were killed by insurgent action.[25] Moreover, according to Paul Rogers, the Taliban are well resourced via the drug trade and have access to over 40,000 fighters based across the border in Pakistan.[26] If this is true then, contrary to the view of the British Government, the Taliban could be a significant threat to the Afghan government.

Moreover, the unexpected resistance from the Taliban in Helmand province has caused a reassessment in British political and media circles and questions are now being asked about why Britain's armed forces are there and what they hope to achieve. As one newspaper journalist put it: 'The debacle of Britain-in-Afghanistan cannot be ignored, because British troops are at risk. They were never meant to be at risk and their presence in that country has nothing to do with British security.'[27] In essence, while not seeking to destroy the British Army in a conventional battle the Taliban's actions have created doubts about the feasibility and cost of this operation among the people of Britain.

The insurgents' strategy is not solely concerned with causing Coalition forces to suffer a constant but steady stream of casualties. Groups such as the Taliban are also making a conscious effort to attack those elements of the Government and Coalition's strategy that are designed to win the hearts and minds of the people. Evidence of this can be seen from the increase in the number of insurgent attacks against aid and charity groups that are working with the Coalition's provincial reconstruction teams (PRTs) to improve the lot of the people. In 2003 only twelve staff belonging to non-governmental organizations were killed as a result of insurgent action, but this increased to thirty in 2004.[28] They have also made a concerted effort to destroy government efforts to provide basic education to all Afghan children, both boys and girls. Over the past year the Taliban burned down over 144 schools and forced another 200 to close following threats against teachers and students. This course of action was justified on the grounds that educating girls is against Islam and their opposition to boys being taught secular subjects.[29] The Taliban are also attempting to kill as many government officials as possible. Included in such attacks are family members of key politicians and bureaucrats and even religious leaders who are known to be strong supporters of the government.[30] The combined effect of such action serves to weaken the authority and legitimacy of the government and reinforces the impression that only the Taliban can guarantee the security of the people.

A variety of measures have also been employed to secure control over the population. While some of these actions are positive in nature, for example, the practical support provided for poppy farming, other measures are designed to intimidate and terrorize the people. A recent example of such behavior concerned the execution of a mother and son by the Taliban, accused of spying for the Coalition in southern Afghanistan. Local people were also being coerced into providing one of their sons to fight for the Taliban to ensure the loyalty of families and villages in the south.[31]

The operational and tactical context

In 2001 the Taliban possessed a significant military capability, but their tactics and operations were deeply flawed. The Taliban military machine consisted of a 'hardcore' of between 2,000 and 3,000 personnel, a further 8,000 supporters who joined after 1995 and between 8,000 and 12,000 foreign volunteers. In addition, support from other warlords and different tribal groups provided a further 25,000 soldiers, but the loyalty of this last group was suspect.[32] So on paper at least they were not going to be an easy nut to crack. Yet their defeat was short, sharp and decisive. Although this success was attributed to American military prowess the truth is that the Taliban made critical tactical and operational mistakes that played to the strengths of the US military.[33]

For example, they allowed their forces to be caught in open ground where air power was used to good effect. Had they remained in the towns and cities they might have been able to negate the effect of air power, cause the US to inflict innocent civilian casualties and, more importantly, inflict casualties on US forces.[34] However, once the air campaign shifted its focus away from targeting the enemy's infrastructure to bombing its forces in the front line, the rate of attrition resulted in the exhaustion of the Taliban's military hard core and the Northern Alliance was able to take advantage of the Taliban's weakened state.

A puzzling aspect of the Taliban's military strategy was that they did not seek to counter America's high-tech blitzkrieg with their own variant of protracted guerrilla war. The prevailing view appears to be that this was not a viable option open to the Taliban because their political incompetence and religious dogmatism alienated the majority of the people. Thus, the rapid collapse of their position throughout the country was caused by their inability to create a viable society or state apparatus through which to govern or develop policies that were likely to win the hearts and minds of most Afghan people. According to Goodson, the Taliban were first and foremost a military rather than a political movement. The senior members of its government divided their time between fighting the war and trying to run the country. They had no policy for reconstruction, education, public services, etc. Kabul and Herat were without electricity for several years and water throughout the country was unsafe to drink.[35]

In contrast the current campaign being conducted by the Taliban appears to demonstrate that they have learned from their mistakes and are now pursuing a more effective strategy that aims to dislocate the reconstruction of the Afghan state. Evidence of this strategy being implemented can be seen from the conduct of recent insurgent actions. It is clear that the insurgents have done their best to stop the government from establishing control over the south of the country. In addition they have sought to inflict casualties on western forces in the hope of forcing their withdrawal.

Currently the level of violence in Afghanistan is at its highest since the collapse of the Taliban. It is estimated that deaths from militant-related violence was in excess of 1,600 killed in 2005 and there has been an increase in the number of kidnappings and roadside suicide attacks. There have already been more suicide attacks in 2006 than in the previous two years combined.[36] Most important is the fact that the attackers are making a conscious effort to target the newly created local security forces. Six hundred Afghan police died between October 2004 and May 2005.[37] The key problem is that the government has been unable to close down the numerous armed groups operating in Afghanistan. Hence 4GW continues to thrive. In April 2006, it was estimated that some 2,000 armed groups were operating within Afghanistan, most of them tribe, clan and family militias.[38] These groups vary in terms of their motivation, tactics and strategy.[39]

Apparently the Taliban have steadily regained their military strength over the last five years and, according to Ahmad Jalali, now have training camps, staging areas and recruiting centers in the form of madrasses in Pakistan.[40] For reasons that are not entirely clear, while the Pakistani Army has been relatively effective in dealing with al Qaeda operating within its borders, it has not dealt with the Taliban and there is a suspicion that the Pakistani military and intelligence services are unwilling to act against a movement they helped to create and bring to power in 1996.[41] As a result, the Taliban have a safe haven in Pakistan and cross the border in groups of up to several hundred insurgents to carry out attacks against the Afghan government and the security forces. Less certain is the success of the Taliban in winning the support of the local population in Afghanistan and it has been suggested that they have been buying support to fight for their cause. Apparently, Taliban soldiers are paid three times as much as soldiers in the Afghan national army. It is estimated that Taliban forces have risen from 2,000 to 6,000 in 2006.[42]

Most interesting has been the recent employment of suicide bombers, a tactic not normally associated with the Afghan way of war.[43] In a recent interview a leading member of the Taliban warned that his organization had recruited 600 suicide bombers to attack the British 16th Air Assault Brigade which was about to be deployed to Helmand province.[44] This threat proved to be a very real danger, in the first week alone the brigade's base was attacked by two suicide bombers. Paradoxically, the effectiveness of Coalition conventional forces in combat might be one reason why the insurgents are relying on this new tactic to inflict casualties against the Coalition.[45] However, it is feared that the Taliban are learning lessons from the insurgency in Iraq and applying them to the war in Afghanistan.[46]

A recent report of the insurgency in Afghanistan warned that the Government was in danger of losing complete control of the three provinces of Helmand, Kandahar and Nangahar. This has been caused by three factors. First, it is important to note that the success of the Taliban in the south of the country is due just as much to the absence of a strong government presence as to improvements in its modus operandi. Equally important, government poppy eradication programmes and anti-terrorist operations have caused financial pain and alienated the local population.[47]

A more recent indication of the success of the Taliban was provided by the British Government's announcement in July 2006 that it would increase the size of its contingent in Helmand province from 3,600 to 4,500 troops. Although this decision was justified on the grounds that an opportunity had been created to accelerate the nation-building programme in the area, according to a senior British commander the decision was actually due to the unexpected tenacity of the Taliban and the rather poor performance of local Afghan security forces.[48] Before the British deployed to Helmand province, senior military officers did not perceive the Taliban to be a real threat. Even a former Taliban minister referred to the movement as a spent force. Subsequent engagements have shown that the Taliban are anything but a spent force, a fact demonstrated by the price they are prepared to pay to achieve their aims. Although only an estimate, it is believed that in recent engagements twenty Taliban are killed for every western soldier lost through combat.[49] British forces have commented on the tactical proficiency of Taliban forces, which has then led to speculation about the role played by the Pakistani army in training the Taliban.

The launch of the US-led operation Mountain Thrust, in June 2006, was designed to eradicate the Taliban and establish a secure environment in which reconstruction could begin in the southern most provinces, provides further evidence of an increasing sophistication on the part of the insurgents. Over 10,000 coalition troops were committed to an offensive against the five southernmost provinces to eradicate the Taliban and al Qaeda insurgents and establish a secure environment in which to begin nation building. Most interesting is the way in which Taliban forces have been able to elude combat or capture. In one attack in mid July, over 1,000 Coalition troops attacked what they thought was a Taliban stronghold that was defended by over 400 Taliban fighters. However, in spite of having first pounded the position with Apache helicopter gun ships, landed over 300 British paratroops by helicopter on the position to assault it, and then setting up a blocking position further down the Sangin valley with over 900 Canadian troops, all that was achieved was a short battle in which ten Taliban were killed. It is believed that the vast majority of the Taliban escaped.[50]

The response of the Taliban to operation Mountain Thrust was to flee from the four provinces where the offensive was concentrated to other parts of the country where there was little in the way of a meaningful security presence. The principal fear of the Afghan government was that guerrilla warfare would begin in these security black holes and indeed there were signs of the Taliban becoming more active in other parts of the country.[51]

The apparent lull in the Taliban's activities in southwestern Afghanistan was also believed to be part of a cunning plan. Apart from sporadic armed guerrilla attacks, a few suicide bombings and the detonation of improvised explosive devices all sustained missions have ceased. Apparently, this halt in offensive operations was made by the Taliban leadership in order to capitalize on the unrest in the Middle East caused by Israel's controversial operations against Hamas and Hezbollah. Their hope was that perceived injustices in the Middle East would have an invigorating effect on the Taliban's campaign against the US-led coalition and increase local support for their cause.[52]

Can 4GW insurgents win in Afghanistan?

Success for the Taliban will depend to a very large extent on the strategy adopted by the international coalition deployed in Afghanistan and the inter-action that results from these competing strategies. On paper, the international coalition has made significant progress in Afghanistan. The initial military campaign resulted in the swift removal of the Taliban from power and the political process set out in the 2001 Bonn agreement has been implemented. It was also recognized that the key to the long-term stability of the country required a sustained and heavy investment in its social and economic infrastructure. Evidence of this can be seen from the launch of the Afghanistan Compact in 2006 which provides the framework for the engagement of the international community in Afghanistan. Most important, the international community pledged $10.5 billion in aid over the next five years to the re-development of this failed state.

But a more detailed inspection of the reconstruction of Afghanistan reveals significant cracks in the implementation of this plan. A fundamental problem was the failure to seize the window of opportunity that emerged after the overthrow of the Taliban at the end of 2001. In economic terms the international community failed to provide sufficient aid to the fledgling Afghan state; only $5 billion over five years, less than allocated to Yugoslavia or East Timor. More important was the stall in the campaign caused because of the need to remove key capabilities from Afghanistan to support the invasion of Iraq in 2003, with at least 50 per cent of key assets shipped out into Iraq. The commando team charged with finding Osama bin Laden and other al Qaeda leaders was reduced to a third of its initial size. On the intelligence side the CIA postponed an $80 million plan to set up a new Afghan intelligence service and moved the Islamabad office to Washington to work on Iraqi issues. In essence, the insurgents were given the time and space to recover from their defeat in 2001 and have made good use of this time to expand and consolidate their control of the southern third of the country.[53]

A further weakness in the international community's strategy is that its coherency is undermined by conflicting objectives. Until recently there were two military missions in operation in Afghanistan: the anti terrorist campaign focused on defeating al Qaeda in Afghanistan led by the US military, and the establishing security for the wider population, the primary responsibility of the International Security Assistance Force (ISAF). Although these objectives are not mutually exclusive, there was a degree of friction caused by a military campaign in the south which alienated much of the local Pashtun population, while at the same time the Afghan Government was trying to win the support of these groups and include them in any final political settlement.

There is even conflict and confusion over how to promote the goal of security. This problem is most apparent in the context of what to do about poppy cultivation in the country and there are reports of friction between the United States and Britain and the Afghan government over the pace and extent of the eradication programme being implemented. The US position focused simply on the destruction of poppy cultivation through a variety of different means. In contrast the approach being pursued by the British and Karzai government is to ensure that alternative livelihoods are available to farmers before implementing such policies and that this action is implemented by local Afghan forces.[54]

Insufficient effort was also made to invest in improving the general security situation of ordinary Afghans. When ISAF was first established in 2002, only 4,500 troops were allocated to this body, which meant that the new Afghan government was unable to extend its control beyond Kabul. It was estimated that at least 40,000 troops were required to establish control of the country, but such a contingent of troops was unavailable.[55] In the absence of such a force the Afghan Transitional Authority was forced to rely on local warlords to govern on its behalf, which exacerbated rather than alleviated many of the internal problems. The problem of finding a lead nation to take over ISAF resulted in NATO assuming control of ISAF in August 2003. By the end of 2005, however, ISAF's area of control amounted to only 50 per cent of the country and although it planned to establish a meaningful presence in the south by summer 2006 it is questionable whether a force of only 16,500 troops will be sufficient to generate a benign security environment throughout the country.[56] In essence, if the 20,000 US troops committed to rooting out and destroying al Qaeda had instead been committed to supporting the ISAF mission, then this would have removed a fundamental contradiction in the strategy which might have led to a very different security environment to the one that currently exists.

The current military campaign being waged in the south is also doing little to win the hearts and minds of the people. The vast majority of the Taliban killed in military operations since 2001 have died from air power rather than ground forces. However, using air power in this way produces other problems that could have an important strategic effect. Of particular importance here are civilian casualties. Approximately thirty Afghan civilians were killed by a US air strike in Kandahar in May 2006, an act that caused much anger among the local civilian population. There are also fears that a reliance on airpower will serve to evoke memories of the Soviet occupation and prompt an armed insurrection among the people.[57]

The problem is not just the use of air power. British forces actions to promote security and neutralize the Taliban have also had the unintended consequence of destroying the local infrastructure as they try to root out Taliban fighters who have hidden in schools, hospitals and other public buildings. This has led to a more general concern that too much stress is being placed on security at the expense of winning hearts and minds. Hamid Karzai, in a speech made in Tokyo in July 2006, condemned the current military strategy saying that they were going in circles. In his view operations were not addressing the root cause of the problem which he believed lay in Pakistan's support for the insurgency.[58]

Of critical importance to the long-term success of the coalition's strategy is the regeneration of Afghan Government forces. There has been significant progress in the training of the Afghan National Army. Currently, this force has approximately 24,000 trained soldiers and is expected to reach its goal of 70,000 personnel by 2010. More worrying is the development of the Afghan National Police Force. By the end of 2005 only 42,000 police officers were trained, 23,000 below the stated target. More important questions were being asked about the quality of this force. Corruption is rife and over 70 per cent of its personnel are illiterate. The state security forces are also part of the problem of rising violence in Afghanistan. Not only are the police and even the army dominated by the Tajiks, a problem that is now being addressed by Karzai, but the pay of the police is so low that commanders are forced to allow their officers to extort money from the Afghan population.[59] A related problem has been the meagre results disarming and demobilising the militias. Although some warlords have complied, this has usually only happened because of veiled threats by the Afghan Government and the US military.[60]

The problem of the warlords was compounded by fact that in the earliest stages of the occupation the US military also relied heavily on warlords to fight al Qaeda and the Taliban. Indeed, it has been argued that the whole venture to rebuild Afghanistan was morally compromised by the US Government's close association with the Northern Alliance, a group that was responsible for much of the devastation and suffering experienced in the country between 1992–1996.[61] In simple terms, too much energy was invested in fighting the war and not enough on reconstruction and pacification. The Afghan Government has also been contaminated by this problem with an estimated 40 per cent of elected representatives having connections with warlords and drug traffickers.[62]

Conclusion

Afghanistan displays many of the features associated with 4GW. However, it is also important to recognize that the experience of Afghanistan does not entirely fit the model of 4GW. The collapse of the Afghan state and its slide into civil war was an extremely complex process precipitated by the local conditions in Afghanistan itself. A more significant problem concerns the general fate of the state and its possible demise, a core assumption of 4GW. There is no doubt that failed and failing states are perceived to be a significant security threat. However, it is not clear that this process is likely to increase in frequency in the future. Moreover, it fails to consider efforts being made by the international community to rebuild failed states. If such a process is successful, what are the implications of this process for 4GW?

It is important to recognize that state failure is not a new concept and has happened frequently in the past without necessarily jeopardising the international system and or producing a new style of war. However, ironically, in spite of the best efforts of the international community to reconstruct states, the refusal to acknowledge the irrelevance of existing national boundaries in states like Afghanistan is simply setting such states up to fail once again, which means that this is likely to remain an enduring phenomenon.[63]

The military challenges posed by 4GW also require further thought. In the case of Afghanistan it is clear that the failure of conventional force was caused by a lack of political will, poor strategy and a lack of resources at critical points in the war. These issues are more than adequately addressed in the literature on insurgency and asymmetric warfare and this leads to the question: what new insights does 4GW offer in terms of developing an effective military strategy for dealing with this threat? In essence, does the construct deserve to exist?

Perhaps not surprisingly, the answer to this question is yes. A classic insurgent strategy such as that articulated by Mao's concept of protracted guerrilla warfare is based on a deterministic model in which the insurgent only wins if they can evolve from fighting guerrilla to conventional regular war; a process that entails preparation, guerrilla war and strategic conventional attack. However, as demonstrated during the Vietnam War, this transition is extremely difficult. Today, there are few insurgent organizations that can call on the almost limitless support provided by the Chinese and Russians to the North Vietnamese, so this dynamic breaks down. Moreover, technological, economic, political and social developments provide new opportunities for insurgents to fight and win without resorting to the creation of a massed conventional army; in essence, we can now by-pass the third phase of a classic insurgent strategy. The concept of 4GW and the example of Afghanistan demonstrates that insurgent groups recognize the new opportunities open to it and provides a clear warning of how such opponents will be able to use these new means to achieve their political ends.

Notes

1 Thomas X. Hammes, 'War Evolves into the Fourth Generation', this volume. See also, Thomas Hammes, *The Sling and the Stone: On War in the 21st Century* (St Paul, MN: Zenith Press, 2004), p. 207.

2 See Foreign Policy and the Fund for Peace, 'The Failed States Index', *Foreign Policy*, July/August 2005, pp. 56–65.

3 For a discussion on the causes of failed states and the problems of reconstruction see Jennifer Milliken (ed.), *State Failure Collapse and Reconstruction* (Oxford: Blackwell Publishing, 2004).

4 Larry Goodson, *Afghanistan's Endless War: State Failure, Regional Politics and the Rise of the Taliban* (Seattle, WA: University of Washington Press, 2001), p. 95.

5 Raymond Millen, *Afghanistan: Reconstituting a Collapsed State* (Carlisle, PA: Strategic Studies Institute US Army War College, April 2005), p. 1.

6 Goodson (note 7), p. 98.

7 Barnett Rubin, 'Post Cold War State Disintegration: The Failure of International Conflict Resolution in Afghanistan', *Journal of International Affairs*, Winter 1993, p. 486

8 Amin Saikal, 'Afghanistan's Ethnic Conflict', *Survival*, Vol. 40 no. 2, Summer 1998, p. 119.

9 Ibid.

10 Rubin (note 7), p. 492

11 Barnett Rubin, 'Women and Pipelines: Afghanistan's Proxy Wars', *International Affairs*, Vol. 72, no. 2, 1997, p. 284.

12 Ibid.

13 Ben Smith, *Afghanistan Where Are We?* Conflict Studies Research Centre, Central Asia Series 05/30, June 2005, p. 8.

14 Kinichi Komano, 'The Role of Elections in the Peacebuilding and Reconstruction of Afghanistan', *Asia Pacific*, Vol. 12, no. 1, 2005, p. 2.

15 See David Keen, *The Economic Functions of Violence in Civil Wars* (Oxford: Oxford University Press, Adelphi Paper, 1998).

16 See Mary Kaldor, *New and Old Wars: Organized Violence in Global Areas* (Cambridge: Polity Press, 1998).

17 Seth Jones, 'Averting Failure in Afghanistan', *Survival*, Vol. 48, no. 1, Spring 2006, p. 117.

18 'Opium, Corruption and the Taliban: The Deadly Alliance that our Troops have to Defeat', *Sunday Telegraph*, 23 April 2006.

19 Jones (note 17), pp. 116–117.

20 Paul Rogers, *Iraq and the War on Terror: Twelve Months of Insurgency 2004–2005* (London: I.B. Tauris, 2006), p. 43.

21 Jones (note 17), p. 117.

22 'Whitehall must give full backing to Afghan forces', *Daily Telegraph*, 11 July 2006.

23 House of Commons Defence Committee, 5th Report, *The UK Deployment to Afghanistan 2005–2006*, Hc 558 (London: HMSO, 2006), written evidence, p. 44.

24 Hansard, col. 2291W, 15 March 2006.

25 House of Commons Defence Committee (note 23), Q11.

26 Paul Rogers, 'Afghanistan's Endemic War', 25 May 2005, www.democracy. net/ articles Accessed 1 June 2006.

27 'A Bad Attack of Beau Geste Syndrome at Our Expense', *Guardian*, 5 July 2006.

28 'Aid Workers becoming "targets" in Afghanistan, Blair warned', *Daily Telegraph*, 22 January 2006, www.telegraph.co.uk/core/Content?displayPrintable.jhtml?xml=/news/ 2006/01/.

29 '4 US soldiers Killed in Afghanistan', *Washington Post*, 20 August 2006, www. washingtonpost.com/wp-dyn/content/article/2006/08/19/AR2006081900585_pf. html.

30 'Afghan Guerrillas Kill 32 with Ties to Legislator', *New York Times*, 20 June 2006.

31 'Taliban Kill a Woman and a Child Seen as Spies', *New York Times*, 10 August 2006.

32 C. Connetta, 'Strange Victory: A Critical Appraisal of Operation Enduring Freedom and the Afghanistan War', *Project Defense Alternatives*, 30 January 2002, p. 31.

33 Donald Rumsfeld, 'Transforming the Military', *Foreign Affairs*, Vol. 81, no. 3, May/June 2002, pp. 20–32.

34 'A Tougher Target: The Afghanistan Model of Warfare May Not Apply Very Well to Iraq', *Washington Post*, 26 December 2001.

35 Goodson (note 28), p. 121.

36 House of Commons Foreign Affairs Committee, *Foreign Policy Aspects of the War Against Terrorism*, HC 573, 2005–2006 (London: 2006), p. 132.

37 House of Commons Defence Committee, 5th Report, *The UK Deployment to Afghanistan 2005–2006*, HC 558 (London: HMSO, 2006), Memorandum from the British American Security Information Council, p. 37.

38 'Restoring Order to a Lawless Land', *Daily Telegraph*, 15 May 2006.

39 See John MacKinlay, *Globalisation and Insurgency* (Oxford: Oxford University Press, Adelphi Paper, 2002).

40 Ali Ahmad Jalali, 'The Future of Afghanistan', *Parameters*, Spring 2006, www.army.mil/professionalwriting/volumes/volume4/may_2006/5_06_3_pf.html.

41 See Ahmed Rashid, *The Taliban* (London: Pan Books, 2002).

42 'Taliban Goes for Cash Over Ideology', *Financial Times*, 26 July 2006.
43 Ali Ahmad Jalali (note 36).
44 'I have 600 Suicide Bombers Waiting for Your Soldiers', *Daily Telegraph*, 26 March 2006.
45 House of Commons Defence Committee (note 23), Q11.
46 Foreign Affairs Committee (note 32), p. 132.
47 The Senlis Council, *Field Notes: Insurgency in the Provinces of Helmand, Kandahar and Nangarhar* (London: April, 2006).
48 'Britain Sends Extra Troops to Afghanistan', *Guardian*, 11 July 2006 and '900 Troops Sent to Fight the Taliban', *Daily Telegraph*, 11 July 2006.
49 'Taliban Force Generals to Rethink Tactics', *Guardian Weekly*, www.guardian.co.uk/guardianweekly.
50 'British Troops Join Raid on Taliban Stronghold', *Guardian*, 17 July 2006.
51 'British Soldier Killed in Taliban Ambush', *Independent*, 6 July 2006.
52 'Taliban Pause for Fresh Breath', *Asia Times*, 19 July 2006.
53 Daniel Benjamin and Steven Simon, *The Next Attack: The Globalisation of Jihad* (London: Hodder and Stoughton, 2005), p. 177.
54 'Afghanistan Close to Anarchy, Warns General', *Guardian*, 22 June 2006.
55 Amin Saikal, 'Afghanistan After the Loya Jirga', *Survival*, Vol. 44, no. 3, Autumn 2002, p. 52.
56 NATO, 'NATO in Afghanistan', www.nato.int/issues/afghanistan/evolution.htm. Accessed on 23 May 2005.
57 'Apaches and Land Rovers Versus a Guy with a Detonator', *Guardian*, 10 July 2006.
58 'Seek the Roots of Terror, Afghan Leader Urges', *Financial Times*, 5 July 2006.
59 Ibid., p. 9.
60 Amin Tarzi, 'How Solid is the New "Afghanistan Compact?" ', Eurasianet, www.eurasianet.org/departments/insight/articles/pp020506_pr.shtml. Accessed 23 May 2006.
61 See Kathy Gannon, 'Afghanistan Unbound', *Foreign Affairs*, Vol. 83, no. 3, pp. 35–36.
62 Ahmed Rashid, 'Afghan Officials Concerned About Pending US Troop Pullout', Eurasianet, www.eurasianet.org/departments/insight/articles/eav010606_pr.shtml. Accessed 23 May 2006.
63 See Jeffrey Herbst, 'Let Them Fail: State Failure in Theory and Practice: Implications for Policy', in R.I. Rothberg (ed.), *When States Fail* (Princeton: Princeton University Press, 2004), pp. 302–318.

17 The end of Israeli omnipotence?

Avi Kober

This chapter examines the Israeli–Palestinian conflict as a potential reflection of Fourth Generation Warfare (4GW). 4GW proponents, particularly Thomas Hammes, present the first Palestinian intifada as a phase in the evolution of insurgency in general and 4GW in particular, demonstrating "both networking and emergence as new characteristics of insurgency."[1] According to 4GW rationale, had the Palestinians conducted insurgency along theory lines, we would have witnessed Israeli omnipotence coming to its end.

Is the Israeli–Palestinian conflict representative of 4GW? And has the Palestinian struggle succeeded in weakening Israel significantly? The Israeli–Palestinian conflict fits many 4GW principles. A deeper examination of the conflict, however, reveals lacunas in the theory itself as well as inaccuracies in Hammes' depiction of the conflict. Contrary to what one would expect based on 4GW rationale, the Israeli–Palestinian conflict shows that the militarily-technologically stronger side does have efficient answers to 4GW waged against it by the weak. I will use the term 4GW throughout the piece despite my belief that 4GW theory does not constitute a novelty but rather only little more than low-intensity conflict (LIC) theory.

The nature of the Israeli–Palestinian conflict

"War is a political undertaking"

Hammes attributes the perception of war as a political undertaking to Mao, heavily inspired by Clausewitz. By political undertaking Mao not only referred to political war objectives that ought to stand behind any use of violence, but also to political mobilization as a means of winning the war.[2] The latter aspect will be addressed later in this chapter; this section relates to the first meaning. Hammes stresses 4GW's appeal to the opponent's rational calculation in an attempt "to convince the enemy's political decision makers that their strategic goals are either unachievable or too costly for the perceived benefit."[3]

But as students of war well know, war as a rational tool in the hands of politics is one thing; what happens in reality when war breaks out or during its course is often another. Unlike most inter-state wars, Fourth Generation wars frequently emerge without any clear political objectives or master plan and creep up incrementally. This usually makes it difficult to appreciate the conflict's character or scope until it is well advanced.[4] Furthermore, the dynamics of war may push violence to the extreme in a spiraling escalatory process, beyond any rational calculation.[5]

Both Palestinian and Israeli behavior have largely been directed by a strong political rationale. The Palestinian struggle challenged Israel's right to exist until the pragmatic mainstream, PLO–Fatah (Palestinian Liberation Organization–Fatah), accepted it as a fait accompli, focusing instead on ending the post-1967 Israeli occupation of the territories and establishing a Palestinian state alongside Israel.[6] In early 2006 Hamas made its first steps in the same political direction. Israel, for its part, adopted "negative" objectives of a thwarting nature, focusing on denying the Palestinians the ability to realize their political ends while trying to convey the message that violence against Israel does not pay.

As Hammes points out, the first intifada of 1987–91 emerged spontaneously; neither PLO–Tunis nor the local leadership planned it. This does not mean that it remained uncontrolled politically. True, once it emerged, the local Palestinian leadership – the Unified Command – lacked any clear vision of where to go from there. Unexpectedly, though, the notion of civil disobedience filled the vacuum and became the platform for the struggle.[7] Civil disobedience was first advocated by Palestinian intellectuals such as Mubarak Awad and Hanna Siniora who believed that it could promote Palestinian self-reliance in the national struggle and put an end to Israeli occupation,[8] but this idea gained no support. With the intifada, the Unified Command called for – and at least for a limited period of time succeeded in – enforcing measures of civil disobedience.

Hammes praises the Palestinian leadership for disarming Palestinian protesters in the streets during the first intifada, "preferring the strategic advantages of pure victims to the ambiguity of losing combatants," and for taking advantage of the Israeli difficulty of reconciling its self-image as a liberal democracy with the actions necessary to suppress the popular uprising. "By using 'non violent' methods, the 4GW warriors can create tactical dilemmas for their opponents," Hammes explains.[9] However, civil disobedience was not in fact introduced onto the scene as a deliberate, conscious choice by the Palestinian leadership. Furthermore, when it did emerge it was applied alongside other, more violent activities, such as burning tires, hurling stones at Israeli troops sent to disperse the rioting civilians, and extensive arson in Israeli forests and fields. Civil disobedience eventually lost its impetus as a result of the economic vulnerability of the Palestinians, which was one of the by-products of civil disobedience.[10]

Hammes also ignores Palestinian fatal diplomatic fiascoes during the first intifada. The PLO's greatest diplomatic failure was the US's decision to suspend its dialogue with the organization as a result of the PLO's terror campaign against Israel and its support for Saddam Hussein before and after his invasion of Kuwait. The PLO's relations with the Gulf states deteriorated too, to the point of the Gulf states expelling Palestinian workers and withholding economic support – which brought about an economic crisis in the territories. This crisis, in turn, served as fertile ground for the strengthening of a fundamentalist, non-pragmatic stream in Palestinian politics and society, particularly the emergence of Hamas as an alternative to the PLO.[11]

As for the second intifada, that began in September 2000, according to Hammes, the Palestinians intentionally reverted to the bombing campaign, motivated by the Israeli withdrawal from Lebanon and confident that they could force the Israelis out of the West Bank.[12] True, many still believe that the outbreak of the al-Aqsa intifada was engineered by the Palestinian Authority (PA) for the sake of improving its political bargaining power after having failed to achieve its goals during the Camp David talks and against the background of the withdrawal from Lebanon.[13] Another interpretation, however, carries more weight. It claims that the second intifada emerged spontaneously, without any prior grand strategy, but was taken advantage of politically and controlled by Arafat at later stages.[14]

In any case, Hammes seems to be wrong in presenting the suicide bombings during the second intifada as violating 4GW rationale. The suicide bombing strategy was rationally chosen because it was both available and inexpensive, and because it was expected to magnify the image of power of the perpetrating organizations, and to damage Israeli morale.[15] The choice was also based on lessons the Palestinians had learned from the experience of the previous two decades – that suicide bombings pay, as shown by the Israeli withdrawal from West Bank cities in December 1995.[16] Unfortunately for the Palestinians, the strategy did not work as expected. In an era where personal safety is perceived by open societies as more important than national security, the extremely high Israeli threat perception only strengthened the Israeli society's staying power. The suicide bombings also proved to be detrimental to Palestinian image in the international community, strengthened Israeli legitimacy, and brought about the construction of the security fence that has created facts on the ground that may affect the final status borderline.

"4GW is ... protracted in duration ... it is the anti-thesis of ... short war"

Having attributed to Israel difficulty in sustaining protracted wars of attrition, the Arabs in general and the Palestinians in particular have tried to impose such wars on it.[17] Palestinian leaders have believed that the Palestinian society's cost tolerance is higher than Israeli society's, and that their greater societal staying power could balance their inferiority in military capabilities.[18] The Israeli withdrawal from Lebanon only strengthened that belief. "If the [Israeli] enemy could not bear the losses on the border strip with Lebanon, will it be able to withstand a long war of attrition in the heart of its security dimension and major cities?" asked Islamic Jihad leader Ramadan Shallah rhetorically in 2001,[19] in the wake of the withdrawal, inspired by Hezbollah secretary-general Sheikh Hassan Nasrallah's spider web "theory" introduced in the early 2000s.[20]

The Palestinians, however, proved to be wrong, and Israeli society has demonstrated high staying power in the wars of attrition against the

Palestinians.[21] Mass killing of Israeli civilians during the second intifada only created a strong sense of solidarity among Israelis, who felt that the conflict was over their home, and perhaps even represented an existential conflict.[22] National unity governments in power during most of the years of the intifadas eased frictions among parties and between the government and the military. Such social and political efforts complemented military measures, whereby Israeli counter-guerrilla and counter-terror operations alongside defensive means enabled Israel to limit the violence against its troops and civilians to a tolerable level.[23]

The conduct of the conflict

A combination of military and non-military means

By characterizing the means used in 4GW as comprising both military and non-military dimensions ("Fourth Generation war uses all available networks – political, economic, social, and military"), Hammes portrays it as an example of modern warfare, which has receded from the actual, direct battlefield. But this does not make 4GW unique. As Freedman rightly puts it, "It is hard to think of any recent conflict, including those involving clashes of regular forces, which did not involve the use of social, economic and political instruments in conjunction with the military."[24]

Hammes also characterizes Fourth Generation warriors as ones who "seek to use international, transnational, national and sub national networks for their own purposes" in order to create a political paralysis both internationally and in the target nation.[25] He praises the PLO for successfully communicating different messages to different audiences during the first intifada. At the same time he criticizes the organization for losing that sophistication and for reverting to pure terror during the second intifada. Yet an Israeli psychological warfare expert claims that during the second intifada the Palestinians rather succeeded in dominating the media's political agenda, presenting Israelis as oppressors.[26] As argued above, it also seems that suicide bombings were not necessarily a violation of Fourth Generation principles. The PA condemned the suicide bombings in order to avoid direct criticism from the international community, but gave at least a yellow light to this mass murder terror, believing in its weakening effect on Israeli society and building on the legitimacy given by the Palestinian society to the bombing campaign. The strategy had the potential of breaking the Israeli will, maintaining the Palestinian people's will and ensuring neutrals to remain neutral or provide tacit support to the Palestinian cause – but it failed.

As for Israel, Hammes is right in claiming that it learned its lessons and started communicating different messages to different audiences. To its own society it communicated the need and the ability to persevere. To the Palestinian society and decision makers it communicated the message that they were unlikely to achieve their objectives and likely to pay too high a price compared to the benefits. To the international community the message was that Israel was using legitimate self-defense means while the enemy was not.

The use of high technology

Hammes presents 4GW as a non-technological force multiplier for the weak against the strong, which enjoys technological superiority. In doing so he draws an inappropriate picture of modern let alone post-modern war, wherein technology has become a tool in the hands of the weak, although the technology may be lower and cheaper.

During the second intifada, at least three homemade technologies were used by Palestinians against Israelis: explosive belts used by suicide bombers; hundreds of homemade *Qassam* rockets launched onto Israeli civilian targets; and mines to blow up Israeli main battle tanks. In June 2006 the al-Aqsa Martyr Brigades threatened to launch rockets with chemical warheads into Israeli territory should the Israel Defense Forces (IDF) invade the Gaza Strip following the guerrilla attack on an Israeli post on the Israeli–Palestinian border near Kerem Shalom.[27] A pro-Palestinian web-based publication was launched in 2001,[28] and it is likely that Palestinian terrorists are already using communication technology to deliver information on plans, tactics, techniques and technology, raise money, secure messages (e.g., via digital cryptography), and conduct other communication.

During the last two decades technology has played a major role in a sophisticated strategy applied by militarily strong Western democracies, not only in high-intensity conflicts (HICs) but also in Fourth Generation wars. The use Western democracies like the US and Israel have made of high technology in Bosnia, Kosovo, southern Lebanon, or the Palestinian territories has been compatible with the post-heroic warfare they have adopted, according to which, one is neither "allowed" to get killed nor to kill – at least not civilians.[29] Although post-heroic warfare could easily be presented as a very inefficient way of conducting war, one should not disregard its positive aspects, particularly for Western democracies. It has enabled them to combine effectiveness and morality, easing the decision to enter wars wherein the defense of the homeland was not at stake and strengthening their sustainability in such wars (for an elaboration on the Israeli–Palestinian case, see below).

Broad coalition/national front

One of the sources of strength for insurgents is their joint action against a common enemy. According to Hammes, "far from being monolithic, today's insurgencies are coalitions of opportunistic groups banded together for the single purpose of ejecting the outsider and then defeating the government."[30] But this has long been typical of national liberation struggles and revolutions in various countries. Such national fronts have often collapsed either during the conflict, e.g. the Iraqi Kurdish factions vis-à-vis the Iraqi government, or once the struggle succeeds and the insurgents seized power, e.g. in Iran after the anti-Shah revolution or Afghanistan after the Soviet withdrawal.

For many years the PLO managed to overcome challenges to its leading status from rival factions and groups. During the first intifada, a Fatah-dominated Palestinian national coalition consisting of secular groups and factions was formed to coordinate and control the anti-Israel struggle.[31] Hammes presents this as an important contribution to the Palestinian successful struggle.[32] However, he ignores two major problems with this national "unity": first, the tension between PLO–Tunis and the young local leadership; second, the rise and gradual strengthening of Hamas as an alternative to the PLO. The intifada, particularly the economic crisis in the territories it created, served as fertile soil for Hamas to win the hearts and minds of the Palestinian people at the PLO's expense. The fact that the Hamas leadership was locally-based in addition to its ties with the Muslim Brotherhood in nearby Jordan served as additional points of strength. This was one of the factors that pushed the PLO to negotiate with Israel so as to maintain its status and authority in the territories.[33]

During the second intifada the PLO's status in the territories deteriorated considerably. The PLO-led PA security agencies weakened because on the one hand they were targeted by the IDF and on the other they were not allowed by the PA to restrain the terrorist organizations. During the initial stages of the intifada the PA encouraged Fatah–Tanzim violence against Israel, but later it lost control of the violence. Israel resumed control of the West Bank, Hamas expanded its control of welfare activities in the territories, and opposition organizations, particularly Hamas and Islamic Jihad, the Popular Front for the Liberation of Palestine (PFLP), and even Fatah-affiliated al-Aqsa Martyr Brigades took both the initiative and the lead in the armed struggle against Israel, gaining more and more legitimacy in the territories. Paradoxically and ironically at the same time, the tensions between the PLO and the opposition organizations loosened as a result of the PLO's inability and reluctance to impose its authority and disarm the terrorist organizations.[34] Palestinian opposition factions reached the highest degree of operational cooperation against the common Israeli enemy. Fatah, Hamas, Islamic Jihad, the PFLP, and al-Aqsa Martyr Brigades activists planned and carried out joint suicide bombing attacks and other terror activities to the point of obliterating the lines of organizational affiliation. This cooperation is not compatible with Hammes' portrayal of the second intifada as a violation of 4GW.

Again, on the Israeli side, the existence of a national unity government during the two intifadas eased frictions between parties and between the government and the military.

Countering Fourth Generation warriors by combining operational effectiveness and morality

Western democracies engaged in Fourth Generation wars often face moral, societal, and political constraints, which are taken advantage of by Fourth Generation warriors. Western democracies are inclined to set the individual and his personal safety before the collective good. They are less disposed to pay a high price in war in which the stakes are not sufficiently high, and would reject the use of harsh measures of suppression against civilians, let alone killing, which are the by-products of many Fourth Generation wars. Sometimes it is the lack of will on the part of their politicians misinterpreting societal resilience that accounts for their societies' low cost tolerance rather than any chronic persever-ance problem.[35]

Given Western democracies' sensitivities, their ability to sustain Fourth Gen-eration wars heavily depends on their operational effectiveness and morality, which are translated into legitimacy. Both normative and cognitive legitimacy[36] are vital for successfully managing the conflict. The weaker the democracy, the more important it becomes to ensure external legitimacy; the more democratic the society and the more prolonged the conflict, the more important it becomes to achieve domestic legitimacy. Greater legitimacy, in its turn, often creates favorable conditions for operational freedom of action. In other words, opera-tional effectiveness, morality, and legitimacy are interrelated.

How has Israel coped with irregular challenges posed by the Palestinian, both operationally and morally? Operational effectiveness in Fourth Generation wars often requires the application of combined, offensive and defensive means against the insurgents. Israel's traditional preference for offense vis-à-vis the Arab states notwithstanding, during its Fourth Generation wars from the 1950s to the 2000s it has adopted a more balanced offensive/defensive approach.[37] Defense advocates (who often also held dovish positions and many of whom belonged to the political echelon) expected defensive methods to strengthen the sense of security among those living in the frontier areas and the rear, to avoid escalation to conventional war, and to have diplomatic benefits. They also pointed to the limited effect of offensive operations as a deterrent against Fourth Generation warriors. In the early 1950s defensive measures were applied in response to the challenge of Palestinian infiltration and *fedayeen* attacks, includ-ing the establishment of a Border Guard responsible for policing the frontier,[38] the establishment of hundreds of new settlements along the border to be integ-rated into an overall defensive system,[39] a shoot-to-kill policy that did not distin-guish between armed and unarmed infiltrators, and the mining of certain areas.

The "activists" among Israel's political and military elite have believed in the cumulative effect of offensive raids. Faithful to its offensive tradition the IDF has never abandoned its belief that there was no better way of defense than going after the enemy, compelling him to stop the 4GW,[40] or deterring him by punishment.[41] This explains the strategy of reprisals of the early 1950s, which Israel has continued to this day, despite its debated effectiveness.

The intifadas posed unprecedented challenges. Terror in populated centers blurred the distinction between frontline and rear and called for a package of defensive measures, consisting of public and private sector security and policing activities, and combining thwarting efforts on the part of the military, the police, and the General Security Service (GSS). The unique nature of the first intifada as a popular uprising dictated the use of measures that did not always belong to the domain of offense or defense in the strict military sense. Curfews, arrests, trials, demolition or sealing of houses of terrorists, deportation of agitators, and administrative measures such as cutting off electricity and telephone communi-cation, administrative detention, and closure of schools. In its activity against rioters and demonstrators, who sometimes used petrol bombs, IDF troops applied a "beating policy" and used non-lethal or semi-lethal weapons such as rubber bullets, plastic bullets, and tear gas. Use of firearms was permitted in life-threatening situations only.[42] The Israeli security forces did not restrict their activity to the territories, attacking PLO activists in Cyprus and killing Arafat's deputy, Khalil al-Wasir (Abu Jihad) in Tunis.[43]

During the second intifada, the unremitting Palestinian campaign of violence provoked harsh Israeli countermeasures. A new offensive doctrine was applied by the IDF and Israeli troops responded forcefully to Palestinian demonstrations, shootings, and suicide bombings.[44] Based on the assumption that there was no longer one front or one line of contact, dozens of simultaneous operations were carried out every day, which were supposed to have a multi-dimensional effect.[45] The Israeli military, the police and the GSS overcame bureaucratic and organizational affiliations and loyalties and carried out joint counter-terror and counter-guerrilla operations. During Operation Defensive Shield in mid-2002, the IDF entered cities, rural areas, and refugee camps in the West Bank, carrying out continuous offensive activity at the tactical level. A sharp decline of over 50 percent in suicide bombings took place in the wake of the operation.[46] In 2003 and 2004 Israel managed to thwart almost 90 percent of the perpetrated terror attacks (88 percent and 89 percent, respectively), as compared to 67 percent in 2002.[47] Since Operation Defensive Shield, targeted killings have intensified in an effort to decapitate terrorist organizations' leaders and operations. Vis-à-vis the Palestinian Authority, the IDF applied piecemeal tactics to flatten its physical infrastructure and undermine the morale of its political leadership and its police and security agencies.

Relying on offense alone was not sufficient for coping with terrorism though. Construction of a buffer zone between Israel and the West Bank began in late 2003, and by the end of 2005, already included more than 400 kilometers – approximately 75 percent of the security fence. Troops deployed along the buffer zone are controlled by the C4I centers, which monitor all ground, air-borne (UAV) and aerostat surveillance assets. Since the creation of the security fence, the number of terrorist attacks dropped sharply – from 73 in the period September 2000–July 2003 (an average of 26 terrorist attacks per year) to five in the period July 2003–August 2004. The number of fatal casualties inflicted by terrorist attacks from the West Bank in the period August 2003–August 2004 dropped, too, by some 84 percent as compared to the period September 2001–July 2002.[48]

Adhering to moral principles while coping with Fourth Generation challenges is important not only from a normative point of view but also politically, as it may determine the chances of gaining internal and external legitimacy. Israeli effort to behave morally during its Fourth Generation wars has its root in both universal and Jewish values. Not only has Israel stressed its commitment to fight morally (*jus in bello*), it has also educated its troops in the spirit of the "purity of arms." The existence of an IDF code of ethics, as well as the public debate in Israel caused by cases of collateral damage, reflect this strong commitment to moral standards despite the difficulties involved and occasional deviations from accepted norms. The murderous nature of the Palestinian struggle against Israel, particularly the suicide bombings during the second intifada, created a legitimacy problem for the Palestinians and at the same time lent justification to Israeli use of harsh measures such as targeted killing and allowed it greater latitude in using military force. On the other hand, this latitude was not without limits. For example, the incident in which an F-16 fired a laser-guided bomb into a building in Gaza City, killing Hamas military leader Salah Shehadeh and 14 other people, including eight children, was criticized both in Israel and abroad.

Three ethical principles are mostly relevant for a Western democracy engaged in 4GW: just cause, discriminate use of force, and proportionality. Just cause means, first and foremost, that the war is considered an act of self-defense. The principle of discrimination forbids the direct targeting of noncombatants.[49] The idea behind the proportionality is to apply the minimum force necessary to achieve one's legitimate objectives, making sure the overall destruction expected from the use of force does not outweigh the good to be achieved.[50] For Israel just cause has been the easiest principle to comply with. Given the fact that its Fourth Generation wars have been imposed on it, it has retained the right of self-defense, only rarely facing a significant public debate regarding the justness and legitimacy of the war.[51] This does not mean that the world has always accepted its right of self-defense. For example, in the mid-1950s, Israel's reprisal policy was criticized by the UN.[52]

Most of Israel's Fourth Generation wars have involved civilians on either side. Unlike the Palestinians, Israel has been committed to the principle of discriminate use of force. Since the Qibya reprisal of October 1953, during which 69 enemy civilians were killed, it became official Israeli policy to refrain from killing civilians, both for moral and utilitarian reasons.[53] Officials have, on many occasions, reiterated the illegitimacy of killing civilians,[54] stressing the Israeli commitment to avoid killing innocent civilians or at least to reduce the amount of collateral damage as much as possible. However, they acknowledged the difficulty in applying such an approach in situations where the distinction between gunmen and innocent civilians is often obliterated, attributing incidents of collateral damage to intelligence failures, poor planning, or poor performance.[55]

Israeli tactics during Operation Defensive Shield in mid-2002, for example, were much gentler than US tactics in Afghanistan, let alone Russian tactics in Chechnya. Despite the fact that Palestinian refugee camps had become home to hundreds of guerrillas and terrorists, the IDF chose to target terrorists selectively, trying to spare the lives of noncombatants. When faced with strong resistance in congested urban areas, IDF troops advanced from house to house by tearing down holes in the walls so as to avoid exposure to snipers. At the same time, they engaged terrorists in house-to-house fighting that spared civilians as much as possible. Noncombatant casualties would have been even lower had the Palestinian terrorists refrained from using civilians as shields and decoys.[56] As a result of these self-imposed restrictions, the IDF suffered more casualties than expected.[57] Israeli engagement regulations were also adapted so as to provide Israeli troops with the tools to cope with situations where unarmed civilians were involved.[58]

Of the various counter-terror methods developed and used by Israel through-out the years, targeted killing, which has been extensively used during the second intifada, seems to have been a classical manifestation of a technology-bent post-heroic warfare (see below) and the option most compatible with the principle of discrimination between combatants and noncombatants.[59] Whereas invading a civilian area inevitably leads to the death and injury of innocent people, with targeted killing, collateral damage is significantly reduced, though not prevented altogether. Between September 2000 and April 2004, Israel carried out 159 killing attempts. Of those killed, 248 (78 percent) were combat-ants, whereas 69 (22 percent) were noncombatants. Later on, Israel managed to improve its performance, and its targeted killings became much more sophistic-ated and selective.[60] According to the Chief of the Israeli Air Force (IAF), not only did the IAF improve the hitting rates in targeted killing from the air, but the number of noncombatant casualties declined from one noncombatant per terror-ist in early 2004 to one noncombatant per 12 terrorists at the end of that year, and one noncombatant per 28 terrorists in 2005.[61]

Throughout the years, though, Israeli operations have on occasion claimed the lives of Palestinian civilians. For example, during the 1981 Small War of Attrition, Israel targeted PLO concentrations in Lebanon from the air, many of which were located in refugee camps. Some 100 people were killed, only 30 of whom were terrorists, and 600 were injured. During the two intifadas, hundreds of Palestinians found their death while participating in hostilities against Israeli troops and as a result of the need to hunt terrorists whose bases of operation and/or refuge were built-up areas. In two famous incidents, Israeli troops unin-tentionally killed innocent civilians. In July 2002, an F-16 plane fired a laser-guided bomb into a building in Gaza City, killing Hamas leader Salah Shehadeh and 14 other people, including eight children, and in May 2004, eight Palestin-ian demonstrators were accidentally killed during an IDF operation in Rafah.[62] When it turned out that innocent people had been killed, Israel usually apolo-gized, in accordance with the doctrine of double effect, which tolerates the killing of civilians as long as it is unintended and accidental.

As for the principle of proportionality, during the intifadas Israel occasionally tolerated the use of excessive force by individual troops as a result of stress, frustration, little or no training, or poor discipline, and sometimes even initiated the use of drastic means such as the beating policy or collective punishment. However, there has never been an official policy to use extreme measures, the Israeli Supreme Court usually ruled against the use of excessive force, and banned the use of "human shields" and torture. In the light of the murderous nature of suicide bombings during the second intifada and Israeli efforts to reduce collateral damage, targeted killings of terrorists seemed to be a propor-tional response.

Israel's success in combining operational effectiveness and morality became possible largely thanks to the post-heroic way of war it adopted in the late 1970s, which reflected demographic, societal, and political constraints, on the one hand, and opportunities created by technology, on the other. Whereas it has been typical of the Palestinians to prefer heroic warfare, Israel has striven to behave post-heroically ever since the 1978 Litani Operation.[63]

Western democracies have in recent years started relating to wars, including Fourth Generation ones, as resulting from the evilness in the enemy's political leadership rather than its people or military. As the people are often considered victims of their leaders, e.g., Milosevic, Aideed, Arafat, Yassin or Rantissi, their lives have to be spared,[64] and the center of gravity should be the enemy's leadership. This shattering of the monolithic definition of the enemy has in recent years been reflected in Israel's attitude toward the Palestinians. For example, Prime Minister Sharon distinguished between "terrorists – whom we will pursue relentlessly – and the civilian Palestinian population that is not involved in terror."[65]

Achieving escalation dominance

Winning the conflict

Escalation dominance is the ability to escalate the conflict to a level where the adversary cannot respond and understands he cannot win.[66] One might get the wrong impression that vis-à-vis Fourth Generation non-state players, like the Palestinians, escalation dominance is more evident than in symmetrical, high-intensity conflicts. This has not been the case in the Israeli–Palestinian asymmetric Fourth Generation war. During many Israeli–Palestinian confrontations Israel has tried to achieve escalation dominance, but calculated escalation as a conflict management tool has often failed to deter the other side or compel it to stop the war.

This was the case in the mid-1950s and the 1960s, when Israel resorted to attacking Arab states instead; in the 1970s–early 1980s, when the Palestinians continued to attack Israel on the northern front and abroad; and during the first intifada. The targeted killing of the political–ideological leadership of Hamas in mid-2004, after three and a half years of targeting military leaders and operatives, was an exception. It accounted for Hamas's decision to accept a truce with Israel, which could be considered an Israeli success in terms of escalation dominance.[67]

Defeating the enemy's military forces

Hammes explains that unlike the previous three generations, in 4GW, battlefield decision has lost its relevance: "4GW does not attempt to win by defeating the enemy's military forces; ... [it] does not attempt to achieve superiority on the battlefield."[68] True, in Fourth Generation wars in particular, battlefield decision has lost its centrality, and is one of fairly "minor" scope, achieved "on points" rather than by "a knockout," if at all. Guerrilla, terror or civil disobedience have been meant to wear down the opponent by demonstrating a higher tolerance for cost.[69] It was precisely Mao's comprehension of the difficulties involved in achieving battlefield decision in an insurgency that influenced him to adopt attrition solely as a stage in an overall strategy.[70] Confronting the strong "conventionally" succeeded in exceptional cases, such as the Communists in China or in Indochina. Attempts to leapfrog the guerrilla-warfare stage and establish a regular army with aspirations of contending with an adversary experienced and powerful in traditional warfare were normally doomed to failure, as had been predicted by Clausewitz and as happened in the case of the post-World War II communist uprising in Greece.[71]

Hammes would have done more justice to the notion of 4GW if, in addition to stressing the obsolescence of battlefield decision, he had pointed to the growing relevance of grand-strategic decision, i.e., denying the enemy. He is right in pointing to the tendency to directly attack the enemy's political will, and in pointing out that it is usually outside the actual battlefield where 4GW is won. But he never uses the concept grand-strategic decision; that is, denying the enemy's ability to carry on the fight not merely from the military point of view, but also from non-military standpoints, such as economic, societal, or political.[72]

When Hammes argues that in the first intifada the Palestinians defeated the dominant military power in the Middle East, i.e. Israel, he does not mean that they did so on the battlefield. He himself points to the fact that the Palestinians knew they were unable to defeat the Israelis militarily. Two clarifications are in place, though. First, alongside attacking the Israeli rear, the Palestinians have often confronted Israeli troops at the tactical level, e.g. in road patrols or at checkpoints, where they did attempt to win militarily. Second, the popular uprising diminished gradually as the social and economic miseries in Palestinian society became intolerable.[73]

Hammes, Lind, Lind *et al.*, and van Creveld claim, either explicitly or implicitly, that the stronger side's chances of coming to grips with the weak, no matter what it does, are low.[74] As van Creveld puts it, "one after the other, the world's most powerful, most advanced, technologically sophisticated forces tried to cope with it but were defeated; often this was done at the hands of people who possessed hardly any formal military training, went barefoot, and could barely read."[75]

The Israeli–Palestinian case seems to refute this contention. During the 1982 Lebanon War Israel proved that a non-state player with irregular force can be defeated militarily by a regular army, and that such defeat can be translated into victory, i.e., achieving the war objectives. In that war Israel destroyed the PLO's military and political infrastructure in Lebanon and the organization's political leadership and troops were expelled from that country to Tunisia. Lind is wrong in asserting that military powers like the Soviets in Afghanistan and the Israelis in Lebanon lost their wars because they could not figure out how to act operationally against Fourth Generation enemies, fighting only an endless series of strategically meaningless tactical engagements.[76] The French in Algeria, the Americans in Vietnam, the Soviets in Afghanistan, and the Israelis in Lebanon learned to cope with the insurgents effectively. Their problem was that they failed in translating their military successes into political gains.

Translating military achievements into political gains

In the past, there used to be a higher correlation between military achievements and victory, no matter if battlefield decision was achieved or not. Today, that linkage has ended. The political war objectives can now be achieved merely by using force, short of battlefield decision. Military superiority can no longer guarantee political victory, while military inferiority does not exclude the possibility of achieving victory.[77] One important reason for the disconnection between battlefield decision and victory is exactly what 4GW theory focuses on – the changing balance between adversaries, which is no longer confined to their relative destructive power but also reflects their relative societal cost tolerance. As Lind puts it:

> Paradoxically, the more the state is successful in winning on the battlefield by turning its immense, hi-tech firepower on guys in bathrobes who are armed only with rusty World War II rifles, the more it becomes disgusted with itself. The weaker the Fourth Generation enemy is physically, the stronger he is morally. And the moral level is decisive.[78]

Not only does the Israeli–Palestinian case prove that battlefield decision is sometimes achievable in Fourth Generation wars, Israeli society has demonstrated impressive resilience during the Israeli–Palestinian conflict. Israel has applied counter-guerrilla and counter-terror operations that have kept violence against both its troops and civilians at a tolerable level. The Palestinians, on the other hand, have gradually moved in the direction of realizing their national vision of a Palestinian state despite their relative weakness, mistakes made by their leadership, and occasional painful defeats. Like a phoenix, the PLO recovered from Lebanon and the Gulf War and again became Israel's negotiating partner in Madrid and Oslo. At the same time, however, the PLO, like Egypt, Jordan, and some other Arab states, moderated its attitude toward Israel during the course of the conflict, recognizing Israel's existence, denouncing terrorism, and recognizing the UN partition plan. Hamas seems to be moving in the same direction. Arafat's death and Abu Mazen's moderation and pragmatism, as well as the public mood in the territories that preferred an end to violence, drove Hamas, which consolidated its public standing and translated it into political power, to institutionalize politically, project an image of responsibility, and moderate its rhetoric vis-à-vis Israel.[79]

Conclusion

4GW theory offers an up-to-date picture of post-World War II insurgencies. Nonetheless, it is incoherent and eclectic and does not constitute any novelty; most of its features already exist in LIC theory and some others are covered by post-modern thought of war. Hammes does not pay enough tribute to the modernity and sophistication of attrition. He also more than implies that attrition serves the weak rather than the strong, whereas the Israeli–Palestinian conflict demonstrates that once the stronger side's vital interests are at stake, its society's cost tolerance and sustainability in attrition situations can be very high, to the point of neutralizing and even overcoming the enemy's staying power.

Violence and diplomacy have been used by the Palestinians sequentially or in combination in order to build internal and external legitimacy, gain self confidence, strengthen the Palestinian people's commitment to national liberation, and weaken Israel socially, economically, and diplomatically. The contention that until the second intifada the Palestinians acted according to 4GW principles but violated them during the second intifada by using the suicide bombing attacks seems to be a blanket statement. During the first intifada the Palestinians witnessed fatal diplomatic fiascoes, whereas the suicide bombing strategy of the second intifada was a rational choice that was based on lessons the Palestinians had learned from the experience of the previous two decades that suicide bombings could pay.

Israel, on the other hand, for many years until the early stages of the first intifada, preferred the use of force to a multidimensional management of its wars against both the Arab states and the Palestinians. Since the late 1980s it has taken both military and non-military measures against the Palestinians. Alongside efforts to improve its operational effectiveness by combining defensive and offensive measures, it has been committed to moral conduct of its Fourth Generation wars, and has learned to strengthen domestic and international legitimacy by communicating different messages to different audiences. The Israeli–Palestinian case shows that not only has technology become a tool – almost a force multiplier – for the weak, in this case the Palestinians, it has also been heavily used by the strong.

The Israeli experience with irregular challenges exemplifies the difficulty of achieving escalation dominance in Fourth Generation wars. Military achievements do not promise political gains, and the weaker side may emerge politically victorious despite the lack of any significant achievements on the battlefield. At the same time it shows that although guerrilla tactics and terror used by the weak might threaten the personal safety of the citizens of the state against which they are operating, thereby demoralizing them, they pose limited risk to national security, let alone national survival, and that guerrilla and terror attacks against the strong can be kept at a tolerable level.

Attributing political achievements to the Palestinians in the course of the conflict is only partially justified. It is true that the Palestinians have gradually advanced toward realizing their national vision, but down the road they have also recognized Israel's existence and committed to stop the violent struggle against it.

Thus, 4GW has not changed the strategic balance between Israelis and Palestinians. Israel has learned to conduct Fourth Generation wars and to use technology in order to combine effectiveness and morality in the Israeli–Palestinian conflict. It has also proved that political gains achieved by the strong, with or without battlefield decision, are no panacea.

Western democracies are likely to experience Fourth Generation wars in the future. In order for their militaries and political leaders to conduct these wars successfully not only do they have to invest in a better understanding of the unique nature of such wars, but also to adapt flexibly to the dynamic nature of the challenges they entail as far as force design, doctrines, strategies, tactics, technology, and jointness are concerned; learn to escalate, if necessary, without losing control; and be operationally effective without giving up high ethical standards.

Notes

1 Thomas X. Hammes, "War Evolves into the Fourth Generation," *Contemporary Security Policy*, Vol. 26, no. 2 (August 2005), p. 201.
2 Mao Tse-tung, *On Protracted War* (Peking: People's Publishing House, 1954), pp. 77, 137.
3 Hammes, "War Evolves into the Fourth Generation," p. 206.
4 Stuart A. Cohen, "Why Do They Quarrel? Civil–Military Tensions in LIC Situations," in Efraim Inbar (ed.), *Democracies and Small Wars* (London: Frank Cass, 2003), p. 24.
5 Carl von Clausewitz, *On War* (Princeton, NJ: Princeton University Press, 1984), pp. 76–7.
6 Moshe Shemesh, "The PLO 1964–1993: From Armed Struggle to Destroy Israel to Peace with Israel," in Moshe Maoz and Benjamin Z. Kedar, *The Palestinian National Movement: From Confrontation to Reconciliation* (Tel Aviv: Maarachot, 1996) [Hebrew], pp. 299–319; Avraham Sela, "Authority Without Sovereignty: The PLO's Way from Armed Struggle to Political Settlement," Ibid., pp. 365–409.
7 Aryeh Shalev, *The Intifada: Causes and Effects* (Jerusalem: Jerusalem Post Press, 1991), p. 85.
8 Ze'ev Schiff and Ehud Ya'ari, *Intifada* (New York: Simon & Schuster, 1990), pp. 204–7; 241–3; Hanna Siniora, "An Analysis of the Current Revolt," *Journal of Palestine Studies*, Vol. 17, no. 3 (1988), p. 2; *Jerusalem Post*, January 10, 1988.
9 Hammes, "War Evolves into the Fourth Generation," p. 212.
10 Yigal Eyal, *The First Intifada: The Oppression of the Arab Revolt by the British Army 1936–1939* (Tel Aviv: Maarachot, 1998) [Hebrew], pp. 125–7.
11 Sela, "Authority Without Sovereignty," pp. 402–5.
12 Hammes, "War Evolves into the Fourth Generation," p. 203.
13 Amos Harel and Avi Issaharoff, *The Seventh War* (Tel Aviv: Yediot Aharonot, 2004) [Hebrew], pp. 62–75.
14 Hillel Frisch, "Debating Palestinian Strategy in the al-Aqsa Intifada," *Terrorism and Political Violence*, Vol. 15, no. 2 (Summer 2003), pp. 63–8; Yezid Sayigh, "Arafat and the Anatomy of a Revolt," www.ipcri.org/files/yezidarafat.html.
15 Yoram Schweitzer, "Suicide Terrorism: Historical Background and Risks for the Future," *PBS.org*, 18 18.6 2004. www.pbs.org/wnet/wideangle/shows/suicide/.
16 Pape, "The Strategic Logic of Suicide Terrorism," pp. 354–5.
17 See, for example, Stewart Reiser, "The Arab–Israeli Wars: A Conflict of Strategic Attrition," in Karl P. Magyar and Constantine P. Danopoulos (eds), *Prolonged Wars: A Post-Nuclear Challenge* (Maxwell AFB, AL: Air University Press, 1994), pp. 67–98.
18 Steven Rosen, "War, Power, and the Willingness to Suffer," in Bruce M. Russett (ed.), *Peace, War and Numbers* (Beverly Hills, CA: Sage, 1972), pp. 167–83.
19 Robert A. Pape, "The Strategic Logic of Suicide Terrorism," *American Political Science Review*, Vol. 97, no. 3 (August 2003), p. 355.

20 Nasrallah cast Israel as a spider web, which only appears sturdy but is in fact fragile, because the Israeli people have lost the will to fight. Hasan Nasrallah, *al-Manar* television, 6 June 2000; Eyal Zisser, "The Return of Hizbullah," *Middle East Quarterly*, Vol. 9, no. 4 (Fall 2002); Daniel Pipes and Jonathan Schanzer, "Winning by Retreating?," *New York Post*, May 22, 2002.

21 Avi Kober, "From Blitzkrieg to Attrition: Israel's Attrition Strategy and Staying Power," *Small Wars and Insurgencies*, Vol. 16, no. 2 (June 2005), pp. 216–40.

22 PM Ariel Sharon in a Speech to the Nation, Israeli television, Channel 1, April 2, 2002.

23 Kober, "From Blitzkrieg to Attrition."

24 Lawrence Freedman, "War Evolves into the Fourth Generation: A Comment on Thomas X. Hammes," *Contemporary Security Policy*, Vol. 26, no. 2 (August 2005), p. 257.

25 Hammes, "War Evolves into the Fourth Generation," p. 207.

26 Ron Schleifer, "Psychological Warfare during the Second Intifada," paper presented at the IAIS annual meeting, Hebrew University, June 6, 2006.

27 www.ynet.co.il/articles/0,7340,L-3267247,00.html.

28 *The Electronic Intifada*, electronicintifada.net.

29 On post-heroic war, see Edward N. Luttwak, "Toward Post-Heroic Warfare," *Foreign Affairs*, Vol. 74, no. 3 (May/June 1995), pp. 109–22; and "A Post-Heroic Military Policy," *Foreign Affairs*, Vol. 75, no. 4 (July/August 1996), pp. 33–44.

30 Thomas X. Hammes, "Response," *Contemporary Security Policy*, Vol. 26, no. 2 (August 2005), p. 283.

31 Yiftach Zilberman, "The Development of Extreme Islam in the Territories Since 1967," in Maoz and Kedar, *The Palestinian National Movement*, pp. 337–8.

32 Hammes, "War Evolves into the Fourth Generation," p. 202.

33 Sela, "Authority Without Sovereignty," pp. 404–6.

34 Anat N. Kurz, *Fatah and the Politics of Violence* (Brighton: Sussex Academic Press, 2005).

35 See, for example, Steven Kull and I.M. Destler, *Misreading the Public: The Myth of New Isolationism* (Washington, DC: Brookings Institution, 1999).

36 On normative and cognitive legitimacy, see Alexander L. George, "Domestic Constraints on Regime Change in US Foreign Policy," in O.R. Holsti, R.M. Siverson, and A.L. George (eds), *Change in the International System* (Boulder, CO: Westview, 1980), pp. 233–62.

37 Avi Kober, "Israel's Wars of Attrition: Operational and Moral Dilemmas," *Israel Affairs*, Vol. 12, no. 4 (October 2006) (forthcoming).

38 Tal, *Israel's Day-to-Day Security Conception*, pp. 71–2.

39 Mordechai Bar-On, *The Gates of Gaza: Israel's Defense and Foreign Policy 1955–1957* (Tel Aviv: Am Oved, 1992) [Hebrew], pp. 93–4, 94–7.

40 For the most compelling works on compellence are Thomas Schelling, *Arms and Influence* (New Haven, CN: Yale University Press, 1966), pp. 1–18; Alexander George and William Simons (eds), *The Limits of Coercive Diplomacy* (Boulder, CO: Westview, 1994).

41 On deterrence-by-punishment as opposed to deterrence-by-denial, see Glenn Snyder, *Deterrence and Defense* (Princeton, NJ: Princeton University Press, 1961).

42 Aryeh Shalev, *The Intifada: Causes and Effect* (Jerusalem: Jerusalem Post Press, 1991), pp. 99–122.

43 Morris, *Righteous Victims*, 552–3.

44 Aluf Ben, "In Israel, Too Much to Leave to the Generals," *Washington Post*, August 18, 2002.

45 Alex Fishman, "Extinguishing the Fire and Gaining Time," *Yediot Aharonot Weekend Supplement*, January 21, 2005.

46 www.intelligence.org.il/sp/10_04/four.htm#2.

47 www.intelligence.org.il/sp/pa_t/det_8feb_05.htm.
48 www.intelligence.org.il/sp/10_04/four.htm#2.
49 Michael Walzer, *Just and Unjust Wars* (New York: Basic Books, 1977), p. 151.
50 James Turner Johnson, *Just War Tradition and the Restraint of War: A Moral and History Inquiry* (Princeton, NJ: Princeton University Press, 1981), p. 198.
51 See, for example, Chief-of-Staff Rabin's words before the members of the General Staff in the midst of "the battle on the water" with the Syrians in the mid-1960s. Ami Gluska, *Eshkol, Give the Order!* (Tel Aviv: Maarachot, 2004), p. 100.
52 Bar-On, *The Gates of Gaza*, p. 249.
53 On the Qibya operation and its aftermath, see Shabtai Tevet, "Has the Operation Order Been Forged?," *Haaretz*, September 2, 1994; van Creveld, *The Sword and the Olive*, pp. 133–134; Shimon Golan, *Hot Border, Cold War* (Tel Aviv: Maarachot, 2000) [Hebrew], pp. 292–7.
54 The government-appointed commission of inquiry for the Sabra and Shatila Massacre in September 1982 found top Israeli officials guilty of the tragedy. In 2002, the Israeli Supreme Court barred the practice of using Palestinian civilians as "human shields" during military operations against terrorists in the Territories.
55 Amos Yadlin and Asa Kasher, "The Ethics of Fighting Terror," *Journal of National Defense Studies*, Nos 2–3 (September 2003), pp. 5–12.
56 See www.palestinefacts.org/pf_1991to_now_jenin_2002.php.
57 James Taranto, *Wall Street Journal*, editorial page, April 10, 2002; Arieh O'Sullivan, "Soldiers' Deaths Won't Affect Defensive Shield," *Jerusalem Post*, April 10, 2002.
58 See, www.btselem.org/English/Publications/Full_Text/Illusions_of_Restraint.
59 Avi Kober, "Targeting Killing during the Second Intifada: Was It Morally Justified and Effective?," Unpublished Paper.
60 Kober, ibid.
61 Chief of the IAF General Shkedi in an interview to *the Israeli Radio*, Channel 2, 29 June 2005; http://www.ynet.co.il/articles/0,7340,L-3224821,00.html. See also Amir Rapaport, "Decision of Existential Significance," *Maariv Weekend Supplement*, July 1, 2005.
62 www.israel-mfa.gov.il/MFAHeb/Diplomatic+updates/Events/Rafiah+19-May-2004.htm.
63 Before Defense Minister Ezer Weizman approved the Litani Operation of March, 1978, he instructed Chief-of-Staff Mordechai Gur that "[the operation] should be conducted very carefully. Ten Fatah [fighters] are not worth even the hand of one of our soldiers. The more lives of our guys we can save, the better. [...] As a pilot, my ideal is that the ground forces should be able to move without shooting even one bullet." Mordechai Gur, *Chief of the General Staff, 1974–1978* (Tel Aviv: Maarachot, 1998) [Hebrew], p. 404.
64 Thomas A. Keaney and Eliot A. Cohen, *Revolution in Warfare? Air Power in the Persian Gulf* (Annapolis, MD: Naval Institute Press, 1995), p. 225.
65 Address to members of the European Parliament, Jerusalem, 27 October 2003, www.kokhaviv publications.com/2003/israel/10/0310281320.html.
66 For this term, see Herman Kahn, *On Escalation, Metaphors and Scenarios* (New York: Pelican Books, 1965), pp. 231, 290.
67 Amos Harel and Avi Isacharoff, *The Seventh War* (Tel Aviv: Yediot Aharonot, 2004), pp. 210–11.
68 Hammes, "War Evolves into the Fourth Generation," p. 206.
69 Such distinctions were inspired by the American experience in the Vietnam War. See, for example, John E. Mueller, "The Search for the 'Breaking Point' in Vietnam: The Statistics of a Deadly Quarrel," *International Studies Quarterly*, Vol. 24, no. 4 (December 1980), pp. 497–519.
70 Mao Tse-tung, *Selected Military Writings*, pp. 181–3.
71 Edgar O'Ballance, *The Greek Civil War 1944–1949* (London: Faber & Faber, 1966), pp. 148, 181–185; Robert Asprey, *War in the Shadows: The Guerrilla in History*

(New York: Morrow, 1994), ch. 42; Walter Laqueur, *Guerrilla: A Historical and Critical Study* (London: Weidenfeld & Nicolson, 1977), pp. 284–5.

72 For the definition of battlefield decision, see Avi Kober, "Has Battlefield Decision Become Obsolete? The Commitment to the Achievement of Battlefield Decision Revisited," *Contemporary Security Policy*, Vol. 22, no. 2 (August 2001), p. 96.

73 Sela, "Authority Without Sovereignty," pp. 402–3.

74 Hammes, "War Evolves into the Fourth Generation," pp. 189–90; Lind, "Understanding Fourth Generation War"; van Creveld, "It Will Continue to Conquer and Spread," p. 231.

75 van Creveld, "It Will Continue to Conquer and Spread," p. 231.

76 William S. Lind, "Operational IEDs," d-n-i.net/lind/lind_12_01_05.htm.

77 See Michael I. Handel, "Clausewitz in the Age of Technology," in Michael I. Handel (ed.), *Clausewitz and Modern Strategy* (London: Frank Cass, 1986), pp. 81–4.

78 Lind, "Critics of the Fourth Generation: the Good, the Bad and the Ugly."

79 Ephraim Lavie, "Hamas's Victory in the Palestinian Elections: What Does it Mean?," *Tel Aviv Notes*, no. 159 (January 29, 2006), p. 2.

18 Fourth Generation Warfare in Africa

Back to the future?

Paul Jackson

The war will be a tedious one, nor can it be glorious, even tho' attended with success. Instead of decisive battles, woodland skirmishes – instead of Colours and Cannons, our trophies will be stinking scalps. Heaven preserve you, my Friend, from a war conducted in a spirit of murder rather than of brave and generous offence.

William Smith, 1763[1]

Introduction

Thomas Hammes' paper on Fourth Generation Warfare (4GW) represents an interesting introduction to the Pentagon's strategic vision of future wars dominated by high-tech, light forces controlled by tightly connected networks allowing US commanders to 'see everything, decide rapidly and execute immediately'. As Hammes points out, this approach to warfare is really a culmination of a series of earlier concepts including the Revolution in Military Affairs. Hammes goes on to point out that, while initial results in Iraq and Afghanistan were promising at the start, the enemy refused to accept defeat and launched a protracted, political, emerging 'Fourth Generation war'.

The central question is whether the current insurgencies are merely aberrations or if the insurgencies represent the evolution of a new generation of war, one that is different from the Pentagon's vision of the future of warfare. An analysis of 4GW is beyond the scope of this chapter and has been the subject of the earlier works.[2] In short, Hammes draws on recent evidence showing that war could be waged by low-tech insurgents against high-tech formal militaries through the use of non-military factors as force multipliers.[3]

This chapter addresses the development of this idea in the specific context of Africa. It begins by outlining the conflict environment and then goes on to analyse similarities with the 4GW approach. In concluding, the chapter also moves on to distinguish what is different about African modes of warfare on a continent that currently contains a significant number of asymmetric, irregular, guerrilla and Fourth Generation wars.

The conflict environment in Africa

In Africa, the discussion of 4GW is linked to the 'New Wars' thesis; that is, qualitative changes have taken place in the nature of conflict in Africa and it is possible to discuss 'new wars' that are distinct from earlier forms of conflict.[4] A literature has also grown around the assertion that Africa is more prone to conflict than other continents and that African wars are driven by economic motivations.[5] At the same time, there have been several case studies of different guerrilla movements and cross-national analysis of the organization of rebellions but there is a significant gap in the analysis of the response of government forces.[6] Given the interference of African militaries in politics, analysis of security has tended to concentrate on political, rather than military analysis.[7]

African wars are complex and messy, even if the modes of warfare are not. There are a number of defining features of conflict across the continent that need to be taken into account in any discussion of 4GW.

Geography

Border regions are central to the nature of conflict in Africa. Although most conflicts begin in a particular country, virtually all conflicts in Africa spill over at least one border and frequently more. In the case of many of the most intransigent conflicts, the border regions are instrumental in maintaining conflicts by providing an exit strategy for armed groups into space that is beyond the reach of conventional African security forces. In Central Africa, the collapse of Zaire has led to a vast area of the Democratic Republic of the Congo (DRC) effectively becoming lawless and supporting a bewildering array of armed groups taking part in conflict within the DRC itself, but also in Sudan, Uganda, Rwanda, and Burundi. In West Africa, the Mano River region provides a similar haven for insurgents, gangs, and smugglers in Liberia, Guinea, and Sierra Leone. Even in relatively calm countries such as Kenya, permeable border regions support violence among, for example, *karamajong* cattle-rustlers that inhabit the Uganda–Kenya border.[8]

Political economy

Economics plays some part in almost all African insurgencies. Resources, frequently in the form of tradeable goods and natural resources such as oil and diamonds, have played a significant part in prolonging conflict in countries as diverse as Angola, Sierra Leone, and the DRC. Whether these resources were the main motivation for conflict remains up for debate, but it is clear that conflict has been prolonged when, for example, a small rebel group gains control of a resource that is then used to fuel further conflict (Sierra Leone) or where one side has control of a resource and the other, a different resource (Angola with oil and diamonds). It is, however, not clear how far resources are a motivation for conflict in a case such as the Lord's Resistance Army in Uganda that has access to no natural resources and yet has been fighting since 1986.[9]

Globalization and networks

One of the defining features of African wars since the early 1990s is their inter-nationalization, and in particular, their links to global networks engaging in illegal trading activities, particularly drugs and arms, but also illegal trading in diamonds (Sierra Leone, Angola), uranium (Sudan), hardwoods (Liberia), and people (Sudan, Liberia). Such illegal trading has given rise to a series of 'shadow states' that are able to become self-financing and to propagate war.[10] David Keen has even gone so far as to suggest that the logic of this approach leads to the conclusion that the continuation of war becomes a war aim in itself if that conflict creates the conditions to profit from 'grey trades'.[11]

The nature of grey trades illustrates a type of globalization that is multi-layered and networked. Most descriptions of illicit trading networks illustrate that warlords may not necessarily have *direct* access to international markets, but they certainly do have *indirect* access via networks of intermediaries. The global pressures placed upon insurgency movements are filtered through a variety of networks that may themselves be specific. Many trading networks in grey trades are family or ethnically run.[12] The nature of the business is high risk, thus trust is the most effective form of mitigation.

At the same time as globalization is filtered, these networks allow access by warlords to international markets. In the case of diamonds, timber, etc. these materials are filtered through the network of companies and organizations to allow eventual entry into legitimate global markets. In the case of, say, arms coming the other way, shipments begin as legitimate arms deals with end-user certificates and then are filtered through a series of companies and agencies, becoming illicit and then being supplied to insurgency movements. The real value of the state in this scenario is that it controls the legitimization of illicit trade operating on 'the periphery of the air cargo industry', to paraphrase the UN Security Council. Regional allies within national governments are also valuable in terms of providing safe havens for weapons (e.g. Togo), or trans-shipment points with false end-user certificates (e.g. Burkina Faso). In other words, the grey areas around legitimate trade provide an avenue to enter international markets.

The importance of geographical space beyond national law and beyond the area over which post-colonial governments can project power is also critical here. The existence of warlord spaces allows the development of these grey trades, while trust networks within these spaces – based on ethnicity, religion or shared identity and usually enforced by violence – is the comparative advantage of these groups in the market place particularly in high value markets.[13]

Orders of battle (ORBATs)

One of the central difficulties facing analysts and militaries in African conflict is accurately identifying various groups involved in violence. This is exacerbated by a continuing flux of alliances and temporary agreements, as well as a cycle of group creation and disintegration, frequently involving specific individuals. Most insurgency groups in Africa start small and then grow. For example, the 27 fighters starting the National Resistance Movement (NRM) in Uganda, the 35 trained soldiers that started the Revolutionary United Front (RUF) in Sierra Leone, and the group of around 100 fighters who crossed into Liberia with Charles Taylor all grew into large groups that are difficult to quantify.

The combatants themselves are difficult to define. Any cursory glance at the literature dealing with rebel movements leads to a number of different definitions: rebels, brigands, subversive elements, gangs, criminals, warlords, militia, etc. All of these are loaded terms.[14] Within any violent armed group in Africa there will be a network of concentric groups with different linkages and loyalties. These will vary from those who are directly loyal to an individual warlord, ethnicity, identity, or clan (or combination). This would include those loyal to warlords within the RUF (Sierra Leone) and National Patriotic Front of Liberia (NPLF) as well as ethnic groups such as the Acholi in Uganda and Eritreans. One of the defining characteristics of African combat groups is the fluidity of the relationship between various armed groups within societies. There is a blurring of the boundary between soldier and civilian as the gap between them in terms of status, values, and systems narrows. In 1996 *Africa Confidential* reported that an area close to the capital of Sierra Leone was controlled by a series of groups including 30–50 sobels; irregular groups of around 50–80 fighters operating under the patronage of senior army officers; around 80–100 escaped prisoners from a local jail; RUF dissidents in bands of around 80 who mounted road blocks to extract 'tax'; and around 50–100 Liberian fighters from the defunct United Liberation Movement for Democracy.[15] The 'government' forces of the time were an equally mixed bag, incorporating demoralized troops from the former army, Nigerian troops, traditional hunters from the south and east, and various mercenaries.

Beyond this frequently small core there will be a loose and fluctuating network of related groups consisting of gangs, breakaway groups loyal to individuals or groups that cannot be ruled effectively. This is encouraged by an emphasis on a pseudo-feudal system of primitive accumulation, whereby territory is only valued for the resources it holds and those resources are granted as a means of paying subordinates.

The final group consists of auxiliaries employed to gain control over resources or to destabilize areas. The expensive end of this method is the employment of mercenary companies by governments, but the far more common feature is the use of auxiliary groups to operate outside territory nominally controlled by states. For example the large number of groups in the Northern DRC, particularly in the Kivu region, can trace support back to Rwanda, Uganda, or Sudan. The prevalence of these groups has led to accusations of Uganda and Sudan carrying out a proxy war in the DRC.[16]

This leads to a complex problem: How can you tell government forces from insurgents? In Africa, Governments themselves frequently lack formal armed forces due to years of under-funding, lack of training and weaponry. During the Sierra Leone War, for example, some of the most effective troops deployed against the RUF were *kamajor* fighters that were indistinguishable from RUF troops.[17] The network structures of many violent groups mean that there is frequently competition over specific auxiliaries, i.e. they change sides. The overall picture, then, is very much one of a series of concentric circles of loosely networked groups with considerable overlap between Government and rebel forces.[18]

Signs, signals and youth

Symbolism has played a critical part in most contemporary African wars. In particular, the use of symbolism as a form of control over predominantly youthful followers has been a feature of most combat groups. While leaders may be older, the majority of fighters are in their teens or twenties having enlisted young. The Lord's Resistance Army (LRA) in northern Uganda has a deliberate policy of kidnapping children allowing a more complete indoctrination and control.[19] The RUF in Sierra Leone also recruited alienated rural youth, usually from unemployed groups or from economically poor areas.

The use of traditional initiation techniques by many groups forms a system of bonding the fighters together in a team through traumatization. There is also some evidence to suggest that violence could also encourage bonding among groups of young men that start from a position of alienation. The life of a rebel is invariably more interesting and exciting than the frustrations of a peaceful life in rural Africa, and, in addition promise a chance of betterment and power through wielding a gun. As Skelt points out, 'deceived by diamonds, bored by agriculture, and powerless against corrupt politicians and lack of opportunities' joining rebel movements was a positive move.[20]

The emphasis on atrocities also has a disciplinary effect. Several returnees from the LRA cite fear of reprisals for their deeds as one reason why they took part in atrocities.[21] The idea of this is that once you have stepped over the mark, you are ostracized from society and cannot go back, either for fear of revenge or through shame at your own actions. One interesting feature of the post-war transformation of Liberia has been the incredibly high number of born again Christians as former fighters seek forgiveness.[22] This is also manifest in the idea that 'it was someone else who did those things and now I am back', an idea that Ellis explores with the idea of fighters adopting metaphorical 'masks'.[23]

For many fighters, technology is represented by the television. The impact of television and video is often mentioned in analyses of violence in West Africa. It is clear that films such as Rambo were in circulation long before the rise of Taylor and Sankoh, and that these videos were popular among the young men who later formed the bulk of combatants. In the West, 'Rambo' has become a caricature of violence and a vehicle for making fun of its star. However, in West Africa there is some identification with the social exclusion elements and the cathartic results of uncontrolled violence, particularly in forcing society to take notice of what it has done in being responsible for alienation. What young Sierra Leoneans see in Rambo is that the young, clever, and strong have a chance to outwit and defeat well-armed but slow-witted opponents even if they are out-numbered.[24] Certainly, fighters routinely adorned themselves with Rambo head-bands and even took names for themselves based on things they had seen within films.[25]

A *New York Times* reporter interviewed a faction leader, General Boley, just as he was putting his fighters through their paces at first light:

> Colonel Action, a reed-thin killer with cane juice eyes, passes me a joint the size of a corn dog. 'Smoke it deep' he says. General War Boss III, General Rambo, General Murder and Captain Mission Impossible all nod encour-agement ... I decline to smoke, but this is a vicious bush weed they grow here and the contact high is head-splitting. General Murder passes me a plastic bottle of cane juice.[26]

And so this Liberian military faction prepared for its days work.

The culture of violence and mutated ideas of US 'youth culture' had led to the adoption of drugs and alcohol as a means of being reckless in action. In particular, the use of amphetamines, alcohol, marijuana, and local drugs such as *khat* is widespread. The youth culture tag so infused the factions that later in the war there was far less wearing of women's clothes or warpaint, and far more aping of celluloid heroes through baseball caps, tee-shirts, Bermuda shorts, flip-flops, bandanas, basketball boots, crew cuts, and even mohican haircuts or braided hair. The one item that continued to be worn was something for spiritual protection, providing an overall effect that mixed pre and post-modern fashion and belief systems.

The mixture of this idea of the 'other', local spiritual beliefs and the cultural influences of Rambo, leads to a militarization based on performance where the actual mode of behaviour on the battlefield is as much designed to instil fear as to gain tactical military superiority. The comic horror dress of many of the fighters was designed to protect and disguise the warrior. By extension, the bizarre assortment of costumes was designed to hark back to traditional African modes of warfare.[27] It is difficult to argue that a fighter dressed in a red *Nike* Tee shirt, some Kung Fu Kit, probably some women's clothing of some description, a *Friday the 13th* horror mask and a Stars and Stripes plastic helmet is either reliving the role of a pre-colonial African warrior or engaged in developing a new generation of warfare.

Heterogeneity

African conflicts are also heterogeneous. Africa is frequently incorporated into international relations discourse as a single entity and on the margin, whereas the level of variety is enormous across the continent and many different actors are involved. Some analysts, like Shaw, see heterogeneity as implying a need for a regional approach to the analysis of African conflict rather than a continent-wide approach.[28]

There are also significant variations within regions drawing on, for example, widely differing colonial experiences. Shaw divides these usefully into three main groups: orthodox inter-state/regime conflicts and responses (Ethiopia, Eritrea, Uganda); semi-orthodox, semi-state conflicts (Angola, DRC, Sudan); and, non-orthodox, mainly non-state conflicts and responses (Somalia, West Africa). Semantics notwithstanding, this is a useful typology for illustrating the sliding scale from formal war through to, effectively, conflict between gangs. Each African country is on a different point on this scale and each has a different mix of combatants. There is no 'one-size-fits-all' theory to encompass this complexity.

Conclusions

Clearly 4GW has been present for some time in Africa and resurfaces when the power of the state declines, creating space for non-state actors to exercise a violent exit strategy. These groups are not necessarily sophisticated and may be successful against some African regimes, but are rarely successful against Western armies or well-trained and equipped African militaries.[29] The problem across most of Africa is that most militaries are not well trained and equipped. Even when they are this tends to lead to a long-term military stalemate in the absence of an acceptable political solution, as even the highly professional South Africans discovered.

What the 4GW thesis misses is the subtlety of the different African actors' motivations, aspirations and modes of warfare. A danger of creating one view of insurgency is that it will inevitably, in US eyes, be based on the experiences of Iraq and Afghanistan. This leaves Africa, the most peripheral global continent both politically and economically, with the highest rates of violent conflict, the most instability and also the highest potential for future 'disorder'. Nevertheless, the 4GW approach does represent a step forward in understanding the nature of many conflicts across Africa.

Despite this, there are three areas where African warfare offers challenges to the theory of 4GW: history, spiritualism, and exclusion.

The first area that 4GW needs to address is the nature of the generational paradigm itself. In Africa, it is by no means clear that warfare has passed through the first, second, and third generations of warfare, let alone entering a fourth. While there are a number of similarities with 4GW, the basic mode of warfare in Africa has not changed significantly since pre-colonial times. In 1896 in his seminal work on guerrilla warfare, Charles Callwell stated:

> The crushing of a populace in arms and the stamping out of widespread dis-affection by military methods, is a harassing form of warfare even in a civil-ized country with a settled social system; in remote regions peopled by half-civilized races or wholly savage tribes, such campaigns are most difficult to bring to a satisfactory conclusion, and are always most trying to the troops.[30]

This is closely linked to the second issue. Virtually all African rebel groups, regardless of other motivation, hark back to earlier warrior traditions. This is not to say that the young rebels of the RUF or LRA are part of a romantic vision of an earlier warrior caste, but there are echoes of earlier ways of dealing with violence. In particular, the use of witchcraft, spiritualism, and secret societies are used as a means of motivation, internal terror, and as a means of using terror to perpetrate war.

In terms of motivation, individual warriors are prepared for battle by invoking earlier ideas of warrior spirits. Secret societies are used as a means of building a sense of togetherness, and also as a means of establishing legitimate authority.[31] Charles Taylor was widely reported to have eaten the heart of his chief rival as a means of gaining magical power, whereas Alice Lakwena was regarded as a witch. At an individual level, symbolism, including becoming 'someone else' to go to war, strengthens the ability of warriors to perpetrate violence.[32] This has implications for rehabilitation and acceptance of combatants back into society through the use of cleansing rituals. This complicates the motivations of insurgents, the nature of combat and their rehabilitation.[33]

Lastly, there is an absence in the debate of a real understanding of the motivations of many insurgents in Africa. A 'classic' 4GW conflict such as Iraq is clearly politically motivated, with religious overtones. However, the rank and file combatants that make up the bulk of insurgency movements may be motivated by simpler, more basic reasons. The average life expectancy in rural Sierra Leone during the war was around 33 years. At the same time there was no access to government services, health or education and youths were excluded from political and social networks and even marriage. Given the conditions, it is hardly surprising that picking up an AK47 and taking to the bush appears to be an attractive way to gain empowerment.[34]

If the 4GW approach represents a step forward in the analysis of insurgency, then it requires further development to encompass the complexity of current African conflicts.

Notes

1 Quoted in Ian Beckett, 'The Future of Insurgency', *Small Wars and Insurgencies*, Vol. 16, no. 1 (March 2005), 22–36. Smith was talking of the impending campaign against the Ottawa Chief Pontiac in the Ohio Valley.
2 There are a number of papers by Evans, van Creveld, Wirtz, Echevarria, Ferris, Sorenson, and Thornton included in a symposium issue of *Contemporary Security Policy*, Vol. 26, no. 2, (August 2005).
3 Thomas X. Hammes, 'War Evolves into a Fourth Generation', *Contemporary Security Policy*, Vol. 26, no. 2 (August 2005) p. 1–51.
4 See, for example, Mary Kaldor, *New and Old Wars: Organized Violence in a Global Era*, Cambridge, Polity, 2001, which takes the former Yugoslavia as a model that is then extrapolated.
5 See, for example, P. Collier and A. Hoeffler, 'On the Economic Causes of Civil War', *Oxford Economic Papers*, Vol. 50, no. 4 (1998), pp. 563–573; and P. Collier and A.

Hoeffler, 'On the incidence of Civil War in Africa', *Journal of Conflict Resolution*, Vol. 46, no. 1 (2002), pp. 13–28.

6 An exception to this is J. Herbst, 'African Militaries and Rebellion: The Political Economy of Threat and Combat Effectiveness', *Journal of Peace Research*, Vol. 41, no. 3 (2004), pp. 357–369, which tries to relate combat effectiveness with mobilization during conflicts. See also C. Clapham, *African Guerrillas*, Oxford, James Currey, 1998; J. Herbst, 'Economic Incentives, Natural Resources and Conflict in Africa', *Journal of African Economies*, Vol. 9, no. 3 (2000), pp. 270–294.

7 See, for example, Herbst, 'African Militaries and Rebellion'.

8 For an interesting view of this conflict, see C. Young, M. Mirzeler, 'Pastoral Politics in the Northeast Periphery in Uganda: AK47 as a Change Agent', *Journal of Modern African Studies*, Vol. 38, (2000), pp. 407–430.

9 See P. Jackson, 'The March of the Lord's Resistance Army: Greed or Grievance in Northern Uganda?' *Small Wars and Insurgencies*, Vol. 13, no. 3 (2002), pp. 29–52.

10 W. Reno, *Warlord Politics and African States*, Boulder, CO, Lynne Rienner, 1998.

11 D. Keen, 'The Economic Functions of Violence in Civil Wars', Adelphi Paper 320, Oxford University Press, International Institute for Strategic Studies, 1998.

12 For example, Lebanese trading networks across West Africa or Asian networks in East and Southern Africa.

13 This could of course be because warlords are clear about what they get out of it, i.e. corruption is explicit, not implicit as it is in dealing with formal government.

14 See M. Bhatia, 'Fighting Words: Naming Terrorists, Bandits, Rebels and Other Violent Actors', *Third World Quarterly*, Vol. 26, no. 1 (2005), pp. 5–22 for an interesting investigation into the 'politics of labelling.' The term 'combatant' is used here since it is simply the broadest and – in my view – the most neutral of the terms purely by being the most technically descriptive.

15 Reported in Alice Hills, 'Warlords, Militia and Conflict in Contemporary Africa: A Re-examination of Terms', *Small Wars and Insurgencies*, Vol. 8, no. 1 (Spring 1997), pp. 35–51.

16 See, G. Prunier, 'Rebel Movements and Proxy Warfare: Uganda, Sudan and the Congo (1986–99)', *African Affairs*, Vol. 103, no. 412 (2004), pp. 359–384.

17 And, notably, turned the RUF's ultra-violent tactics back on to them. In one meeting in Bo Town in Sierra Leone, one former combatant told me that they regularly executed RUF infiltrators and either sent them back in pieces to the rebels or divided them up between the different commands to encourage teamwork!

18 This raises an interesting issue from the point of view of 4GW in that it no longer becomes an asymmetrical conflict, but rather a conflict of equals.

19 See Jackson, 'Greed or Grievance in Northern Uganda' for a more detailed discussion of the importance of youth in recruitment and indoctrination. One of the reasons for employing child soldiers is their reputation for disregard for danger and human life, and susceptibility to brainwashing through traumatization as initiation.

20 Joanna Skelt, *Rethinking Peace Education in War-Torn Societies: A Theoretical and Empirical Investigation with Special Reference to Sierra Leone*, Cambridge, International Extension College, 2002.

21 Jackson, 'Greed or Grievance in Northern Uganda'.

22 Stephen Ellis, *The Mask of Anarchy: The Destruction of Liberia and the Religious Dimension of an African Civil War*, London, Hurst, 1999.

23 Ellis, *The Mask of Anarchy*.

24 Richards, *Fighting for the Rain Forest*. It should be pointed out that Richards uses Rambo as an example and does not suggest that all of the fighters were systematically watching the film and then picking up guns.

25 Richards also cites an eyewitness who states that the NPFL in Liberia had five generator-powered video parlours operating twenty-four hours a day and showing US films in the vein of *Rambo: First Blood*.

26 Quoted in Ellis, *The Mask of Anarchy*, p. 120. It should be noted that in the original article in the *New York Times Magazine*, 22 January 1995, the reporter notes that the General introduces him to the 'professional fighting men' of his faction, which begs the question what were the less professional ones like?

27 But was actually represented by that most post-modern of American materials – plastic.

28 T. Shaw, 'Regional Dimensions of Conflict and Peace-Building in Contemporary Africa', *Journal of International Development*, vol. 15, (2003), pp. 487–498.

29 This is clearly illustrated by the collapse of the combatants in Sierra Leone during the intervention of British Special Forces troops during Operation Barras in 2000.

30 Charles Callwell, *Small Wars: Their Principles and Practices*, 3rd edn, HMSO, 1972, p. 26. This is a summary of much previous British thinking on counter-insurgency and is only one of an entire library of Imperial counter-insurgency manuals.

31 Stephen Ellis, *The Mask of Anarchy*.

32 For example, Charles Taylor's troops were originally from Nimba County in Liberia and were frequently pictured with faces painted white and in women's clothing. This was held to be part of a ritual whereby an individual had to become a different person.

33 Particularly when there is a general belief in, for example, immunity from bullets.

34 As Paul Richards points out, following Durkheim, there are elements of slave revolt in the development of many armed groups, or at least a violent expression of the dispossessed. Paul Richards, 'To Fight or to Farm? Agrarian Dimensions of the Mano River Conflict', *African Affairs*, Vol. 104, no. 417 (2005), pp. 571–590.

Part V

The implications of Fourth Generation Warfare

19 Combating Fourth Generation Warfare

F.G. Hoffman

In the twenty-first century, the doctrine of maneuver warfare is less an operational doctrine and more a way of thinking, a new kind of security shield created by creative thought and imagination.[1]

The events of September 11, 2001 punctuated the end of one era of war, and heralded the dawning of a new one. This new era presents policy makers and national security with its own method of conflict, one that makes conventional thinkers uncomfortable and traditional solutions unworkable. This kind of war, as Mao suggested long ago, has several constituent components and overwhelming military power alone is insufficient. Regardless of some unfounded speculation, this does not eliminate the utility of the timeless Prussian sage, Carl von Clausewitz or some 15 centuries of recorded military history before Westphalia. Quite the contrary, he recognized that every age has its own conception of war.[2] But Osama Bin Laden and his ilk shook the West from its long-standing strategic complacency, reintroducing the need for a reassessment of security challenges and the corresponding means of meeting these threats.

Today's "Long War" makes the originators of Fourth Generation Warfare (4GW) more than merely prophetic.[3] More than a decade's worth of unipolar delusion and unilateral triumphialism went up in smoke on 9/11. European illusions fell later after London, Madrid and Paris gave pause to the idea that war and savage violence was something in the Continent's collective past. American hubris about its invulnerability and over-financed Pentagon were the principal victims of 9/11 and the subsequent war in Iraq. Kaplan's "Coming Anarchy" has arrived with full force, but with more transnational connectivity and political direction.[4] Rather than anarchy, today's security is being challenged more by a violent but politically organized reaction to the alienation and fragmentation fostered by globalization and the internal factions of the Middle East.[5]

The future portends an even more lethal strain of perturbation. A study sponsored by the National Intelligence Council argued that "lagging economies, ethnic affiliations, intense religious convictions and youth bulges will align to create a 'perfect storm' for internal conflict" in the near future.[6] Other analysts point out that Iraq's insurgents and jihadist foreign fighters will benefit from their education in Iraq, and will soon return home or to alternative battlespaces with greater motivation, lethal skills and credibility.[7] Their Darwinian evolution against America's vaunted military has refined their methods and emboldened their plans, while the clash within Islam continues unabated. The West remains unprepared to provide security against a stateless entity that deliberately targets its weaknesses and never plays to its military strength.[8]

I am very sympathetic to the arguments, made by commentators in this volume and elsewhere, that the "generational" framework of 4GW is flawed or that it represents a new form of war. Yet whatever one may think about the concept, the reality of 4GW is now difficult to dismiss. What is not debatable is the intensity of this new form of conflict, or the West's relative vulnerability. Numerous analysts have begun pointing to the increasingly blurred nature of future warfare, a mode of hybrid warfare, combining the lethality of state-based armies, with the cunning adaptation of insurgencies.[9] It is not just that conventional warfare or interstate conflict is on the decline, there is a fusion of war forms emerging, one that blurs regular and irregular warfare.[10] As Hammes noted, wars have been "a mixed bag of conventional and unconventional." Since World War II the mix has leaned toward the conventional and we are seeing a reverse of that combination today. The merging modes of war will remain essentially irregular to Western democracies and their even more conventional armies, but increase in scope and lethality. To avoid the generational history debate, I prefer the term Complex Irregular Warfare (CIW) over 4GW.[11]

Whatever the terms used, it is quite simply a defining challenge, not because of its monolithic status or existential threat, but because of our cultural predisposition to miscomprehend its pervasiveness, to underestimate its protracted nature, and to ignore our own lack of preparedness. We are not prepared for the passions of tribal warfare on the global stage.[12] Nor are we ready to compete actively with the viral contagion that rages both in the Zone of Peace and that of Chaos. This infectious and destructive virus must be offset with a dose of reality and a clear and compelling positive alternative. We need to be willing and able to "discredit, delegitimize and dismantle barbaric ideas" to win at CIW.[13]

The theory of 4GW may be viewed as ineloquent in its historical foundation but its relevance is unquestionable. While the proponents have done an excellent job of laying out the nature of this challenge, this essay lays out some basic fundamentals to combat the rise of CIW for consideration.[14]

Strategic considerations

The traditional way to approach strategic options to impose our will upon an opponent is Delbruck's two major options. One is the strategy of *annihilation*, which calls for the substantial if not the total destruction of the enemy force. The alternative approach, more common to the weaker side, is to employ a strategy of *exhaustion*. A strategy of exhaustion seeks to wear down the opponent and his will by raising costs and protracting a conflict over time. Neither strategy is exclusive, there will be violent and destructive moments within the latter strategy, and annihilation is often set up by exhausting maneuver in one domain or another to establish the conditions for a decisive and overwhelming victory. But these time honored choices are too simplistic for today's world.

Another way of looking at strategy is to compare destructive versus constructive strategies. This may be a far better way of examining overall strategies and subcomponents in 4GW or CIW in the future. As seen in Table 19.1, there are a number of components or sub-strategies to each of these fundamental approaches. The more destructive approaches emphasize kinetic destruction and physical properties. Annihilation of the adversary and repression against his supporting base are the oldest approaches, and imperial powers of the past have gained temporary success with such measures going back to Alexander. Russian failures in Afghanistan and Chechnya in the twentieth century suggest that this approach is just as often a colossal failure. The decapitation of the key cadre or elites of an organization is another approach with a long history, but not one recommended to stem modern CIW opponents or well networked adversaries like today's global insurgent.[15] Decapitation may work against opposition groups dependent upon a charismatic leader, but are largely irrelevant against well-distributed networks.[16]

Isolation, in the physical sense, is a common security measure during insurgencies and rebellions. Creating a means of physically isolating a threat or at least negating the ability to easily enter and plunder one's own population has been a component of strategy since Emperor Hadrian ordered the construction of the Roman fortification line across Britain. This technique has little application when the adversary is not located in a contiguous position, or when avenues of approach are unlimited. Likewise, isolation in the physical sense is unlikely where the opponent is already infiltrated throughout society and cannot be isolated from the population.

"Incapacitation" may be more appropriate in many cases. We rarely intend or need to annihilate a rebel force, and may find it counterproductive to do so with respect to long-term political objectives. The more destruction we create in the early phases, only elongates the missions and raises resistance to our presence and effort. But some offensive forms of direct action may be needed to minimize the enemy's freedom of action or neutralize his ability to interfere with the counter-CIW force. By raising the costs for his operations or limiting his freedom of action, our relative ability to control tempo is enhanced. Keeping the CIW off balance, dispersed and limited only to the periphery is a supporting objective to improved security for both the general population and our own security. Incapacitation is limited to attacks upon critical vulnerabilities, including communications, arms caches and other resources.[17] This component is probably only a supporting aspect of a broader approach that emphasizes more positive aims, but it may remain critical to maximizing the credibility of the host government and demonstrating its ability to protect the population.

More constructive approaches are needed to stem a CIW approach. A constructive strategy seeks to undermine the true source of strength of the adversary in CIW, his ideological base and the attractiveness of his appeal for support,

Table 19.1 Destructive versus Constructive Strategies

Strategies	Approaches	Description
Destructive	Annihilation	Can include ethnic cleansing and mass violence against both combatants and population
	Repression	Mostly focused on population
	Decapitation	Solely targeted against leadership
	Incapacitation	Targeted against critical nodes or key supporting infrastructure
	Isolation	Physical barrier to control or eliminate interaction
Constructive	Subversion	Generate mistrust/confusion/paralysis within or between the opposing leadership, cadre, combatants or support base
	Penetration	Physically penetrate and subvert either by deed or mistrust
	Political Reform	Negotiated or preemptive change
	Economic	Redressing employment or distribution of society's resources, includes land reforms
	Ideological	Focuses on the psychological and informational domain
		Crucial to non-kinetic isolation

intelligence, or resources. There are a number of indirect approaches within this broader and less kinetic suite of strategies.

Subversion is a well worn strategy for counteracting an insurgency, and generally involves sowing internal discord or mistrust into the adversary organization. Insurgents historically have reflected internal divisions and a "divide and conquer" strategy has been offered since Machiavelli to exploit this weakness.[18] Attacking inconsistencies or shortfalls within the adversary organization's purpose, structure, or achievements is conducted in order to subvert its internal cohesion, or undermine its attractiveness to current or future members.[19] A center of gravity for many networks is their internal cohesion or trust. In that many groups have multiple factions, internal leadership struggles, or internal arguments about goals and methods, subversion may be a way of introducing increased friction or higher operating costs on the enemy. Subversion can be accomplished by effective information operations including leaks, street gossip, or introducing items into broadcast media or even the communications links of the adversary system.

An advanced but risky form of subversion entails what are called Pseudo operations.[20] Pseudo operations have been used in past counterinsurgencies, and require the use of indigenous or foreign units to dress, arm and behave as an insurgent organization. Pseudo techniques were used successfully by the British in Kenya against the Mau Mau, by the US MAC-V-SOG in Vietnam, and by Rhodesian Selous Scouts. Pseudo operational techniques may be oriented on gathering intelligence, luring insurgent units into ambushes in their own backyard, or they may repress a supporting populace in order to separate an insurgent from his popular base. This latter technique is fraught with risk if the true nature of the unit is ever revealed, and could be counter-productive.

Penetration is another potential approach. Against CIW opponents the chances of a significant penetration is unlikely but not impossible. American law enforcement officials were successful in penetrating the Cosa Nostra or American Mafia over time, using both turncoats and its own agents. British intelligence has had success in penetrating the IRA in Northern Ireland from time to time. But modern cells of the Islamic movement are widely distributed and built upon group dynamics that make penetration very improbable.[21]

Both subversion and penetration may be extremely effective forms of inciting factionalism within complex organizations such as networked entities conducting CIW. Recent research suggests that even absent external provocation or deliberate intervention, complex insurgent networks are vulnerable to internal fissures and destructive behavior.[22] Of course, this requires a fairly comprehensive understanding of the network, and its internal values, leadership and behavior. Western military forces and their intelligence organs have not demonstrated any virtuosity so far in this undertaking, and should seek to leverage the local expertise of the host nation and expatriates to better advantage.

Negotiation for political or economic reforms is another. Few insurgencies have been defeated outright, many more have been "defeated" by governments making the necessary improvements in governance and by the redistribution of society's power. Most of the so-called success by British counterinsurgencies can be tied to negotiated removal of colonial control and the removal of economic reforms that were central to the grievance of the insurgency.

Ideological confrontation is another key strategic option. Ideas and grievances are the seeds of CIW and ideological contests are the principal battleground and often the central strategy. This is nothing new; words and ideas are recognized weapons in this form of warfare.[23] Modern information technology has given anyone with access to a computer the ability to spread a message globally at a fraction of what it used to cost, and at the speed of sound. Given that CIW are ultimately won or lost in the political and psychological dimension, the importance of communications and information dissemination is vital. The velocity of information flows and the power of imagery can now be readily transmitted instantly. This can generate significant support for one's cause throughout the international system or through a network of sympathizers and supporters. It can be a force multiplier to the side that can employ the informational domain to secure and sustain a positional advantage in the moral or psychological dimension. Since popular opinion or support may be the center of gravity or a critical vulnerability in the conduct of CIW, the importance of these technological shifts cannot be overlooked. While the US military has a demonstrated capacity to dominate a situation with its technological supremacy and computer software, its performance in Iraq suggests it remains handicapped by its techno-lust and well short of mastering modern Information Warfare, where the most important software exists between the ears of the local population. At the strategic level, the American government has just about unilaterally disarmed itself.

The American military has myopically focused on Information Warfare and its cousin, net-centric warfare, to enhance traditional functions and missed the larger strategic influence of cyber tools. The US military has repeated the most frequent mistake of military innovation, attempting to laminate new technology on top of old processes, and underestimating the imagination of our enemies. Recent scholarship has persuasively compared the ongoing cyber-mobilization of Muslims around the world to the French Revolution and the *levée en masse*.[24]

Modern cyber-mobilization benefits from numerous parallels to the French revolution. These include a democratization of communications, an increase in public access, sharp cost reductions in both production and distribution of media, and an exploitation of images to create and reinforce a mobilizing ideology or narrative. Today's computer and media saturated audience has an astonishing array of cyber choices that also have clear analogues to France's rising: blogs are today's revolutionary pamphlets, websites are the new dailies, and list services are today's broadsides.

Like the *levée en masse*, the evolving character of communications today is altering the patterns of popular mobilization, including both the means of participation and the ends for which wars are fought. It is enabling the recruiting, training, convincing and motivating of individuals. "Today's mobilization may not be producing masses of soldiers, sweeping across the European continent" – a modern day French *Grande Armée* does not threaten Europe – but it has produced a globally distributed uprising. The end result has produced real-world effects and magnified the influence and means of today's global guerrillas.[25] As Audrey Cronin perceptively warns, "Western nations will persist in ignoring the fundamental changes in popular mobilization at their peril."[26]

To counter the ideology or narrative of the CIW opponent at the strategic level, a counter narrative is needed.[27] A narrative is a sociology or anthropological term for any group's compelling story line which structures how information is processed and events explained. These narratives reinforce identity and group cohesion, generating a sense of purpose or rallying cause. The counter narrative should provide the central theme for resolving the conflict, delineate the major aspects of the subsequent information operations activities used by friendly forces, and provide general guidance to subordinate components, including the military. The US government continues to struggle with the basics of strategic communications, public diplomacy, public affairs and related information activities in this area.

An effective counter narrative will speak to the entire international community, serving to rally international support, isolate support to the insurgency and minimize its attractiveness and viability. As Hammes noted, the 4GW antagonist is going to talk to multiple audiences with his message, and so too must the counter-CIW narrative. This grand narrative must be able to deal with the various audiences of the global "deep fight" making the proverbial Three Block War into a Three Screen War, including CNN, Al Jazeera and the BBC.[28]

In sum, there are two very broad approaches and a subset of components to combat CIW. These two approaches may also be thought of in terms of being

Counter Force or Counter Value. While these are terms normally associated with the strategic or nuclear priesthood, they have compelling applications in the new world of CIW.[29] The "Counter Value" approach is recommended as the primary strategy, and that physical or kinetic methods be limited to incapacitation.

Operational considerations for combating the CIW adversary

I disagree with Colonel Hammes' conclusion that the rise of 4GW can defeat maneuver warfare.[30] What the US Marine Corps has documented as maneuver warfare philosophy is perfectly suited for winning against CIW foes because it accepts the inevitability of chaos, complexity and friction and the preeminence of the human element in conflict. Recognizing that even the simplest things in war are difficult, maneuver warfare places a premium on intelligence, flexibility and adaptability – essential attributes of a successful counter CIW force. Just as important, the emphasis in maneuver warfare on human intelligence, adaptive enemies, surprise, relative tempo and "maneuver" broadly defined, provide the cognitive foundation for CIW or 4GW.[31] Thanks to the foresight of John Boyd, William Lind and Colonel Mike Wyly, an intellectual framework for CIW exists.

Achieving battlespace synergy in the disaggregated battle

But ultimately, success against the protean nature of the transnational adversary requires the attainment of synergy by a broader coalition of national agencies. This is the essence of the leadership and organizational challenge posed by the CIW opponent, since his operations do not present easily templatable targets for traditional military operations, and occur over a wider or more accurately "disaggregated" battlespace which respects neither international borders nor the dysfunctional bureaucratic stovepipes of many Western governments.[32] Achieving this degree of coordinated synergy must be gained, and new forms of planning and integrating "combat power" in its broadest sense must be achieved. This may require an entire re-conception of operational art as we know it today. We do not have the planning processes to design and execute campaigns against CIW combatants at this time. As General Anthony Zinni, probably the foremost expert in the application of operational art against irregular opponents once suggested,

> The planning process, the decision-making process, the thinking process, is remarkably different. You need to be much broader based in your knowledge. You need to be much more flexible in your thinking. You've go to be prepared to take things that all your life have been completely logical – and understand that it does not apply. You may have to think entirely differently about cultures, about history, and the effects of the environment that will lead you to do things that you would never arrive at using your normal, logical, thinking process.[33]

Intelligence

The CIW planner views the battle space very differently from that of the conventional planner. Planners must expand beyond conventional enemy analysis to focus more on the local population, its cultural terrain, its connectivity to external sources of support, and probable reactions to potential US actions. This emphasis requires acute cultural intelligence; detailed knowledge of the ethnic, tribal, racial, economic, technical, religious and linguistic groups in the host nation, as well as the underlying cultural beliefs and narratives that distinguish their value system, from which we can attempt to think about how they would perceive and react to our operations. Bernard Brodie observed that "good strategy presumes good anthropology and good sociology," going on to add that, "Some of the greatest military blunders of all time have resulted from juvenile evaluations in this department."[34] But the study of culture and anthropology has been given short shrift in a country that assumes it can dictate changes to the very nature of war.[35]

In conventional warfare, destruction is the norm, whereas in small wars, persuasion and influence are more often the objective. This shift in emphasis from destruction to persuasion creates a radically different context for intelligence gathering and processing. In conventional conflicts, the warfighter's intelligence and information requirements are largely concerned with physical entities such as locations and dispositions of enemy armed forces. In CIW, these requirements are more often subjective evaluations of intentions, aspirations, and relationships. US forces are normally at a significant disadvantage in foreign areas because they lack local knowledge and have an ingrained Order of Battle mentality. Our national security community has experts who monitor and rigorously study the strategic and military culture of adversarial states, and assessing an opponent's military capabilities. During the Cold War, we created an entire cadre of experts in Russian history, language and culture. We became what Zinni calls Order of Battle oriented, focused on quantifying a known opponent and laying out his capabilities in neat templates.[36]

This orientation treats physical attributes such as armored vehicles and command posts as key nodes and capabilities for identification and tracking. In CIW, the cultural terrain and the relationships between groups and leaders is more relevant. This turns the intelligence collection process of Western militaries on its head, fixated on collecting mass quantities of intelligence from technological sources and packaging it for dissemination downwards to tactical units. In the context of CIW, much more information will come from the bottom up. A lot of information will be acted upon immediately, to leverage its value. Much more will have to be collected, painstakingly connected to other sources to generate true intelligence. All source fusion of this intelligence is what brings fidelity to the commander's estimate and ongoing planning. Commanders must ensure their entire organization becomes an indications and warnings system. Every patrol, every convoy, every visit to a local tribal leader is a potential collection source. Maintaining close contact with the civilian population, intensive patrolling and observation of populated areas, and developing networks of local sources, all create opportunities. Only such intimate interaction provides the level of understanding necessary to develop accurate situational awareness and any chance of anticipatory planning.

The Commander must ensure that intelligence drives operations, but may have to "fight" for it by conducting operations or exploiting routine actions in which intelligence may be garnered. In CIW, the conduct of operations will produce pieces of information that if properly processed could lead to further operations occurring at a tempo faster than the enemy can react. A clearing operation or a raid on a suspected arms cache may generate information on other sites or about future operations that can be leveraged to produce decisive results. A disk from a lap top computer left behind may unravel an entire network. Being prepared to exploit intelligence rapidly is key to success in CIW.

Maneuver

The essence of maneuver warfare is the creative and bold application of forces to generate and exploit opportunity. Maneuver means more than just the literal term, it is not limited to movement in a spatial sense. This is an area where I am surprised by Hammes' more narrow take on maneuver warfare. This would limit us to the mobility of units over terrain to gain a positional advantage versus an adversary. However, in the context of maneuver warfare, the term maneuver has a much broader context. It seeks to generate an advantage in several dimensions. As defined in Marine Corps doctrine, "That advantage may be psychological, technological, or temporal as well as spatial."[37]

Because of the need to reduce violence and to generate an advantage with a civilian population in CIW, this conception of maneuver takes on special meaning. Rather than focus on using fires to attrite an adversary's forces by physical destruction, the counter CIW force must maneuver in the broader sense to create multi-dimensional advantages to secure the civilian population, build up the local government, protect and enhance its critical infrastructure and economic resources. The counter CIW force may seek a physical positional advantage with military or security forces in order to preserve its freedom of action, and appearing able to move freely throughout the entire battlespace. But more often it will exploit non-military forms of maneuver to build up its credibility or capacity to influence events.

Civil Military Operations (CMO) are one of those nontraditional forms of maneuver employed to achieve advantage. CMO describes the efforts made to build and use associations with civilians in order to facilitate our primary military actions. At times, CMO itself may be the focus of our efforts, especially in CIW. Whatever the mission, CMO is a constant element throughout the planning and execution of military operations, and not merely an adjunct specialty that occurs before or after hostilities. These kinds of operations, sometimes referred to as post-conflict stability operations, are not secondary to the resolution of the conflict, they should be considered primary. If we consider this dimension in the design of a campaign or battle, we can limit problems that may lead to greater violence and a more costly campaign. Because of the nature of CIW, CMO is a critical shaping capability and potentially a decisive form of "maneuver" for the commander.

Fires

Another traditional concept in military operations is the employment of fires. Fires are employed to delay, disrupt, degrade or destroy enemy capabilities, or reduce his will to resist. Fires can also be used as a shaping action to facilitate or mask maneuver. Consistent with the concept of combined arms, fires are usually integrated with maneuver to shape the battlespace and establish conditions for decisive action. Fires in the context of a conventional conflict involves the collective and coordinated employment of target acquisition systems – fires from direct and indirect weapons, armed aircraft including UAVs – to destroy or neutralize military forces, physical targets or the electromagnetic spectrum.

But in CIW conflicts, we need to reconsider the nature of fires, and accept the primacy of the political and psychological dimensions of the conflict and employ our "fires" to seek influence and results in these dimensions. There is a classic statement in the venerable *Small Wars Manual*, "instead of striving to generate maximum power with forces available, the goal is to gain decisive results with the least application of force and the consequent minimum loss of life."[38] As a non-kinetic form of combat power, information operations (IO) and activities must be a significant part of a CIW campaign plan. CIW campaigns are battles of ideas and battles for the perceptions and attitudes of target populations.

Traditional military forces are good at applying kinetic solutions, which are a form of influence as well, and they will play a support role in CIW. Other non-kinetic military tools however, such as psychological operations, civil affairs, engineer and medical, are the fires and maneuver of CIW. They frequently are the main effort simply because of the criticality of the functions they perform. Their efforts, when backed-up by traditional military forces and combined with the entire panoply of other instruments of national power (government and civilian resources, including political or diplomatic, economic and information, as well as intelligence, financial, judicial, law enforcement and humanitarian), are the primary means toward achieving the desired end state in many CIW situations. Not surprisingly, the growing importance of IO has been added to the original Three Block War concept.[39]

Psychological Operations (PSYOPs) are a critical supporting arm in CIWs. PSYOPs also has a counter-propaganda role to negate an adversary's attempt at influencing local, US and coalition audiences. Commander's must be alert to this threat, and have prepared "counter-battery fires" in the informational domain to offset or negate this influence. An effective enemy propaganda campaign can have enormous impact on operations; from prompting neutral parties to resist military operations to causing a coalition partner to withdraw support. If

IO can turn the people who tacitly support the adversary, it can decisively affect both the adversary's material support and morale. American IO procedures are notoriously slow and unresponsive to this aspect of CIW.

An overall objective during CIW is to compete in the informational battle, and win the battle of ideas and the politico-military struggle for power. The IO capabilities and supporting of related activities enable or support military operations that create opportunities for decisive battles. These capabilities, when synchronized, counter the CIW opponent and subversive activity while seizing and maintaining the initiative with a steady broadcast or delivery of information. It is for this reason that Lawrence of Arabia observed, "the printing press is the greatest weapon in the armoury of the modern commander."[40] It may now be the video camera or the DVD copier.

Planning considerations

Battlespace geometry

The commander and his staff must consider the altered nature of battlespace geometry in CIW. The battlefield framework lays out the way the commander will organize his assigned area of the battlespace and arrays the main effort, reserve and security forces. The counter CIW force will not be sweeping through a battlespace or "maneuvering" some number of miles per day. The concept of deep and rear areas are different. Strategically the "deep area" could be thought of as regional support for a host nation, and the support of its own population. Actions the Coalition or Joint Task Force can take in the deep area include many long-term projects that build up the government and its political and service institutions. The "rear area" is our own population at home, an area in which the current US administration took for granted for too long. In the close fight, operationally, we expect anti-CIW forces to routinely occupy noncontiguous areas and conduct more distributed forms of operations.[41] Instead of a traditional battlespace organization, it may be more likely that the counter CIW force will take up a series of small and often changing battle spaces within an AOR for the conduct of nonlinear operations with noncontiguous deep, close and rear areas.[42]

At the strategic level, the battlespace has to be considered at least at the theater if not the global level, depending upon the nature of the opponent. Obviously, when dealing with the likes of al Qaeda, a global dimension must be considered, necessitating a strategic capacity to think holistically and operate in the "virtual dimension" across many theaters.[43] The nature of globalization and information technology extends the potential support base of the adversary to a global dimension. This extended support base can provide financial, material or personnel support to the cause. Of particular relevance to future CIW, the availability of modern information technology radically changes the manner by which potential adversary's acquire and disseminate strategic intelligence, how they recruit and rehearse. Al Qaeda's globally dispersed operations, facilitated by the Internet and modern telecommunications technology, make them a truly network-based adversary and vastly complicates the definition of the battlespace to well beyond the geographic or territorial dimension that has dominated warfare for the past few centuries.[44]

Shaping actions

In purely military operations, shaping is defined as the use of lethal and/or non-lethal activities to influence events in a manner that changes the general condition of war to our advantage as steps toward decisive operations. In the context of CIW, shaping actions refer to the application of various elements of national power; political, diplomatic, economic, military, social, legal and informational to modify or shape conditions. It is by shaping the mental conditions in the opponents mind or in his supporting population that decisive operations are achieved. As part of the "close fight," local security efforts and security assistance efforts will be conducted. The day-to-day interaction between Marines and the local population occurs in the close combat area, as do many CMO projects that target social and economic development opportunities.

Information operations are a significant element in shaping actions. They are the modern "fires" used to mold perceptions and inform target populations of ongoing efforts that impact their lives and aspirations. The difficulty of achieving effective IO in foreign cultures cannot be underestimated. It requires an acute understanding of the culture and belief systems of a people. The prevalence of new information technologies and the pervasive presence of modern media require that we redouble our public diplomacy and educational efforts and begin focusing on shaping the informational dimension of the battlespace. Because CIW has a very high informational component, it is possible that successful shaping operations can be sufficient to accomplish the desired end-state and thus can become "decisive" operations.

Decisive operations

In CIW "decisive" may not be decisive in the traditional military meaning of the term. In this context, "decisive" means achieving a clear decision or final resolution on a specific objective or goal rather than necessarily reaching a broad and definitive conclusion. Once multi-dimensional shaping has set the stage for successful decisive operations, the concerted application of all elements of national power must be used to accomplish the desired end-state. Frequently, the military will play a prominent role during the decisive stage, but close coordination among all agencies is still vital for lasting success.

The cumulative impact of many discrete shaping actions can eventually achieve a "tipping point" in the minds of the civilian population that describes a point in time where they accept and desire the existing government as its legitimate vehicle for the representation of its views and authorizes it to act on their collective behalf for the delivery of services and governance. Likewise, at some point in the protracted series of military and non-military activities directed at the counter-governmental force, it too reaches a "tipping point" where it recognizes that it cannot attain popular support, resources or a decision. This is the decisive point in the conflict.

Single battle

The most important aspect we must consider during CIW is focusing holistically on the problem presented, and the integrated use of all the tools available to accomplish it. Ultimately, we want to influence foreign audiences to behave in certain ways. We have a wide range of tools available with which to influence them, from traditional kinetic resources to more subtle ones such as civil military and psychological operations. The trick is to consider them all and carefully select what, how and when you will use them. The harder trick is coordinating the message and the Joint Task Force's maneuver, synchronizing the delivery of both CMO and IO, and integrating them to gain synergy and success. The important thing to understand is that in CIW, all aspects of national power must be integrated into the campaign and the execution of operations. In a sense, the terms Civil–Military Operations and Information Operations are misnomers. They are not operations in their own right. They are functions or activities that must be integrated into counter CIW to *influence* the adversary and the populace. That's the basic challenge in CIW, fighting the "single battle" with many tangible and intangible assets into a cohesive campaign.

The difficulty of integrating both military and non-military forces and capabilities should not be taken lightly. It cannot be thought of in Jominian or linear terms, using eighteenth- and nineteenth-century operational art, including Lines of Operation and Decisive Points. It must be planned holistically from beginning to end, and execution of the plan must attain the synergy we traditionally associate with combined arms at the operational level of war.

Operational activities

Although there is no prescribed set of phases for the conduct of CIW, it is useful for commanders and their staffs to consider the nominal set of activities listed below. The acronym "MINDOPS" offers a useful mneumonic device for thinking about the nature of the operational efforts involved to successfully thwart a cunning CIW adversary. This provides a useful grouping of tasks that may allow the commander to envision the application of interagency task force's efforts in time and place. These activities may be phased but should not be considered sequential. They are a point of departure for considering how a campaign may unfold. The actual missions and tasks assigned to the Coalition force or Joint Task Force commander may vary this set.

Mission analysis

This analysis is an iterative process that never actually ends, as long as the opponent is contesting our own interests and will. It must be based upon a detailed appreciation of the political object assigned by higher authority and the physical terrain and culture of the target country/region. In addition to a profound grasp of the nature of war, we need to gain a deep and nuanced understanding of the conflict we are about to embark on and acquire as thorough a grasp of the nature of the adversary as possible. This includes becoming well informed about the culture of the adversarial social and political system as well. It has become a cliché to intone Clausewitz's most important warning about "The first, the supreme, the most far-reaching act of judgment that the statesmen and commander have to make is to establish ... is the kind of war on which they are embarking." This particular judgment on the part of civilian and military leaders is difficult to establish for numerous reasons. Commanders and planners who are examining a potential contingency need to assess the nature of the conflict in very detailed terms, often with limited time and information to access experts or databases.

As in any war, large or small, a thorough mission analysis is necessary to determine specified and implied tasks from the higher headquarters' mission statement. This also includes determining centers of gravity and associated critical vulnerabilities, determining the desired end-state and establishing measures of effectiveness. In the case of CIWs, the conduct of a mission analysis is not always easy. Commanders may be left to plan what is required based upon inferred information due to the suddenness of a crisis. Likewise the development of centers of gravity and critical vulnerabilities is complicated by the amorphous nature of the opponent. However, no matter how nonlinear or adaptive the enemy, his requirement to gather resources and intelligence, or to recruit new supporters, as well as operate against the government to sustain his movement or position will open any network or structure to analysis and a determination of potential critical vulnerabilities. New and sophisticated forms of network and link analysis are being developed to assist planners in this task.

Unfortunately, these are exactly the kinds of conflicts we will be involved in for the next few decades. "Fault line" wars place a premium on an in-depth knowledge base of the other component of a nation's strategic culture – its societal culture. The roots of victory or defeat often have to be sought far from the battlefield, in political, social or economic factors.[45] Nor is this news to those familiar with the Marine's classical *Small Wars Manual*, which notes, "The campaign plan and strategy must be adapted to the character of the people encountered."[46] It is impossible for US forces to succeed without an intimate appreciation of the local culture.

As Zinni observed more than a decade ago:

> What we need is cultural intelligence. What I need to understand is how these societies function. What makes them tick? Who makes the decisions?

What is it about their society that is so remarkably different in their values, in the way they think compared to my values and the way I think in my western, white-man mentality.[47]

Isolate insurgent/contending elements from support

Physically and psychologically separate the insurgents or opponents from both external and internal sources of support. Here the counter CIW force must use both military force and information operations to demoralize the active or armed elements, but more importantly de-legitimize their underlying ideology or political movement. To use a common medical metaphor, one should begin to "cauterize" around the insurgency to keep it from spreading or acquiring support.[48] Despite the wide range of case studies explored, the physical and psychological isolation of the insurgent was a key contributor to all successful examples. Isolation cuts off resources and other sources of support, from within the host nation or from contiguous territories used as sanctuary. Physical isolation by barrier or other means makes interference with the host government harder, maximizes freedom of action within other domains such as economic development, and limits the ability of the insurgent to intimidate or coerce friendly or neutral indigenous personnel. From Hadrian's Wall in Britain to Israel's latest effort, physical defense barriers or strings of blockhouses and posts have been a regular feature in this mode of war.[49]

Isolation in the ideological or political sense is also critical to both neutralize the insurgent's message or appeal, as well as reduce potential forms of intelligence gathering, recruiting or funding. The classic experts in irregular warfare, including Lawrence, Mao and Galula, have all pointed to the importance of information as a weapon. However, its mastery has proven to be elusive even to modern powers. Galula went on to add, "If there was a field in which we were definitely and infinitely more stupid than our opponents, it was propaganda."[50] This is a poignant comment given the paucity of effective informational activities in Iraq. This aspect of CIW could rise in salience as future irregular combatants continue to exploit modern Information Age tools to broaden their appeal and their resource base. "Winning hearts and minds" may have a more global orientation thanks to the ubiquitous and diffuse nature of modern communication techniques. Proponents of 4GW would have you believe this is a new phenomenon. But the old *Small Wars Manual* noted the rapidity by which a revolution could develop due to the modern communications technologies.[51] Today's 24/7 news cycles and graphic imagery produce even faster and higher response cycles from audiences around the globe and offer powerful new "weapons" to those who can master them.[52] It has taken almost four years for the Pentagon's leadership to understand its own limitations in this regard. The US Secretary of Defense himself has acknowledged, "If I were grading I would say we probably deserve a 'D' or a 'D-plus' as a country as to how well we're doing in the battle of ideas that's taking place in the world today."[53]

Neutralize anti-government forces

Employ military operations to neutralize and incapacitate identified anti-government elements that pose a security threat to coalition, US or host nation operations and infrastructure. This requires extensive patrolling and intensive intelligence collection, followed by aggressive but discriminate engagements.[54]

Neutralization requires the counter CIW force to minimize the use of blunt military force. It is possible to conduct a brilliant series of tactical actions with overwhelming force and firepower and lose the larger strategic goal. The classic *Small Wars Manual* advised that "instead of striving to generate the maximum power with forces available, *the goal is to gain decisive results with the least application of force and the consequent minimum loss of life.*"[55] History rarely offers such a consistent finding – a lack of rectitude or an excess of violence leads ineluctably to prolonged conflict.[56]

The excessive application of military firepower can significantly alter the strategic situation. Firepower intensive operations may antagonize both external and internal parties that are neutral to the insurgent, swinging support and resources to the opponent. Excessive collateral damage or accidental injuries to noncombatants will undermine the credibility of efforts to assist a host nation, and make our intervention longer and more costly. The Russians also employed more firepower than necessary, and did not adapt their tactics in Afghanistan, and then repeated their own mistakes in Chechnya.[57] In Vietnam, US forces inappropriately applied technological superiority and firepower, frequently in a manner at odds with American policy objectives.[58]

CIW conflicts include deliberate acts of provocation, designed to generate a kinetic response for which the antagonist is fully prepared to counter, or to exploit in the informational realm. The recent experiences in Fallujah during April 2004 are germane. Its important to remember that CIW contests will pit US forces against acutely agile opponents with no qualms about killing innocents by the thousands. Such opponents recognize no bounds, and are not easily deterred, nor can they be deflected by clever appeals to their conscious. Today's warrior class cannot be argued into submission.[59] Some elements in today's world cannot be persuaded or deterred from violence. This places a premium on *discriminate force*, and forces that are prepared to deal with the ambiguity and provocations posed by their adversaries. The issue is not restraint or holding back as much as finding the right balance between force and restraint based on the facts on the ground.[60] It also involves expanding our conception beyond just the use of force, and realizing that other forms of action may be just as effective at neutralizing the key links and relationships that comprise a complex adaptive system, without requiring the kinetic destruction of a node in the system at all.

Develop host governance mechanisms

As required, military forces may be employed to assist in enhancing state and local level governance. This could include a wide range of civil–military operations, to provide for administration, public services or the restoration of needed functions including critical infrastructure, road/transportation networks, or educational facilities. In intra-state conflicts not involving a counter-insurgency, the coalition or national task force will generally be supporting diplomatic efforts to create new political and security mechanisms acceptable to both parties. The US military had a lot of experience in this area in the past, and has not maintained an adequate doctrinal or experience base to meet current demands despite some positive learning experience in the Balkans.

After its failures in Somalia, the American military returned to its professional roots and adroitly attempted to ignore the chaotic conditions extant in the Balkans. Despite this reluctance to participate, US interventions over the past decade have grown broader in scope and in commitment. As Ambassador James Robbins has eloquently put it, "Nation building, it appears, is the inescapable responsibility of the world's only superpower."[61] For too long the US military has tried to stay away from this responsibility and not view it as part of its overall mission. Those days are now over.[62]

That should not be taken as a blanket endorsement for military solutions. There is a consensus on the requirement to reformulate the national security architecture of the United States to better address the challenges posed by weak or collapsed states, and the challenges of CIW. The requirement for effective and holistic planning and coordination mechanisms is clear. So is the need for integrated civil–military organizational models in complex contingencies. Satisfying these demands for more constructive strategies is a necessary element for success in CIW.[63]

Organize indigenous security and intelligence mechanisms

Success in fragile or failed states will require an intensive investment in bringing the local security and intelligence apparatus up to requisite levels. This may take specially trained units and intensive training to make local forces effective. It is important in most conflicts to put a local face on the solution, and to try to make foreign forces not a mirror image of our own.[64] One of the more obvious American shortfalls in Iraq was the noted lack of emphasis on creating an Iraqi police and security bureaucracy to displace the one they toppled in 2003. The United States lost a valuable year in which leadership development and a solid training base could have been established.[65] Why this was allowed to occur is unfathomable, especially given the early decision to disband the existing Iraqi Army (such as it was).[66]

Penetrate (if possible)

The military theorist John Boyd placed a great emphasis on penetration as a key task in conducting counter-guerrilla operations.[67] We have already discussed how difficult this may be against cohesive CIW opponents, but it may still be possible, especially later in a campaign where success has been achieved at turning former insurgents over to the counter force. Whenever possible, the use of indigenous assets to penetrate the opposing group and/or its support networks is useful. These sources should be used to develop actionable intelligence, prevent operational surprise, and make the adversary less secure in his planning and operations. Penetration may be achieved earlier if possible against less committed or less homogenous groups. Penetration is most probably going to occur later against today's networked elements but should be pursued ultimately to ensure the elimination of key cadre and leadership "die hards" who may not accept the finality of their lost cause.

Sustain and reintegrate

Success against a persistent and virulent CIW force is a protracted challenge, and momentum must be sustained throughout the campaign. Ultimately, a number of former adversaries must be reintegrated back into civil society. Ongoing security assistance efforts and economic development projects will be needed to achieve an acceptable result realizing that some conflict may remain. The reintegration of previously hostile elements into mainstream political and economic activity will be needed to ensure long-term stability. Finally, amnesty programs or judicial reviews are often critical to reconciliation, and must be conducted as openly as possible. The seeds of the next conflict are often planted by a failure to make the necessary socio-political and judicial compromises needed to affect a long-term solution. The difficulty of reconciliation and justice should not be underestimated, as it is protracted and often requires difficult compromises between justice and settlement.

Conclusion

According to one noted traveler, "Knowing the future is easy, if only we were willing to see the present."[68] We may want to extend that by adding, "if only we are willing to study the past as well." Whether you buy into the 4GW construct or CIW, there is nothing new, "What is new is not the phenomenon itself, but our perception of it."[69] I have been in continuous disagreement with 4GW proponents regarding their less than holistic grasp of history, but I do support the need for increased attention to the nontraditional components of what they describe as 4GW. These have been fundamental aspects of conflict for two millennia, in varying degrees at different times. I also agree with their criticism that war is evolving in a manner that is inconsistent with the technophilia represented by the Pentagon's infatuation with Revolutions in Military Affairs and a Transformation agenda that put the United States at a disadvantage with today's threats.[70] I also concur with the assessment that confronted by today's global insurgency, today's "third generation" militaries are going to have problems with today's virulent strains of CIW.

The conflicts in Afghanistan, Chechnya and Iraq reveal how difficult it is for old habits to die. The US military establishment, like its former Russian antagonist, as a whole was unprepared to advise, plan and conduct an irregular contest.[71] Moreover, it was slow to learn and resistant to operational adaptation. The 4GW school offered a lot of insights into the nature of the challenge. But understanding the present and the nature of the threat is important but insufficient. Only through the deep study of history and culture can we build the broad intellectual foundation necessary from which to interpret and counter emergent CIW challenges.

Defeating the CIW adversary will require alterations in how military and national security organizations think about strategy and how leaders are educated. It will require commanders throughout the military that can work without positional authority, across organizational boundaries, with coalition members, international organizations, and non-military agencies of government. It requires entirely new forms of operational art and campaign design. It will also require changes in the way military organizations acquire and exploit intelligence, and how they leverage information in their command and control systems.[72] This is not the type of information that can be quickly absorbed by satellites and sensors, the Pentagon's default solution to sticky problems. Nor will this problem be resolved by an intelligence community slavishly devoted to data mining huge hordes of digital transmissions, or tagging and tracking of human subjects in tomorrow's densely populated mega-cities.

Instead, it requires a degree of understanding that must be acquired or interpreted by a more enlightened security community imbued with a deep understanding of the historical and cultural context that has generated the conflict to begin with. This will require an ability to outreach to different sources of expertise, and new ways of fusing diverse insights and perspectives into multidimensional campaigns. The planning process and manifest failures that led to the post-conflict debacle in Iraq are hopefully instructive. Thus, calls for culture-centric warfare should have great resonance in any military challenged by this mode of warfare.[73]

Combating CIW threats is ultimately an intellectual challenge, certainly one more complicated than a bayonet charge or an armored thrust across the Russian steppe. The "MINDOPS" mnemonic device was purposely contrived to reinforce the cognitive requirements levied by the rise of CIW. But we should not underestimate the lethality or the significant costs of CIW. Containing the social costs and negating the human casualties of CIW poses the most serious doctrinal challenge to US military organizations since the dawn of the nuclear age. This shift says more about the American preoccupation with battles than with the better peace these are supposed to contribute to, than about the uniqueness of nontraditional conflict.[74] There is more than a grain of truth to the charge that in 4GW, or CIW, we are the weaker side. Whether or not Western militaries or the US national security brain trust has the requisite intellectual capacity to succeed remains problematic as long as they resist the underlying basis of tomorrow's wars and cling to a more comforting conventional and kinetic paradigm. Hopefully this book brings us one step forward toward increasing our readiness for what surely will be "another bloody century."[75]

Notes

1 Gary Hart, *The Shield and the Cloak: The Security of the Commons*, New York: Oxford University, 2006, p. 165.
2 For more on how Clausewitz remains an invaluable guide to war, see Colin Gray, "How Has War Changed Since the End of the Cold War?," *Parameters*, Spring 2005, pp. 14–26.
3 William S. Lind, Keith Nightengale, John Schmitt and Gary I. Wilson, "The Changing Face of War: Into the Fourth Generation," *Marine Corps Gazette*, November, 2001. Additionally, see Martin van Creveld, *The Transformation in War*, New York: Free Press, 1991.
4 Robert Kaplan, *The Coming Anarchy, Shattering the Dreams of the Post Cold War*, New York: Vintage, 2001.
5 Michael J. Mazarr, "Extremism, Terror and the Future of Conflict," online essay. Accessed at www.policyreview.org/000/mazarr.html. on March 10, 2006.
6 National Intelligence Council, *Mapping the Global Future: Global Trends 2020*, Washington, DC: Central Intelligence Agency, 2005, p. 97.
7 Statement of Dr. Bruce Hoffman, RAND Corporation, testimony presented to the House Armed Services Committee, Subcommittee on Terrorism, Unconventional Threats and Capabilities on February 16, 2006. Accessed at www.rand.org/ pubs/ testimonies/CT255/.
8 Thomas X. Hammes, "4th Generation Warfare: Our Enemy Plays to Their Strengths," *Armed Forces Journal International*, November 2004, p. 40; see also Thomas X. Hammes, *The Sling and Stone, On War in the 21st Century*, St. Paul, WI: Zenith Press, 2004.
9 Michael Evans, "From Kadesh to Kandahar: Military Theory and the Future of War," *Naval War College Review*, Summer 2003, p. 136; Lieutenant General James N. Mattis and Lieutenant Colonel Frank Hoffman, "Future Warfare: The Rise of Hybrid Warfare," *Naval Institute Proceedings*, November 2005, pp. 30–32.
10 Colin S. Gray, *Another Bloody Century: Future Warfare*, London: Weidenfeld & Nicolson, 2006.
11 For a detailed explanation of the terms and its implications see Frank G. Hoffman, "Complex Irregular Warfare: The Next Revolution in Military Affairs," *Orbis*, Vol. 50, Iss. 3, Summer 2006, pp. 395–411.
12 David Ronfeldt, "Al Qaeda and Its Affiliates: A Global Tribe Waging Segmental Warfare?," *First Monday*, Vol. 10, no. 3, March 2005.
13 Fareed Zakaria, "How to Stop the Contagion," *Newsweek*, August 1, 2005, p. 40.
14 The most notable exception is William Lind, *et al.*, *Draft FMFM 1-A, Fourth Generation War, Imperial and Royal Austro-Hungarian Marine Corps*, undated but circa 2004.
15 Stephen Hosmer, *Operations Against Enemy Leaders*, Santa Monica, CA: RAND, 2006. Accessed at www.rand.org/pubs/monograph_reports/MR1385/index.html.
16 Kurt Campbell and Richard Weitz, "Non-Military Strategies for Countering Islamist Terrorism: Lessons Learned from Past Counterinsurgencies." Accessed at www.wws.princeton.edu/ppns/papers/ counterinsurgency.pdf.
17 As suggested in MCDP 1–2, *Campaigning*, Washington, DC: Headquarters, US Marine Corps, 1997, p. 105.
18 Thomas H. Henriksen, "Divide et Impera," *Hoover Digest*, no. 1, 2006. Accessed at www.hooverdigest.org/061/henriksen.html.
19 Rick Brennan, Adam Grissom, Sara Daly, Peter Chalk, William Rosenau, Kalev Sepp and Steve Dalzell, *Future Insurgency Threats*, Santa Monica, CA: RAND, 2005.
20 Lawrence E. Cline, *Pseudo Operations and Counterinsurgency: Lessons from Other Countries*, Carlisle, PA: Strategic Studies Institute, June 2005.

21 See Marc Sageman, *Understanding Terror Networks*, Philadelphia, PA: University of Pennsylvania Press, 2004.

22 Ibid., pp. 47–49.

23 John Shy and Thomas W. Collier, "Revolutionary War," in Peter Paret, ed., *Makers of Modern Strategy: From Machiavelli to the Nuclear Age*, Princeton, NJ: Princeton University Press, 1986, p. 821.

24 Audrey Kurth Cronin, "Cyber Mobilization: The New Levee en Masse," *Parameters*, Summer 2006, pp. 77–87.

25 A term employed by John Robb at his invaluable blog site of the same name.

26 Cronin, p. 87.

27 Lawrence Freedman, *The Transformation of Strategic Affairs*, London: International Institute for Strategic Studies, Adelphi Paper 379, March 2006, pp. 22–24.

28 Tony Corn, "World War IV as Fourth Generation Warfare," *Policy Review*, January 2006, p. 2. Accessed at policyreview.org/000/corn.html.

29 I am indebted to Lieutenant Colonel David Kilcullen, formerly of the Australian Army, for this suggestion.

30 Gavin Bulloch, "Military Doctrine and Counterinsurgency: A British Perspective," *Parameters*, Summer 1996, pp. 4–16. Brigadier Bulloch describes a quintessentially maneuverist approach to counterinsurgency.

31 For more support on this issue see Hart, *The Shield and the Cloak*, pp. 67–69.

32 The term "disaggregated battlespace" is found in the Australian concept paper "Complex Warfighting," October 2004. Accessed at www.defence.gov.au/army/lwsc/.

33 Anthony Zinni, "Non-traditional Military Missions: Their Nature, and the Need for Cultural Awareness and Flexible Thinking," p. 269, in Joe Strange, *Capital "W" War: A Case for Strategic Principles, Perspectives on Warfighting*, no. 6, Quantico, VA: Marine Corps University, 1998.

34 Bernard Brodie, *War and Politics*, New York: MacMillan, 1973, p. 332.

35 See Montgomery McFate, "The Military Utility of Understanding Adversary Culture," *Joint Force Quarterly*, Vol. 38, 2005, pp. 42–48; and Montgomery McFate, "Anthropology and Counterinsurgency: The Strange Story of Their Curious Relationship," *Military Review*, March/April 2005, pp. 24–38.

36 Zinni, in Strange, p. 266.

37 MCDP 1, *Warfighting*, p. 72.

38 *Small Wars Manual*, pp. 1–17.

39 Mattis and Hoffman, "The Rise of Hybrid Warfare."

40 T.E. Lawrence, "The Evolution of a Revolt," *The Army Quarterly and Defence Journal*, October, 1920.

41 See Brigadier General Robert E. Schmidle, "Distributed Operations from the Sea," *Marine Corps Gazette*, August, 2004.

42 MCDP 1–0, *Marine Corps Operations*, pp. 6–23.

43 John MacKinlay, *Defeating Complex Insurgency: Beyond Iraq and Afghanistan*, London: Royal United Services Institute, Whitehall Paper 64, 2005.

44 See the three part series by Susan B. Glasser and Steve Coll, "The Web as a Weapon," *Washington Post*, August 7–9, 2005, p. A1; as well as Gabriel Weimann, "How Modern Terrorism Uses the Internet," *Journal of International Security Affairs*, Spring 2005, pp. 91–105.

45 Michael Howard, "The Use and Abuse of Military History," *Parameters*, Summer, 1980.

46 *Small Wars Manual*, p. 13.

47 Zinni, "Non-Traditional Military Missions", p. 267.

48 Steven Metz and Raymond Millen, *Insurgency and Counterinsurgency in the 21st Century*, Carlilse, PA: Army War College, Strategic Studies Group, 2004, p. 21.

49 Paul Staniland, "Defeating Transnational Insurgencies: The Best Offense is a Good Fence," *Washington Quarterly*, Winter 2005–2006, pp. 21–40.

50 David Galula, *Pacification in Algeria, 1956–1958,* Santa Monica, CA: RAND 1964 (reissued in 2006 with a foreword by Bruce Hoffman), p. ix.

51 *Small Wars Manual*, p. I-13.

52 Frank. G. Hoffman, "Small Wars Revisited: The United States and Nontraditional Warfare," *Journal of Strategic Studies*, December 2005, pp. 913–940.

53 Donald Rumsfeld, Speech at the Council on Foreign Relations, New York, February 17, 2006 accessed at www.cfr.org/publication/9902/news_brief.html.

54 Here I am building on arguments first presented in my essay, "Principles for the Savage Wars of Peace," pp. 309–311 in Anthony McIvor, ed., *Rethinking the Principles of War*, Annapolis, MD: Naval Institute Press, 2005.

55 *Small Wars Manual*, p. 32.

56 Anthony James Joes, *Resisting Rebellion: The History and Politics of Counterinsurgency*, Lexington, KY, University Press of Kentucky, 2004.

57 Lester Grau, ed., *The Bear Went Over the Mountain: Soviet Combat Tactics in Afghanistan*, Washington, DC: National Defense University, 1996; Anatoly S. Kulikov, "The First Battle of Grozny," in Russell Glenn, ed., *Capital Preservation: Preparing for Urban Operations in the Twenty-first Century*, Santa Monica, CA: Rand, 2001.

58 See Robert H. Scales, Jr. *Firepower in Limited War*, Novato, CA: Presidio, 1997.

59 Ralph Peters, "The New Warrior Class Revisited," *Beyond Baghdad: Postmodern War and Peace*, Harrisburg, PA: Stackpole, 2003, pp. 44–60.

60 Sam Mundy, "No Better Friend, No Worse Enemy," *Naval Institute Proceedings*, April, 2004.

61 James Robbins, John McGinn, Keith Crane, Seth G. Jones, Rollie Lol, Andrew Rathmell, Rachel Swanger and Anga Timilsina, *America's Role in Nation-Building, From Germany to Iraq*, Santa Monica, CA: RAND, 2003, p. xv.

62 Nadia Schadlow, "War and the Art of Governance," *Parameters*, Autumn 2003, pp. 85–94.

63 Seth Jones, Jeremy M. Wilson, Andrew Rathmell and K. Jack Riley, *Establishing Law and Order after Conflict*, Santa Monica, CA: RAND 2005; Brent Scrowcroft and Sandy Berger, *In the Wake of War: Improving U.S. Post-Conflict Capabilities*, New York: Council on Foreign Relations, 2005; Clark A. Murdock and Michele A. Flournoy, *Beyond Goldwater Nichols: U.S. Government and Defense Reform for a New Strategic Era*, Phase 2 Report, Washington, DC: Center for Strategic and International Studies, 2005.

64 T.E. Lawrence captured this with his quip that "Better to let them do it imperfectly than to do it perfectly yourself, for it is their country, their way, and your time is short." T.E. Lawrence, "Twenty-Seven Articles," *Arab Bulletin*, August 20, 1917.

65 James Fallows, "Why Iraq Has No Army," *The Atlantic Monthly*, December, 2005.

66 Robert Cassidy, "The Long Small War: Indigenous Forces for Counterinsurgency," *Parameters*, Summer 2006, pp. 47–62.

67 Email from Chuck Spinney to the author, dated August 2004. See also Grant Hammond, *The Mind of War*, Washington, DC: Smithsonian, 1999.

68 Robert. D. Kaplan, "Cultivating Loneliness," *Columbia Journalism Review*, Iss. 1, January 2006. Accessed at www.cjr.org/issues/2006/1/Kaplan.asp.

69 Shy and Collier, p. 838.

70 See my "Complex Irregular Warfare.

71 Robert M. Cassidy, *Counterinsurgency and the Global War on Terror: Military Culture and Irregular Warfare*, Westport, CT: Praeger, 2006.

72 James W. Harris, "Building Leverage in the Long War: Ensuring Intelligence Community Creativity in the Fight Against Terrorism," pp. 341–356, in Roger George and Robert D. Kline, eds, *Intelligence and the National Security Strategist:*

Enduring Issues and Challenges, Washington, DC: National Defense University, 2004.

73 Robert H. Scales Jr, "Culture-Centric Warfare," *Proceedings,* October 2004, pp. 32–36.

74 Antulio J. Echevarria, II, *Toward an American Way of War,* Carlisle, PA: Army War College, Strategic Studies Institute, March 2004.

75 Gray, *Another Bloody Century.*

20 Information operations in 4GW

Thomas X. Hammes

Fourth Generation War (4GW) uses all available networks – political, economic, social and military – to convince the enemy's political decision makers that their strategic goals are either unachievable or too costly for the perceived benefit. It is an evolved form of insurgency. Still rooted in the fundamental precept that superior political will, when properly employed can defeat greater economic and military power, 4GW makes use of society's networks to carry on its fight. Unlike previous generations of warfare, it does not attempt to win by defeating the enemy's military forces. Instead, via the networks, it directly attacks the minds of the enemy decision makers to destroy the enemy's political will. Fourth generation wars are lengthy – measured in decades rather than months or years.

Obviously, 4GW places a premium on ideas and the use of information networks to transmit key messages to the various actors involved in the conflict. They are at the heart of this kind of war. As a result, information operations should be central to all efforts from the strategic to the tactical level. Information operations are much tougher in war than in normal political discourse. While politics includes the fog, friction and uncertainty of war, it rarely includes the primordial violence that is the distinctive character of war. The results to date in Iraq indicate that the insurgents understand this clearly while the US cannot even develop an effective definition for information operations.

This chapter will examine current US doctrine on information operations, how that doctrine essentially misses the target, then briefly examine how the US has failed miserably to produce any coherent information campaign either in Iraq or in the Global War on Terror (GWOT). It will contrast the poor US performance to the insurgents' successful execution of information operations both globally and in Iraq specifically and make some minor recommendations to improve US performance.

US doctrine

Over the last five years, the US military has adapted extensively to adjust to the fourth generation wars they are fighting in Afghanistan and Iraq. From strategic to the tactical level, American military personnel are rethinking how they fight insurgents. They have rewritten doctrine and updated those tactics, techniques and procedures that have been successful against previous insurgents to face the constantly evolving insurgencies they are now fighting. Of particular importance has been the dramatic shift in professional education at all levels, from a focus on fighting high-tech short wars to the ideas and concepts necessary to fight the protracted, political struggles America faces today. There has also been some progress in other elements of the US government. People are looking at ways to make the US government as a whole more effective in counterinsurgency.

Thus, it is particularly puzzling that the United States has made so little progress in Information Operations. On October 30, 2003, the Department of Defense (DOD) released its *Information Operations Roadmap*. In it, DOD defined Information Operations as:

> The integrated employment of the core capabilities of electronic warfare [EW], computer network operations [CNO], psychological operations [PSYOP], military deception, and operations security [OPSEC], with specified supporting and related capabilities to influence, disrupt, corrupt, or usurp adversarial human and automated decision making while protecting our own.

The Roadmap then stated:

> Three integrated IO functions are of overriding importance
>
> - Deter, discourage, dissuade and direct an adversary, thereby disrupting his unity of command and purpose while preserving our own.
> - Protect our plans and misdirect theirs, thereby allowing our forces to mass their effects to maximum advantage while the adversary expends his resources to little effect.
> - Control adversary communications and networks and protect ours, thereby crippling the enemy's ability to direct and organize defense while preserving effective command and control of our forces.

Obviously, the Roadmap is a product of Cold War thinking. It focuses almost exclusively on enemy military command and control. It assumes an enemy with "unity of command" that has a central communications system that can be crippled to prevent him from organizing a defense. In essence, this doctrine still sees warfare as essentially a contest between the armed forces of nation states. Oddly, this definition does not even consider the type of enemy we were actually fighting at the time – a loosely affiliated "coalition of the willing" that was on the offensive worldwide. It does not even offer a possibility of dealing with the much wider range or problems inherent in the broad political, social and economic issues of 4GW. An even more critical oversight is the fact the document makes no mention of the importance of friendly, neutral and enemy populations to the fight. While it does mention PSYOPS, it seems almost as if PSYOPS is rolled in simply because there is no where else to put it in the hierarchy.

However, given the very long time lines required to attain concurrence on a DOD document, it is not surprising that the roadmap was sorely out of date before it was published.

Yet almost three years later on March 13, 2006, the Pentagon released *Joint Publication 3–13 Information Operations*. It repeats the 2003 Roadmap almost word for word. In its Executive Summary, *Information Operations* states:

> Information is a strategic resource, vital to national security, and military operations depend on information and information systems for many simultaneous and integrated activities.
>
> Information operations (IO) are described as the integrated employment of electronic warfare (EW), computer network operations (CNO), psychological operations (PSYOP), military deception (MILDEC), and operations security (OPSEC), in concert with supporting and related capabilities, to influence, disrupt, corrupt, or usurp adversarial human and automated decision making while protecting our own.... The principal goal is to achieve and maintain information superiority for the US and its allies.

Clearly the Pentagon still sees large scale conventional war as the primary threat. This is prudent, given the potential catastrophic effects if a near peer competitor should arise in the next couple of decades. Unfortunately, that competitor is most likely to use 4GW concepts and techniques rather than the 3GW the Pentagon is preparing for. Thus, the Pentagon's failure to integrate the wars we have been fighting for five years into its new IO doctrine is truly remarkable.

Stranger yet, the ultimate goal remains information superiority. This is despite the fact that in the three conflicts the United States is currently fighting – Iraq, Afghanistan and Global War on Terror – it is fighting at a significant information deficit. The new document ignores the hard knocks the United States is taking daily and continues to base its future on the assumption it will have information dominance and fight a conventional, nation-state army. It fails to understand the information requirements for conflicts with either nation states or non-state actors.

The inability of the US to develop an effective definition of IO is caused by two major factors. First, the DOD bureaucracy is naturally conservative. It uses a collegial approach, heavily weighted to the need of existing constituencies. Second, is the persistence of the senior leadership in doggedly clinging to their "vision" of a high-technology military fighting short wars. In this vision, there is no need to expand IO beyond the very limited definition and concepts provided in the joint publication.

Despite our worldwide failure to deliver an effective message and the mismatch between IO's "new" definition and reality, the Pentagon is not even seeking a new definition for information operations.

US execution of IO

While the United States has clearly failed to develop an effective working definition of IO, the White House appeared to understand the importance of IO when it appointed Karen Hughes, a very trusted Bush advisor, to the position of Undersecretary of State for Public Diplomacy. Yet even as they announced the position, the White House made it clear they did not see this as an urgent task. The announcement of the office was made on March 12, 2005 yet admitted that Ms. Hughes would not actually start work until sometime in the autumn. Her first trip to the Middle East in September 2005 was a major embarrassment, for it revealed weak staff work, cultural ignorance and an assumption that American ideas would appeal to any audience (without reference to actual American actions such as Abu Ghraib). Since then her office has essentially dropped out of the news but US blunders have continued.

While there are a wide variety of mistakes to choose from, the most important has been the complete disconnect between our stated strategic plan for Iraq and the actions we have taken. President Bush has stated repeatedly that we will "stay the course" and rebuild Iraq. He has declared that our strategy is "Clear, Hold, Build" and we will not "Stand Down Until the Iraqis Stand Up." Yet in January of 2006, he unilaterally announced that there would be no more reconstruction funds provided for Iraq. Later in the spring, the administration drastically cut funds for democratization programs in Iraq. It then announced a budget which cut the funds (and personnel) of the US Army and Marine Corps – the two services most involved in the war. Throughout the period, the administration kept telling the American people that we would have major troop withdrawals in 2006.

This highlights one of the fundamental rules of IO – "What I do speaks so loudly you cannot hear what I say." While Bush kept saying the US was staying for the long haul, many administration actions indicated it was planning to leave soon. As a result, ordinary Iraqis started turning to ethnic and secular militias to insure the security for their families. It was obvious the Iraqi government could not provide security – and with the US indicating it was leaving, the situation would only get much worse.

Another fundamental disconnect is the US emphasis on freedom, when what the Iraqi people consistently say they want is security and justice. By pushing freedom and ignoring the message that would reach the Iraqis, the US government further undercuts its credibility. Worse, the inability to adjust its message despite its failure indicates the administration lacks the flexibility that is an absolute requirement to deal with a networked, agile enemy.

In the wider GWOT, the US has also failed to back its words with action. While stating the United States was essentially about freedom, security for the people and opportunity, it failed miserably to back its words with action. The actions at Abu Ghraib and subsequent failure to either investigate or prosecute those responsible combined with the Guantanemo Bay camps and secret rendition programs directly contradicted the statements about freedom. The failure of the US to honor even modest promises for rebuilding in Afghanistan have given the Taliban a new lease of life.

Insurgent execution of IO

In contrast, al Qaeda is clearly attuned with both its core supporters and the broader Islamic audience. This is not to say al Qaeda does not make mistakes. The beheadings of bound victims and the bombing of three hotels in Jordan were both major mistakes. Yet its subsequent actions and the correspondence between al Qaeda leaders indicate the terrorists constantly analyze their operations and adapt. Based on the response of their audiences, al Qaeda stopped broadcasting beheadings but still made them available via CD or passworded website to those elements of the movement that are motivated by viewing them. The reaction of Jordanians and Jordan's subsequent assistance in the killing of al-Zarqawi made it clear to al Qaeda in Iraq that bombings in adjacent Arab states was not a productive activity. Bombings continue in various locations such as Egypt but these are conducted by affiliated groups not under al Qaeda control. Further, al Qaeda is acutely aware of the requirement to keep its message in front of its supporters and opponents. Using a series of over thirty taped statements since the beginning of 2005, al Qaeda continues an aggressive worldwide public information campaign. In essence, the United States is losing the public communications battle to an organization that wants to take the world back to the seventh century!

Al Qaeda understands that the massive, worldwide communications revolution has fundamentally changed not only how people communicate but how they get their information and form their opinions. The Pentagon insists that information technology (IT) has transformed war. Unfortunately, it cannot seem to see that the real impact of IT goes far beyond the conventional operations the Pentagon loves and funds. The impact of IT has been felt much more strongly in the political, economic and social spheres than in the military arena. In short, IT has greatly strengthened the spheres where 4GW outflanks superior military forces.

While in the military sphere superb connectivity allows faster decision cycles and greater awareness of where conventional enemies are, it has yet to provide major dividends in fighting an enemy that chooses to use 4GW techniques rather than earlier forms of war. In contrast, the new communications technologies have literally transformed how our 4GW enemies are using IO to recruit, train, motivate and direct a widespread web of people with similar ideas. In fact, it is in developing, implanting and nurturing those ideas that our enemies are making transformational use of cell phones, text messaging, chat rooms, streaming videos and email.

Starting with a self-selecting group of dissatisfied males, al Qaeda on line provides a closed virtual environment where they can express their dissatisfaction, have their concerns echoed by like-minded people and then have them reinforced by al Qaeda's fourth generation warriors. The very nature of the group excludes any opposing views so it becomes a self-reinforcing, closed-loop that confirms and reinforces the radical Islamist teachings of the group. In addition to the on line reinforcement of initial beliefs, these web sites provide contacts at radical mosques near where the patrons live. These mosques further reinforce both their view and their isolation from other viewpoints. Using online chat rooms, a person can be identified, contacted, proselytized, recruited and even trained with streaming video of everything from religious lectures to firing an SA-7 missile. The terrorists are showing a sophisticated ability to use two different information media – the 1,000-year-old mosque sermon and the decade-old internet – to promulgate and amplify their messages.

Al Qaeda and other insurgent groups have used the information pathways to conduct truly broad spectrum information operations that contact like-minded zealots across the world. Further they do it largely out of sight of the security services. The March 11 bombings in Spain and the July 7 bombings in England were done by people who had minimal contact with any recognizable element of al Qaeda. Rather they had simply acted on the message al Qaeda had been putting out through various paths using techniques easily available on the internet.

These activities are all based on al Qaeda's understanding that the population is the correct target of IO, not the enemy's command and control system. Further, they understand they do not have to control each group. Al Qaeda is not a centralized group – rather it is a coalition of franchises of locals who make use of the al Qaeda brand and philosophy to attract and motivate followers.

The West has essentially ceded the IO battlefield to the Islamist radicals. Other than the truly weak efforts by the White House Office of Communications, the West does not have a system to identify the false themes being pushed by the Islamists, find the online and real time venues where these themes are being pushed and then provide a truthful alternative message to counteract the Islamist message. Al Qaeda and its associates are winning the battle of IO because the West has conceded the field to them. While our European allies harp on the United States for failing to talk rather than fight, they have utterly failed to put out an effective counter message within their own nations. The 2006 riots in France, the comic wars throughout the world and the bombings and murders conducted by completely independent elements heeding al Qaeda's message all originated within the radical Islamic populations within Europe.

Redefine IO

So how does a bureaucratic Western democracy fight this information battle?

First, we have to broaden our definition of IO. IO is not about disrupting an enemy's command and control system or attacking its communication technology. It is not about technology at all. It is about people. It is about influencing a number of distinct audiences – the population of the country where the conflict is being fought, the population of the region, potential sympathetic populations worldwide (to neutralize the support for the insurgents) and our own populations (to reinforce our political will).

We have to understand that IO has offensive and defensive aspects in both reaching and protecting populations. Offensive IO should focus on getting our message out. Of course, our leaders have to understand that the message must be based in truth. If we say one thing and do another, it weakens our credibility and hence influence. Defensive IO means finding the enemy messages that are false and then providing the truth via a wide variety of media. When we do screw up (such as Abu Ghraib and potentially Haditha), we have to deal with the problem by admitting the mistakes and then taking corrective and disciplinary action. Abu Ghraib still haunts us because no senior officer has been held responsible and we continue to operate both Guantanamo Bay and the rendition program. No matter what we try to say about our belief in justice and accountability, al Qaeda can simply run real news stories highlighting our failure to deal with Abu Ghraib and continuing activities in other parts of the world. We have to define IO to include the concept that truth matters!

Once we are grounded in a broader concept of IO, we must develop the cultural and language expertise to work effectively within the targeted audiences. National level decision makers must decide the key themes to be used by our IO campaign but the specific messages must be left to the regional and country experts who can frame the message in a culturally appropriate way. In essence, we apply one of the key concepts of maneuver warfare – commander's intent – to IO.

We need to develop high standards for the language skills and cultural knowledge essential to crafting a strong message. To be rated as a cultural expert one must have near native proficiency in the language as well as years studying and living in that culture. If we are going to demand these kinds of skills, the US government will have to create some kind of super SES billets that provide sufficient compensation to attract those people now. At the same time, we need to establish long-term scholarships and subsidies to provide a new generation of students with the opportunities to become true experts in their areas.

Frankly, bureaucratic resistance has been and will remain the single biggest obstacle to success in this area. While no single agency wants to be responsible for the message, none wants to give up whatever portion of that message it has. And of course, none of the agencies are interested in changing their firmly entrenched and sadly antiquated personnel systems to create a system that will attract the type of people needed for this effort. However, this effort must be made.

When we have both the message and the experts, then we can use those experts to determine the channels that are most effective within the target societies to reach our audiences. Obviously our interconnected world means that any message we deliver anywhere in the world will bounce around the world. Therefore, it is essential that regional and country teams craft their messages in consonance with the guidance provided from the national level. It is just as important that national decision makers do not attempt to approve each message. The excruciatingly slow bureaucratic process inherent in the US government has crippled our IO efforts in Iraq simply because by the time the message is approved it has been overcome by events on the ground.

Only mission type orders based on a clear intent should be provided from the national level. Draft and release authority must reside at local level. This will allow our field operators to compete effectively against insurgent IO campaigns by either anticipating or responding quickly to insurgent messages. It will also allow them to coordinate closely with host nation and regional officials to make use of their much greater cultural knowledge and to tie IO themes together. In places like Iraq, this will be particularly challenging given the separate goals of various Sh'ia, Sunni and Kurd groups. Thus IO must be closely tied to the overall campaign plan to reflect the strategy through our messages.

For example, in Iraq, the Administration would set the major themes. These themes must be more concrete than simply bringing democracy and freedom to Iraq. They should include specific goals that can be measured. (In fact, we did initially have such goals but when it became clear we were not making progress toward them, we simply stopped talking about them. Remember when 4,000 MW of power was the goal?) Once the national goals are set, the in-country team should develop methods to inform the public how we are doing. Something as simple as widely available progress reports would be good. Perhaps graphs showing the status of water, sewer, oil production, gasoline delivery, power availability and security by province or perhaps even cities within the province. While the news in Baghdad is clearly bad, there should be successes elsewhere in the country. If the successes are most clear where there is no insurgent activity, this is a theme we could use. Unfortunately, you can look in vain for such information on US government websites. And of course, we would have to invest the time and money to have these properly translated into Iraqi Arabic. Even if this means bringing Iraqis to the United States so they can work in safety, we need to do it. Where the charts show lack of progress, we need to explain why. If we cannot, it shows we have a much greater problem than a bad IO campaign. Local commanders would expand on the themes to show how their interaction with Iraqis is contributing to the overall plan.

One final caveat about IO is necessary. If your campaign plan is failing, then all the information operations in the world will not convince the people you are winning. For instance, if failing to provide security, you cannot claim you are. Instead, you must lay out the campaign plan to provide that security. If you cannot keep to the security plan, you need to rethink your entire campaign, not just the IO segment.

In summary, to date, the West has failed miserably in the information arena. To recover, the West must get in the game. First, we have to understand IO is much broader than our current definition. Then, we have to find talented people with the language and cultural knowledge to be effective in IO – and establish a system to educate the next generation. Finally, we have to overcome the bureaucratic inertia that inhibits effective people from producing effective IO campaigns for the targeted audiences. Until we do all three, we will continue to lose the war of ideas to a group that wants to take the world back to the seventh century.

21 The flight to irrelevance?

Air power and Fourth Generation Warfare

Donald A. MacCuish[1]

Introduction

In writing this chapter, Robert Frost's *The Road Not Taken* comes to mind. One ought not take the road less traveled simply to make a statement or to go against the grain, rather it should be trod when it makes sense. This is the case here as I intend to go against the conventional wisdom, because it is the right thing to do.

I happen to like the notion of Fourth Generation Warfare (4GW) because it breaks the paradigm that both restrains and constrains our thought processes. The idea of 4GW requires that we ask questions the answers to which take us outside our comfort zone and evaluate whether or not our perception of reality needs some adjustment. Unfortunately, far too many people are wedded to a form of warfare that no longer exists, if it ever did. If we, especially the US Air Force, continue down the path they recommend, we will most certainly lose this Global War on Terrorism (GWOT). I would prefer almost any idea to what is put forth by the dogmatists from the Jominied–Clausewitzian camp if it will force me to think critically (as contrasted with groupthink), question my own comfort zone, and get off the plane to Abilene.[2]

This chapter focuses on the US Air Force and 4GW rather than the much wider notion of air power. As a result, the research question is not about air power and 4GW, but rather the Air Force itself. As we will come to realize, if the US Air Force continues its flight path to Abilene, it will be on an irreversible Flight to Irrelevance.

The impossible dream

The reality of air power is not quite 100 years old. The existence of a United States Air Force, as a separate service, is a little more than half that age, but her leadership clings to the dream, born during the Great War, that has yet to materialize and probably never will. Specifically, I am referring to the notion that air power, meaning the air force, alone can win wars. That is the quintessential impossible dream.

In his work, *The Command of the Air*, General Guilio Douhet, the first of the airpower advocates to publish an authoritative treatise on air power, contended that aeronautics opened a new form of war. He was certain that an independent air force with scores of airplanes under the able command and leadership of an aviator, could in short order, bring any country to its knees. He noted that the only defense against an aerial offensive was to attack your enemy first and more forcefully than he could ever attack you. Nothing, he asserted, was sacred, not the cities, nor the civilian population, nothing.[3] In fact, the goal was to demoralize the population so that the enemy's government would sue for peace. The fact that Italy was, and still is, a party to both The Hague and Geneva Conventions, i.e. the Laws of War, seemed to have escaped the General's notice.

The American General Billy Mitchell's position on an independent air force and its capability to win a war single handedly was similar to that of Douhet. Mitchell, however, was not as convinced that the Battleplane, one aircraft for all missions, was the best approach. Mitchell's concept of an independent air force included pursuit planes (fighters), bombers, and attack (ground support).[4] Further, he thought a strong partnership with civil and commercial aviation was necessary, as it was from these ranks that transport and aerial refueling needs would be satisfied.[5] However, he did note that during the insurgency in Mesopotamia, the British successfully used military transport aircraft thereby inferring the independent air force should also have this inherent capability.[6] Mitchell, as did Douhet, supported the idea of carrying the attack to the civilian population through the bombardment of cities.[7]

The British experience was quite different. Initially, as was the case with the United States and Italy, both the Royal Army and Navy had aviation assets in the Great War. Between Christmas 1914 and the autumn of 1916 German aircraft bombed England. Airships, not airplanes, carried out most of the bombing raids. These bombings were ineffective and the populace, especially the Londoners who tended to be the primary recipients of the gifts from heaven, considered them a nuisance. At the time, the people considered the air defense provided by the Royal Naval Air Service and Royal Flying Corps an effective countermeasure. That all changed on July 13, 1917 when the first squadron-sized Gotha bomber attack on London killed over 600 civilians. The reaction of the civilian community was such that in November 1917 the Parliament passed the Air Force Bill thereby establishing the Royal Air Force.[8] Most assuredly, American and Italian aviators looked on with envy.

With the conclusion of the Great War the experiences of these three allied nations diverged as their respective independent air forces were developed. Douhet based his theory of airpower on a strict geographical context. Water surrounds Italy on three sides. A vast mountain range – the Alps – protects Italy's fourth side. Two oceans separate the United States from potential adversaries, except for the difficult to cross Baring Strait. Mitchell's sinking of the ex-German dreadnought *Ostfreisland* by air finalized the American context.[9] Enter now the Air Corps Tactical School (ACTS) and the birth of the Bomber Mafia and Jomini's contribution to airpower theory.[10]

The necessity to rebuild her post-war economy and maintain her Empire forced the British to take a different route. Trenchard, like Douhet and Mitchell, was an advocate of the strategic bombing concept.[11] Lord Trenchard realized that in an insurgency, however, there were no strategic targets to bomb. More-over, as we learned in Iraq precision bombing is not always that precise. An analysis of insurgencies involving great powers since the Great War, therefore, will be instructive.

The antecedents

During the inter-war years, both Britain and the United States were involved in a number of successful counterinsurgency campaigns or small wars. Interestingly, since World War II there have been twelve counterinsurgency campaigns involving Britain, France, Israel, Russia (including the USSR), and the United States. The results suggest an unhappy outcome for the major power. Fortu-nately, we can learn from both the successful and the not so successful provided we are willing to change our mindset, which the anti-4GW group seems reluct-ant to do.

Shortly after the Great War, the British were forced to wage counterinsur-gency campaigns in both Somaliland and Mesopotamia (modern day Iraq). In Somaliland, the British ground forces could not stop the insurgents, led by Mohammed bin Abdullah Hassan, who had been ravaging havoc in the region since 1899. The resourceful Brits put together a Royal Air Force (RAF) expedi-tion with the classified designation of Unit Z.[12] This unit working in close coordination with the ground forces neutralized Hassan's forces and forced him into exile where he was assassinated.

The success in Somaliland convinced then Colonial Secretary, Winston Churchill, that the proper use of airpower could quell an insurgency. He tasked Air Marshall Trenchard to develop a workable plan for Mesopotamia. The resulting plan placed the counterinsurgency operation under the command and control of an RAF officer, Sir John Salmon. Everyone realized that the RAF alone could not quell the insurrection. Initially the British reduced the number of British and Indian soldiers, but as the insurgency progressed, the numbers remained substantial.

A number of factors, relevant to the Global War on Terrorism, contributed to the success of this campaign. First, the British realized that their two-phased approach of a punitive expedition followed by a military occupation was not successful because of the friction generated between the locals and the occupa-tion forces. This led the British to develop more subtle techniques for dealing with the problem. Second, it became obvious that to be successful the British had to commit to a long-term effort designed to ensure political stability, provide essential services to the populace, and win the hearts and minds of the people. Third, the British minimized violence. When violence was necessary, they directed it against the insurgents alone.

It was readily obvious that the British lacked an in-depth knowledge of the culture and the people.[13] They rectified this by bringing in Arab linguists who divided their time between living among the tribes building lasting relationships and participating in air operations.[14] This group of people developed a detailed knowledge of the culture, tribal leaders and the breadth and depth of tribal lands, method of living, and state of mind of the people.[15] Because of these efforts the teams not only collected actionable intelligence, but also were able to "smell" trouble before it erupted into overt disobedience. Further, this group of resident experts conducted a variety of humanitarian missions that brought such things as modern day medical services to those who needed them most. Essential to success was the ability of the RAF to move security forces to trouble spots quickly, isolate the insurgents from the general population, and help restore confidence in the central government.

So, what did the British learn about airpower and counterinsurgency? From the effort in Somaliland, they learned that airpower could be an influencing factor in a counterinsurgency campaign. In the decade-long counterinsurgency in Mesopotamia, they learned a number of lessons that served them well in Malaya after World War II. The most important lesson learnt was to minimize the violence. Intimate knowledge of the culture, the people, their language and customs is essential. Actionable intelligence coupled with persistent reconnaissance and surveillance is paramount. The local-commander must have control of all air assets. Decentralized control and execution of operations are mandatory. Protecting the populace and their local leaders by isolating the insurgents (includes the employment of mobile strike teams) is vital. Providing the local populace with essential services, humanitarian assistance, and meaningful employment is critical. Moreover, establishing or reestablishing confidence in an indigenously controlled government is paramount to success. The smaller the footprint of the occupational force the better.

Captain M.B. Ridgway discussed the Marine Corps experience in the Nicaraguan insurgency in his Notes to the Chief of Infantry dated October 1928.[16] He noted that the major problems counterinsurgency forces faced were in the areas of intelligence, mobility, logistics, and communications. Marine and Naval air assets were most helpful, he noted, in conducting reconnaissance, close air support of ground forces, courier and supply services, transportation of combat forces, and evacuation of the sick and wounded missions. Further, he reported that insurgent tactics stressed ambushes and dynamite bombs (commonly referred to as improvised explosive devices or IEDs).[17] Throughout his report, Captain Ridgway stressed that success was a result of a synergistic effort of all arms of the Navy. The lessons learned by the Marines in Nicaragua were thusly quite similar to those of the British and were the basis for the *Small Wars Manual* published in 1940.

Three years after the end of World War II, the British found themselves in a counterinsurgency in Malaya that lasted twelve years. One of the factors that contributed to British colonial success was their policy of retaining traditional social institutions and political divisions throughout the areas they controlled.[18] At first, the British and Malayan authorities blamed the populace for not assisting them in eradicating the insurgents. They soon realized that the sooner they took aggressive steps to protect the people from the insurgents, the sooner the people would stop their fence sitting and support the authorities.[19] Fortunately, the authorities came to this realization before the local police forces became ineffective. The authorities moved military units close to friendly villages so they could quickly respond to emergencies and support the police. Villages that were suspect or areas beyond government control were relocated to government controlled areas. A national registration system with identity cards was also established to help separate the insurgents from the populace. Additionally, one person was accountable for the governing of the country and control of the counterinsurgency effort. The critical focal point was at the village level and the coordination of a unified effort involving local political figures, police, infantry company commander, and other civic officials responsible for health, education, and sanitation services.[20]

In Malaya, the British integrated a variety of air assets to create a synergistic civil–military force that included helicopters, small fixed-wing and larger air-craft.[21] These assets emphasized logistics support, transportation of combat forces, reconnaissance and surveillance, and efforts designed to separate the population from the insurgents.

The US–Philippine success against the Hukbalahap (Huk) insurgency was again built around a civil–military synergistic effort designed to build the people's confidence in the national government. Air assets conducted intelligence gathering, reconnaissance and surveillance operations, close air support, and transport of combat troops, air evacuation of sick and wounded.[22] Counterinsurgents forced the Huks out of built-up areas and into areas where the likelihood of collateral damage was virtually nil. The Air Force added bombing missions against concentrated insurgent forces to its repertoire of offensive operations. During this phase of the insurgency, the Air Force conducted effective psychological operations and ferried civic action groups throughout the countryside to build popular support for the central government among the rural population.[23]

Following the end of World War II the Viet Minh assumed that Vietnam would be given her independence. The United States tried to convince the French to recognize Ho Chi Minh as head of a new Vietnamese government. However, as the Japanese left, the Viet Minh temporarily filled the void. In 1946, the French began to re-occupy her former colony, promising to make it a part of an ill-defined "French Union."[24] After an unsuccessful conventional operation, the Vietnamese forces adopted a strategy of insurgency.[25] For the most part the southern portion of Vietnam remained free of large-scale Viet Minh forces. Throughout northern Vietnam, the French Army built a series of fortifications to control and pacify the country. They were not successful as the Viet Minh simply avoided the fortified areas and intermingled with the peasant population, convincing them that they offered a better future than the colonials did. They also received massive logistics and training support from the Chinese Communists after they expelled the Nationalists.

Either the French were not aware of the British colonial experience or they were unwilling to learn from it. Unlike the British, it was not French policy to leave intact the social and cultural institutions or the traditional political boundaries of the territories they occupied. In addition, the French were not keen on developing the necessary bonds with the locals that were essential for success. Although the series of fortifications were intended to be a vehicle to help isolate the population from the insurgents, the French did not follow up with an effort to win the "hearts and minds" of the general population.

In addition, the French misread their success with the "air–land" base concept that enabled them to win at Na-San. When they attempted to try the tactic again at Dien Bien Phu, General Giap refused to fight until he was able to surround the French force of 16,000 soldiers and six Grumman F8F fighters with his force of some 40,000 troops supported by well-camouflaged artillery and anti-aircraft batteries.[26] The results were inevitable.

The French counterinsurgency effort in Indochina was a dismal failure. There was no concerted civil–military integrated effort. Thus, there was no credible civic actions program. Further, the French did not have a unified military strategy that integrated land, air, and naval forces. The French Air Force in Indochina can best be described as vintage, at least until the end of the conflict by which time their fate had already been sealed. Thus, the lessons to be learned from the French experience are all in the negative realm and could be the subject of a paper titled "How to lose a counterinsurgency in grand style."

In Algeria, the French won the military battles, but lost the political war. Unlike the air force they had in Vietnam, the one they fielded in Algeria was modern. They readily adopted new tactics, and were good innovators.

Interestingly, prior to the insurrection, Algeria was a faithful colony that provided loyal troops to fight for the French in both world wars and throughout her colonial possessions. Years of broken promises of reform and poverty culminating in the Setif massacre eventually took its toll and insurrection broke out.[27] When the Algerian insurgency was at a tipping point, French paratroopers fresh from their humiliating defeat in Indochina were called upon to crush the insurgent elements in Algiers. The French heavy handedness in Algiers created an insurmountable schism between European (Colons) and North African (Arab and Berber) residents that drove almost the entire indigenous population into the waiting arms of the insurgents. It was policy to break down doors, torture, and wreck havoc on guilty and innocent alike. In a manner of speaking the French did win the "Battle for Algiers," but at a terrible political price. French forces drove the insurgents into the countryside where the insurgents made sure there were no neutrals. You were either on their side or dead. They created sanctuaries in the newly independent states that bordered Algeria. The civic actions program the French instituted was too little too late to have any effect on the outcome.

By the time the insurgency developed in Aden, the major powers should have learned enough to not lose either the military or the political war. What sets Aden apart from the other insurgencies discussed here are two factors. First, it was a real part of the Cold War and, second, it became a part of Nasser's pan-Arabism Movement. It is for these two reasons that we will concentrate on the air force lessons learned. When combat missions are required, close air support is essential. Pilots flying counterinsurgency close air support missions must be able to fly low and slow with relative safety. The aircraft must have a long loiter time and be able to carry the right mix of ordnance to meet a number of different contingencies.[28] In Aden, the British had a modern fighter – the Hunter FGA9. In Aden one ravine or mountain pass looked like another. Unfortunately, it was not a slow aircraft and at the speeds these aircraft flew, once the pilot began his run, he only had three seconds to make sure he had a positive identification before making his decision to engage or abort. To overcome this difficulty the British instituted Forward Air Controllers or Forward Observers co-located with ground units to help the pilots with target identification. FACs and FOs were not always success-ful, resulting in a needless expansion of munitions or an unacceptable delay in fire when needed.[29] Another lesson is that terrain dictates pursuit after contact. Readily available air mobility of combat forces across the battlefield or strike forces requires having the right kind of aircraft available, usually helicopters. The British had modern helicopters, but they did not have enough of the right kind to be influ-ential. British air assets were never able to solve the actionable intelligence dilemma, especially in built-up areas where the ground forces needed it most to be successful.[30] Lastly, the British were never able to isolate the insurgents from their sanctuaries and logistics support bases in Yemen.

The USAF's contribution to the counterinsurgency effort in Vietnam was the continued embrace of Douhet and Mitchell's misguided notion that airpower in its own right could produce decisive results. General Momyer embraced the independent air campaign as the economical, crucial, and determining ingredient for victory in Vietnam.[31] H.R. McMaster's work, *Dereliction of Duty*, articulates quite well the total ineffectiveness of the Air Force's notion of the proper employment of air power in a counterinsurgency.[32] By 1971, two years before the final withdrawal of American troops from Vietnam, many in the Air Force considered the war to be "a loser."[33] Whatever the spin placed on it by the Air Force, the air power strategy employed in Vietnam was a total failure.[34] Thirty-two years after the American counterinsurgency debacle in Vietnam the US Air Force continues to insist that the airpower thesis espoused by the "Bomber Mafia" in the 1930s is correct, that Vietnam was an anomaly, as are the coun-terinsurgencies in Afghanistan and Iraq.

It seems as though the senior leadership in the Air Force refuses to learn from the mistakes of Vietnam, steadfastly insisting on translating an insurgency into a conventional war it better understands,[35] and is preparing to fight the next war rather than adapting itself to fight and win the war of today. Admittedly, every organization does have to concern itself with the future, but to ignore the present is sure folly. If the Air Force continues this flight to Abilene, it is most certainly will be the Flight to Irrelevance as well.

Learning the right lessons

To paraphrase Fox Mulder, the right lessons to be learned are out there. With regard to the role of the Air Force, is the leadership willing to seek them out, adapt them as necessary, and become relevant? The late Colonel John Boyd would suggest that in order to do this the Air Force would have to first change its orientation, particularly its cultural attitude with regard to the notion of airpower; then and only then would the Air Force be able to play a pivotal role in 4GW, specifically the GWOT.

There are important lessons to be learned from both the successful and less than successful counterinsurgency campaigns waged by the major powers since the Great War. First, counterinsurgency operations are long-term affairs. Democratic governments have found it difficult to maintain focus on long-term efforts. The basic rule for an insurgent is to outlast your opponent. Second, the goal of the counterinsurgency is to maintain or restore the central government. This requires that the populace have faith in the government's ability to maintain order and safety, provide essential services, and ensure economic opportunity. In other words, the people must be convinced that the government's way is better than the promises of the insurgents. One way to accomplish this task is for the host country's ground, sea and air forces be as visible as possible. It is understood that the visibility is in a positive light. If an effective host country military does not exist, then it is incumbent on allies to train host military forces to an acceptable level as soon as possible so they can be seen as the protecting force. Further, this means that the government must isolate the insurgents from the general population, physically, mentally and morally.[36] It is vital that the counterinsurgent forces have an in-depth knowledge of the indigenous population to include their culture, their religious beliefs, and their value system. Along with this, counterinsurgency forces must respect the people they are fighting for and reach out to them not as occupiers but as neighbors. A successful counterinsurgency can only be successful if there is a united politico-military-civic actions effort. Actionable intelligence is paramount as is mobility, good logistics, reliable and secure communications, and the proper equipment to get the job done. Finally, violence must be minimized. When violence is necessary, targeting must be accurate. There is no such thing as collateral damage in the abstract.

Successful counterinsurgencies are fought at three levels, the physical, mental, and moral.[37] One of the major problems with Air Force doctrine is the emphasis on the kinetic or physical level. An action at any one of these three levels has simultaneous implications on the other two. A counterinsurgency is won at the moral (values) level. The abuse of detainees by American soldiers at Abu Ghraib is an example of conflict at this level, and American forces have been feeling the repercussions of this incident ever since. The abusive actions of a few can have serious long-term consequences to the success of a counterinsurgency campaign.

Relevance in a counterinsurgency is measured by presence and contribution. There are over 135,000 ground forces in Iraq alone, yet there are less than 17,000 Air Force personnel in the Southwest Asia Theater of operations, which includes Kuwait, Saudi Arabia, Afghanistan, Qatar, Oman, and the United Arab Emirates.[38] The Air Force constantly argues high operations tempo, yet relevance is hard to prove when your service represents less than 10 percent of the total military forces committed.

We are involved in a global insurgency, there is much the Air Force can and ought to do. Its contribution is not necessarily limited to Iraq and Afghanistan. It can provide a proactive contribution elsewhere. In the next section, I provide several examples of what the Air Force needs to do to get out of the Flight Path to Irrelevance in 4GW. Each of the illustrative examples provided are based on lessons that were learned by the British in Somaliland, Mesopotamia, Malaya, and Aden; by the Marines in Nicaragua; and we all should have learned from the French in Vietnam and Algeria and reinforced through the American experience in Vietnam.

The road to relevance

The most important step the Air Force can take to become a relevant partner in 4GW is to develop a comprehensive counterinsurgency doctrine. Current Air Force Doctrine on Foreign Internal Defense (AFDD 2–3.1) and Special Operations (AFDD 2–7) are simply inadequate. A coherent counterinsurgency doctrine would guide the Air Force in counterinsurgency operations and provide a basis to train host country aviators in counterinsurgency operations. In his article on airpower against guerrillas, Dr. Thomas Searle quoted Dennis Snow, a professor at the School for Advanced Airpower Studies (SAAS), by noting that USAF counter guerrilla doctrine is "a short journey to confusion."[39] An effective counterinsurgency doctrine implies you have both the interest and wherewithal to carry the fight to the insurgents even though it is not the war you want, rather than opting to sit on the sidelines waiting for the war you do want.

According to Robert Coram, "Maj. Gen. David Deptula of the Air Combat Command ordered a subordinate to draft a memo justifying the decommissioning of the A-10 Fleet."[40] Coram argued that the purpose of the memo was to help save both the F/A-22 (Raptor) and F-35 (Joint Strike Fighter). As early as 1996, F.C. Spinney, a Department of Defense analyst, wrote about the Air Force's effort to procure the F-22 and JSF for use against a yet to be defined adversary at some ill-defined point in the future.[41] In other words, preparing for the next war before the one we are now fighting is over. What this means in practical terms is had he been successful in phasing out the A-10 (Warthog), the United States would not have an effective counterinsurgency aircraft in its inventory. The lessons of Somaliland, Mesopotamia, Nicaragua, Vietnam (by both the French and US), Algeria, and Aden illustrates that aircraft capable of providing close air support to counterinsurgency forces is vital. Nevertheless, that is not the only mission a good counterinsurgency aircraft can perform. Effective counterinsurgency aircraft can also conduct surveillance and reconnaissance, intelligence collection, target identification, and similar types of missions.[42] These aircraft can help isolate insurgents from the populace by patrolling remote locations and international borders. The inability of US Air Force aircraft to effectively perform this function in Iraq and Afghanistan is hurting our counterinsurgency effort in those two countries because additional foreign fighters, munitions, and money flow in from Syria and Iran.

There are four options available to the Air Force with regard to providing the US with an effective counterinsurgency aircraft to meet today's needs. The A-10 is an outstanding close air support aircraft. It can withstand a lot of punishment and one option is to update and upgrade the A-10. A second option is to adopt either the Thrush Vigilante or a modernized version of it.[43] The Thrush Vigilante is a low-cost surveillance and close air support platform with a ceiling of 25,000 feet and it has a loiter time of approximately seven hours. This aircraft can be equipped with infrared sensors, defensive systems, and has hard points for a variety of weapons systems. Third, the Air Force can develop a new fully capable counterinsurgency aircraft. No such aircraft is currently on the drawing boards. Frankly, the US Air Force is not interested in performing close air support missions, let alone counterinsurgency missions. This runs counter to the prevailing consensus, at least to those outside the Air Force, that for the foreseeable future the most likely enemies the US will face are entities that practice or adhere to the principles of 4GW (e.g. insurgencies and guerrilla operations). The fourth alternative is for the Air Force to relinquish both the close air support and counterinsurgency air missions to the army, along with the personnel, aircraft, and funding to support such missions. Since the Air Force is already willing to cut its personnel strength by 57,000 to fund the F-22 and F-35, this ought to be a reasonable Air Force alternative. Such a move, however, would represent one more phase line crossed in the Flight to Irrelevance.

Lack of a coherent Air Force counterinsurgency doctrine has other implications as well. Without such a doctrine Air Force, internal defense and development teams cannot train host country air force personnel in counterinsurgency operations. This has two implications. On the one hand, it suggests to the air force of the host country that they do not have a role to play in fighting the insurgents. On the other hand, assuming that another ally does have a counterinsurgency doctrine, it means the US Air Force looses an opportunity to influence the development of the host country's air force.[44] The Air Force cannot, and must not, delegate this role of developing local aviation to other nations!

The Air Force needs to conduct additional research in the development of air and space sensors to improve intelligence collection, surveillance and reconnaissance, and identification of potentially hostile forces.[45] This is particularly true with regard to the five spaces that characterize urban terrain. These five dimensions are airspace, supersurface space, surface space, subsurface or subterranean space, and information space.[46] By monitoring these five spaces of urban terrain, the counterinsurgency forces have a much better chance of isolating the insurgent from the general population. At the same time, the Air Force cannot overlook sensors that identify potential insurgents in mountainous terrain as well as regions with dense foliage and undergrowth. This included air deployable sensors. In Vietnam the US deployed these types of sensors. For the technology available at the time they were quite effective. We seem to have lost sight of that type of technology, concentrating instead on space-based and aerial platforms.

In addition, research is needed to create a sensor capable of either "smelling out" improvised explosive devices (IEDs) and the like, identifying recently disturbed ground where such devices are planted, or neutralizing radio waves within a certain radius of counterinsurgent personnel. Miniaturization of these types of sensors is also most important. Why continue to maintain the Air Force Institute of Technology (AFIT), granting masters and doctoral degrees in the sciences and engineering or fund numerous aerospace laboratories if you are not going to develop capabilities such as the above? The Air Force, of course, can abdicate these to either the Army or the Marines and continue its Flight to Irrelevance.

In the area of unmanned aerial vehicles (UAVs) and unmanned combat aerial vehicles (UCAVs), the Air Force has concentrated on costly high-end intelligence collection and attack vehicles like the Predator and Global Hawk. There are no UAVs in the inventory that are simple, low cost, and useable at the base or local level. An effective series of UAVs and UCAVs that can be used in built-up areas are essentially nonexistent. Miniature/micro aerial vehicle (MAV) research is necessary![47] A large number of inexpensive MAVs each equipped with a different set of sensor packages flooding an area will not only improve intelligence collection, reconnaissance, and surveillance of potential danger areas, but will force insurgents to maintain a constant state of high vigilance. Over time, this causes exhaustion and becomes wearisome, thereby dulling the senses. A large number of these unmanned vehicles would have a psychological effect as well. This is especially true if not all the operating MAVs carried sensors, thereby sowing doubt and uncertainty. One cannot overlook the fact that MAVs can also help monitor Captain Thomas's five spaces of urban terrain.

The notion that the Air Force cannot and should not participate in certain ground operations, convoy duty, perimeter sweeps and security, etc. has to change. Not that the Air Force has to adopt the "every marine is first a rifleman" philosophy of the Marine Corps, but relevance means doing things you may never have done before because, if for no other reason, the current American military force structure no longer allows that luxury. As Captain Troy Thomas had argued, the Air Force will fight in cities. One reason for his prognosis is that the number of cities with one million or more inhabitants will increase from 270 in 1990 to over 516 by 2015.[48] Further, cities are usually strategically located, have symbolic importance, are centers of power, and facilitate the insurgents' blending-in with the general population as well as offering them a safe haven.

Current US Air Force Doctrine calls for centralized control and decentralized execution.[49] In an insurgency the local commander, who is usually an Army or Marine Corps officer, is the individual who must have complete control of air force assets.[50] Since this is contrary to Air Force thought, the counterinsurgency doctrine statement must include provisions for decentralized command, control, and execution of counterinsurgency missions.[51]

With this change in doctrine the Air Force would enable friendly forces to co-locate a six-plane flight of counterinsurgency aircraft to provide continuous 24/7 over-head air cover to Army or Marine Corps ground troops.[52] This operational concept is an adaptation the small outpost concept employed by the British in colonial America to protect the frontiers. By employing this or a similar concept, US and other counterinsurgency forces could significantly improve their ability to isolate the insurgents from the populace, their cross-border sanctuaries, and impede the flow of money and vital materials to the insurgents.

For illustrative purposes only, the concept would be to construct reinforced squad or platoon-sized outposts along the frontier (for example the Syria–Iraq and Iraq–Iran border areas). Headquarters units with a limited mobile reaction capability would be placed at strategic locations behind the line of outposts. A battalion headquarters adjacent to an improvised airfield with a six-plane flight of counterinsurgency aircraft along with maintenance personnel would be located in a relatively secure area, yet close enough to the outposts to provide 24/7 protection air cover.[53] Several knowledgeable air force pilots recommended the six-plane flight concept as the minimum size required having 24/7 over-flight protection by two aircraft and at the same time have a sound aircraft maintenance program in place. This type of air control operation is not new, but has proven itself in successful counterinsurgency conflicts.

As noted previously in this chapter, building and maintaining the infrastructure of the host government is vital to winning a counterinsurgency campaign. If the Air Force is to become a reliable and relevant partner in counterinsurgency operations and the GWOT, it needs to broaden it focus. Building and maintaining a governmental infrastructure, to include providing vital services requires a variety of vocational disciplines, e.g. engineers, police officers, construction workers, healthcare professionals, and administrators to name but a few. As an organization, the Air Force has large numbers of these types of skilled personnel who can contribute to providing essential services to indigenous personnel and helping to isolate them from the insurgents. The army and other coalition forces simply cannot satisfy the demand. Governmental, international, and nongovernmental organizations cannot be expected to assist if there is concern for the safety of their personnel. Members of the Air Force can and ought to help provide this type of support.

There is another way Air Force personnel can proactively help in the GWOT. In addition to humanitarian operations, which the Air Force has done quite well, the Air Force can become proactive GWOT participants.[54] They could be a part of each Combatant Commander's Regional Assistance and Development Plan helping various governments in the respective regions provide their people essential services, train professionals and volunteers, and lend assistance in building and maintaining governmental infrastructure. By acting proactively, as it did in the recent devastating mudslides in the Philippines,[55] the Air Force can help eliminate the conditions that tend to set the climate that fosters an insurgency in the first place.

We cannot leave this discussion without giving the Air Force the kudos it deserves. Although combat search and rescue is not highlighted in previous successful counterinsurgency operations, combat search and rescue of downed aviators or extraction of small units in dangerous situations is important to maintaining the morale of counterinsurgency personnel. In this field of operations, there is no air force in the world that compares. The US Air Force receives five stars.

The US Air Force provides a mobility capability equaled by none. Yet, the Air Force has left a void in the small intra-theater mobility capability. In Vietnam the C-7 Caribou served a vital function of providing US Army Special Forces camps with vital supplies and munitions. The C-130, the intra-theater workhorse, simply could not get into or out of the improvised airstrips adjacent to the camps. The closest comparable aircraft in the inventory today is the C-23 Sherpa, which is only found in Army reserve units. Currently the Army and Air Force are negotiating a Future Cargo Aircraft that can fill this void. The Air Force is not keen on providing this capability, thus the negotiations. Mobility, the reader will recall, is one of the essential counterinsurgency airpower functions. The Air Force receives three stars.

Aero Medical Evacuation is the last of the essential counterinsurgency functions of airpower. The C-9A Nightingale, is now out of service. The C-141 is being phased out of service. That leaves the C-130, an inter-theater aircraft, and the C-17 an aircraft with "longer legs" available for this essential mission. Both of these aircraft are capable of performing multiple missions. The C-17 is an outstanding aero medical evacuation aircraft. This aircraft has multiple oxygen and electrical outlets throughout that are compatible with currently used medical equipment. The cargo bay has great lighting and has full temperature control. Litter stanchions are easy to assemble and disassemble so the aircraft can be changed over quickly for a different mission. Air Force performance and capability in aero medical evacuation, another critical counterinsurgency mission is excellent. The Air Force receives five more stars.

Wrap up

There is an old cliché that states you know what is important to your boss by observing what he monitors or pays attention to. This is a basic truth all military people understand quite well. Lieutenant Colonel David Dean, in his book *The Air Force Role in Low-Intensity Conflict*, phrased it slightly differently when he wrote "Another way to judge the commitment of the Air Force to its various missions is the emphasis given to efforts to procure, maintain, and improve the equipment dedicated to each mission."[56] Although the Air Force's Special Operations Command is a Major Command, the only counterinsurgency aircraft it has is the AC-130H/U Gunship. This aircraft is capable of performing a variety of counterinsurgency missions, but it simply is not well suited for many of the missions cited in this chapter.

Currently, the Air Force has approximately 359,000 uniformed personnel. It is in the process of reducing this force by some 57,000 over the next several years. Somehow the Air Force is convinced it needs to fund the F-22 Raptor, which currently costs $187 million each. Originally the program called for 750 aircraft at a total cost of $67 billion. Because of cost overruns the number of aircraft has since dropped to 339, and the Government Accounting Office projects that in the end only 224 planes will be purchased. The various aircraft the F-22 replaces are already the most capable aircraft in the world. The USAF is the largest air force in the world, the Marines field the eighth largest and the Navy's is somewhere in between. Colonel Brilakis suggests we need this new advanced capability to force the Martian High Command to rethink its interplanetary invasion of earth.[57] An Air Force colleague disagrees with Brilakis, arguing instead his belief that the reason we need the F-22 Raptor is to out-fly al Qaeda's flying SUVs, as they have recently upgraded from their flying carpets.

Air Force Doctrine contends that airpower is inherently strategic and that air superiority is a prerequisite for all other combat operations.[58] Evidently our enemies have not read our doctrine. The United States had air superiority in Vietnam, Lebanon, and Somalia. We lost! We currently have it in Afghanistan and Iraq. Air superiority is not the issue; having an air force that is capable of and desirous of relevance in a counterinsurgency campaign is. It makes no sense to plan for the next war when you are "up to your ears" in one now. The Air Force, if it is to be relevant, must adjust its fighter-bomber mindset from its "breaking things" mentality to one of "buildings things" and winning counterinsurgencies.

Air Forces played a vital role in all successful counterinsurgency campaigns. Perhaps the most important lesson to be learned was best expressed by General Rene Emilio Ponce, who said of the insurgency in El Salvador during the 1980s, 90 percent of a counterinsurgency is political, social, economic, and ideological in nature, while only 10 percent is military.[59] Several thoughts branch out of this observation. A 500-pound precision bomb usually is not, especially when the target is a house in a crowded neighborhood. Violence must be minimized and there is no such thing as collateral damage, which may be an abstract term for the Air Force, but it has another meaning to the innocent civilian who just lost his home. Among other things, it violates the principle of protecting the populace and local leaders. When violence is necessary, for example, strike and close air support missions, it must be timely and accurate, placed where the person on the ground requires. There are not enough trained Tactical Air Control personnel available to do the job; bringing back the FAC might be the solution.[60] Countering terrorism requires decentralized responses under the command of the commander on the ground.[61] The Air Force's notion of centralized control and decentralized execution is counter productive.[62]

The Air Force needs to provide persistent aerial reconnaissance and surveillance. This support needs to deliver actionable intelligence to all counterinsurgent forces including the host country's military and police. Better sensors and additional research into the development of low cost and easy to maintain UAVs, UCAVs, and MAVs deployed in large numbers as well as the operators to operate them is required. This author does not agree with the Air Force belief that Federal Aviation Administration (FAA) certification of operators is a requirement, especially when outside the continental US.

The US needs a relatively inexpensive aircraft that is easy to maintain and operate, has a long loiter time, and can take off and land in short unimproved airfields in the bush. It must also have the capability to perform multiple missions, e.g. reconnaissance and surveillance, strike, intelligence collection, etc. is essential. Our only counterinsurgency aircraft in the Air Force inventory is being forced out to pasture before its time for questionable reasons and, to make matters worse, there is none on the drawing boards to replace it.

The Air Force does an adequate job in the area of mobility and transportation even though it lacks an aircraft smaller, more nimble, and flexible than the C-130 series. It is in the fields of combat search and rescue and aero medical evacuation, however, where the Air Force shines. It has no equal, except for perhaps the Navy and Marines. Both are essential in a successful counterinsurgency.

Without all of the capabilities noted above, the Air Force cannot build an effective local aviation capability. If positive long-term results are expected, then the host government must be able to stand on its own two feet. An effective air arm is essential.

In conclusion, a counterinsurgency can be successful when the insurgents are isolated from the population and the population has confidence in the central government. Essential services must be provided. Counterinsurgent forces need actionable intelligence, which is a result of persistent reconnaissance and surveillance. Violence must be minimized, but when required it must be on target, timely, and under the control of the ground force commander. Decision making and responsibility for ones actions must be delegated to as low a level as possible. This also means that everyone must be held accountable for his or her actions. Fiscus type double standards are not acceptable.

The unfortunate conclusion drawn is that the Air Force is long on promise and short on delivery. It is obvious that the Air Force is maintaining its course to Abilene and its Flight to Irrelevance. Unless it alters course, it may find that Congress and the nation as a whole may start to seriously question the notion of a separate and independent Air Force.

Notes

1 The views expressed in this chapter are the author's own and do not necessarily reflect those of the US Air Force or the Air University.
2 See Jerry B. Harvey (1988). *The Abilene Paradox*, San Francisco, CA: Jossey-Bass Publishers.
3 G. Douhet (1983). *The Command of the Air*, trans. Dino Ferrari, Washington: Office of Air Force History. This work was first printed in 1921. The cited version is a reprint of the second edition published in 1927.
4 W. Mitchell (1925). *Winged Defense*, New York: Dover Publications, pp. 181–198.
5 Ibid., pp. 77–96.
6 Ibid., pp. 23, 24. The British waged a successful counterinsurgency campaign in Mesopotamia (Iraq) from 1920 to 1930 through the doctrine of Air Control which synergized both air and ground forces and by focusing on winning the hearts and minds of the populace. For further information see *The 2005 Air and Space Strategy Conference* proceedings (FOUO) and/or D.J. Dean (1985). *Airpower in Small Wars: The British Air Control Experience*, Maxwell, AFB, AL: Air University Press.

7 Ibid., pp. 9, 10, 14, 165 (he also advocated the use of chemical weapons), 204, and elsewhere.
8 D.E. Omissi (1990). *Air Power and Colonial Control: The Royal Air Force, 1919–1939*, Manchester: Manchester University Press, pp. 3–4.
9 Mitchell, op. cit., pp. 42–43, 66–73.
10 J. Shy (1986). "Jomini," in Peter Paret, ed., *Makers of Modern Strategy* Princeton, NJ: Princeton University Press, pp. 181–185.
11 C.K.S. Chun (2001). *Aerospace Power in the Twenty-first Century*, Maxwell AFB, AL: Air University Press, pp. 50–53.
12 Dean, op. cit., p. 3.
13 *2005 Air and Space Strategy Conference* proceedings, Executive Summary, p. 5.
14 The author would like to point out that the USAF has approximately 120 college educated anthropologists in its officer corps. Yet this knowledgeable group has yet to be leveraged in the War on Terrorism.
15 Dean, op. cit., p. 10.
16 Captain M.B. Ridgway (30 October 1928). *Notes on Military Operations of United States Naval Forces in Nicaragua July 1927–October 1928*.
17 Captain M.B. Ridgway (30 October 1928). *Notes on Military Operations of United States Naval Forces in Nicaragua July 1927–October 1928*, esp. pp. 2–14,
18 R.O. Tilman (1966). "The Nonlessons of the Malayan Emergency," *Military Review*, 46, December, p. 65.
19 C.C. Too (1967). "Defeating Communism in Malaya," *Military Review*, 47, August, p. 87.
20 R.L. Clutterbuck (1963). "Communist Defeat in Malaya: A Case Study," *Military Review*, 43, September, pp. 67–73.
21 J. Weller (1966). "British Weapons and Tactics in Malaysia," *Military Review*, 46, November, p. 21.
22 R.R. Smith (1965). "The Hukbalahap Insurgency," *Military Review*, 45, June, pp. 40–43.
23 J.S. Corum and W.R. Johnson (2003). *Air Power in Small Wars*, Lawrence, KS: University Press of Kansas, pp. 129–131.
24 Ibid., p. 143.
25 Ibid., p. 230.
26 Ibid., p. 231.
27 It is estimated that approximately 6,000 Algerians died in this massacre that was reminiscent of World War II SS reprisals.
28 J. Walker (2005). *Aden Insurgency: the Savage War in South Arabia*. Staplehurst, England: Spellmount, p. 101.
29 This was one of the problems experienced by US forces during Operation Anaconda in Afghanistan. See Major General F.C. Hagenbeck (2002). "Afghanistan: Fire Support for Operation Anaconda," *Field Artillery Journal*, (September–October), pp. 5–9.
30 Walker, *Aden Insurgency*, op. cit., pp. 117–140.
31 D.J. Mrozek (1988). *Air Power and the Ground War in Vietnam*, Maxwell AFB, AL: Air University Press, p. 22.
32 H.R. McMaster (1998). *Dereliction of Duty*, New York: Harper Perennial, pp. 214–225, 235, 256, 261, 265.
33 Comment by Secretary of the Air Force Robert C. Seamons Jr, quoted in E.H. Tliford (1991). *Setup: What the Air Force did in Vietnam and Why*. Maxwell AFB, AL: Air University Press, p. 215.
34 B.S. Lambeth (2000). *The Transformation of American Air Power*, Ithaca, NY: Cornell University Press, p. 12.
35 Lambeth, op. cit., p. 30.
36 See John Robb's post titled, "Boyd on al Qaeda's Grand Strategy." Available at

globalguerrillas.typepad.com/globalguerrillas/2005/05/journal_boyd_on.html (accessed 8 June 2005).

37 D.A. MacCuish (2005). *Toward a Better Understanding of the OODA Loop.* Available at www.d-n-i.net/.

38 These are the latest unclassified figures as of February 13, 2006 posted on www. globalsecurity.org/military/ops/global-deployments.htm. The total figures reported in theater are 170,000 ground forces, 17,000 Naval personnel and 17,000 Air Force or 8 percent of the total force.

39 T.R. Searle (2004). "Making Airpower Effective Against Guerrillas," *Air and Space Power Journal,* Fall 2004.

40 R. Coram, (27 May 2003). "The Hog that Saves the Grunts," discussion thread titled *Terminate the Hog that Saves the Grunts!!!.* Available at www.d-n-i.net/fcs/ comments/c483.htm (accessed 1 February 2006).

41 See F.C. Spinney (March 6, 1996). *Defense Time Bomb: Background F-22/JSF Case Study Hypothetical Escape Option.* Also, F.C. Spinney (2000). "The JSF: One More Car in the House," *Proceedings of the Naval Institute,* August.

42 Current doctrine requires that ground attack pilots positively identify their targets, the acronym SPINS is the term used. If a Forward Air Controller (FAC) is not flying overhead, or if a trained airman is not with the unit requiring assistance, then counterinsurgency aircrafts of the type discussed could perform this task for the pilots of high performance aircraft.

43 W.B. Downs (2005). "Unconventional Airpower," *Air and Space Power Journal,* Spring.

44 Chairman of the Joint Chiefs of Staff (2006). *National Military Strategic Plan for the War on Terrorism,* Washington, DC: US Printing Office, pp. 7, 25. Described in the NMS as Military-to-Military contacts.

45 Toady's space-based sensors, for example, are still severely limited in collecting signals intelligence and imagery. See W.B. Danskine (2005). "Aggressive ISR in the War on Terrorism," *Air and Space Power Journal,* Summer.

46 T.S. Thomas (2000). *Slumlords: Aerospace Power in Urban Fights,* pp. 17, 18. Available at call.army.mil/products/mout/misc-pubs/slumlords-v21.pdf (accessed September 29, 2003).

47 M.S. Pardesi (2005). "Unmanned Aerial Vehicles/Unmanned Combat Aerial Vehicles," *Air and Space Power Journal,* Fall 2005.

48 Thomas, op. cit., p. 4.

49 *Air Force Basic Doctrine* (2003) *Air Force Doctrine Document 1.* Washington, DC: US Government Printing Office, pp. 28–30. The September 1997 edition of this Doctrine Document stated that centralized control "will ultimately cost blood and treasure … ," p. 23. Nothing could be further from the truth. Context matters.

50 Ibid., p. 21.

51 S. Atran (2006). "Risk in the Wild: Reassessing Terrorist Threats from the Field," paper presented at the AAAS Annual Meeting, "Risk and Society" Panel, February 19, p. 3.

52 *Organizing and Employment of Aerospace Power* (2000). Air Force Doctrine Document 2. Washington, DC: US Government Printing Office, p. 40. Air Force Doctrine holds that Air Force units, with few exceptions, do not deploy below Squadron level (e.g. explosive ordnance disposal (EOD) teams, security forces, liaison teams, etc.

53 These aircraft would have the capability to simultaneously conduct intelligence collection, surveillance and reconnaissance, and close air support missions when called upon to support the outposts.

54 A.H. Cordesman (2003). *The Iraq War: Strategy, Tactics, and Military Lessons.* Washington, DC: The CSIS Press, pp. 556, 557.

55 February 17, 2006 was devastated by a mudslide that killed an estimated 1,800 people. Air Force personnel from Yokota AFB, Japan responded as did elements of the US Army, the Marine Corps and US Navy to provide humanitarian assistance.

56 D.J. Dean (1986). *The Air Force Role in Low-Intensity Conflict*, Maxwell AFB, AL: Air University Press, pp. 106, 107.
57 M.A. Brilakis (2006). "Martian Alert!," *Proceedings*, January, pp. 1, 4. Downloaded on February 13, 2006 from www.usni.org.
58 AFDD 1, pp. ix, 19.
59 B. Hoffman (2004). *Insurgency and Counterinsurgency in Iraq*. Santa Monica, CA: The Rand Corporation, p. 5.
60 B.R. Pirnie, A. Vick, A. Grissom, K.P. Mueller and D.T. Orletsky (2005). *Beyond Close Air Support*, Santa Monica, CA: The Rand Corporation, pp. 167–171.
61 S. Atran (2006). "Risk in the Wild: Reassessing Terrorist Threats from the Field," paper presented at the AAAS Annual Meeting, February 19, p. 3.
62 AFDD 1, p. ix.

22 Venus calling

Can NATO cope with 4GW?

Colonel Dr. Frans Osinga[1]

> Today's security environment bears no resemblance to the Cold War. Today's challenges are very different. They require us to act – sometimes in faraway regions; where we know our soldiers' lives will be at risk; where the costs can be high; and where the engagements can seem long.[2]

4GW: icebergs all around

The idea of 4GW has been strongly and deservedly criticized. But like the thesis of the so-called Revolution in Military Affairs and the topic of asymmetric warfare of the 1990s, 4GW serves as a fruitful icon for our time. It highlights what needs highlighting in the current era, it stimulates debate, and while describing familiar territory it also points at new features in the terrain, it captures the problems we currently face, and it poses questions that need answering, such as the one above: Can NATO cope with 4GW? This is not a trivial question. Indeed, it touches the health and very relevance of NATO as an institution, an institution often described as bureaucratic, averse to change, and manifestly unable to make headway in improving its capabilities to cater for security challenges around its borders, let alone those at 10,000 kilometers away from Brussels.

The answer to this seemingly simple question depends first of all on the problem one sees 4GW to point at. Second, it depends on what one regards as the counter to the 4GW problem. Third, it depends on one's view of what NATO is, should be, wants to be or can be, and the challenges it faces, both internally and externally. Is NATO adapting sufficiently in terms of geo-political outlook? Is it adjusting its internal structures and processes? Does it have the right military capabilities and doctrines? Is it addressing 4GW at all? Answering these questions begins by briefly examining 4GW literature. Based on that reading four postulates are developed that, combined, provide the answer to the question whether NATO can cope with 4GW.

Postulate #1: NATO will never fight 4GW

Venus calling

4GW is also a very American discourse.[3] In Europe one finds many studies on the problem manifested by 9/11, but none so starkly put as in 4GW literature.[4] This helps explain how, while certainly not in denial of the problems that 4GW literature captures, Europeans are very reluctant to accept the grand-narrative of good against evil, of a clash of civilizations or images of World War IV. This forms the starting point of the first postulate.

Simply put, NATO will not wage 4GW. It does not feature in the institutional language. NATO recognizes security problems and threats, it talks of missions and conducts operations, but not 4GW. Another obvious reason is that as an institution NATO is endowed with only a limited mandate and set of instruments, not nearly as broad as a nation-state such as the "hyperpuissance" United States, the prime target of the 4GW authors, nor will it ever have those.

More profound is the issue of strategic culture in relation to 4GW as a mainly and distinctly American discourse, because what NATO "does" and is allowed to do "with" 4GW, is in part dependent on the European perception of the problems noted in the 4GW literature. The US has been a driving force behind many NATO developments, but the recent transatlantic rift over Iraq pointed at the fact that European nations, some more than others, have their own views on the problems of international security in the twenty-first century, some of which are not in line with the dominant views of American elites.[5] Yes, in Europe too, it is recognized that the different theaters in which 4GW or global jihad plays out, and the groups within them, are connected through a nested series of links into an aggregated pattern.

Some of this risk, it seems, is avoidable by being selective in choosing where to intervene and where not to, and in the motives for intervention. This feeds into the discussion of European views on current future security threats, and the "Venusian" attitude, as Kagan famously coined the European strategic culture. As 4GW currently deals primarily with radical Islamic terrorism and the situation in Iraq, the European position toward 4GW can be gleaned from the response to the Global War On Terror (GWOT).[6] Many European politicians and the public at large have not bought into GWOT. First, there was a discussion whether it warrants the label of war at all, as this suggests a defined end state and perhaps accords the perpetrators an elevated political and legal status that they certainly do not deserve, and because the "Terror" in GWOT refers to a tactic, without addressing the underlying causes. Second, terror attacks are regarded as a regrettable but not totally eradicable risk of modern society. This risk does not warrant the overhaul of the architecture of the international system nor the circumventing of international law as the US National Security Strategy with its infamous frequent reference to preemptive measures seems to suggest. Nor does it warrant drastic legal changes that would impinge on the freedoms and privacy of citizens. Besides, it is an open question to many whether the terrorist threat has been given too much priority compared to other challenges such as environmental security, crime and migration. Overreaction is a distinct danger and precisely the aim of terrorists.

This also applies to engaging in the "clash of civilizations" thesis. While quite a few European commentators acknowledge the war of ideas, most European politicians are reluctant to engage in it by launching broad brush blueprints for the future, by bashing about the superiority of the Western victorious model of liberal democracy, or by entering in a "West versus Islam" discourse at all. This is no denial of identity. Instead it is motivated by an awareness that *the* European or Western identity is an ambiguous, diffuse and evolving concept. The profound discussion on the question whether or not to include reference to the Christian heritage in the EU constitution made this manifest. Moreover, any simplistic framing of the complex terror problem in religious and civilization terms may fire up an unnecessary and unwelcome backlash, and would in effect be tantamount to playing exactly the game jihadists want to play.

The European view on the ideological dimension that 4GW refers to is probably captured by Lawrence Freedman when he notes that there is as of yet no serious ideological challenge to the transatlantic countries. Time may prove an ally for the West in that liberal democracy, as it has done in the past, sends a subversive message to authoritarian states, working at a symbolic level by representing values and standards against which others will be judged by their own people.[7] Virtual presence may succeed where physical military presence may be risky, uncalled for, ineffective or counter-productive. Indeed, the temptations of Western civilization are corrosive, Laqueur posited recently. Other religions had to face these temptations over the ages and by and large have been fighting a losing battle. Thus in the longer term al Qaeda's allure may diminish due to lack of spectacular success or due to changing views internal to the Muslim world (for instance because of the awareness that more Muslims fall victim to Islamic extremism than infidels). In any case, the present fanaticism will likely not last forever as religious-nationalist fervor does not constantly burn with the same intensity.[8] Moreover, the attacks of 9/11 so far seem to be al Qaeda's single "lucky shot," and the record of other attempts at mass casualty terror attacks suggests that it may be difficult to match that catastrophic event.[9] Mass terrorism is not yet a defining threat of strategic proportions.[10]

At the same time Western society, at large, has proven rather robust. While psychologically vulnerable, and its so called "critical infrastructure" in particular, the very survival of Western nations has not been really at stake, and the threat is subsequently probably not existential. In that light the costs of the US GWOT appears staggering in both loss of life and treasure, and perhaps not in direct comparison to the direct effects of the 9/11 attacks. Indeed, the war against Iraq may have opened a new front for Bin Laden no one but the late al-Zarqawi and Bin Laden asked for. Finally, without denigrating the danger of terrorism, John Mueller nevertheless has a point when he states that within the US on a yearly average as many people die of lightning strikes or taking a bath as people die because of terror attacks worldwide.[11]

Third, Europeans discern not only an extra-national/European aspect but also recognize there is a substantial domestic side to the problem due to the fact that, on average, 2.5–8 percent of the population of most Western European nations are Muslim. The bomb explosions in Madrid and London, the assassination of Dutch filmmaker Theo van Gogh, and the recent societal unrest caused by the Danish cartoons, feed this perception of the problem. Indeed, European security experts are fully aware that much of the campaign against jihadist terrorism will be fought out in Western Europe, as well as in the Middle East, and share the view that the most dangerous people are not pious Muslims in the Middle East but alienated and uprooted young people in Hamburg, London and Amsterdam. We should not see too many similarities between the insurgency causing the American forces huge problems in Iraq and the threats to internal security in European nations.

Similarly, there is a variety of problems underlying the threat of jihadism in each European nation, some of them are comparable – radicalization of second generation immigrants – but some of them also unique to a specific country. Here too we need to get away from the view of al Qaeda as the global mastermind and central coordinating agency for the global *jihad*. The London bombings in July 2005, for instance, were of a purely local home grown nature. A report by the Dutch Intelligence Service in March 2006 noted the emergence of home grown "polder" jihad – local and regional groups, sharing al Qaeda's ideology, finding inspiration and practical tips on the internet, but operating autonomously and requiring no outside assistance whatsoever.[12]

From the start most Europeans have regarded the problem as one with many underlying causes, and considered it dangerous to focus primarily on the manifestation of a complex problem. There is a tendency to assign a large role to judicial departments, to internal security and intelligence forces, to police organizations and customs organizations, and to fostering international cooperation between these organizations, on disrupting financial flows, on improved airport security and the protection of critical infrastructure. In addition, European nations emphasize consequence management, disaster response, the organization of emergency health care, i.e. homeland defense and on adjusting policies thereby limiting the flow of immigrants to European countries. And to some effect, as terrorism expert Paul Wilkinson recently noted.[13] In other words, Europe has translated 9/11 into primarily an internal security problem, and only secondary as a problem of security policy and defense. It regards the anti-jihadist campaign more as an enduring intelligence and police operation rather than a war, and certainly not a war with a large part of the Arab world. World War IV overstates and mis-frames the problem.

Turning to the external side of the problem, because of the different perception of the problem, due to capability limitations as well as cultural disposition, and because 9/11 points in no small measure to a conflict internal to the Muslim world, European nations in general will not put such an emphasis on the military dimension to solve the problem as the US did from 2001–2005. There is generally a suspicion of attempts at "enforced social engineering" aimed at implementing democracy in foreign countries. Instead, the favored approach is marked by conflict prevention and dialog, rather than threat prevention, in key regions using a range of multinational diplomatic, political and economic measures, with military action as the very last resort, rather than an early preference.[14] In that sense, there is not really a categorical difference in approach in the way Europeans treat the security environment before or after 9/11, only in intensity of political attention.

Disaggregating the problems incorporated in 4GW shows NATO will only partially play in the 4GW "game." NATO as an institution does not deliberately wage a war of ideas. It does not possess the full gamut of instruments for developing and applying a coherent grand strategy. Neither does NATO deal with the decline of the nation-state or the West. In fact, in contrast to the EU, most of the internal dimension of the problems 4GW points at is beyond NATO's purview. Consequently, there will be less coherence in dealing with 4GW opponents than called for. Finally, NATO is unlikely to get involved in risky military endeavors reeking of attempts at social engineering, of visions of a speedy enforced democratization of areas that appear in Thomas Barnett's map of the disconnected non-globalized non-democratic and therefore terrorist-prone parts of the world.[15]

Postulate #2: NATO has done 4GW, and won

The benefit of old news

On another point however, the European views cohere nicely with those of 4GW authors. When dealing with terrorism and the problems of radical Islam, NATO cannot be expected to address it exclusively through military means, and when military forces are employed, it will not only be for fighting insurgents, but will probably look more like the operations of the 1990s, that is, as part of a broad approach to the security challenge, much like the recommendations of 4GW papers.

Indeed, 4GW points at problems NATO has encountered before. Much like the fading distinction between terrorism, irregular warfare and insurgency, there is a convergence in the underlying dynamics of current security problems as well as in the solutions, as far as solutions to such problems go. Whether the problem involves peace keeping in the Balkans, peace enforcement, stability and reconstruction, the fight against the global radical Islamist inspired insurgency, or humanitarian operations, the underlying strategic dynamic as well as imperatives are comparable and/or overlapping. As Julian Lindley French observed, the distinctions between peace keeping, peace making and war fighting are becoming rapidly meaningless.[16]

Solution convergence: been there, done that, gave away NATO T-shirts

This goes some way to answering the question whether NATO can cope with 4GW. Some of the tools that were applied in peace keeping and humanitarian intervention, humanitarian aid, and stability and reconstruction also have relevance for conducting 4GW. The methods to address the crises of the 1990s aimed to create effects that are also beneficial in 4GW or counterinsurgency.

Critical to peace keeping proved the relationship between consent, force, endurance and impartiality. If a peace operation uses too much force it risks losing its impartiality and crossing the consent divide into open conflict. At the same time, peace keepers must be prepared to use minimum yet sufficient force to counter peace spoilers and induce consent for the operation to succeed. As in 4GW, another critical element is endurance. Often peace keeping operations and their aftermaths involve and require lengthy commitments of the intervening powers in order to rebuild and democratize.

It follows that, in hindsight it can be argued that NATO has built up a track record in 4GW, and one that bodes favorably for the future. NATO has been involved in several peace keeping and peace enforcement operations in the Balkans, signifying that NATO was willing and able to operate "out of area" to address a crisis in an adjacent area that posed a significant danger of spilling over to impact peace and stability in Europe.[17] A lot of ink has been justifiably spilled over the measure of effectiveness of those operations, their legitimacy, the drawn-out political decision making processes and inertia and the humanitarian disasters that could perhaps have been avoided. Here those experiences bear relevance to our discussion for, as General Sir Rupert Smith recounts in his recently published tome, the Balkans environment he operated in bears a nice resemblance to the challenges of 4GW.[18]

Indeed, NATO has proven it has stamina in that it has continued its engagement in the Balkans since 1992 up to this very day. To be sure, there were grave problems and institutional problems to be surmounted, and frequently only a looming crisis provided the leverage to push nations into concerted actions and accept drastic policy changes. From an institutional point of view peace keeping operations and out-of-area intervention in internal conflicts fell beyond the traditional interpretation of self-defense and Article 5 of the North Atlantic Treaty. Second, such operations – terminating conflict and providing peace – were complex, with humanitarian, economic, political and military elements, and often a variety of non-governmental and supranational organizations to engage with. NATO possessed only military means and was thus not materially nor institutionally equipped to deal with all the challenges. Peace keeping and enforcement doctrine only developed ad hoc or even post hoc, and often in response to institutional failing and human suffering as a consequence, such as NATO's response to launch Deliberate Force – finally a robust coherent operation – after the massacre of Srebrenica had unmistakably pointed at the dysfunctional complex and sluggish NATO–UN command structures and the inappropriate Rules of Engagement. Both Deliberate Force and Allied Force moreover highlighted the difficulty NATO has in coordinating diplomatic overtures, collectively or by individual nations, with military actions.[19]

Yet, while perhaps not always neatly executed either militarily or politically, and perhaps with only a small dose of legality, nevertheless the operations in the Balkans have had a very positive effect on the region. Moreover, while it took a painful learning process, it proved that NATO forces could develop an appropriate doctrine, adjust their training, display a sufficient level of cultural sensitivity, build up a perception of legitimacy, and offer (in addition to coercive incentives) an attractive alternative to civic strife. Manifesting the political commitment, NATO nations deployed 60,000 troops for IFOR in 1995, for KFOR in 1999 the number was 50,000. NATO troops saw to cease-fire agreements, oversaw transfer of territories and the disarmament of factions, assisted UN bodies in implementing UN accords, providing a secure environment for civil and political reconstruction. It involved patrolling, supervising de-mining operations, arresting individuals charged with war crimes, assisting the return of refugees and displaced persons to their homes.

Seen clinically as a learning experience, it showed NATO could do more than fight interstate wars, and endure. As Julian Lindley French noted in 2004, even without substantial US support European nations have the capabilities to mount significant humanitarian, peace keeping and peace making operations, up to a limited level of intensity of violence. So too can they perform medium scale counterinsurgency strikes with special forces almost anywhere in the world against terrorists.[20] NATO has done 4GW, and done so successfully, albeit in a somewhat ad hoc fashion, through a long learning process and not directly against al Qaeda or another jihadist opponent.

Postulate #3: NATO will get better at it

From the brink of irrelevance

After Kosovo it became evident for all that European nations lacked severely in expeditionary capabilities, and in the means to conduct high intensity combat operations. This combination produces a very limited capacity to deal with the external dimension of 4GW and not surprisingly, in the immediate aftermath of 9/11, many questioned the capacity for NATO to deal with this challenge. After all, if it could only barely manage an effective small scale operation of limited complexity within Europe, what did that imply for threats emanating from remote regions? If it did not have the wherewithal to find and destroy mobile Surface to Air Missiles, and precisely track and engage Serb infantry across mountains, what does that mean for the ability to target small groups of insurgents?

Since the publication of the new Strategic Concept in 1999, as an institution NATO has recognized the threats and challenges of terrorism and it has been trying to get nations to improve the collective power projection – expeditionary – capabilities as well as their defense against non-traditional threats. The 1999 strategic concept marked a distinct effort to redefine NATO's fundamental security tasks, shifting its focus outward from the European mainland toward the arguably much wider Euro-Atlantic security environment.[21] It also reflected a decade of experience in crisis management in the Balkans when it listed two security tasks: crisis management, including conflict prevention and crisis response operations; and partnership, including dialogue and cooperation, with other nations in the Euro-Atlantic region. Compared to its predecessor of 1991, the new concept also paid more attention to deter and counter the proliferation of WMD. Most importantly from the perspective of this chapter is the attention it paid to terrorism, calling for the protection of Alliance forces and infrastructure against terrorist attacks.

Since 1999 terrorism has only increased as a core focus for NATO defense planning. NATO responded immediately to the attacks of 9/11, invoking – albeit rather symbolically – Article 5, no less than the cornerstone of the Alliance; it was considered an attack against all. NATO also agreed on a package of measures such as greater intelligence sharing, provision of assistance to states threatened as a result of their support for coalition efforts and increased security for facilities of the US and other Allies on their territory. On December 18, 2001 NATO Defense Ministers tasked the NATO Military Authorities to prepare a *Military Concept for Defense Against Terrorism*.[22]

During that same meeting (and subsequent ones), with renewed self-confidence emanating from the victory of Operation Enduring Freedom, US Defense Secretary Donald Rumsfeld reminded European NATO members to start making good on their promises to solve the military shortfalls among European NATO member states, and to work on the burden sharing issue. The US would no longer wage war by committee in these conditions, reflecting a shift in the US toward coalitions of the willing. In recognition of the failure of the *Defense Capabilities Initiatives* of 1999, and in response to some US pressure, during the Prague Summit in November 2002 European nations agreed upon the US initiative to embark on a limited program of focused accelerated modernization – transformation – and expansion of military capabilities.

To embryonic globocop

Laid down in the Prague Capabilities Commitment, those measures in broad terms concerned flexibility, interoperability, sustainability and deployability.[23] In practical terms it involved concrete targets to increase combat effectiveness, including precision attack munitions; air-to-air refueling capabilities; sea and air lift assets; the means to suppress enemy air defenses; command, control and communications; intelligence, surveillance and target acquisition; deployable combat support and combat service support. Moreover it was decided to create a *NATO Response Force*, a small but rapidly – globally (!) – deployable force, modeled after the forces and doctrine the US employed in Operation Enduring Freedom. NATO wants agile, rapidly reconfigurable forces, consisting of smaller units, lighter logistic support trails, with much improved sophisticated command and control facilities, and ample support of surveillance and reconnaissance assets. In launching the *NATO Networked Enabled Capability* initiative NATO made an effort to introduce the US Network Centric Warfare concept into the Alliance, so as to improve interoperability with the US and provide timely relevant information to all levels. Such capabilities would also shorten the "sensor-to-shooter" time – enabling so called "time-sensitive-targeting" – not unimportant if one wants to find, track and target small mobile groups of insurgents. NATO also tried to increase transparency but above all coherence and focus in the defense planning activities of nations through the implementation of a regular *Defense Requirements Review*, which pays particular attention to expeditionary operations. In short, NATO aimed to improve its expeditious capabilities and to close the capability gap that had become manifest during Allied Force. Combined with an overhaul of the outdated and redundant command structure, and a review of its internal decision making procedures, its force generating and funding processes aiming to promote more expeditious and responsive decision making at the political and military strategic levels, this package became known as NATO Transformation.

More so than the Strategic Concept of 1999, the Prague Declaration effectively killed the out-of-area discussion and brought terrorism and 4GW themes much more into focus, by stating that NATO was to meet "challenges to the security of our forces, populations and territory, from wherever they may come." NATO needed the ability to "field forces that can move quickly to wherever they are needed, sustain them over distance and time, including in an environment where they might be faced with nuclear, biological and chemical threats." This specifically included "the threat posed by terrorism and the proliferation of WMD and their means of delivery." Terrorism, it noted, "poses a grave and growing threat to Alliance population, force and territory, as well as to international security." In firm terms it continued to proclaim that "we are determined to combat this scourge for as long as necessary."

Both themes – expanding geopolitical scope and terrorism – were explicitly emphasized in 2006 during the important Munich Conference on Security Policy when De Hoop Scheffer stated that "we have broadened our strategic horizon far beyond Europe. We have begun tackling terrorism as a main mission – indeed, in Afghanistan, we are engaging terrorism at the source. We are projecting and sustaining forces well beyond our traditional area of operations."[24] Forging close relations with partner nations – "from Austria to Finland and from Armenia to Kazakhstan" – are part of this trend, and one that may in the future include "Australia, New Zealand, South Korea or Japan." On a subsequent occasion he added that NATO nations faced a "lethal breed of terrorism, the proliferation of WMD, failed states spreading instability and criminal networks trafficking in people, drugs and weapons" – "new, complex, and truly global threats to our security." He was also frank about "certain countries and regions" where NATO needed to foster democracy and stability, mentioning Russia, Ukraine, Central Asia, "a string of countries in Northern Africa and the Middle East, from Morocco to Israel" and the Gulf Region.[25]

DAT or NWOT

In more practical terms too developments suggest 4GW is being tackled. An important element of the 2002 Summit was the endorsement of the *Military*

Concept for Defense Against Terrorism, (DAT), or NATO's War On Terror, (NWOT).[26] It follows a threat assessment of terrorism which, somewhat predictably, concluded that terrorism may emanate from religious extremism, emerging ideologies and unresolved conflicts. It recognizes the risk of state sponsorship providing terrorists with safe havens and resources. Finally, it warns of the risk of terrorists seeking weapons of mass destruction. It stipulates that NATO actions against terrorists and those who harbor them should help deter, defend, disrupt and protect against terrorist attacks or threat of attacks, against populations, territory, infrastructure and forces of any member state. NATO can also act, if requested, in support of the international community's efforts against terrorism and provide assistance to national authorities in dealing with the consequences of attacks.

NATO's role becomes more prominent in the counter terrorism role, which is defined as offensive military action designed to reduce terrorists' capabilities. This may involve actions against specific individuals, groups or training sites, as well as psychological and information operations. Force protection too gains in significance here, because expeditionary operations will be vulnerable to the type of insurgency currently seen in Iraq. Critical for effective counter terrorism operations are procedures and capabilities that support accelerated decision cycles, responsive precision strikes and specialized anti-terrorist forces.

Action!

Several ongoing NATO operations also specifically address the threat of terrorism and insurgencies. Operation *Active Endeavour* is a maritime surveillance and escort operation in the Mediterranean, aiming to detect and deter terrorist activity and keeping the trade routes open. It includes boarding and inspection of civilian ships. Started in October 2001, by January 2005 the operation had hailed approximately 59,000 vessels. Ongoing operations in the Balkans are now also put in the context of the campaign against terrorism by focusing on the illegal movement of people, arms and drugs.

NATO's presence in Afghanistan in particular defines the extent of NATO's evolving ambitions and capabilities against 4GW opponents. Operating under the mandate of an evolving set of United Nation Security Council resolutions, the International Security and Assistance Force (ISAF) started in 2003 with a Dutch and German contingent. In the words of Lord Robertson, it established NATO firmly as a key actor in the international struggle against terrorism.[27] Initially the aim was limited to assist the Afghan Transitional Authority in the maintenance of security in the Kabul area so as to enable United Nation's personnel to work in a secure environment, facilitate fair elections, spread the rule of law, and reconstruct the country. After October 2003, ISAF's role widened beyond Kabul with the introduction of Provincial Reconstruction Teams. These are teams of international civilian and military personnel working in Afghan provinces to extend the authority of the central government and to provide a safer and more secure environment in which reconstruction can take place. By

October 2004 NATO had 10,000 troops deployed across Afghanistan, including quick reaction forces. In May 2005 NATO expanded ISAF into the west of Afghanistan by taking command of four additional PRTs in western provinces.[28] In the summer and autumn ISAF assumed command of all forces in the southern and eastern parts of Afghanistan, with a total of approximately 31,000 troops in the theater.

Initially ISAF was, at least formally and as far as command and control arrangement were concerned, kept separate from the US-led Operation Enduring Freedom, which focused much more on combating Taliban and al Qaeda remnants in and around Afghan border areas.[29] While ISAF will not conduct counter-terrorist operations even when ISAF will cover the entire country in 2007, its range of activities now include robust counterinsurgency operations being conducted by British, Canadian, Dutch and American forces that are engaged in fierce combat with Taliban forces.[30] It is perhaps the riskiest and most ambitious operation in NATO's history.[31]

Introducing a comprehensive approach

Despite these significant changes since 1999, NATO has opted not to open the Pandora's box of drafting a new strategic concept, not least because the existing one offers sufficient latitude to incorporate the evolving range of missions and threats.[32] Another reason is that NATO has circumvented the issue by launching a number of other high level documents, that, while not raised to the ministerial level, potentially have far reaching implications and have inspired high level discussions, leaving no doubt about the status of the ideas incorporated in those documents. If those views take effect they would bolster NATO capacity to "do" proper strategy, and deal more effectively with the complex threats, indeed they answer the call of the DAT Concept for the development for an overarching strategy for defense against terrorism.

One such document is the *Strategic Vision: The Military Challenge,* promulgated by Allied Command Transformation in 2004–2005.[33] Picking up on the imperative of military cooperation as mentioned in the DAT Concept, the *Strategic Vision* emphasizes that such operations need close cooperation with international organizations. Within Allied Command Transformation this has been referred to as Enhanced Civil Military Cooperation. This initiative aims to improve the ability of NATO units on all levels of command to cooperate effectively with civil actors, ranging from local authorities to international and non-governmental organizations. This development, the coupling of military and non-military instruments, and the institutionalization of relationships with other organizations, should lead to achieving a capacity to implement a so called "Effects Based Approach to Operations," the cornerstone of the document titled *Concepts for Allied Future Joint Operations* that was developed within ACT and released in 2006.

It is based on the idea of coherence and interdependence, and the realization that peace, security and development are more connected than ever.[34] It recognizes that, apart from the military instrument, there are three other instruments that need to be coordinated in concert: political, economic and civil. The political instrument refers to the use of political and diplomatic power to influence an actor or to create conditions that are advantageous to the Alliance. It involves efforts within and among the various regional and international organizations and actors. The use of the economic instrument refers generally to financial incentives or disincentives. This instrument is most likely to be exercised not by NATO but by nations or international organizations. Third, the civil instrument refers to areas such as judiciary, constabulary, education, public information and civilian administration and support infrastructure, which can lead to access to medical care, food, power, water and administrative capacities of nations and non-governmental organizations.

Strategic Vision had no formal status beyond the two strategic commands, but did arouse significant debate within the Military Committee and the International Staff, resulting in the *Comprehensive Political Guidance* to the two strategic commanders effectively endorsing the ideas laid down in *Strategic Vision*. EBAO has become a major topic of high level exercises and experiments such as Allied Reach 06 and the Multi-National Experiment 04. The principles have also been agreed upon at the Ministerial meeting in December 2005, when the *Final Communiqué* notes that today's challenges demand improved cooperation among international organizations.[35] In Oslo on March 2006 de Hoop Scheffer noted that intense interagency cooperation was already a reality on the ground, whether in the Balkans, Afghanistan, Iraq or Darfur, stressing however, that these ad hoc methods of cooperation need to become structured relationships at the institutional level – to be able to coordinate strategically, not just tactically.[36] Thus, in a way, NATO is not only attempting to institutionalize the *3 Block War* concept, as coined by the US Marine Corps, at the tactical level, but also at the operational and strategic levels.

Value-based security policy

NATO is now about "projecting stability,"[37] not dissimilar to what the EU endorses as "preventive engagement."[38] Capturing the identity of the Alliance, the first paragraph of the 2004 Istanbul Summit explains that the 26 nations are united in the values of "democracy, individual liberty and the rule of law."[39] Paragraph two goes on to say "to defend our security and our values" it will promote stability and take on a full range of missions.[40]

In February 2006 the Secretary General told a Polish audience that the transatlantic community that NATO helped create, is bound by the values of pluralism, freedom, democracy and tolerance, values that are vulnerable and have been under direct attack since 9/11 by al Qaeda and like-minded extreme terrorists. It is only through active engagement that we can protect our values; NATO operations in the Balkans, Darfur and Afghanistan, but also NATO's expansion, are the most visible manifestations of such a policy.[41] In a way NATO is leveraging "the tremendous potential of networked systems," as

Hammes has argued for.[42] All in all, as Robertson concluded, a venerable old dog can indeed learn new tricks.[43]

Postulate #4: NATO may also not win

Good intentions, however, are often not translated into actions and tangible results. No one pretends the capability gap is closing rapidly. Indeed, with ongoing US modernization and stagnant or decreasing investment levels in Europe, the US military is in a league of its own. European dependence on US transport and intelligence assets is only gradually decreasing. Long after the fall of the Berlin wall, many European armed forces still betray force structures oriented toward territorial defense, with a consequence that out of a total of 1.7 million uniformed personnel, only 10 percent can actually be deployed. As SACEUR General Jones remarked, there is a political will for the alliance to do much more, but there is an equal and offsetting political desire to cut defense budgets. If we do not reconcile those impulses, there is a train wreck out there waiting to happen.[44]

Second, internal decision making procedures at the political level are still cumbersome, as the prolonged and continuing discussions concerning deployment, funding and manning for ISAF contingents once more demonstrated. This pertains to the identity of NATO. While for the US NATO's future relevance is a function of its capacity to operate more globally, it is probably true that for most European politicians the willingness to embark on long and risky missions is tied to the specific stakes involved. The more abstract the goal – fighting global terrorism – and the greater the distance, the less European publics are inclined to initiate NATO intervention. As during the 1990s, NATO will change most rapidly when nations need to respond to crisis and urgent real-world demands in which interests, humanitarian in particular, are unmistakably at stake, as became visible in the disaster relief operation in Pakistan in October 2005. Arguably, the more successful the US and European nations are in fending off terrorist attacks on their own soil, the more abstract the threat to the Alliance of al Qaeda located in remote barren parts of the world will appear.

Third, apart from the internal challenges in turning NATO's ambition into reality, there are external problems and risks. NATO's own benevolent image is not shared in all parts of the world. In reaching out to spread its message and convince other nations of NATO's agenda and mutual interest, the magnitude of countering negative views of NATO is enormous, as two scholars recently noted.[45] For the Arab public NATO has no separate identity from those of the Western powers and states that constitute its members. Until recently NATO was viewed as a powerful, aggressive alliance, an imperialist, pro-Israeli, colonist club. Also NATO has often been equated with US foreign policy, and operations like ISAF, or the *Istanbul Cooperation Initiative* are subsequently regarded as a US-proxy. The Alliance's policies and objectives have thus been prejudged. Against a backdrop of such prevailing attitudes it is unwarranted to expect to gain credibility and a perception of legitimacy, i.e. to gain ground in the ideological dimension, anytime soon, no matter how good the intentions or benign NATO's policies.

Related to the context of hostile perception toward NATO is the rising risk of NATO's mission in Afghanistan, where Europeans remain reluctant to make good on their promise to deploy the number of troops they promised. Not surprisingly Michael Gordon noted during a visit to the area that "I couldn't help getting a queasy feeling thinking about whether NATO truly has the capability and staying power to see the Afghan mission through, especially if the going gets tough."[46]

Conclusion

Set within a distinctly European Venusian strategic approach toward terrorism, *institutionally* NATO seems to be coping quite appropriately with 4GW, albeit primarily in regards to the manifestations of 4GW outside the territory of NATO nations. NATO can build on a decade of bringing stability in the Balkans which demonstrated that the Alliance can bring a substantial collective political and military power to bear on security problems, as well as a welcome dose of legitimacy, credibility and acceptability in its operations. Moreover, the Alliance has proven to be dynamic. Within six years, NATO nations have proved willing to straddle strategic distance, close the capability gap, take on terrorism and WMD, enlarge its membership, improve its institutional processes and cooperation mechanisms, expand its framework of partner and dialogue nations, take a broad approach to security, and expand its range of tasks to include fighting fleeting terrorists, coerce rogue states and "do" nation building. Explicitly, it now also addresses 4GW problems in the ideological dimension, its diplomats spreading a moderate but distinctly Western message. While NATO does not have the ambition or the means to become a "globocop," a word coined by de Hoop Scheffer, these developments certainly indicate a deliberate and wide-ranging effort at the policy level to change NATO into a security organization with a wider range of missions, capabilities and reach, and one that is specifically focusing on issues identified in 4GW.

But clearly the jury is still out whether NATO can cope with 4GW *in practice*. It is unlikely that the security of NATO nations will suffer directly if NATO is forced to withdraw from Afghanistan. In that sense, NATO will likely not lose against 4GW opponents. But the fact that it would not win, would likely be perceived and exploited as a victory for and by any *jihadist* insurgent force. No doubt NATO's credibility and relevance would dramatically suffer.[47] Interestingly, however, it was precisely the potential damage to NATO's credibility during Operation Allied Force that amalgamated NATO nations into more forceful action, escalate and show it could persevere. Analogously and paradoxically perhaps, if through their actions 4GW warriors raise the stakes for NATO high enough, NATO can be expected to rise to meet the direct challenge of 4GW.

Notes

1 The views expressed by the author reflect a personal opinion and are not in any way representative of either the Netherlands Ministry of Defence nor of NATO.

2 Speech by Jaap De Hoop Scheffer, NATO Secretary General, Munich, February 4, 2006.

3 See for a recent entry in the list of American articles debating the nature of modern wars (including direct references to 4GW) for instance Michael Mazarr, "Extremism, Terror, and the Future of Conflict," *Policy Review*, March 2006, Web Special, www.policyreview.org (accessed April 28, 2006).

4 See for instance Gilles Kepel, *The War for Muslim Minds, Islam and the West*, Harvard University Press, Cambridge, MA, 2004; Oliver Roy, *Globalized Islam: The Search for the New Ummah*, Columbia University Press, New York, 2004; Roger Scruton, *The West and the Rest, Globalization and the Terrorist Threat*, Continuum, London, 2002; and John Gray, *Al Qaeda and What it Means to be Modern*, Faber and Faber, London, 2003.

5 For the heterogeneity of European perspectives, see, for instance, Adrian Hyde-Price, "European Security, Strategic Culture, and the Use of Force," *European Security*, 13(4), 2004, pp. 323–343. For a concise overview of studies on the transatlantic crisis post 9/11 see Leslie Gelb, "The Iraq War and U.S.–European Relations," *Orbis*, Fall 2004, pp. 719–731.

6 For a broad representative European perspective (with a French accent) see Gilles Andréani, "The 'War on Terror': Good Cause, Wrong Concept," *Survival*, 46(4), Winter 2004–2005, pp. 31–50. For two philosophical commentaries see Jurgen Habermas, "Interpreting the Fall of a Monument," *German Law Journal*, 7 (July 1, 2003); and Vivienne Jabri, "War, Security and the Liberal State," *Security Dialogue*, 37(1), March 2006, pp. 47–64.

7 Lawrence Freedman, "The Transatlantic Agenda: Vision and Counter-Vision," *Survival*, 47(4), Winter 2005–2006, pp. 36–37.

8 Walter Laqueur, op. cit. For the corrosive influence of Western ideas on traditional communities, see Benjamin Barber's *Jihad vs McWorld*.

9 See, for instance, Robert Jervis, "An Interim Assessment of September 11: What Has Changed and What Has Not," *Political Science Quarterly*, 117(1), Spring 2002, pp. 37–54; and Francis Fukuyama, *America at the Crossroads*, Yale University Press, New Haven, CT, 2006, p. 69.

10 Andréani, op. cit., p. 48.

11 John Mueller, "Six Rather Unusual Propositions about Terrorism," *Terrorism and Political Violence*, 17, 2005, p. 488. For another such balanced view on the threat of terrorism see, for instance, Richard Betts, "How to Think About Terrorism," *The Wilson Quarterly*, Winter 2006, pp. 44–50.

12 Algemene Inlichting en Veiligheids Dienst, *De Gewelddadige Jihad in Nederland*, Den Haag, Maart 2006. For similar observations see, for instance, Scott Atran, op. cit.; and David Martin Jones and M.L.R. Smith, "Greetings from the cybercaliphate: some notes on homeland insecurity," *International Affairs*, 81(5), 2005, pp. 925–950.

13 See Paul Wilkinson, *International Terrorism: The Changing Threat and the EU's Response*, Chaillot Paper no. 84, October 2005, EU Institute for Security Studies.

14 For this see Cornish, op. cit.; Lawrence Freedman, op. cit.; Michael Cox, "Beyond the West: Terrors in Transatlantia," *European Journal of International Relations*, 11(2), 2005, pp. 203–233; and, in particular, Wyn Rees and Richard J. Aldrich, "Contending Cultures of Counterterrorism: Transatlantic Divergence or Convergence?," *International Affairs*, 81(5), 2005, pp. 905–923.

15 Thomas Barnett, *The Pentagon's New Map*, Putnam, New York, 2004.

16 Julian Lindley-French, "Big World, Big Future, Big NATO," *NATO Review*, Winter 2005.

17 Terry Terriff, "Fear and Loathing in NATO: The Atlantic Alliance after the Crisis over Iraq," *Perspectives on European Politics and Society*, 4(3), December 2004, p. 4.

18 See General Sir Rupert Smith, *The Utility of Force*, Allan Lane, London, 2005, in particular ch. 7.

19 For NATO's learning process see, in particular, Henning-A. Franzen, *NATO and Peace Support Operations 1991–1999*, Frank Cass, London, 2005, in particular ch. 4.

20 Julian Lindley-French and Franco Algieri, *A European Defence Strategy*, Bertelsmann Foundation, Gutersloh, 2004, pp. 28–32.

21 See North Atlantic Council, *Strategic Concept*, April 24, 1999 for the following, in particular paras 6 and 24.

22 See for the full array of measures *NATO and the Fight Against Terrorism*, NATO Briefing, Brussels, March 2005.

23 See the *Prague Summit Declaration*, NATO Press Release, November 21, 2002, also for the following paragraphs.

24 Speech by Jaap De Hoop Scheffer, NATO Secretary General, Munich, February 4, 2006

25 *A New NATO*, speech by Jaap De Hoop Scheffer, NATO Secretary General at the Norwegian Atlantic Committee, Oslo, March 3, 2006.

26 For a full survey of all of NATO's initiatives see *NATO's Military Concept for Defence Against Terrorism*, NATO International Military Staff, Brussels, October 2003; *NATO and the Fight Against Terrorism*, NATO Information Briefing, Brussels, March 2005; *Istanbul Summit Communiqué*, June 28, 2004; and *Final Communiqué*, Ministerial Meeting of the North Atlantic Council, December 8, 2005.

27 George Robertson, "Transforming NATO to Meet the Challenges of the 21st Century," in Daniel Hamilton (ed.), *Transatlantic Transformations: Equipping NATO for the 21st Century*, Center for Transatlantic Relations, Washington, DC, 2004, p. 31.

28 See *NATO in Afghanistan*, NATO Press Factsheet, Brussels, January 19, 2006;

29 See *Istanbul Summit Communiqué*, June 28, 2004, para. 5.

30 Nicjolas Fiorenza, "ISAF to be Commanded by Composite Headquarters," *Jane's Defense Weekly*, March 15, 2006, p. 6.

31 James Kitfield, "Divided We Fall," *National Journal*, April 7, 2006.

32 For a full analysis see David Yost, "NATO's 1999 Strategic Concept," in NATO Defense College Occasional Paper, Rome, March 2005, pp. 21–33.

33 *Strategic Vision: The Military Challenge*, NATO BiSC Unclassified Publication, Mons/Norfolk, August 2004. For similar statements see also *Understanding Military Transformation*, unclassified publication, Allied Command Transformation, Norfolk, Fall 2005.

34 I have made use of *Concepts for Allied Future Joint Operations*, Unclassified BiSC Document, Norfolk, VA, February 20, 2006. This is a draft version but one that has already passed through many iterations and is considered balanced and nearly complete.

35 *Final Communiqué*, Ministerial Meeting of the North Atlantic Council, Brussels, December 8, 2005.

36 *A New NATO*, speech by Jaap De Hoop Scheffer, NATO Secretary General, at the Norwegian Atlantic Committee, Oslo, March 3, 2006.

37 *NATO's Istanbul Summit: New Missions, New Means*, speech by Jaap De Hoop Scheffer, NATO Secretary General, at the Royal United Services Institute, June 18, 2004.

38 See *EU Security Strategy*, Brussels, December 2003.

39 *Istanbul Summit Communiqué*, June 28, 2004, para. 1.

40 *Istanbul Summit Communiqué*, June 28, 2004, para. 2.

41 *NATO: Defending Values and Security*, speech by Jaap De Hoop Scheffer, NATO Secretary General, Warsaw, Poland, February 16, 2006.

42 Hammes (2004), p. 285.
43 Robertson, op. cit., p. 32.
44 Cited in Kitfield, op. cit.
45 See Mustafa Alani, "Arab Perspectives on NATO" and Francis Ghilès, "Bridging Cultural Divisions," both in *NATO Review*, Winter 2005.
46 Cited in Kitfield, op. cit.
47 As Hikmet Cetin, NATO's senior civilian representative in Afghanistan admitted. See Kitfield, op. cit.

23 Transforming NATO for a Fourth Generation Warfare world

Diego A. Ruiz Palmer[1]

[T]ransformation is about the physical end of things, certainly how you use your soldiers, your sailors, airmen, Marines and their equipment; but it's also a cultural transformation, a mind-set, if you will, a philosophical shift for the 21st century that says that the new NATO is going to be more proactive, more involved at greater strategic distances than it was in the past, and has the capacity and the will of the member nations to be involved, to look at new missions and new ways in which the alliance can be utilized. And this is vastly different than the reactive, static, defensive alliance that was successful during the Cold War.[2]

Asking whether NATO can cope with Fourth Generation Warfare (4GW) – the central question addressed in the companion chapter by Colonel Dr. Frans Osinga – and whether it is transforming successfully to that end, raises fundamental questions about the nature, purpose and utility of the Atlantic Alliance in the emerging global security environment. In this rapidly evolving environment, where adversity and complexity reign supreme, it is still unclear today whether NATO will continue to prosper, propelled to assume its destiny as the world's premier "hard power" security organization (but, increasingly, with "a soft touch") or, ultimately, wither away, abandoned through a lack of vision, resolve and capability on the part of its members.

Giving an answer to the question of whether NATO can cope with 4GW, therefore, is of central importance, beyond the confines of the academic debate over the intellectual persuasiveness of the notion of "generational warfare," for addressing the wider and topical issue of NATO's enduring relevance to Euro-Atlantic and world security. And in this endeavor, the concept of 4GW can act as a magnifying glass, highlighting the continuities and discontinuities, as well as the challenges and opportunities, which NATO faces as it continues to chart its transition from the Cold War to this new age of danger and hope.

The central premise of this chapter is that 4GW, as a metaphor for the risks associated with the emerging global security environment, the diffusion of lethal technologies, and the rise of non-state actors, constitutes a double paradox for NATO. First, 4GW represents an operational challenge to the Alliance, but with far-reaching strategic implications, because in the later stages of the Cold War, with maneuver warfare reaching its apex, NATO had in effect mastered Third Generation Warfare (3GW). The strategic competition with the Warsaw Pact in Europe, with its focus on the deterrence of general war, including through preparations for it, was for forty years the prism through which NATO defined its identity and its legitimacy. In that world, NATO had scarcely any reason to worry about irregular warfare or expeditionary operations outside the North Atlantic Treaty area. Even when some NATO member nations engaged militarily in distant theaters in Africa, Asia or the Middle East during the Cold War, including in counterinsurgency operations, they did so in an individual capacity and not under NATO auspices. During the Cold War, the most "exotic" dimensions of 3GW for NATO were preparing to defend against special operations by Soviet *Spetnaz* units, execute the rapid reinforcement of Europe's northern and southern flanks by maritime expeditionary forces, and provide civil support to military operations through host nation support, lines of communications and other such agreements involving cooperation between civilian and military agencies (although nuclear weapons and the risk of nuclear warfare cast a long shadow). NATO's Secretary General, Jaap de Hoop Scheffer, succinctly described the operational challenge for NATO associated with moving beyond 3GW as "(...) how we prepare ourselves militarily, how we need to change heavy metal armies into much more agile forces."[3]

Second, and at a higher level of abstraction, 4GW may present a near mortal challenge to NATO as an institution. This is so because traditionally NATO has been chiefly concerned with the defense aspects of the security of its member states, whereas 4GW encompasses an overlap of foreign and domestic risks posed by a constellation of state and increasingly non-state actors. Furthermore, by its very nature, 4GW presents a central challenge to the military establishments of Alliance member nations. Whereas traditional military establishments operate along recognized hierarchical lines from which they draw their effectiveness and their cohesion, Fourth Generation warriors excel in flat, dispersed networks, in which lines of authority are often fluid and not easily recognizable. Where military establishments seek order and linearity, to overcome the fog of war and prevail by bringing order to an inherently disorderly environment, Fourth Generation warriors aim for chaos as an asymmetric method.[4]

Yet, it is not inevitable that 4GW would doom NATO. 4GW posits that in such a "post-modern" security environment the cultural dimension of warfare – the cultural and intellectual awareness of opponents and of their mindsets, values and tactics – would be paramount. In such a world, the Alliance, through its increasingly varied partnerships and consultation and cooperation mechanisms, can provide a framework for mobilizing core skills, such as adaptability and innovative spirit, in support of the cause of global security. These skills have been the hallmark of NATO's member nations and act as a beacon for an increasing number of like-minded, non-NATO nations. If 4GW, in essence, is a "war of ideas," in which societal values and strengths are more important than material assets and physical capabilities, this is a form of warfare which NATO, as part of a concerted grander strategy of engagement, cannot only cope with but, possibly, leverage successfully for a noble cause.

As suggested above by General James Jones, NATO's former Supreme Allied Commander, Europe, both of these challenges relate to NATO's ability to manage successfully its transition from the Cold War to the emerging global security environment. Militarily, this transformation involves evolving operational concepts, force structures and capabilities from a 3GW to a 4GW paradigm and, as importantly, in the political domain, from an "introspective", comparatively static and reactive, defense-focused organization to an inclusive, outward-looking, pro-active, security-oriented organization. To help answer whether NATO can cope with 4GW, these two challenges will be addressed in turn.

Biding farewell to the NATO of the Cold War

Sounding the tocsin for NATO? The retreat from major war

In September 1988, the United States European Command sponsored, in Germany, the largest ever US field training exercise – *Certain Challenge* – in NATO's then 39-year-long history. It involved the participation of nearly 100,000 US and allied troops and thousands of armored and other vehicles. *Certain Challenge* was the key event of REFORGER 88, the large-scale reinforcement exercise staged annually since 1969 to test the capability of the United States to rapidly return to Europe forces stationed in the Continental United States but whose equipment was stored at designated sites in West Germany, Belgium, Luxembourg, The Netherlands and the United Kingdom.[5] In many ways, *Certain Challenge* was the culminating event of two 3GW trends in NATO's operational art tracing their origin back to World War II, as well as the crowning achievement in NATO's quest to master armor-centric maneuver warfare.

By the time allied forces were congregating in Bavaria in the fall of 1988 for *Certain Challenge*, NATO's quest to master the art of maneuver warfare – the apex of 3GW – appeared almost totally anachronistic, even though the exercise, in a concession to a rapidly changing strategic reality in Europe, did not have opposing forces operating as if they were the Warsaw Pact. Here was NATO exercising on a massive scale for an improbable general war scenario fourteen months before the fall of the Berlin Wall. While Operation *Desert Storm* in 1991 against a Soviet- (poorly) trained and -(well) equipped Iraqi Army was a virtually unprecedented demonstration of successful 3GW mastered on a grand scale, it also appears today as an anachronism in the context of the world's retreat from major war at the Cold War's end.[6] The Gulf War was perhaps 3GW-style maneuver warfare's last hurrah.[7]

It is this contrast between NATO's focus on 3GW high-intensity armored warfare for decades – prompted by the success of the "D-Day" operational paradigm and the Soviet infatuation with Great Patriotic War-like theater-scale offensive operations involving tens of thousands of tanks and other armored vehicles and the associated air support – and the amorphous nature of 4GW which perhaps best illustrates the transformation challenge faced by NATO forces after the Cold War. Transforming NATO forces for the new post-Cold War security environment of "mass disruption" has meant more than gradually disestablishing the Alliance's Cold War infrastructure by closing down bunkers and excess communications networks, disbanding redundant units and disposing of obsolete capabilities. It has meant, as indicated by General Jones in his March 2006 briefing at the Pentagon, engaging in wholesale cultural transformation, changing NATO's mind-set from a reactive posture of static defenses "on the Fulda Gap" to a pro-active posture of expeditionary operations on the Khyber Pass.

NATO's first encounters with 4GW in the Balkans and Afghanistan

Much of this transformation has been driven by events, notably NATO's gradual, but steady involvement in bringing the Balkan wars of the 1990s under control and eventually to an end. The Balkan wars represented NATO's first encounter with 4GW. In Bosnia and Herzegovina, NATO had to support the United Nations Protection Force (UNPROFOR) in contending with three warring factions made up of irregular combatants, organized in not easily identifiable but heavily armed formations, rather than with the regular army of a sovereign state. In many instances, these groups of marauding warriors enjoyed extensive moral and material support from the civilian population of their own ethnicity and maintained covert links to shadowy death squads and criminal networks. For both UNPROFOR troops on the ground and NATO pilots, the adversary was alien, multi-faceted and elusive. Ethnic, cultural and religious factors blurred the moral and operational clarity that had traditionally been associated with purposeful military planning. In Kosovo, Yugoslav forces cleverly dispersed their Soviet-equipped air defense and armor units to negate NATO airpower and, behind this shield, conducted a campaign of ethnic cleansing where Kosovar refugees were used de facto as hostages. In this environment of unrestricted warfare, where enemy combatants operated among and often against civilians, with little regard for the laws of warfare, rules of engagement became the indispensable, although not always reliable, compass for helping ensure that political and legal legitimacy – and moral clarity – were preserved at all times.

This was transformation by trial and fire. It had the merit of driving home to all the Alliance's members the need to acquire deployable forces, logistics and communications and information systems, and provided the impetus to the further development of expeditionary capabilities. Operations in the Balkans also underscored the growing requirement to complement "content capabilities" – war-fighting and logistical assets – with "context capabilities" – specialized units and skills to enable NATO forces to "connect" with the civilian population in the pursuit of their priority mission to establish and maintain a safe and secure environment. Context capabilities include predominantly combat support and combat service support assets, such as engineering, transportation, medical support, intelligence, psychological operations, civil affairs and civil-military cooperation, public information and constabulary units. Of particular significance in this regard, NATO established in SFOR in Bosnia and Herzegovina and in KFOR in Kosovo an Allied Multinational Intelligence Battalion, as well as Multinational Specialized Units, made up mostly of French *gendarmes* and Italian *carabinieri*.

NATO's engagement in Afghanistan since 2003 has represented an even greater challenge, but also an unprecedented opportunity to carry NATO's transformation forward. The Alliance's growing engagement on the ground in Afghanistan through its leadership of the International Security Assistance Force (ISAF) represents its most ambitious and demanding operation to date. It has put the "out-of-area" debate, which dogged NATO for decades during the Cold War, firmly behind it, and it is now helping translate NATO's commitment of 2002 to "meet the challenges to the security of our forces, populations and territory, from wherever they may come,"[8] into reality. If NATO "can do Afghanistan right," it will have demonstrated its ability to take on the most difficult missions in one of the world's most difficult theaters.

ISAF has broken new ground by propelling NATO into a distinctly 4GW environment combining a recovering state; often contending centers of powers in the provinces; insurgent and terrorist groups; a web of militias, warlords, narco-traffickers and other criminals; and a constellation of International Community partners. Unlike the Balkans, in Afghanistan there is no formal truce to enforce and NATO's role is one of providing security assistance to the sovereign Afghan authorities. Operationally, the security environment is more challenging. Whereas in Bosnia and Herzegovina and in Kosovo, the military challenge to NATO forces has come from the rare sniper and from occasional civil disturbances, in Afghanistan the Alliance has had to face groups of *Taliban* insurgents in the hundreds against the background of the enduring presence of irregular armed groups, large-scale poppy cultivation and drug trafficking, and other criminal activities. To cope with this diverse set of challenges, the provision of security assistance by NATO in the sense of helping ensure a safe and secure environment has had to be embedded in a wider network of connected Security Sector Reform activities aimed at facilitating the disarmament, demobilization and reintegration of former militia members; the training and mentoring of the Afghan National Army and Police; the disruption of drug trafficking; and judicial reform and the enforcement of the rule of law.

Although NATO is in a supporting role vis-à-vis these activities that are led by the government of Afghanistan with the assistance of lead nations from the G-8 group of nations, its security assistance role in Afghanistan has placed ISAF forces resolutely at the center of a 4GW-like web of military and non-military security challenges. At the same time, NATO's engagement in support of the legitimate government of the Islamic Republic of Afghanistan has given further credibility to the proposition that NATO has an established record of taking action on behalf, and for the protection of, Muslim societies and communities, whether in Bosnia and Herzegovina, Kosovo or Afghanistan, as well as in Iraq through NATO's support for the Polish-led Multinational Division and the provision of training to Iraqi security forces. This is an important, if often neglected, consideration in the context of making cultural awareness a "center of gravity" for the Alliance's expanding engagements beyond Europe.

NATO's engagement in Afghanistan has also represented a series of operational "firsts". Before taking command of ISAF in August 2003, NATO supported the Force's third rotation (ISAF III) with the provision of intelligence and a planning capability. This marked the first time ever that NATO's Supreme Headquarters Allied Powers Europe (SHAPE) had assisted with the planning and force generation of a non-NATO operation.[9] In Bosnia and Herzegovina and in Kosovo, NATO relied on traditional force structures of multinational divisions and brigades to enforce the peace. In Afghanistan, however, the type of mission – multi-task security assistance – and the size, remoteness and barren nature of the country have mandated the use of a new type of civil-military unit, the Provincial Reconstruction Team (PRT). PRTs bring together a military component entrusted with the tasks of establishing a local presence, maintaining a safe and secure environment throughout their area of operation, mentoring the Afghan Army and Police forces, and providing force protection, and a civilian component responsible for supporting reconstruction efforts, facilitating economic and social development, and fostering respect for the rule of law.

Making NATO militarily agile

To be sure, the remarkable adaptability of NATO to new missions, despite important political and operational constraints, was facilitated by the transformation of NATO's force and command structures following the end of the Cold War. In 1991, NATO approved the concept of establishing a UK-led Allied Rapid Reaction Corps (ARRC), which became operational in 1994, two years after the disbandment of the Cold War Allied Mobile Force (AMF).[10] The ARRC became the centerpiece of a wider initiative to create a pool of high-readiness, mobile "Reaction Forces," alongside the more traditional, armor-heavy "Main Defense Forces." While the ARRC was still heavily mechanized, its mindset was clearly expeditionary. When NATO led large peace-enforcement forces into Bosnia and Herzegovina and Kosovo, in 1995 and 1999, respectively, involving the large-scale movement of forces into the Balkans, the ARRC was in each case deployed as the lead headquarters.

By the late 1990s, the ARRC had become the model for similar rapid deployment corps established as successors to the venerable armored army corps of the Cold War.[11] The terminology Reaction Forces vanished from the NATO vocabulary in favor of Graduated Readiness Forces (GRF), a pool of multinational, mostly European, land and maritime headquarters at various levels of readiness, but with an orientation to high responsiveness.[12] The significance of the establishment of the GRF should not be minimized. GRF were devised by European military establishments as a clever concept to spearhead the development of genuine expeditionary capabilities, as well as to stave off the rapid reduction of

European armies following the end of the Cold War. In effect, the GRF allowed the armies of European Allies to rebound. Moreover, the GRF provided the necessary backbone for the creation of the US-inspired NATO Response Force (NRF) in 2003,[13] to which the GRF land and maritime headquarters provide the land and maritime component commands. In effect, the European-inspired GRF and the US-inspired NRF are the two sides of the same NATO rapid deployment coin. Together, the NRF and the GRF provide the initial and the follow-on elements, respectively, of a larger land-based or sea-based Combined Joint Task Force (CJTF), the third pillar in NATO's expeditionary triad.

In addition to providing the NRF's land and maritime component commands, the High Readiness Force HQs of the GRF pool have also provided on rotation the core headquarters of ISAF in Afghanistan. Starting with the Eurocorps in 2004, the Turkish and Italian-led NATO Rapid Deployment Corps and the ARRC have led ISAF in succession. This clever scheme has allowed these various corps both to bring into the NRF the experience of having deployed to a distant theater in an expeditionary mode and into ISAF the expertise derived from having stood on a high-readiness alert to deploy on short notice. Remarkably, European Allies and Canada have been able to deploy to Afghanistan a major land force headquarters every six to nine months, together with brigade-size battle groups, a feat that few observers would have considered achievable only a few years ago.

In parallel with this reformed NATO Force Structure, NATO has down-scaled and transformed considerably its Command Structure, from sixty-five headquarters in 1990, to twelve today, of which eleven have an operational role.[14] Furthermore, the most recent Command Structure blueprint, agreed at the November 2002 NATO Summit in Prague, for the first time in the Alliance's history has no territorial focus and is expeditionary-oriented. Under SHAPE,[15] which acts as the strategic-level headquarters for all Alliance operations, three operational-level headquarters – Joint Force Commands Brunssum and Naples, located in The Netherlands and in Italy, respectively, and Joint Command Lisbon in Portugal – are configured to provide a deployable command and control capability. On rotation, the three headquarters are responsible during a six-month alert period for generating a tailored NRF package on demand. Furthermore, Brunssum and Naples are designated as the parent HQ for a land-based CJTF, whereas Lisbon is the parent HQ for a sea-based CJTF.[16] In addition to their NRF and CJTF responsibilities, Brunssum, Naples and Lisbon have been assuming the expanding front-line role of leading and managing NATO's ever more varied operations, from the Mediterranean and the Balkans to Afghanistan, Iraq and Darfur.

This interaction and overlap between NATO's operations and NATO's transformation – one feeding into the other and vice-versa, on the ground as well as institutionally through the cooperation between the two strategic commands for operations (SHAPE) and for transformation (HQ SACT) – underscore the increasingly symbiotic relationship between the two: operations pull transformation forward; transformation facilitates operations. Feedback from successive ISAF rotations provides operational context to experimenting with such new concepts as an "Effects-Based Approach to Operations", "reach-back" and "intelligence-driven operations."[17] In turn, changes brought about by transformation – streamlined command and force structures; innovative operational concepts; and new technological applications, such as NATO Network-Enabled Capabilities[18] – can make an important contribution to making inherently complex operations easier to plan and conduct.

Following NATO's "transformational summit" in Prague in 2002 and the transformations brought about by NATO's expanding operational engagements across a range of geographically diverse theaters, today's NATO bears little resemblance to the "Grand Daddy NATO" of the Cold War once evoked by Lord Robertson, the then NATO Secretary General. As suggested above, in the 1990s NATO gradually shed the vestiges of its former 3GW self, with REFORGER exercises part of a rapidly receding past, and by the early part of this decade had ably completed its post-Cold War military transformation. Yet, has NATO transformed sufficiently to defend against 4GW, let alone wage 4GW on its terms? Even if it has, will that be enough to maintain NATO's military effectiveness and political relevance? Assuming that it could be enough, what are the possible costs of "getting there" in terms of preserving NATO's identity, distinctiveness and cohesion?

Surfing on the 4GW wave: the promise of a grand strategy

How much transformation is enough?

4GW represents potentially an existential threat to NATO because it threatens the fabric of both the allied military establishments that form the core of NATO's distinct capability to act and the institution itself. How far can and should allied militaries transform to cope with the varied, amorphous risks and adversaries associated with 4GW, before they begin to lose their operational coherence and spiritual cohesion, and ultimately their effectiveness and fighting ethos? Similarly, how far can and should NATO itself transform institutionally by possibly taking on some of the trappings and responsibilities of other organizations, before it begins placing at risk its distinctiveness as a political-military alliance without peers?

Transforming armor-heavy formations into expeditionary-type forces and improving their deployability and sustainability in distant and austere theaters will not, in itself, guarantee their effectiveness and endurance in adverse circumstances. Are NRF/GRF/CJTF force packages sufficiently agile and "culturally sensitive" to operate effectively against warriors, insurgents, terrorists and thugs, as well as among displaced, dispossessed, malnourished and dying civilian populations?[19] How much further do NATO forces need to divest themselves of the influence of the "D-Day" model of warfare, with its clearly recognizable army divisions, air force wings and naval task forces, and move toward "network-centric"[20] joint and combined structures associating adaptable force packages from various armed services and defense as well as civilian agencies?[21]

Is "three-block" or "four-block" warfare viable with one set of forces?[22] Does NATO need to have or retain specialized "one block" forces for single, specialized tasks? What is the proper balance – is there a proper balance? – between forces optimized for rapid deployment, forcible entry and high intensity combat operations and those configured for lower intensity, enduring peace enforcement and stabilization operations? If Alliance military forces risk "losing their soul" in 4GW, because it is so antithetical to almost everything present-day military establishments, as they have developed since Napoleonic times, stand for, what is their future? Should they retreat into some clearly specialized functions – perhaps serving as a deterrent-like force of last resort – and leave a good part of the more "mundane" 4GW heavy lifting to paramilitary or constabulary forces patterned after the French *Gendarmerie*,[23] to civil police and other law enforcement agencies, or possibly, to new, purpose-built, multi-task, civil–military "influence" formations combining a range of assets and skills?[24]

How far should Alliance consultation, planning and decision-making processes be transformed to incorporate non-military aspects of operations, such as military support for reconstruction, improved law enforcement and enhanced governance? And now that NATO is engaged in distant and geographically diverse theaters that bear little resemblance to NATO's more familiar Western moorings, how important does "cultural transformation" become? And how should such transformation be pursued institutionally? Lastly, if transformation is a process rather than an end-point, is there a milestone beyond which the costs and the risks of transforming forces and institutions outweigh any possible additional advantages, when transformation has exhausted its usefulness and threatens the survival of the institutions it is designed to serve?

These are hard questions to which there are as yet no easy or readily available answers, and the vast 4GW literature – which is extensive on the causes and manifestations of 4GW and much less so on its implications, notably for institutions, except for general speculation on their likely demise – is in this regard of little help. Yet these questions strike at the heart of the relationship between NATO and 4GW.

To help answer these questions, NATO's transformation will need to address four sets of issues:

1   adapting Alliance and Partner forces to an emerging global security environment where the "engagement space" at the tactical level will be civilian-dominated and unfamiliar;
2   extending further the notion of security beyond the defense sphere;
3   preserving NATO's institutional distinctiveness as a unique enabler for international security across a broad risk spectrum; and
4   embedding NATO's transformation into a wider, grand strategy of engagement.

The challenge of operating tactically in complex, civilian-dominated environments

Unlike the Cold War where a hypothetical conflict in Europe would have extended the employment of military forces on the battlefield to society as a whole, the environment in which Alliance and Partner forces have been deployed while on operations since the end of the Cold War is in most cases a civilian-dominated one. In such an environment, the broad focus of missions on protecting or ensuring the general welfare of the civilian populations in the theater of operations, as well as concern over civilian casualties and collateral damage to property and natural resources, will displace more traditional war-fighting tasks and place important and likely growing constraints on the use of force. The center of gravity of operations in this environment will shift radically from *dominating* the "battle space" to *influencing* the "engagement space." In this contest for the hearts and minds of "the man in the street," as well as the local community leader – where the "main street" is the rallying place for sup-portive crowds, not the locale for firefights – the highest form of operational art will be achieving such influence through "non-kinetic" means, without large-scale engagements and with a minimal level of violence.

In these civilian-dominated environments, where friend and foe intermix, NATO and Partner forces will face two key challenges. The first challenge will be to diversify "non-kinetic" skills, to achieve a higher level of tactical effec-tiveness while enhancing force protection, without sacrificing proper war-fighting skills. The second will be to develop greater cultural awareness, while averting the risk of losing moral cohesion and operational integrity through osmosis with these environments. Forces will need to be operationally adaptable and resilient, as well as culturally savvy, yet be able at all times to remain faith-ful to their core professional and moral values.

The mix of relevant military capabilities between "content" and "context" referred to above will have to be adjusted to reflect this emerging reality, in such a way that NATO and Partner forces can "plug" easily and seamlessly into the environment, operationally as well as "culturally." To this end, two multina-tional civil-military cooperation (CIMIC) groups have been established in Italy and The Netherlands; the latter will become the home of a new NATO center of excellence to develop CIMIC doctrine and provide CIMIC training. Satisfactory cultural awareness is also a function of improved knowledge of foreign coun-tries and cultures. Accordingly, building upon the lessons learned in the Balkans,[25] SHAPE recently established an Intelligence Fusion Center (IFC), co-located with the US European Command's own Joint Analysis Center at Molesworth, UK, to provide all-source, timely and targeted intelligence to NRF and other NATO operations.[26] In effect, the IFC will become NATO's "window on the world." Lastly, education will play an increasing role both in helping inculcate lasting commitment to enduring values and develop greater cultural awareness of the countries and societies in which the Alliance is or might be engaged. Here, NATO's partnerships with an increasing number of countries of the Mediterranean Sea's southern rim and the Middle East could prove particularly useful.

Straddling the civil–military divide at the strategic level

In the 4GW-like environments of the future, terrorism will be a constant risk at the tactical as well as the strategic level. At the tactical level, this risk will frustrate the best-intentioned efforts to "blend" with the local environment. At the strategic level, terrorism will aim to achieve a psychologically "decapitating" impact on its targets. Terrorists will generally operate among the civilian population and target civilians, both in deployed operations and in home territories. Terrorist attacks could take many forms and include a variety of destructive means, including, potentially, the use of weapons of mass destructions (WMD). Attacks on the territory of NATO and Partner nations from abroad could be aimed at instilling fear in the civilian population and generally undermining the resolve of governments, or at deterring the initiation or precipitating the termination of a specific NATO-led military operation. Attacks in overseas theaters where NATO and Partner forces are deployed will aim at undermining support for the deployment of those forces among the local population and political and community leaders, and at home. In these circumstances, the "engagement domains" of military forces and civilian intelligence and law enforcement agencies will increasingly overlap.

The invocation of Article 5 of the North Atlantic Treaty following the terrorist attacks on New York and Washington, DC, on September 11, 2001, established that NATO's collective defense clause also applied to major acts of aggression against an Ally by non-state actors, such as a terrorist movement like al Qaeda. While the 9/11 attacks marked the intrusion of 4GW-like mass terrorism into the heart of NATO's post Cold War strategic calculus, the invocation of Article 5 usefully provided a legal basis for NATO to address this new, high-voltage risk. Accordingly, some NATO member nations, pursuant to the United Nations Security Council Resolution 1373 of September 28, 2001, contributed forces and capabilities to the US-led Operation Enduring Freedom on an individual basis. The Alliance initiated Operation Active Endeavor, aimed at disrupting terrorist networks and activities in the Mediterranean Sea, and later agreed a NATO military concept for defense against terrorism. These steps eventually opened the way in 2002 for NATO initially to provide planning support to ISAF in Afghanistan and, a year later, to take command of ISAF.

Anchoring a substantive and enduring NATO contribution to international peace and security in an environment characterized by multiple stabilization operations and pervasive terrorism has meant gradually embedding this contribution in a wider set of arrangements that straddle the once water-tight civil–military and foreign–domestic boundaries. The expanding operational domain of Operation Active Endeavor illustrates, in a microcosm, the scope of the change. Since this maritime interdiction operation was initiated in the fall of 2001, there has been a growing recognition that terrorism at sea overlaps with

other maritime-borne risks, such as covert weapons of mass destruction proliferation, small arms trafficking and illegal immigration. It requires both a global
approach to these risks and information sharing arrangements that extend beyond
the military sphere. To that end, Active Endeavor operations at sea are supported
ashore by a Joint Information and Analysis Center (JIAC) located in Naples, Italy.
The JIAC is an experimental, all-source, information fusion center aimed at facilitating the exchange of information among a variety of agencies.[27] As a result,
NATO has been able to "target" the Active Endeavor's limited assets more effectively and efficiently and to cover a wider spectrum of suspicious or illegal activities across the Mediterranean, thereby making a tangible contribution to overall
security along vital sea-lanes. Beyond Active Endeavor, NATO also established in
Turkey in 2005 a center of excellence for defense against terrorism to provide education and expertise to Alliance and non-NATO nations.[28]

As suggested above, NATO has readily acknowledged that its transformation
must extend beyond the military transformation of Alliance and Partner forces
for expeditionary operations. It must also embrace the development of capabilities and procedures that will enable these forces to deal effectively with a
range of overlapping risks, from nation-states recovering from war and civil
strife to terrorism and the proliferation of WMD. And, as operations in both the
Balkans and Afghanistan have underscored, NATO's engagements will need to
be embedded in a wider web of cooperative relationships, to ensure that NATO
and Partner forces can interact effectively with the range of non-NATO actors
which they will encounter on the ground: the host government and population,
non-NATO countries, other international organizations, non-governmental
organizations and media outlets. Success in terms of achieving a sustainable
end-state will only come through this higher form of multi-dimensional engagement.

Preserving NATO's distinctiveness

Transforming its military forces for this emerging global security environment,
however, poses additional dilemmas for NATO. While enhanced agility and ver-
satility are a necessity in order for Alliance and Partner forces to be able to
operate in 4GW-like environments, because they are likely to become more
prevalent, NATO must also retain a capacity to field a force of sufficient size
and capability to deter a regional hegemon intent on disturbing the international
system and possibly threatening core allied security interests or even threatening
the Alliance's territorial integrity. If NATO's military capabilities are "disaggregated" into a collection of capabilities optimized for relatively "small" contingencies, there is a risk that the Alliance might not be able to reconstitute a
coherent force for a "big" contingency in a timely fashion. In pursuing the transformation of its military forces, the Alliance will therefore need to aim for a
point of equilibrium between the competing requirements of relevance and cohesion, of responsiveness to a "coming anarchy"[29] and eternal vigilance vis-à-vis
possible existential threats looming distantly beyond the horizon.

Transforming institutionally poses yet another dilemma for NATO. While it must be able to act effectively in environments in which military forces are no longer the principal actors and in which NATO is not in the lead, the Alliance must guard against the risk of "banalization." Its greatest strength will always be its distinctiveness, i.e. its unique ability as a political-military alliance to combine political purpose and military capability, to "make a difference" in a crisis or in a theater in ways that no other international organization today can. This suggests that there are limits to NATO's institutional transformation into something different from what it fundamentally is. While NATO should enhance, for instance, its ability to plan and conduct stabilization operations and provide military support to reconstruction efforts, because such an ability will place the Alliance on a good footing to deal with growing 4GW risks, it should do so partly by developing its own capabilities internally, but mostly by relying on, and, as appropriate, bringing into its own planning, the expertise and skills of other international organizations. This is what Denmark has skillfully termed "concerted planning and action."[30]

A grand strategy for a great Alliance

Developing a compelling vision of NATO's enduring roles in the emerging global security environment, characterized by a mounting 4GW challenge, and of the scope of the military and political transformation required to sustain successfully such a vision, will therefore become a central concern for the Alliance in the run up to its sixtieth anniversary in 2009. In the end, it is NATO's own early history which may provide the best recourse for formulating a way forward for the Alliance to meet this concern. When faced with exceptional international circumstances, such as those prevailing at the dawn of the Cold War in the late 1940s, the West was able to formulate a *grand strategy of containment* that spanned the political, economic, military and information spheres – in effect the various levers of power – in order to rise to the challenge of the new security environment brought about by the onset of the Cold War.[31] While NATO was established to promote political cooperation among allied nations and provide for their common defense, the Organization for European Economic Cooperation (OEEC) assumed a similar role for the economic recovery of Europe and the implementation of the Marshall Plan.[32] In addition, the grand strategy of containment involved the creation of the Coordinating Committee for Multilateral Export Controls (COCOM) to restrict the transfer of sensitive technologies beyond COCOM member nations, and of various Western radio stations for broadcasting into Soviet Bloc countries.[33]

While the emerging global security environment bears no resemblance to the early years of the Cold War, and the type of complementary institutional arrangements of that time in many cases would not be relevant or applicable to tomorrow's circumstances, the comprehensive approach to security followed then bears all the hallmarks of the kind of intellectual foresight – thinking "NATO smart" – that is required to bring greater clarity and purpose to policy.

This grander approach – a *grand strategy of engagement* – should encompass the following:

1   a dedication by all Allies to translating into action the commitment to "(...) strengthening NATO's role as a forum for strategic and political consultation and coordination among Allies (...)";[34]
2   a readiness to consult within NATO, among Allies and with partner nations, on all security issues of common concern, including those having primarily a non-military dimension but which could have important security implications, and irrespective of whether, institutionally, NATO has an a priori claim on them or not;
3   a broader approach to security that encompasses maritime security and the protection of energy infrastructure, in addition to collective defense, crisis management, the prevention of the proliferation of weapons of mass destruction and defense against terrorism[35];
4   a higher level of institutional relations with the United Nations and relevant UN agencies and, where appropriate, with other international and regional organizations;
5   an improved capacity to plan and conduct stabilization operations and to provide military support to reconstruction efforts, through regular consultations, concerted planning and an expanded access by NATO to civilian experts in NATO and Partner nations and in specialized UN agencies and non-governmental organizations;
6   enhanced military capabilities to perform stabilization and military support to reconstruction operations in the inventories of NATO and Partner nations, including a larger and more capable pool of special operations and psychological operations forces; and
7   an enhanced information-handling capability at NATO HQ, in order to interact more effectively with the media, convey NATO's image and messages with greater impact and influence positively the perception of NATO in the general population in theaters where Alliance forces are deployed.

Such a grand strategy would encompass a wider vision of security, a broader set of core tasks to reflect a larger spectrum of risks and defense requirements, more intensive political consultations on emerging factors and regions of concern and an expanding web of partnerships with a variety of non-NATO nations.

In effect, whether NATO flourishes or flounders in coping with 4GW may well depend, to a large extent, on whether it is successful in embedding its ongoing transformation in a grand strategy of engagement, as outlined above. Such a grand strategy should address the diverse and acute security challenges of the emerging global security environment and set out the ambition to give a transformed NATO a wider and more central role in helping to maintain international peace and security for which it is uniquely qualified. The record of NATO's transformation since the end of the Cold War suggests that it can meet successfully the emerging security challenges of the early twenty-first century. The task for Alliance member nations in the run-up to NATO's sixtieth anniversary is to ensure that it will continue to do so in the decades ahead.

Notes

1 The author is Head of the Planning Section, Operations Division, International Staff, NATO Headquarters, Brussels, Belgium. The views expressed in this chapter are the author's own and do not necessarily reflect those of NATO or Alliance member nations. The author is indebted to Ludwig Decamps, Morten Henriksen, Jonathan Parish and David S. Yost for their comments on earlier drafts of this chapter.

2 DoD news briefing with General James L. Jones, March 7, 2006. General Jones was Supreme Allied Commander, Europe (SACEUR) and Commander, United States European Command (COMUSEUCOM) between January 2003 and December 2006.

3 *A new NATO*, speech by NATO Secretary General, Jaap de Hoop Scheffer, at the Norwegian Atlantic Committee, Oslo, March 3, 2006.

4 Barry D. Watts has convincingly argued that all belligerents have and will continue to experience friction in war, because friction is an inherent part of war, but what matters "(…) is not the absolute level of friction that either side experiences but the *relative frictional advantage* of one adversary over the other (…)" (emphasis in the original text). See Barry D. Watts, *Clausewitzian Friction and Future War*, McNair Paper 52 (Washington, DC: Institute of National Strategic Studies, National Defense University, October 1996), p. 132. A key asymmetry between 3GW traditional armed forces and 4GW warriors is that while the former will attempt to overcome friction, the latter will attempt to exploit it.

5 REFORGER stood for "REturn of FORces to GERmany." The last REFORGER took place in 1991. The 1992 edition was cancelled owing to the end of the Cold War.

6 The notion of the obsolescence of major war is elaborated upon in John Mueller, *Retreat from Doomsday* (New York: BasicBooks, 1989).

7 Although, from the perspective of operational art, US land operations during the joint campaign against Iraq in 2003 were extremely successful, they paled in terms of their size and scope in comparison with land operations during the 1991 Gulf War.

8 NATO Prague Summit Declaration, November 21, 2002, p. 3.

9 See Diego A. Ruiz Palmer, "The Road to Kabul," *NATO Review*, Summer 2004.

10 "*Allied Command Europe Mobile Force Land Headquarters to be Dissolved in Autumn 2002*," SHAPE press release, August 12, 2002.

11 "*Four New Multinational, Rapidly Deployable Headquarters Assigned to NATO*," SHAPE press release, September 23, 2002.

12 This pool includes now nine land HQ – the ARRC, the Eurocorps, the 1st German–Netherlands Corps, the Italian, Spanish and Turkish-led NATO Rapid Deployment Corps, the Rapid Reaction Corps-France, the NATO Deployment Corps-Greece, the Multinational Corps Northeast – and five maritime HQ – the French, Italian, Spanish and United Kingdom Maritime Forces and the Striking and Support Forces-NATO (STRIKFORNATO). Among these fourteen GRF headquarters, the last HQ is the only one that is US-led.

13 "*NATO Launches Response Force*," SHAPE press release, October 15, 2003.

14 In addition to SHAPE, there are three joint commands, two land, two air and two maritime component commands, and a submarine command. The twelfth command is HQ Supreme Allied Commander, Transformation, in Norfolk, Virginia, which has no operational responsibilities.

15 "*A New Name for Allied Command Europe (ACE): Allied Command Operations (ACO)*," SHAPE press release, 1 September 2003.

16 The link between the HQ Lisbon staff ashore and a sea-based capability is ensured

through the triple-hatting of the commander of the Joint Command Lisbon as commander of STRIKFORNATO and the US Sixth Fleet, whose flagship, the USS *Mount Whitney*, would provide the command platform for a sea-based CJTF.

17 Effects-Based Approach to Operations refers to the principle of basing the planning and conduct of operations on the effects being sought. Reach-back refers to the ability of a deployed headquarters to rely on planning support from usually a higher headquarters located to the rear, often outside the theater of operations. Intelligence-driven operations are operations whose design is driven by the ability to collect, fuse and distribute intelligence on a near-real time basis, with the aim of achieving higher levels of effectiveness and efficiency in their conduct.

18 NATO Network-Enabled Capabilities is a NATO concept for enhancing the effectiveness of distinct but complementary military capabilities, through the establishment of purpose-built connectivity among them via networks.

19 Major General Scales, US Army (Retired), has introduced the concept of "cultural warfare" to highlight the importance of sensitivity to cultural differences in planning and conducting operations. See Robert. H. Scales, "Culture-Centric Warfare," *Proceedings*, October 2004, pp. 32–6. Lieutenant General Peter Chiarelli, former Commander of the Multi-National Corps-Iraq and second in command of coalition forces in Iraq, has made cultural awareness a central tenet of his command. See James Rainey, "Aiming for a More Subtle Fighting Force," *Los Angeles Times*, May 9, 2006.

20 It is important to guard against the fallacy of opposing "culture-centric" and "network-centric" approaches to warfare; each is aimed at meeting a different set of sometimes overlapping requirements. Each has its strengths and shortcomings.

21 A large amount of work in this area has been done over the last fifteen years by the US Joint Forces Command (USJFCOM) and by its predecessor, the US Atlantic Command (USACOM).

22 "Three block warfare" refers to the concept championed by the former Commandant of the US Marine Corps, General Charles Krulak, which envisaged at the tactical level Marines being involved in executing nearly simultaneously high-intensity, peace enforcement and humanitarian assistance tasks all within a few city blocks. See General Charles C. Krulak, "The Strategic Corporal: Leadership in the Three Block War," *Marines Magazine*, January 1999. The Marines have subsequently added a "fourth block" represented by psychological and information operations. See Lieutenant General James N. Mattis, USMC and Lieutenant Colonel Frank G. Hoffman, USMCR (Retired), "Future Warfare: The Rise of Hybrid Wars," *U.S. Naval Institute Proceedings*, November 2005, p. 19.

23 Rapid deployment units from France's *Gendarmerie*, Italy's *Carabinieri*, Spain's *Guardia Civil*, and equivalent forces from The Netherlands and Portugal have been regrouped in a European Gendarmerie Force, headquartered in Vicenza, Italy, to provide a readily available multinational constabulary force. See Enrique Esquivel Lalinde, "The new European Gendarmerie Force," ARI No. 48/2005, Real Instituto Elcano, Madrid, 9 May 2005.

24 The Joint Inter-Agency Coordination Groups (JIACG) attached to the headquarters of each of the US regional combatant commands and the Provincial Reconstruction Teams deployed in Afghanistan and in Iraq represent two different, embryonic models of what could in time be a much larger and more potent civil–military capability. On the JIACG, see Lieutenant Colonel Harold Van Opdorp, "The Joint Interagency Coordination Group: The Operalization of DIME," *Small Wars Journal*, July 2005, pp. 1–12; and Neyla Arnas, Charles L. Barry and Robert B. Oakley, *Harnessing the Interagency for Complex Operations*, Defense and Technology Paper #16 (Washington, DC, Center for Technology and National Security Policy, August 2005). There are currently 25 PRTs operating in Afghanistan and four in Iraq. On PRTs see Michael J. McNerney, "Stabilization and Reconstruction in Afghanistan: Are PRTs a Model or a Muddle?," *Parameters*, Winter 2005–06, pp. 32–46.

25 Commander Eileen Mackrell, "Combined Forces Support: The Evolution in Military (Intelligence) Affairs," *NATO Review*, no. 6, November–December 1997, Volume 45, pp. 20–2.
26 *"Launch of the Intelligence Fusion Center in Support of NATO"*, SHAPE press release, January 17, 2006.
27 See Vice Admiral Roberto Cesaretti, "Combating Terrorism in the Mediterranean," *NATO Review*, issue #3, Autumn 2005.
28 *"EUCOM Commander Signs Agreement at NATO Center of Excellence-Defense Against Terrorism,"* SHAPE press release, October 10, 2005.
29 On the prospects of a "chaotic" international environment, see, in particular, Robert D. Kaplan, "The Coming Anarchy," *Atlantic Monthly*, 273, February 1994, pp. 44–76; and Therese Delpech, *L'Ensauvagement* (Paris: Grasset, 2005).
30 Kristian Fischer and Jan Top Christensen, "Improving Civil–Military Cooperation the Danish Way," *NATO Review*, Summer 2005.
31 S. Nelson Drew (editor), *NSC-68: Forging the Strategy of Containment* (Washington, DC: Institute of National Strategic Studies, National Defense University, September 1994).
32 OEEC was established in April 1948, NATO in April 1949. OEEC eventually evolved into the present-day Organization for Economic Cooperation and Development (OECD).
33 The Coordinating Committee for Multilateral Export Controls was established in November 1949 and disbanded in 1992. Unlike OEEC and NATO, COCOM was not a treaty-based institution. In the 1950s, all three had their headquarters in Paris.
34 Statement issued by the Heads of State and government participating in a meeting of the North Atlantic Council in Brussels, February 22, 2005.
35 See Julian Lindley-French, "For the Crucial Alliance, a Day of Decision," *International Herald Tribune*, May 30, 2006.

24 Fighting Fourth Generation wars

The Indian experience

*Rajesh Rajagopalan**

Introduction

Fourth Generation Warfare (4GW) theorists argue that future wars are likely to pit traditional state forces against non-state guerrillas who are politically astute and skilled in communications technology. The central plea of such theorists to modern conventional militaries is to remember that political objectives are the key to winning modern unconventional wars, or what they term 4GW. Thus, thinking of the use of force in ways that simply increase military technical efficiency will leave them unprepared for fighting wars in which the primary dynamic is not military efficiency but rather understanding the intricacies of political violence and communication. Suicide bombing maybe a crude instrument but its effects are to be measured not so much by the sophistication of the tactic but the political effect it produces. Though all wars (hopefully) are politically driven, conventional second and third generation armies tend to think of wars largely as an inter-state phenomenon and the political objectives they serve are in the context of traditional inter-state politics: deterrence, defense, coercion, military victory and such. 4GW requires that these militaries change: it is, as James Wirtz put it nicely, politics with guns.[1]

Nevertheless, as Martin van Creveld points out, 4GW theorists are somewhat short on suggesting practical solutions to fight such wars.[2] Even critics of 4GW theory agree that the US and other conventional militaries need to re-orient their forces away from purely technological solutions to future war. This is of course not a new debate: an earlier iteration can be seen in the disagreements about the nature of the Vietnam War and how the US should have fought that war, best represented by the opposing perspectives of Harry Summers and Andrew Krepinevich.[3] But even if we agree that conventional militaries should change to meet the requirements of fighting unconventional wars, *how* they should do this is less clear. Adaptability and flexibility are valid recommendations, but they are far too general to be of practical help to military commanders facing the task of procuring weapons and training soldiers for future war.

India's long experience with counterinsurgency provides some useful pointers both about some of the elements of an appropriate doctrine as well as the difficulty of re-orienting traditional military forces in directions that 4GW theorists suggest. India has had longer experience with such wars than most other countries. Since its independence from British colonial rule in 1947, India has faced a large number of domestic insurrections, many of them ethnic separatist movements. Most of these conflicts have yet to be resolved, though military action and political initiatives have reduced the levels of violence associated with many of these conflicts.

The Indian Army has been the primary agency tasked with controlling such movements.[4] Paradoxically, however, the Indian Army has never considered fighting such wars as its primary task, and it does not do so still. Its primary mission is seen as preparing and defending the country from traditional adversaries Pakistan and China. Despite the continuing large scale commitment to domestic 4GW adversaries, from Kashmiri terrorists to Maoist insurgents in rural India and violent ethnic separatists groups in northeast India, the Indian Army is reluctant to see 4GW as a primary mission, repeatedly stressing that such missions are secondary to preparing for conventional, high-intensity wars.

Nevertheless, the Indian Army has managed to evolve a doctrine for such wars that incorporates many of the central tenets of 4GW theorists. The Indian experience suggests important lessons for studying such conflicts, but because these were domestic conflicts rather than foreign ones, there are also significant differences between this experience and most of the other wars that are normally characterized as 4GW.

Overview of the Indian experience

India's first 4GW campaign was against a motley group of communist insurrectionists in a region known as Telengana, in what is now the state of Andhra Pradesh, in southern India. Only the barest details are available of this brief war, and most histories of the Indian Army do not even mention it.[5] There have been brief Maoist insurrections in other parts of India too, especially in the 1960s. But much of the Indian experience with 4GW have been with sub-nationalist rather than ideologically driven groups. This may change in the near future: there are individual Maoist rebellions in several Indian states, and indications that these groups are beginning to work together.

Most of the sub-nationalist rebellions within India have taken place in India's northeast, a region that is culturally and racially distinct. The first significant 4GW that India fought was against rebels from the Naga tribes of northeast India. The entire northeastern region of India had been kept out of bounds for outsiders by the British colonial administration. This prevented the Indian independence movement from having any impact in this region. It also led to a natural sense of distinctiveness among the tribal population of the region. Encouraged by some British colonial administrators, some Nagas demanded their own independent state. By 1956, their agitation had turned into a violent rebellion and the Indian Army was dispatched to control the situation. The central government in Delhi also began negotiating to meet some of the demands of the more moderate sections of the Nagas, leading to the creation of the state of Nagaland within the Indian Union. Nevertheless, a section of Naga rebels continue to fight.

In 1966, another rebellion broke out in the Mizo hills, also in northeastern India. Again, the Indian Army was dispatched, and as before, the central government offered to create a separate state of Mizoram for the Mizos within the Indian Union. Unlike the Naga rebellion, however, the Mizos reached a settlement, and the fighting ended in the mid-1980s. This illustrates one aspect of the Indian strategy: political compromises, including the creation of new provinces and autonomous regions, giving special privileges and political power at the local level, are as integral to the Indian effort as military force. In essence, only one demand is non-negotiable: secession.

By the mid-1980s, a number of minor insurgencies had broken out in other parts of the northeast. Though none of these insurgencies are a serious threat to the Indian state, none have been resolved either. They continue to simmer, with violence erupting intermittently. Two other Indian 4GW experiences, however, require some explanation.[6] In the mid-1980s, the Tamil minority in Sri Lanka rebelled against the Sinhala government in Colombo.[7] In 1987, the Indian government assisted the two sides in reaching a settlement and sent the Indian Peace-Keeping Force (IPKF), drawn largely from the Indian Army, to monitor and implement the ceasefire. But neither the Liberation Tigers of Tamil Eelam (LTTE), the leading Tamil rebel group, nor the Sri Lankan government, were particularly happy with the agreement. As the agreement collapsed in recriminations, the IPKF found itself at war with the superbly organized, trained and LTTE-led guerrillas. Though the IPKF managed to seriously maul the LTTE, it could not defeat them despite devoting as many as four infantry divisions to the fight. The IPKF was withdrawn in 1990, joining the long list of powerful conventional armies that failed to defeat much smaller adversaries in 4GW.

The rebellion that broke out in Jammu and Kashmir, the state at the center of a long-standing dispute between India and Pakistan, has probably been the most serious internal rebellion that India has faced. Though the specific cause for the outbreak of the violence lies in political ineptness and bureaucratic incompetence in both New Delhi and Srinagar, the capital of the state, Pakistan's support to the rebels made them far more potent than they otherwise would have been. The Indian Army did introduce some limited innovations during the Kashmir campaign by creating an entirely new dedicated 4GW force called the Rashtriya (National) Rifles (RR) but the difficulties it faced does provide pointers to the difficulty that conventional forces face in fighting 4GW. In the next section, I examine the Indian Army's approach to fighting such 4GW, and the possible lessons that can be gleaned from this experience.

The Indian army's 4GW doctrine

4GW theorists, as I suggested earlier, emphasize more the problems with current 2GW- and 3GW-based militaries in dealing with 4GW than on suggesting specific recommendations of how to deal with 4GW. Nevertheless, there are some similarities, as well as differences, between their recommendations and the doctrine that the Indian Army has developed.[8]

Five elements make up the Indian Army's 4GW doctrine.[9] The *first* is the limitation on the quantum of force used in operations. This is probably the central, most important element in the Indian 4GW doctrine, and is crucial to the success that the Army has had in 4GW campaigns. The army is careful about this issue not only because of concerns about human rights, but also because of operational effectiveness. Thus, units that are deployed in 4GW operations are devoid of all heavy fire-power equipment. Indian forces engaged in 4GW operations get no artillery or close air support. And this principle has almost never been violated: even in Sri Lanka, when the troops of the IPKF were under severe pressure, their use of fire-power remained restrained. The few uses of helicopter gunships were confined to unpopulated areas, such as Tamil Tiger camps in the Vanni jungles south of the Jaffna peninsula. Within the country, the prohibition on the use of air support or heavy firepower has been violated only a couple of times. One was when Indian Air Force (IAF) planes strafed and bombed parts of Aizawl, the capital of Mizoram, during the first few days of the Mizo rebellion in March 1966.[10] The second instance was 'Operation Blue Star', the assault on the Sikh rebels holed up in the Golden Temple in Amritsar, which included the use of tank guns.[11]

This limitation on the use of force is partly the consequence of the strict civilian control over the military in India. Prime Minister Jawaharlal Nehru was the first to impose these limits, when the Army began operating in the northeast. He emphasized the political nature of the Naga problem, arguing that the Nagas had never developed Indian nationalism because they had been kept isolated from the rest of the country by British colonial rule.[12] This was coupled with Nehru's ambivalence about the development project of modern India as applied to the northeast. Nehru, as a Modernist, believed that Development had a lot to offer, but was uncertain about the impact that it would have on the way of life of the tribal population of the region.[13] All these uncertainties suggested a carefully moderated policy that emphasized the need for understanding the context of the Naga rebellion, and a strategy that sought political accommodation rather than military victory. Many of these values were accepted and assimilated by the Army, though not without resistance. Young officers complained about having to fight 'with their arms tied behind their backs',[14] while the Army itself asked for air support during the early operations against the Nagas.[15] These, however, were not a serious challenge to the political, and moderate, approach, and even these quickly disappeared.

Part of the reason why such a political approach was not seriously questioned was that it complemented the military's own professional understanding of the phenomenon of insurgency. This had two sources: the British view of counterinsurgency warfare, and the Chinese view of People's War. Brought up in the British tradition, the Army looked to Britain for its doctrinal underpinnings. This was no different in 4GW. Moreover, the British army was one of the few that had extensive 4GW experience. The British experience suggested both the need for political compromise as well as limitation on the use of firepower. (It also emphasized the importance of small unit operations, such as the Ferret Force, but for various organizational reasons, this was not particularly appealing to the Indian Army). The idea that 4GWs were essentially political in nature was also stressed by Mao, another source of Indian thinking about the problem of 4GW – and an important source of much of the recent literature on 4GW.[16] This is a principle that has repeatedly been violated by most conventional forces engaged in 4GW campaigns, including the US Army in Vietnam, the Soviets in Afghanistan, and even the Israeli forces in southern Lebanon.

The *second* element in the Army's approach to 4GW is isolating the insurgents from the general population. The Army has assimilated one of the truisms of guerrilla war, which is that in such wars the support of the masses is the key. Thus both sides seek to gain the support of the people. There is a positive and negative side to this: each side not only has to gain the support of the populace, it also has to deny the opposite side such support. 'Winning the hearts and minds' of the people through public service is one approach; but preventing the opposing side from doing the same thing is an equally key objective. Thus, one of the objectives of the Army in operations is to prevent the insurgents from getting support from the general populace. Though there are different methods for achieving this, and all are attempted in tandem, one of the most important methods is attempting to physically isolate the insurgents from the population. This is easier said than done, as the insurgent wears no uniform, and is usually indistinguishable from the general population.

Over the years, the Army has used a variety of methods to attempt to 'sanitize' the population from the insurgent. Taking a leaf out of the British experience in Malaya in the 1950s, the Indian Army attempted to create centralized, sanitized villages, access to which was controlled by the Army.[17] This had the advantage of making the task of monitoring the populace easier, and of preventing the insurgents from mixing with the populace. Such 'Protected and Progressive Villages' (PPVs) were tried in Nagaland in the late 1950s and early 1960s, and in Mizoram in the late 1960s.[18] There was, of course, a fundamental difference between Malaya and India's northeast – the former was a colony while the latter was not. The Indian government and the Army had to take into account the feelings of the citizens of the northeast. The PPVs were always controversial, and in 1968, the Assam High Court put a stop to the scheme before its implementation in Mizoram.[19] Subsequently, the Army has come to rely entirely on 'cordon-and-search' operations to accomplish the same task. But such operations have also faced criticisms because of the dislocation it causes to civilian life and the charges of human rights abuses that accompany such operations. These tactics are therefore less often resorted to now, and usually only in those instances when there is good intelligence information about the presence of terrorists or insurgents.

This element has not been stressed by the recent theorists of 4GW, who emphasize the cellular nature of 4GW adversaries. Clearly, al Qaeda, as a terrorist organization, does not depend as much on direct popular support as a means of protecting themselves as classical Maoist theory suggested. Dealing with such organizations represents an additional difficulty. But in most other cases, including the current US campaign in Iraq, the guerrillas do require popular support or at least acquiescence to be effective, and denying such support has to be an important element of any 4GW doctrine.[20]

The *third* element in the Army's approach is dominating the affected area. This does not always mean that the Army has to be in full control over the area. But 'showing the flag' through large-scale deployment of troops has a psychological effect that is important in preventing the insurgents from claiming success. Thus the stress is on blanketing the area with troops more than conducting offensive operations.[21] Over time, this also helps to wear down militants, illustrating to them the sheer resilience of the Indian State and Army, and the impossibility of any ultimate victory. This approach is somewhat unique to the Indian experience, and it is premised on two important elements: a huge infantry pool, including several large para-military forces that are used as adjuncts to the Army, and an acceptance of the inevitable higher casualties.[22]

A corollary to this is the *fourth* element of the doctrine, which emphasizes the need to maintain larger forces at all times in the combat area. Since the ambush was the most prevalent type of combat, and since the guerrilla adversaries were likely to break contact before reinforcements could arrive, there was an emphasis on keeping all deployed forces sufficiently large as to be able to deal with any contingency.[23] This also means that though small-unit operations are stressed, this remains primarily an intellectual thrust in professional writings, without it necessarily being transferred to actual operational doctrine. For example, an internal assessment in 1970 by the 8th Mountain Division, one of the formations with the longest experience in 4GW, noted that small unit operations were more likely to succeed than large-scale ones.[24] But operational practices do not appear to have changed. For example, the 'cordon-and-search' remains the favourite field tactic despite the fact that these rarely net insurgents, usually result in human rights complaints, and require at least company strength to successfully implement even the smallest cordon.

One alternative to maintaining large forces in combat areas is to have indirect fire support from artillery or close air support, an option that American forces in Vietnam and Iraq have exercised, and which the Soviets followed in Afghanistan. However discriminate and careful such fire is, it is bound to create civilian collateral damage that will play into the hands of the terrorists. Such fire causes more harm than good, creating the additional impression of a giant flailing helplessly against ants, an image that boosts the standing of the terrorists and does little practical good to the 4GW campaign.

A more appropriate alternative is to emphasize small unit operations, including the deployment of a large number of patrols to keep the insurgents off-balance and deny them the initiative. An example would be the 'ferret force' that the British deployed during the Malaya insurgency. On the other hand, the favourable conditions that British forces enjoyed in that campaign – an insurgency confined largely to one ethnic community, insurgents who were isolated from trans-national assistance, a war fought well out of public sight even by the standards of an age before CNN and the internet, and a permissive global political culture that allowed Britain to adopt measures such as village groupings – are unlikely to be enjoyed by any modern state fighting a 4GW campaign.

The *fifth* element of the Indian Army's approach to such wars is the belief that there are no military solutions to such wars. The Army has come to believe, since at least the mid-1970s, that such wars represent political problems which need to be resolved through political dialogue with the rebels. Though the Army had always recognized that 4GWs are ultimately political in nature (something most other Armies also tend to recognize, at least intellectually), the evocation of the mantra that 'there are no military solutions' was noticeably absent until sometime in the 1980s. Since the 1980s, it is difficult to find any essay written by Indian Army officers on 4GW that does not include this formulation. The Army's objective in such wars, then, is not victory but the restoration of normalcy, usually defined as a reduction in violence that permits normal political processes to resume.[25]

This vital element is absent even in the most recent iteration of the debate about the appropriate doctrine for such wars. Much of the debate assumes that insurgents can actually be militarily defeated. In that sense, the fundamental aim of 4GW theorists is the same as that of the 2GW and 3GW militaries that they critique. A more appropriate approach might be to carry the notion of 'politics with guns' to its logical conclusion, to assert that 4GW adversaries need to be defeated not just through military force but through political resolution of these conflicts that eliminate the political space for such terrorists to operate. Though military force is necessary, its role might be even more limited than current 4GW theorists assume.

The conventional war bias

Despite developing the elements of a counterinsurgency doctrine, the Indian Army is primarily designed to fight a Second Generation war. The Army sees its main mission not as fighting 4GW adversaries, but rather as fighting large-scale conventional wars with either – or both – China and Pakistan. Much of the Indian Army's training emphasizes large-scale (division and corps-level) exercises designed for a slug-fest with similarly structured opponents. Most of the innovations that the Army is considering respond primarily to change in this environment. Thus, the nuclearization of the region, and the experience of the Kargil crisis (1999) and Operation Parakram crisis (2001–02), led to doctrinal innovations such as the 'cold-start' and experiments with new types of more flexible field formations.[26] The Indian Army's first written and public doctrinal statement, released in 2004, largely emphasizes the need to move from a Second Generation to a Third Generation force. The 'Foreword' written by the then Chief of Army Staff, General N.C. Vij, does not even mention the challenge of 4GW or counterinsurgency, emphasizing rather the need to move towards net-centric and maneuver warfare.[27] And the doctrine itself categorically states that 'asymmetric wars cannot replace conventional wars' and that the primary mission of the Army is to protect the country from 'external threats' while the secondary role is to deal with 'internal threats'.

This is not a new bias, and despite the long experience with 4GW, it is deeply embedded in the Army's doctrinal culture. There are legions of examples of this 'conventional-war bias', but a telling one is in the 'Forward' written for the official divisional history of the 8th Mountain division – a formation that has almost entirely been involved in 4GWs since it was founded in the early 1960s – which states that '... counterinsurgency is only a subsidiary role of the formation. Its main role is in a war situation, to defend the country against external aggression'.[28] This 'conventional war bias' has limited the evolution of the Army's doctrine to those aspects of the doctrine that do not challenge this primary mission. In particular, the Army has been unable to assimilate small unit operations, or change the doctrine to develop such capabilities. Perhaps the motto of the Indian Army's Counter-Insurgency and Jungle Warfare School at Vairengte (CIJWS) says it best: 'Fight a Guerrilla like a Guerrilla.' Unfortunately, the Army has been unable to translate this motto into a doctrine that emphasizes the spirit of the motto, primarily because such a transformation would challenge the fundamental conventional-war values of the Army.[29]

The Army's failed efforts at creating specialized units to fight 4GW only provide further indications of the strength of the conventional war bias within the Army. The first such force, called the I (Insurgency)-battalion, was created in the late 1960s. The experiment itself was a somewhat limited one, involving the 'lightening' of several standard infantry battalions by removing their heavy equipment and logistical components.[30] Such 'light' battalions could have been much more agile, and probably more adept at 4GW, though there is little to indicate that the creation of these new units was accompanied by any new operational doctrines. But the experiment itself was short-lived. In less than two years, all of the I-battalions were converted back to regular infantry battalions. What is crucial here is the reason why this experiment was abandoned: the Army believed that such 'light' battalions would not do well in the Army's primary mission, fighting in conventional, high-intensity wars.[31]

Two decades later, the Indian army created another dedicated 4GW force called the Rashtriya Rifles (RR).[32] The RRs, despite teething troubles, appear to have now become well-established. They have grown from just a handful of battalions to nearly seventy now. Nevertheless, their success owes less to their effectiveness in actual operations, which has had mixed reviews, and more because they have allowed the Army to expand somewhat surreptitiously. Most importantly, with the exception of their permanent basing in combat theaters,[33] there is little operational or doctrinal difference between the RR and any other Indian Army infantry battalion. Thus, despite understanding that 4GW requires a different approach, the Army has been unwilling to undertake any radical restructuring to make such an approach possible. These failed experiments are further evidence of the presence of a conventional-war bias that emphasizes preparations for high-intensity conventional war, and rejects any innovation that might challenge this central mission.

Lessons from the Indian experience

Are there lessons that the Indian experience with 4GW suggest for other such campaigns, as in Iraq? I have suggested some above, and I will reiterate those, but an important caveat needs to be made first. Indian 4GW campaigns have been domestic campaigns, with the exception of the intervention in Sri Lanka. Domestic campaigns eliminate one serious disadvantage that fighting a 4GW campaign on foreign territory faces: the limitation on time. India's 4GW campaigns have taken decades to yield results. India's successful campaign against Mizo separatists took two decades to conclude, and the Punjab campaign took more than a decade. The Naga rebellion, which was the first major secessionist movement in India, has continued in fits and starts now for the last half-century. The insurgency in Assam started in the 1980s, and it has yet to be resolved. And the Kashmir insurgency, the most serious of these rebellions, is already a decade-and-a-half old. Nevertheless, because these are internal rebellions, giving up the fight does not seem to have been an option that was considered within the Indian government at any time, and it clearly is not an option that has been publicly discussed by non-governmental experts and commentators. That suggests great commitment to the idea of the Indian nation, but such staying power will be difficult to muster and sustain when fighting on foreign soil. Indeed, the Indian withdrawal from Sri Lanka in just four years suggests that New Delhi's extraordinary staying power is limited to internal conflicts. This suggests the need for great caution in attempting to draw lessons from the Indian experience for other 4GW contexts when the fighting is taking place on foreign soil. With this caveat made, the implications of the Indian experience can be reiterated.

The first is that 4GW is very difficult to win militarily. Military force can only create conditions which need to be exploited through additional political compromises for a final settlement. As Indian Army officers repeat almost by rote, such wars can only be solved through politics, not military force. It is unlikely that political compromises can be made with terrorists, but there are always moderates who are cowed by more extremist sections of their own community. Political compromise must focus on giving these elements tangible political goods to take back to their communities, which will have the additional benefit of isolating the extremists. In the Indian case, carving out new provinces for rebelling ethnic groups, or autonomous regions within existing provinces, helped to satisfy many grievances. Thus an important lesson for 4GW is the necessity of compromise and political solutions to conflict.

The second lesson is that such political compromises become difficult unless the use of force is drastically curtailed. Though Indian Army 4GW operations are far from gentle, and Indian forces have repeatedly been accused of human rights violations (many times with good reason), the absence of heavy firepower or close air support in such operations do significantly limit the level of violence. Both Naga and Mizo rebels demanded – and were given – a place in the Indian Army or other Indian security forces. Such assimilation would probably have been difficult in the absence of the restrained use of force by the Indian Army. Though 4GW theorists do emphasize the need to think of the use of force differently than in conventional wars, the theory needs to stress the limitation on the use of heavy firepower more.

A final implication is that militaries that face other conventional threats may find it difficult to transform themselves in the fundamental manner that 4GW theorists suggest. In the Indian case, despite recognizing the need 'to fight a guerrilla like a guerrilla', the Army found it difficult to ignore the requirements of preparing for conventional threats from across India's borders. We can disagree about whether the Indian Army has gone far enough in meeting the requirements of 4GW, but it is difficult to ignore the fact that there are real conventional threats that the Army has to prepare for. In the US context, as Edward Luttwak points out, it would be foolish to ignore the conventional challenge that future great powers such as China might pose.[34] Preparing for 4GW needs to be stressed while understanding the limitations imposed by the need to prepare also for traditional conventional high-intensity wars. A unipolar world might not see many inter-state wars because of the dominance of the US, but a unipolar world might not last forever.

Conclusions

The Indian Army's long experience with 4GW suggests both that the Indian Army has gone farther than other conventional armies in crafting a politically-driven doctrine to fight such campaigns, and the limitations inherent in such doctrines. The Indian Army's doctrine is successful precisely because its objectives are limited to reducing the levels of violence, which it accomplishes by saturating the affected area with troops. Such tactics work by ensuring low-level but long-term commitment. But such commitments are probably impossible when fighting on foreign territory. The Indian experience suggests that the old adage continues to be relevant to 4GW: you can only lose a 4GW, not win one.

Notes

* Associate Professor in International Politics, Centre for International Politics, Organization and Disarmament, School of International Studies, Jawaharlal Nehru University, New Delhi, India.
1 James J. Wirtz, 'Politics with Guns: A Response to T.X. Hammes', *Contemporary Security Policy* 26:2 (August 2005), pp. 222–6. Hammes approvingly cites Wirtz in Thomas X. Hammes, 'Response', *Contemporary Security Policy* 26:2 (August 2005), p. 280. Approaching the subject from a more traditional framework, David Kilcullen nevertheless expresses the same idea, calling it 'armed social work' in 'Twenty-Eight Articles: Fundamentals of Company-level Counterinsurgency', manuscript available at www.d-n-i.net/fcs/pdf/kilcullen_28_articles.pdf
2 Martin van Creveld, 'It Will Continue to Conquer and Spread', *Contemporary Security Policy* 26:2 (August 2005), pp. 231–2.

3 Harry Summers, *On Strategy: A Critical Analysis of the Vietnam War* (Novato: Presidio, 1982); and Andrew Krepinevich, *The Army and Vietnam* (Baltimore, MD: The
   Johns Hopkins University Press, 1986).
4 The only exception was in the case of the Punjab separatist movement, which was
   largely handled by the local police, though even in this case the Army did play a
   significant supporting role.
5 A brief account is provided by Vivek Chadha, *Low Intensity Conflicts in India*,
   (London: Sage Publications, 2005), pp. 392–4.
6 The Sikh rebellion that convulsed Indian Punjab in the 1980s is not included here
   because this was largely dealt with by the local police force, with only an intermittent
   supporting role for the Army.
7 For a general history, see Allan J. Bullion, *India, Sri Lanka and the Tamil Crisis*
   (London: Pinter, 1995).
8 The Indian 4GW doctrine was, until recently, not a written doctrine. The Army has
   now prepared a written 4GW/COIN (counterinsurgency) doctrine. But the document
   remains restricted, and does not appear to have been widely circulated even within the
   Army. The outline of the Indian 4GW doctrine presented here is gleaned from essays
   written by Indian officers in professional journals, military operational and unit histories, military memoirs, and interviews.
9 For a fuller narrative, see Rajesh Rajagopalan, ' "Restoring Normalcy": The Evolution of the Indian Army's Counterinsurgency Doctrine', *Small Wars and Insurgencies*
   11:1 (Spring 2000), pp. 44–68.
10 Animesh Ray, *Mizoram* (New Delhi: National Book Trust, 1993), p. 162.
11 Mark Tully and Satish Jacob, *Amritsar: Mrs Gandhi's Last Battle* (New Delhi: Rupa,
   1985).
12 Sarvepalli Gopal, *Jawaharlal Nehru: A Biography, Vol. 2, 1947–1956* (Cambridge,
   MA: Harvard University Press, 1979), p. 212.
13 Verrier Elwin, *A Philosophy for NEFA*, second edition (Shillong, India: Government
   of Assam, 1959), pp. (iii), 55.
14 P.D. Stracey, *Nagaland Nightmares* (New Delhi: Allied Publishers, 1968), p. 114.
15 Gopal, *Jawaharlal Nehru: A Biography, Vol. 2*, p. 211.
16 Most professional Army writings stressed the importance of Mao in understanding
   4GW. For example, see Major P.B. Deb, 'Thoughts on Guerrillas', *USI Journal* 92
   (July–September 1962), pp. 254–61.
17 Lieutenant D.R. Seth, 'Malaya: A Geopolitical Study', *USI Journal* 84 (July 1954),
   pp. 293–300; Lieutenant Colonel S.P. Anand, 'Counterinsurgency Theory and Practice in Mizo Hills', *USI Journal* 101 (April–June 1971), pp. 150–6; K.C. Praval, *The
   Indian Army After Independence* (New Delhi: Lancer International, 1987), p. 561.
18 Nirmal Nibedon, *Mizoram: The Dagger Brigade* (New Delhi: Lancer Publishers,
   1980), pp. 105–7; Major-General D.K. Palit, *Sentinels of the North-East: The Assam
   Rifles* (New Delhi: Palit & Palit, 1984), p. 271.
19 Profulla Roychoudhury, *The Northeast: Roots of Insurgency* (Calcutta: Firma KLM,
   1978), pp. 162–3.
20 Some recent writings also stress this point, even if they do not identify themselves as
   4GW theorists. See, for example, Kilcullen 'Twenty-Eight Articles: Fundamentals of
   Company-level Counterinsurgency'.
21 Lieutenant-General V.K. Nayar, 'Management of Insurgency in the North-East',
   Indian Defence Review 7:4 (October 1992), p. 20; K.V. Krishna Rao, *Prepare or
   Perish: A Study of National Security* (New Delhi: Lancer Publications, 1991), p. 258.
22 The Indian Army has 356 infantry battalions and the combined strength of the various
   national para-military forces is over 340 battalions and growing.
23 Major R.V. Jatar, 'Counterinsurgency Operations', *USI Journal* 97 (October–
   December 1968), pp. 415–23.
24 R.D. Palsokar, *Forever in Operations, A Success Story: A Historical Record of the*

8th Mountain Division in Counter-insurgency in Nagaland and Manipur, and in the 1971 Indo-Pakistan Conflict, 1963–1989 (n.p.: Headquarters, 8 Mountain Division, 1991), p. 80.

25 Rajagopalan, ' "Restoring Normalcy": The Evolution of the Indian Army's Counterinsurgency Doctrine'.

26 Gurmeet Kanwal, 'Strike Fast and Hard: Army Doctrine Undergoes Change in Nuclear Era', *The Tribune*, 23 June 2006, available at www.tribuneindia.com/2006/20060623/edit.htm

27 Indian Army, *Indian Army Doctrine*, available at indianarmy.nic.in/indianarmy-doctrine.htm.

28 'Foreword' by General K.V. Krishna Rao in Palsokar, *Forever in Operations*, p. vi.

29 The Army Doctrine does emphasize the importance of small unit operation, though they appear to have difficulty in translating that into actual operations. See *Indian Army Doctrine*, paras 5.12–5.14, pp. 19–21.

30 There is very little information about this experiment. I have based this on interviews and occasional references in unit histories. See Rajagopalan, ' "Restoring Normalcy": The Evolution of the Indian Army's Counterinsurgency Doctrine'.

31 This conclusion is based on interviews with several senior Army officers. The Army has released little information on the formation or the quick dismantling of the I-battalions. See ibid.

32 Rajesh Rajagopalan, 'Innovations in Counterinsurgency: The Indian Army's Rashtriya Rifles', *Contemporary South Asia* 13:1 (March 2004), pp. 25–38.

33 Traditionally, the Indian Army prefers to rotate entire battalions through higher formations and theaters. In the case of the RR, the battalions themselves stay in place, while the troops rotate individually or in small groups.

34 Edward N. Luttwak, 'A Brief Note on "Fourth-Generation Warfare" ', *Contemporary Security Policy* 26:2 (August 2005), pp. 227–8. I disagree with Luttwak, though, that 4GW should therefore be left to police forces.

Part VI

Conclusion

25 Can we adapt to Fourth Generation Warfare?

Terry Terriff, Regina Karp and Aaron Karp

That the character of warfare can and will change constantly should not be surprising. Yet the Western world has been surprised and often shocked by the violence of this transformation in the early years of the twenty-first century. That war and warfare was evolving was evident to many during the 1990s. Much of the debate on the changing character of warfare during the 1990s, however, focused on the so-called Revolution in Military Affairs (RMA). This focused on the application of new technology, particularly information technology, to the means of war-making. This RMA debate ranged widely, but when all was said and done, much of the argumentation about the implications of information technology, particularly in the United States, centered exclusively on enhancing the form of warfare successfully demonstrated by the American-led Coalition in the 1991 Gulf War.

The 1991 Gulf War may have represented the epitome of conventional warfare, and it certainly was the form of war that our military organizations preferred to wage. But through the 1990s this conventional form of warfare, at least as we styled it, seemed more to be the exception to the general rule. Liberia, Bosnia, Somalia, Rwanda, Haiti, Chechnya, Kosovo, among far too many other wars in all regions of the world, furnished evidence that warfare, both its practice and the ends force was being used to achieve, were undergoing some form of change that was different from that being extolled in the RMA debate. During the 1990s any number of analyses emerged that sought to make sense of what these changes entailed, and indeed what they implied both for our ability to manage them and for what they implied for the future.[1]

When the concept of 'Fourth Generation Warfare' (4GW) was first proposed in 1989, its authors – William S. Lind, Keith Nightengale, John F. Schmitt, Joseph W. Sutton and Gary I. Wilson – were not intent so much on defining a particular form of warfare, rather their main argument was that warfare does evolve and that we would be wise to explore how war might change to be better prepared. Subsequently, a small cadre of military mavericks and civilian analysts sought to develop the idea of 4GW and influence American military thinking about future war. Their work appeared almost exclusively in military journals, where it had virtually no effect on civilian strategic thought. A special impetus came not from official military audiences – these remained hostile or at least unconvinced – but from the maturation of the World Wide Web, the same resource that would serve a crucial role for al Qaeda and other 'Fourth Generation warriors'.[2] Even so, the dissemination of 4GW was limited to a sub-culture of military officers and academic specialists. Even within these audiences it was not clear to what extent the idea gained serious acceptance.

Welcome to the fourth generation of warfare

One advantage of the idea of 4GW was that its advocates sought to distil general features of the changing character of warfare rather than attempting to stipulate a set of tactics, techniques and procedures that would specifically define a new form of war. The idea of 4GW as they were articulating it comprised general trends which they believed would broadly inform how warfare would be, indeed increasingly was being, conducted. A critical aspect of 4GW was that the changes it anticipated were likely to be very difficult for our military organizations to meet successfully.

In spite of their efforts, and the efforts of other analysts, we continued to march eyes wide shut through the 1990s into the twenty-first century, sure that the conventional form of warfare that we preferred and were so obviously very good at would sweep all before it. So we were surprised by the horrifying attacks of 11 September. Even though 11 September made clear in a very devastating manner that the use of violence was undergoing a change, and even sparked an outbreak of wider thinking about how war was changing, we seemingly continue to be caught by surprise. The US Army and Marine Corps forces that attacked Baghdad in the spring of 2003 with destructive efficiency, for example, were caught by surprise. As Lieutenant Colonel Bryan McCoy, commander of the 3rd Brigade, 7th Marines, complained during the initial campaign:

> The enemy has gone asymmetric on us. There's treachery. There are ambushes. It's not straight-up conventional fighting.[3]

An inherent problem was that US forces entered Iraq expecting the Iraqis to fight much the same way our military organizations prefer to fight.[4] To a substantial degree the Iraqis did, but there were those, both military and Fedayeen, who did not. Certainly US forces overcame the challenge that was posed, but the non-traditional forms of warfare used by Iraqis did trouble them. The US-led Coalition forces were perhaps fortunate that the Iraqis using irregular forms of warfare were not well trained, not very disciplined, not really prepared and not very well armed.[5]

In Lebanon, Hezbollah in the summer of 2006 was, for its part, an irregular force too, but one that was much better trained, disciplined and prepared. Moreover, it was well armed, with an array of sophisticated modern weapons, such as anti-tank and anti-ship missiles and large artillery rockets, and it demonstrated a real capacity to mate twenty-first century information technologies with these modern arms in innovative ways.[6] The very professional and successful Israeli military was caught by surprise when they attacked Hezbollah; to be fair, as was most of the rest of the world. As Yaron Ezrahi, of Hebrew University, observed, 'This war will be studied in all military academies in the world as a new kind of war which requires new and unprecedented definitions of how to fight it and how to win it.'[7]

Ezrahi is almost certainly correct in this assessment. For Hezbollah seemingly represents what may be euphemistically termed a 'professional' networked irregular fighting force, with an adaptive and agile mindset and approach to warfare – that is, a professional Fourth Generation force – that was able to fight a traditional hierarchical state military organization to a draw on the battlefield. Jon Alterman, of the Center for Strategic and International Studies in Washington, observed that the form of combat between Hezbollah and the Israeli forces is 'more difficult to resolve' than the more traditional style of battles our military organizations are equipped, trained and prefer to fight. Alterman went on to say about Hezbollah that, 'The groups have made a living out of having few tangible assets to attack. In many ways, they exist principally as a set of ideas ... and they enjoy wide support among their target communities.'[8] Ezrahi captured another element of the conflict with his observation that 'The problem for the army and the problem for the Israeli government is the concept of military victory which was inscribed in the minds of Israelis in wars like the Six-Day War or even the Yom Kippur War. That is utterly irrelevant to this kind of war, to the war of a regular army against a terrorist network.'[9] Nor is it just 'battlefield victory' that is suddenly in question – who can legitimately claim to have won the conflict (assuming that it is not just in remission) is seemingly up for grabs as well.

The main innovative features of this conflict largely came from Hezbollah, but there were also novel aspects to the conflict that emerged on the Israeli side of the fighting as well. For example, Israeli Defense Forces telephoned individuals and families in Lebanon to warn them that their houses were about to be bombed in an apparent effort to reduce civilian casualties.[10] And has anyone taken close note of the fact that Israeli reservists privately commissioned an opinion poll, in the midst of the fighting, as a way to influence their political and military leadership, not to reconsider the war but to reconsider how the war was 'being waged'?[11] Gerald Steinberg, of Bar-Ilan University, is regrettably not far wrong when he said, 'I don't think anybody had any way to really grasp the implications of this kind of war.'[12]

The hard question is why many of the implications of the ongoing changes in warfare were not at least broadly comprehended before the war? Indeed, why was the Israeli political and military leadership, first, so blithe in their belief that they could destroy through aerial bombing a dispersed, networked, opponent?[13] And second, so off the mark in their ability to comprehend what likely awaited the ground forces they sent across the border into Lebanon?[14] Many elements of Hezbollah's approach were quite evident in the activities of the Iraqi irregulars in 2003, while many others were evident in the activities of Iraqi insurgent forces over the past three years. The main difference is that Hezbollah was more sophisticated, more professional, and better armed.

Certainly the specifics among the many changes in warfare that we have seen were not foretold by the original analysts of 4GW, but they are generally consistent with the key features and trends these analysts identified. On balance, they seem to have gotten far more right than they got wrong. At the very least, in the broad description they argued about the changes occurring furnished a good starting point for thinking carefully about how these general trends might manifest in the details. This alone gives good reason to go back to the original 1989 article as well as the subsequent analysis they developed. There is a range of views on most aspects of 4GW, ranging from the nature and character of Fourth Generation groups, general trends, information operations, cultural intelligence, among other aspects of 4GW.[15] There is even a draft doctrinal manual on 4GW produced by a seminar of officers from the US Marine Corps, Royal Marines, US Army and Air National Guard, led by Bill Lind.[16] Even if one disagrees with these analyses and attendant policy prescriptions, they force us to think critically and imaginatively about the changes that are occurring and what we may do to be prepared.

Change and history

In spite of 4GW receiving wider interest in the aftermath of 11 September, use of the label is largely eschewed in official terminology.[17] One can arguably ascribe any number of reasons for the apparent marginalization of 4GW and many of its advocates. One set of reasons may be personal in nature. Many of these individuals appear to be perceived as trouble makers, for they are mavericks, and some of them previously were keen, and at times publicly provocative, advocates for the adoption of maneuver warfare by the US military. Their past success as members of the Defense Reform Movement in the US during the 1970s and 1980s may colour the attitude of some towards their work.[18] No good deed goes unpunished.

Another set of reasons have to do with the concept itself. These have been admirably debated in detail in Part III of this volume. One critical line of argument is that there is no need for the 'generations of warfare' concept to explain the changes we are witnessing. In effect, the argument is that the changes occurring do not constitute a new form of war. They correctly note that most if not all of the approaches increasingly being utilized in many conflicts, whether at the tactical, operational or strategic level, have been employed in one form or another in the past, in some cases as far back as Alexander the Great or farther. These approaches are merely reoccurring and becoming more central, they are not something new. We would do well to take heed of the concern inherent in this critique that if we label what we see as being a 'new form of warfare', we may fail to examine history closely for measures that will help us to meet the challenges posed. Regardless of whether or not we believe that 4GW is a new form of war, we can and should learn lessons from the past on how, and how not, to meet the challenges of the twenty-first century. Whether one accepts that what is being described as the onset of 4GW is a new form of human violence, or merely the reappearance and repackaging of approaches and techniques used in the past, is perhaps a matter of taste so long as we still struggle to cope with it.

The second and more damning critique of the 'generations of warfare' idea that the commentators in this volume point to is the use, or perhaps abuse, of history. This issue is a telling one, particularly with respect to the underlying model that is employed for the evolution of generations of warfare. In the spirit of fairness, the complaint about the selective use of history is one that historians have been rightly levelling at social science theorists for many a long year. This observation, however, does not obviate the problem which the misuse of history poses to the concept, particularly if one approaches the underlying 'generation concept' as a model, or theory, of change.

Very evident is that the intent of the original authors, or indeed of those that followed, was not to develop a social science theory of change in warfare. Rather their interest, having been directly involved in the long debates to convince the US military to adopt maneuver warfare as its strategic, operational and tactical concept, was to convince it not to rest on its laurels. Thus, it is not unexpected that the first three generations of warfare discussed mirror fairly closely the episodic evolution of the US military's conceptual approaches to warfare over its 200-plus year history.

While reducing the model to basics – by focusing on change in warfare essentially since Napoleon – may have been a conceptual simplifying ploy used to facilitate reaching the US military audience, it also tended to eviscerate the concept as a model of change. An inherent problem, at least from a social science perspective, is that the methodology employed was never really explicated. At best this remained a latent element of the work that followed in the subsequent years, evident mostly in the fact that most if not all are followers of the remarkable Colonel John Boyd and practitioners of the approach to thinking about war and warfare he developed.[19] The original authors in essence based the development of 4GW on Boyd's work, essentially applying his concept of the Observation–Orientation–Decision–Action Loop, or OODA Loop, to generate ideas of what the form of war after maneuver warfare might look like.[20] The OODA Loop they used, however, is not really the one that military personnel normally refer to, as in 'we got inside their OODA Loop' or 'we need to get inside their OODA Loop'. Boyd, with his boundless curiosity, voracious appetite for learning, and keen ability to pull together and synthesize concepts from disparate fields into a coherent whole, in time moved beyond his earlier conceptualization of the OODA Loop to, as Grant Hammond puts it, 'a general theory of change'.[21] This 'theory' is captured in Boyd's 1992 briefing, 'The Conceptual Spiral', with the spiral referred to being the central insight 'around which [his] "A Discourse on Winning and Losing" itself revolves'.[22] It is in this more sophisticated variation of Boyd's OODA Loop where the methodological approach used by the original authors of 4GW may be found.

Here is not the place to explicate Boyd's 'conceptual spiral', not least as it is at heart a way of thinking. Suffice it to say that the essence, as explained by

Hammond, is that a world that is uncertain, ever-changing and unpredictable generates mismatches, and hence 'one must continue the whirl of reorientation, mismatches, analyses and syntheses to comprehend, shape and adapt to unfolding, evolving reality that remains uncertain, ever-changing, and unpredictable'.[23] One of the hoped for aims of the original symposium in *Contemporary Security Policy* was that the debate might contribute to a refinement of the 'generation of warfare' model.[24] The historical critique of many of the scholars who have contributed to the symposium/volume, with several of the analyses of specific conflicts that highlight lacunae in the 4GW concept and/or aspects not considered by its advocates, combine to delineate issues that constitute 'mismatches'. The critiques thus strongly suggest that there is a need to re-engage in the 'whirl'. Freedman's observation that 4GW is 'an evolved form of unconventional warfare' that historically has and continues to run parallel to the evolution of conventional war, may be a useful insight. Or perhaps the idea, mentioned by Hammes and taken up by Hoffman, that the dominant way of warfare switches episodically through history between conventional and unconventional forms may furnish another, or even additional, insight. The current 'generations' model for change in warfare, based as it is on selective history, probably is flawed. As Freedman has noted elsewhere, however, this 'is not in itself reason for neglecting its prescriptive aspects'.[25] The application of the methodology of Boyd's 'conceptual spiral' to a more rigorous use of history may generate some interesting insights to help us, if we are imaginative, be better prepared to meet the unknown country of the future.

Differential change

Several of the contributors address the issue of the 'unknown country' from a different perspective. In Part IV, Chet Richards, Greg Wilcox and Gary Wilson, Warren Chin, Avi Kober, and Paul Jackson each present an analysis of a specific conflict or region of conflict. These four analyses provide considerable insight into differences in who is fighting, what they are fighting for, how they are organized and how they are fighting. They are thus very instructive in two main ways.

One is that they offer food for thought for any effort to refine the concept of 4GW itself, as well as for thinking about the dynamics of how warfare is changing or may evolve. Even if many of the tactics and strategies are generally similar, how each of these 4GW antagonists fights reflects differences in their own levels of sophistication. The way fighting is conducted in Iraq, Afghanistan and the Holy Land bear close similarities, but the Darwinian pressures of the war in Iraq appear to be driving faster improvement in sophistication and innovation there than in the other two conflicts. But while there are differences in the refinement in their approaches, the diffusion of ideas, such as we have seen happen from Iraq to Afghanistan,[26] will occur and will influence how other groups wage war.[27] Further, the particular dynamics of each conflict will be determined by specific factors, such as situation, opponent capabilities, culture, motives, armaments, among many others. This creates a real prospect that war will evolve differently in different places and regions even if diffusion does occur. This possibility is most evident in Jackson's examination of 4GW in Africa, where the evolution of warfare has barely even reached the level of the first generation of warfare. The character of conflict in Africa, as he makes clear, is a mixture of pre-modern and modern, particularly with respect to the mindsets of the combatants. As these groups are exposed to ever more modern or post-modern ideas and technologies, they very likely will innovate, either in a very original fashion or through diffusion. The process seems almost certain to result in a form of warfare that diverges considerably, even radically, from other regions.

The other instructive aspect is that the Fourth Generation warriors currently fighting around the world – in Iraq and Afghanistan, Hezbollah and Hamas, the LTTE in Sri Lanka or various African factions and others elsewhere – have very little in common. If one compares the make up of the assortment of opponent forces in Iraq and Afghanistan, the differences in various groups, factions and militias that are working together is considerable. In Iraq, the opposing forces encompass groups allied to al Qaeda, members of the Ba'ath Party and/or loyal supporters of Saddam Hussein, and variegated numbers of Sunni and Sh'ite groups of different sizes opposed to the Coalition forces, as well as a growing diversity of groups, whether Sunni or Sh'ite, militias or rogue police and military. They appear to be unified exclusively through their participation in what can only be considered a civil war of intimidation, assassination and ethnic cleansing. In Afghanistan the fighters include the Taliban, possibly al Qaeda, regional warlords, drug lords and smugglers, amongst others, which largely are arrayed to oppose the NATO, US forces and the Afghan government. In the case of Palestine, Hamas and the PLA are different yet again, just as insurgent and guerrilla groups in Africa display even more variance in comparison to the other three examples as well as across Africa itself.

The wide range in 'who is fighting' is the foundation for wide differences in 'why they are fighting' and 'how they are organized'. In Afghanistan and Iraq, and in Africa, various groups will work together in tight or loose 'networks of the willing' because they perceive they share a common goal. In these three cases the common goal generally is to force out the government and/or force out those they deem to be 'occupiers'. This shared aim, however, is often as not an operational goal for most groups, for it is a means to the ends they really seek. And these strategic goals as often as not are different across the cooperating groups. For example, al Qaeda in Iraq and drug lords in Afghanistan are fighting against the government that represents order. These two groups prefer disorder so that they can flourish, whereas many other factions with which these two cooperate are looking to replace the current government so that they can seize control or at least create circumstances so that they can negotiate with the government a better political position or more benefits for themselves. Much the same applies to the way these actors are organized, both in terms of each one's internal organization and of how they are organized to cooperate with other groups. Groups may be based on friendship, family, tribal or clan ties; they may be based on loyalty to a particular leader or idea; they may be based on a shared desire for economic gain or simple survival; or they may be based on a shared sense of cultural or social alienation and disenfranchisement. The structure and dynamics of individual groups will vary widely, as will the degree of centralized control. Moreover, while we can say that these various groups coordinate and cooperate with each other in a networked fashion, the structure and dynamics of the functioning of those 'networks' will vary widely as well.

These many differences make the prospect of managing and indeed resolving individual conflicts extremely problematic. The lesson is that each case is unique. Careful heed should be taken of Jackson's admonition that we should not formulate new concepts of warfare, and attendant doctrines and means, based on one operational experience. The growing appreciation of what retired US Army Major General Robert Scales termed 'culture-centric warfare'[28] and on-going efforts to incorporate cultural awareness, cultural knowledge and cultural intelligence into our military organizations is a significant step forward to forestalling this problem.[29] Yet it will take more than simply being cognizant of the importance of local culture, social linkages and mores. During the Cold War NATO's member militaries focused almost exclusively on fighting one enemy in one environment, with the result that they developed rigid and specialized structures and doctrines to fit. Over a decade on, these militaries, in spite of efforts to move from their Cold War structures and mindsets, have not fared well in other forms of warfare. Such a way of thinking about and preparing for challenges is not tenable in the twenty-first century. Cookie-cutter 'how to' doctrines that often have far too much in common with manuals for how to strip a rifle or fix an engine may work in one specific place but may not work nearly as well in another conflict – indeed, they are a potential recipe for failure. What is required are new ways of thinking about war and warfare, and concepts and doctrines that stress 'understanding' and 'knowledge' rather than specific practices and implementation if our military organizations are to be able to deal successfully with the evolution of war and the resultant challenges across geography and cultures.

Meeting the challenges of change

Western military organizations, and indeed Western governments, are more concerned with today than tomorrow, as they are seeking to develop the means to meet the immediate challenges of a '4GW world'. In Part V, Frank Hoffman, Thomas Hammes and Don MacCuish furnish insightful, and at times provocative, analyses that set forth many aspects of what can and indeed needs to be done to accomplish this. Frans Osinga and Diego Ruiz Palmer provide penetrating examinations of how well NATO is prepared to address the challenges and what it needs to further do, while Rajesh Rajagopalan offers a discerning analysis of the Indian Army's experience of fighting Fourth Generation-style warriors. Other possibilities are also evident in some of the analyses that focus on particular cases of conflict in Iraq, Afghanistan, Israel and Palestine, and

Africa. Some of the perspectives brought to bear in these analyses question the concept of 4GW, enhancing their insights, for the recommendations are not dependent on accepting the concept of 4GW in whole or part.

A common theme that runs through many of the analyses is the capability and prospects of our military organizations being able to adapt and change to meet the challenges of the twenty-first century. This theme resonates strongly. The originators of 4GW were first and foremost motivated by their desire to convince the US military that it needed to prepare for the future instead of just preparing better to fight the last war. Their starting point was that war continually evolves and hence military organizations must continually adapt and change to meet future challenges that will arise as a consequence. They toiled long and hard, mostly in obscurity, in their efforts to convince others of this important point. It almost goes without saying that military organizations, much as is the case of any large organization, generally tend to be resistant to change, particularly substantial change to their organizational goals, actual strategies and/or structure. There is more than just a passing element of truth to the old saw that 'Generals always prepare to fight the last battle of their last war'. One certainly sees this in the case of the US-led invasion of Iraq in 2003, where the US military, focused exclusively on the conventional conflict which was essentially the Son of the first Gulf War, was ill-prepared to meet the challenges of the post conventional phase of the fighting.[30] And it seems that there may be an element of this in the case of Israel in the summer of 2006, for there are hints that the Israelis may have perceived Hezbollah as, in effect, the twin of Hamas.[31]

Military organizations nonetheless can and do make changes in terms of whom and how they prepare to fight. Today, most or all military organizations of the liberal, democratic Western states are seeking to innovate (or at least claiming they are) the means and measures to meet the challenges they face today. This is very evident in the US military. Engaged in very difficult counterinsurgency campaigns in Iraq and Afghanistan, the global campaign of the 'long war' against organizations such as al Qaeda and affiliated groups, and a range of nation building or conflict prevention operations around the globe, among other operations, the US military is seeking to come to grips with the intricate and multifaceted character of battle and war in the twenty-first century. Indeed, the growing awareness of the complexity of the change in the ways, means and ends utilized by opponents is a significant driver for the move towards developing a more comprehensive approach to thinking about the ends, ways and means of war. This is most apparent in the recognition in the US and many other NATO states of the requirement to employ the political, economic, social and cultural aspects of national power, along with military power, in an integrated manner at the strategic, operational and tactical levels.

The changes required, however, are far deeper than simply developing new technologies or new doctrines. The pressure and demands of ongoing operations is a well understood spur for such developments, and certainly is a key stimulus for the US military. For example, three long, difficult and problematic years in Iraq has impelled the US Army, well known for having very deliberately and firmly turned its back on counterinsurgency in the aftermath of Vietnam, to develop jointly with the Marine Corps a new, modern manual on counterinsurgency.[32] This is well and good, indeed necessary, given the conflict environments in Iraq and Afghanistan in which the US Army and Marine Corps can currently expect to conduct operations over the next several years. But the international security environment is in a state of flux, and warfare will continue to evolve. Much more crucial, then, is the requirement for a real change in the mindset of the US Army, to stay with the example, for the problems encountered in Iraq ultimately stemmed less from the lack of counterinsurgency training than from the fixed (or perhaps fixated) mindset that was the foundation underpinning this lack.

Without a change in the mindset, or organizational culture, of our military organizations,[33] the innovations and changes adopted to meet current operational realities may be rejected or allowed to fade away once those operational demands reduce or peter out, or current innovations may give the appearance of adjustment without resulting in a substantive change in function or practice. Expedient adaptations that are transitory or superficial may seem suitable today, yet may be much less so tomorrow. What the concept of 4GW makes clear is that what is required today and tomorrow is enduring and even persistent change in our military organizations and the civilian counterparts with which they must learn to closely cooperate.

Notes

1 Among the more prominent of these were Martin van Creveld *The Transformation of War* (New York: Free Press, 1991*)*; Kalevi Holsti, *The State, War and the State of War* (Cambridge: Cambridge University Press, 1996); Mary Kaldor, *New and Old Wars* (Stanford, CA: Stanford Univeristy Press, 1999); and Ralph Peters *Fighting for the Future* (Mechanicsburg, PA: Stackpole Books, 1999).

2 This theme is developed at greater length in the editors' *Introduction* to this volume.

3 Quoted in Romesh Ratnesar, 'Sticking to His Guns', *Time*, 30 March 2003, available at: www.time.com/time/magazine/printout/0,8816,438861,00.html (accessed 2 April 2003).

4 As Lieutenant General William S. Wallace, US Army, candidly noted on 27 March 2006, 'The enemy we're fighting is a bit different than the one we war-gamed against, because of these paramilitary forces. We knew they were here, but we did not know how they would fight.' Quoted in Jim Dwyer, 'A Gulf Commander Sees a Longer Road', *New York Times*, 28 March 2006, available at www.nytimes.com/2003/03/28/international/worldspecial/28GENE.html?ex=1161489600&en=9f2bbaa7f5e18 6f4&ei=5070 (accessed 28 March 2003).

5 For example, in the US military's Millennium Challenge exercise in 2002, which effectively reflected aspects of the real invasion to come, the Red Team, led by Lieutenant General Paul van Riper, USMC (retired), employed a range sophisticated unconventional approaches and techniques to such effect against the more powerful invading Blue (US) Team that referees were essentially forced to halt and restart the exercise from point zero. See Sean D. Naylor, 'War Games Rigged?', *Army Times.com*, 16 August 2002, available at www.armytimes.com/story.php?f= 1–292925–1060102.php (accessed 16 October 2006)

6 See, for example, Conal Urquhart, 'Computerised Weaponry and High Morale',

Guardian, 11 August 2006, at: www.guardian.co.uk/print/0,,329550690–103552,00. html (accessed 11 August 2006).

7 Quoted in Molly Moore, 'Israelis Confront "New Kind of War"', *Washington Post*, 9 August 2006, p. A11.

8 Quoted in Associated Press, 'Analysis: Hezbollah May Have the Edge', *New York Times*, 30 July 2006, available at www.nytimes.com/aponline/world/AP-Mideast-Fighting-Hezbollahs-Edge.html?pagewanted=print (accessed 30 July 2006).

9 Quoted in Moore, 'Israelis Confront "New Kind of War"'.

10 Ian MacKinnon, 'Phone Calls Mean Your House is Jet Target', *Times Online*, 19 August 2006, available at http://www.timesonline.co.uk/printFriendly/0,,1–3-2319379–3,00.html (accessed 19 August 2006).

11 Commissioning a public poll is a significant evolution beyond the war blogs being written by US soldiers and Marines in Iraq. See Ilene R. Prusher, 'At War, Israeli Reservists Wield New Weapon: Opinion Polls', *Christian Science Monitor*, 16 August 2006, available at www.csmonitor.com/2006/0816/p10s01-wome.html (accessed 16 August 2006).

12 Quoted in Moore, 'Israelis Confront "New Kind of War"'.

13 On the inherent fallacy of believing that their air strikes would be effective, see Philip H. Gordon, 'Air Power Won't Do It', *Washington Post*, 25 July 2006, p. A15.

14 On this point, see Jim Hoagland, 'Spy Lessons From Israel', *Washington Post*, July 30, 2006, p. B07; Ian Black, Inigo Gilmore and Mitchell Prothero, 'The day Israel Realised that this was a Real War', *Observer*, 30 July 2006, available at observer.guardian.co.uk/print/0,,329541424–119093,00.html (accessed 30 July 2006); and Steve Erlanger and Richard A. Oppel Jr, 'A Disciplined Hezbollah Surprises Israel With Its Training, Tactics and Weapons', *New York Times*, 7 August 2006, available at select.nytimes.com/gst/abstract.html?res=FB0D11FD355B0C748 CDDA10894DE404482 (accessed 07/08/06).

15 Websites that provide links to a range of publications and analyses on 4GW include *Defense and the National Interest: Fourth Generation Warfare* (http://www.d-n-i.net/second_level/fourth_generation_warfare.htm) and *Small Wars Journal* (www.smallwarsjournal.com/).

16 Lind, *et al.*, 'Draft FMFM 1-A Fourth Generation Warfare', accessed from www.d-n-i.net/second_level/4gw_continued.htm.

17 The US Navy appears to be using the term, at least unofficially. See, for example, Admiral Mike Mullen, Remarks delivered to the Current Strategy Forum, Naval War College, Newport, RI, 14 June 2006. In contrast, the new joint US Army and Marine Corps manual, *Counterinsurgency*, does not mention it at all.

18 On the Defense Reform Movement, see James Fallows, *National Defense* (New York: Random House, 1981); Gary Hart, with William S. Lind, *America Can Win: The Case for Military Reform* (Bethesda, MD: Adler & Adler, 1986); and James G. Burton, *The Pentagon Wars: Reformers Challenge the Old Guard* (Annapolis, MD: Naval Institute Press, 1993).

19 That they were followers of Boyd and his ideas likely did not endear them to many in the US military. For all that Boyd did for the US military, many generally did not much appreciate him, his ideas, or what they saw as his interference and caustic manner.

20 Email message to Terriff, from Colonel Gary I. Wilson, 6 October 2006.

21 Grant T. Hammond, *The Mind of War: John Boyd and American Security* (Washington, DC and London: Smithsonian Institution Press, 2001) p. 174.

22 Hammond, *The Mind of War*, p. 174.

23 Hammond, *The Mind of War*, p. 173.

24 Certainly this is an important reason why Thomas Hammes was willing to write his contribution to that issue and subject it to open debate.

25 Lawrence Freedman, *The Transformation of Strategic Affairs*, *Adelphi Paper 379* (Oxford: Oxford University Press, 2006) p. 21.

26 The sophistication of Hezbollah's tactics may also reflect a degree of diffusion of ideas and innovations from Iraq, or even other conflicts, as well as internal learning and innovation.

27 For an examination of the dynamics and impact of the diffusion of military innovations, see Emily O. Goldman and Leslie C. Eliason, eds, *The Diffusion of Military Technology and Ideas* (Stanford, CA: Stanford University Press, 2003). Also see chapters by Farrell, Goldman and Terriff in Theo Farrell and Terry Terriff, eds, *The Sources of Military Change: Culture, Politics, Technology* (Boulder, CO: Lynne Rienner, 2002).

28 General Robert F. Scales, 'Culture-Centric Warfare', *Proceedings*, Vol. 130, Iss. 10 (October 2004) pp. 32ff.

29 For the military utility of culture, see Montgomery McFate, 'The Military Utility of Understanding Adversary Culture', *Joint Force Quarterly*, Iss. 38 (2005) pp. 42ff.

30 It may be equally or more apropos in this example of it being 'politicians fighting the last battle of the last war'.

31 There is a sense that many Israeli soldiers, including reservists, if not the Israeli military leadership, were expecting in effect to be fighting 'Hamas' all over again – only to find a different enemy fighting in a different way. As one senior Israeli officer noted, 'This isn't like the war we fight in the territories [the West Bank and Gaza]'; quoted in Black, Gilmore, and Prothero, 'The day Israel realized that this was a real war'. For expressions of Israeli soldiers' growing appreciation of the differences, see Conal Urquhart, 'We thought Gaza was pretty tough ...', *Guardian*, 10 August 2006, available at www.guardian.co.uk/print/0,,329549400–103552,00.html (accessed 10 August 2006); and Greg Myre, 'Wounded Israelis Tell of a Tough, Elusive Enemy', *International Herald Tribune*, 10 August 2006, available at www.iht.com/bin/print_ipub.php?file=/articles/2006/08/10/news/israel.php (accessed 11 August 2006).

32 Headquarters Department of the Army, *FM 3–24/MCRP 3–33.5: Counterinsurgency*, draft, September 2006.

33 On changing military organizational culture, see Terry Terriff, 'Warriors and Innovators: Military Change and Organizational Culture in the US Marine Corps', *Defence Studies*, Vol. 6, no. 2 (2006) pp. 215–247. For a failed effort to alter the organizational culture, or mindset, of the US Marine Corps in the 1990s, see Terriff, 'Of Romans and Dragons: Preparing the Marine Corps for Future Warfare', *Contemporary Security Policy*, Vol. 28. no. 1 (April 2007) pp. 143–162.

Index